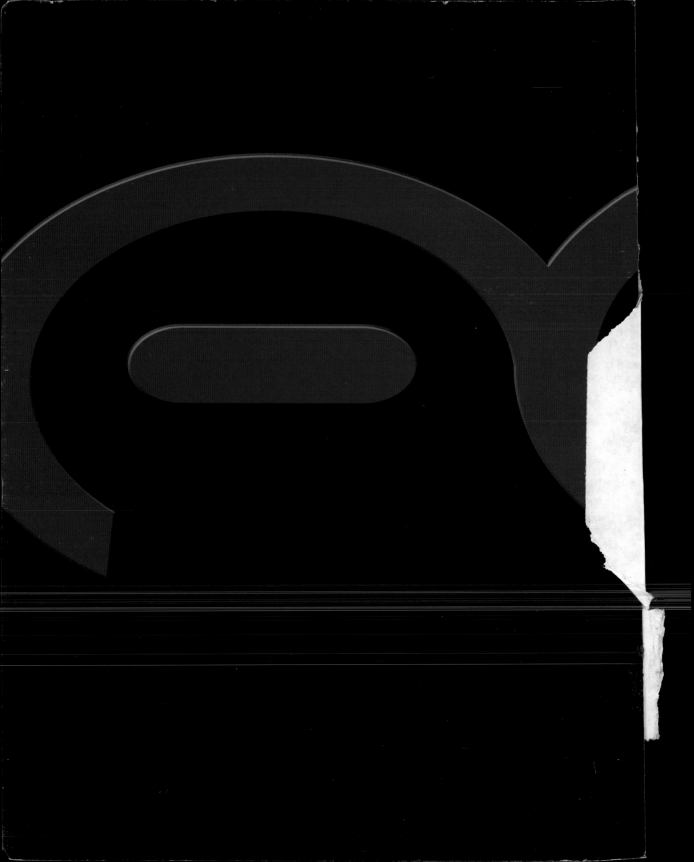

mohammad f. haque ■ ananth panagariya

applegeeks™

② weird science

PUBLISHER
mike richardson

EDITOR
samantha robertson

DIGITAL PRODUCTION
dan jackson + ryan hill

DESIGNER
tina alessi

APPLEGEEKS™ VOLUME 2: WEIRD SCIENCE

This volume collects comic strips from the Applegeeks website, originally published online from January 2005 through November 2006. This volume also collects comic strips 845 and 847 from the Megatokyo website, which were created by Mohammad F. Haque and Ananth Panagariya as part of a crossover story between applegeeks .com and megatokyo.com. As a result of this crossover, several *Megatokyo* characters appear in this volume without satiric intent. These characters are copyright © 2000–2009 by Fred Gallagher. "Megatokyo" is a registered trademark of Fredart Studios LLC.

Published by Dark Horse Books, a division of Dark Horse Comics, Inc., 10956 S.E. Main Street, Milwaukie OR 97222

darkhorse.com • applegeeks.com

To find a comics shop in your area, call the Comic Shop Locator Service toll-free at 1-888-266-4226

First edition: October 2009
ISBN 978-1-59582-337-3

10 9 8 7 6 5 4 3 2 1
Printed in China

For you.

—*Ananth*

I would like to dedicate this book to my family, Jess, and Ananth. They always encourage me to push myself further, and I am eternally grateful. I also would like to thank our readers, who stayed with us this long and motivate me to keep going. Thanks.

—*Hawk*

contents

Foreword

I hate writing forewords as much as you hate reading them.

You already know you like *Applegeeks*, or at least you know you like the look of it enough to have spent the money. You have all this vibrant, amazing art waiting for you just a page or two away, and this blowhard Kurtz is holding you up. Meanwhile, do you really expect you'll buy into all the smoke I'm about to blow up your ass about how awesome *Applegeeks* truly is? Obviously they asked me to write this thing. They wouldn't have asked me if they expected I was going to sit here and tell you that I consider *Applegeeks* to be . . . meh . . . okay, I guess.

So let's keep this short. For your sake and for mine. And let's keep it honest, 'cause nobody likes to be pandered to.

For the longest time, I never read this comic strip. I was totally aware of it. It's impossible not to be because Mohammad Haque's art is so amazing that every time I see it, I can't decide if I want to punch him or myself in the face. Every time I think that he can't get any better, he does. One time I watched a YouTube video of Hawk coloring on his Wacom Cintiq and at least three times I yelled "@$%& YOU!" at the screen.

No, to be honest, I avoided *Applegeeks* for a while. I assumed, falsely, that it was just another one of these manga-influenced comics that pandered to its audience. While I certainly admired the art, I wasn't going to invest the time to read the comic. There are a lot of webcomics out there, and I simply don't have the time to read all of them.

But I'll tell you something, two things happened that turned me around and got me invested in *Applegeeks*: I met Hawk, and I learned more about Eve.

If you go by what you see online, you might think that Hawk is some hardened art god adorned in flowing black robes, who wields a giant Wacom pen like Poseidon might wield a trident. While that might be true ONLINE, let me tell you . . . offline he's a real teddy bear. Hawk is such a sweet, genuine guy, who is truly passionate about art. He's eager to learn and he's even more eager to share what he already knows. I had the honor of spending a lot of time with Hawk at last year's New York Comic Con. Hawk kept me company in my booth. He even watched the booth for me while I had to step away. I was sad to say goodbye.

And that led me to check out the strip in more detail. Which is when I learned all about Eve.

Now anyone who owns a Mac knows we all fetishize our machines. The brushed aluminum, the polished glass, the vibrant display, and those sleek, sleek lines. Ooh-la-la. I'm sure Hawk is not the first Apple geek to consider the idea of building a robot girlfriend out of Apple hardware. But what makes *Applegeeks* so special, and what really is a strong testament to both Hawk and Ananth, is that with the character of Eve, these guys didn't take the obvious path.

How easy it would have been for Eve, the hot anime-style robot babe made out of Apple parts, to fall instantly in love with her creator (modeled after the artist himself). But instead, Eve didn't turn out as expected. Once activated, Hawk's comic alter ego discovered that she had a childlike mind, prone to wonder and emotional outbursts. He wanted a girlfriend, he got a child. He wanted a screw, he got a huge responsibility. That threw me. That SURPRISED me. That was compelling as hell. I wanted to read more.

Applegeeks doesn't always take the easy way out. Yes, the strip is about tech nerds who drool over the latest offering from Cupertino. But it's also a strip about friendship, heritage, growing up, the hardships of love, and ultimately, deciding who it is you're supposed to be.

If you think about it, *Applegeeks* is designed a lot like the wonderful Apple products it celebrates. Initially, you're drawn to it by the classy design. However, the reason you stay, the reason you get passionate and return again and again, is because of the user experience.

You can't fake that. That's talent and passion channeled through discipline.

And it's all made on a Mac.

@$%& PCs!

—*Scott R. Kurtz*
Dallas, Texas
May 2009

I was in elementary school when I was first introduced to the Internet. My dad had a dial-up connection he was able to use through work, so sometimes he would let my brother and me log on and muck around. My first real exposure to chat rooms was at my best friend's house, through his AOL account. It wasn't until years later that I realized we were what people now call "trolls."

I certainly had friends in middle school and high school, but, like many people, many of my closest buddies were from the Internet. There were a lot of us—congenitally shy kids who were just more comfortable expressing ourselves online rather than in person— whose cyber friendships persisted over the years, from the Internet into real life. One of my closest friends, Jess, has been with me since I was ten. Nowadays if Hawk and I have to do a show, she'll often come stay with us. We've found we get on even better in person than we did over the Internet—I didn't think she could become a closer friend than she was, but that's what happened. We don't always get to hang out, but the time we spend together has had a positive effect on our conversations online.

The Internet is pretty cool sometimes.

It shouldn't really surprise anyone that *Applegeeks* started on the Internet. For people like Hawk and me, it is an ideal arrangement—we grew up on the Internet, and we have some experience forging relationships there. I think it's part of what has helped us become so connected with our readers. My sincerest hope is that these print collections of our comics will help deepen that connection with you too.

Will it work? Come see us at a convention and let us know! We're always happy to chat, whether it's online or off.

—Ananth Panagariya
Washington DC
May 2009

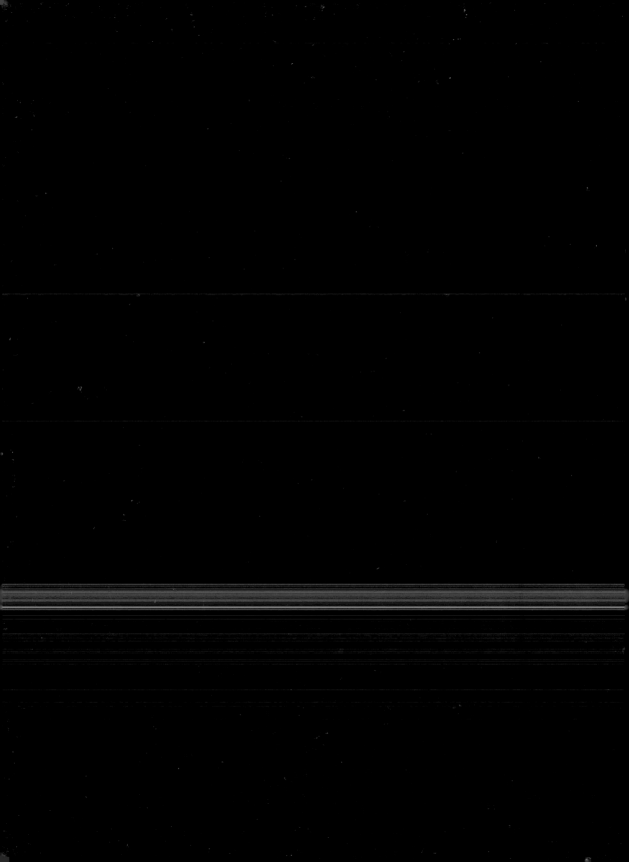

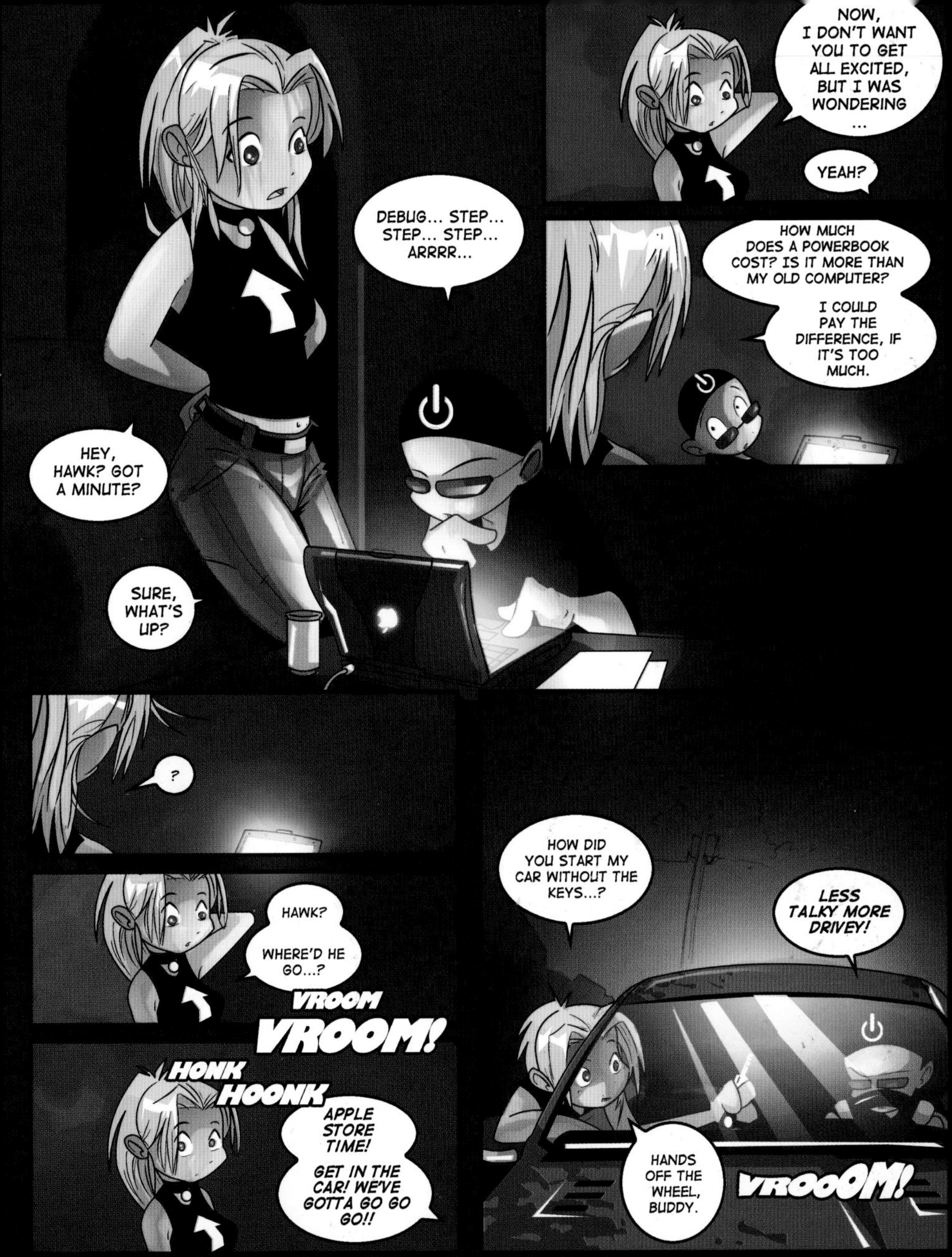
DEBUG... STEP... STEP... STEP... ARRRR...
HEY, HAWK? GOT A MINUTE?
SURE, WHAT'S UP?
NOW, I DON'T WANT YOU TO GET ALL EXCITED, BUT I WAS WONDERING ...
YEAH?
HOW MUCH DOES A POWERBOOK COST? IS IT MORE THAN MY OLD COMPUTER?
I COULD PAY THE DIFFERENCE, IF IT'S TOO MUCH.
?
HAWK?
WHERE'D HE GO...?
VROOM
VROOM!
HONK
HOONK
APPLE STORE TIME!
GET IN THE CAR! WE'VE GOTTA GO GO GO!!
HOW DID YOU START MY CAR WITHOUT THE KEYS...?
LESS TALKY MORE DRIVEY!
HANDS OFF THE WHEEL, BUDDY.
VROOOM!

This is a pretty accurate portrayal of Hawk's behavior. It doesn't matter what he has on his agenda—if there's even a *remotely* good reason for him to drop everything and go to the Apple store, he'll do it. Some people look at porn ... Hawk goes to apple.com.

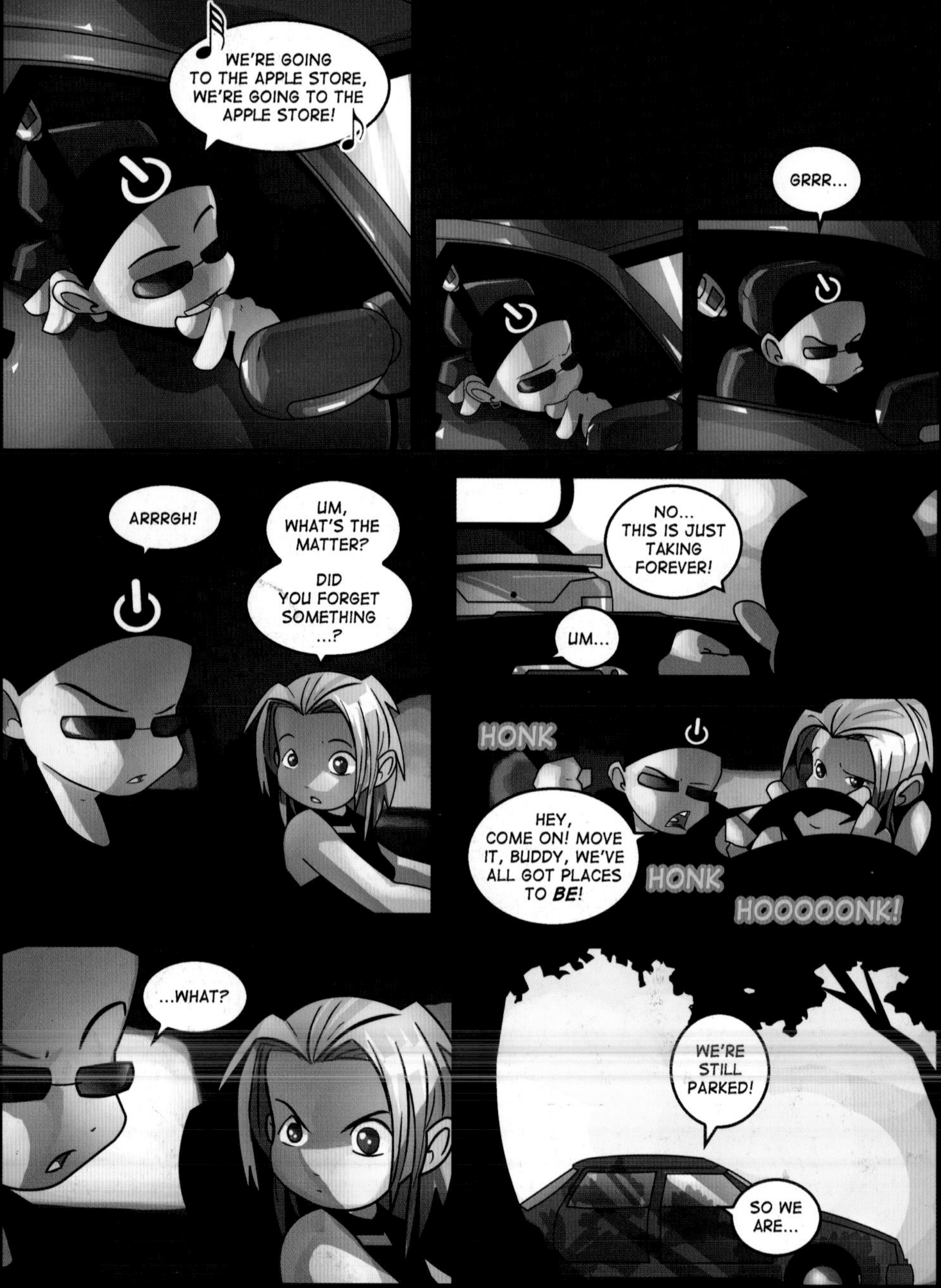
WE'RE GOING TO THE APPLE STORE, WE'RE GOING TO THE APPLE STORE!
GRRR...
ARRRGH!
UM, WHAT'S THE MATTER?
DID YOU FORGET SOMETHING ...?
NO... THIS IS JUST TAKING FOREVER!
UM...
HONK
HEY, COME ON! MOVE IT, BUDDY, WE'VE ALL GOT PLACES TO *BE*!
HONK
HOOOOONK!
...WHAT?
WE'RE STILL PARKED!
SO WE ARE...

Sometimes impatience is a virtue.

A lot of things happened between the last volume and this one! Hawk built a house out of old G4s. I started my first

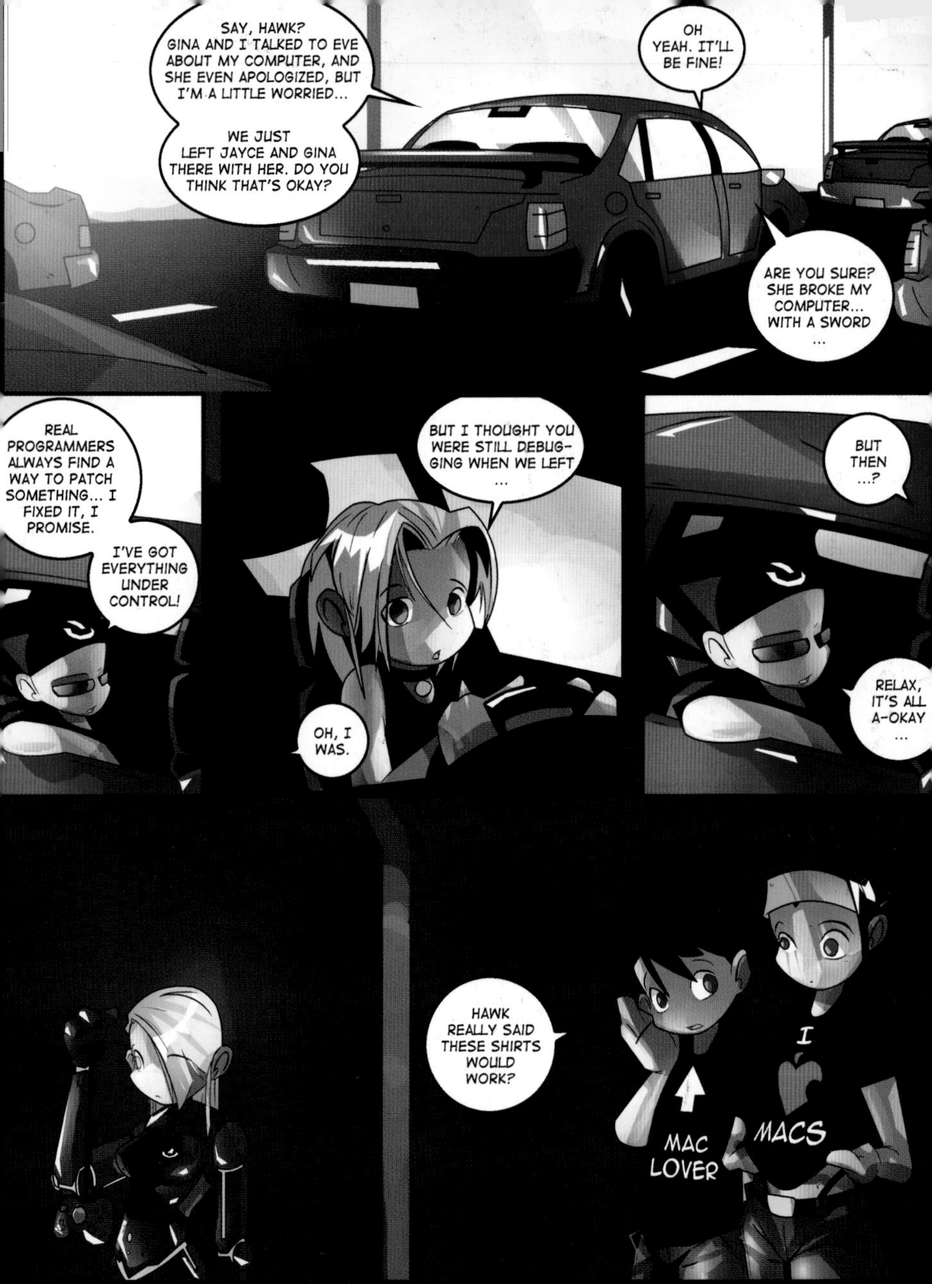
SAY, HAWK? GINA AND I TALKED TO EVE ABOUT MY COMPUTER, AND SHE EVEN APOLOGIZED, BUT I'M A LITTLE WORRIED...
WE JUST LEFT JAYCE AND GINA THERE WITH HER. DO YOU THINK THAT'S OKAY?
OH YEAH. IT'LL BE FINE!
ARE YOU SURE? SHE BROKE MY COMPUTER... WITH A SWORD ...
REAL PROGRAMMERS ALWAYS FIND A WAY TO PATCH SOMETHING... I FIXED IT, I PROMISE.
I'VE GOT EVERYTHING UNDER CONTROL!
BUT I THOUGHT YOU WERE STILL DEBUG-GING WHEN WE LEFT ...
OH, I WAS.
BUT THEN ...?
RELAX, IT'S ALL A-OKAY ...
HAWK REALLY SAID THESE SHIRTS WOULD WORK?
MAC LOVER
I
MACS

netimes we need lo-fi solutions to high-tech problems! Although it *does* seem likely that Hawk left his fri
die at the hands of his homicidal robot girlfriend while he went off to the Apple store on a flight of fancy

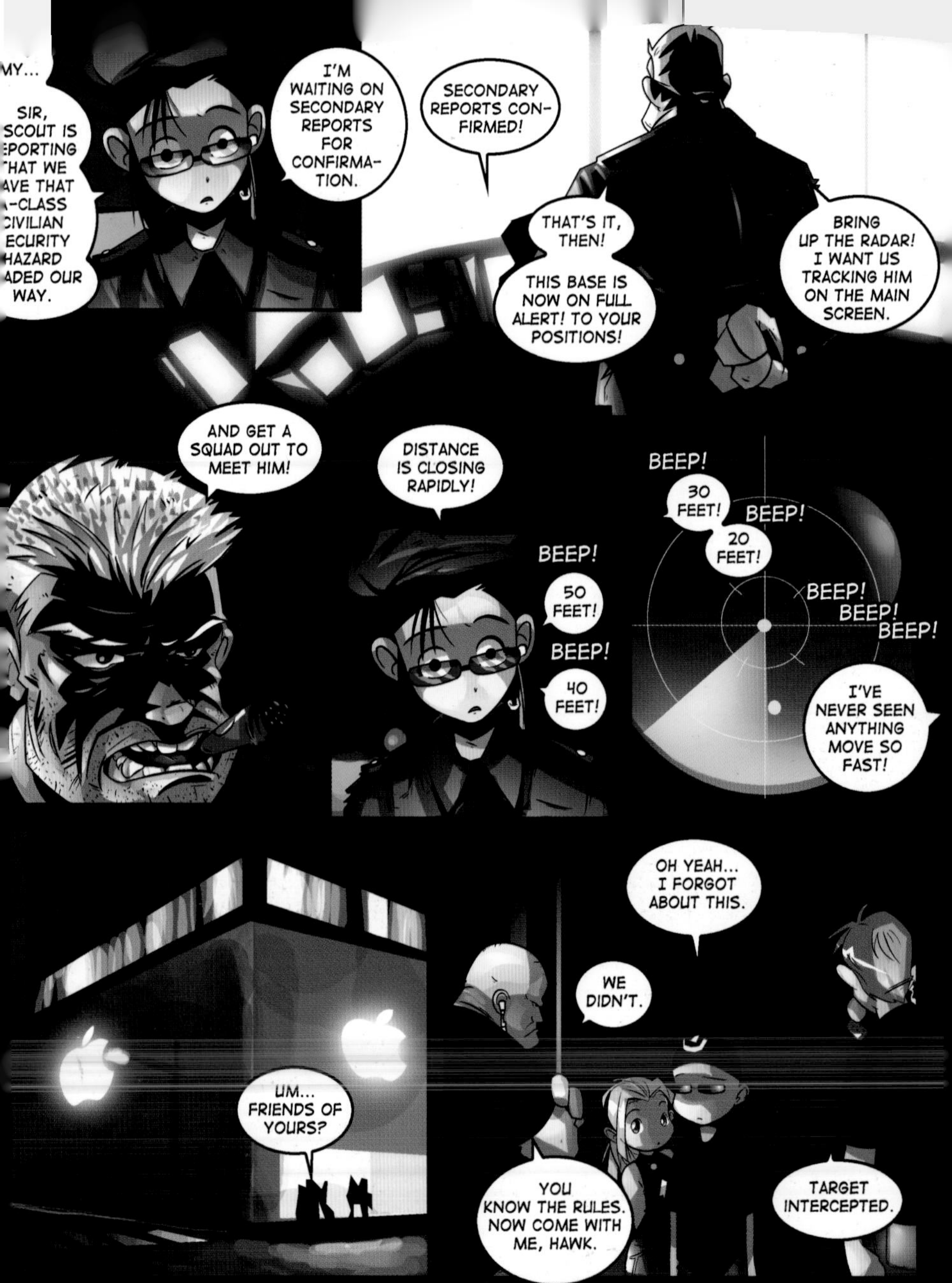

MY...
SIR, SCOUT IS EPORTING THAT WE AVE THAT -CLASS CIVILIAN ECURITY HAZARD ADED OUR WAY.
I'M WAITING ON SECONDARY REPORTS FOR CONFIRMA-TION.
SECONDARY REPORTS CON-FIRMED!
THAT'S IT, THEN!
THIS BASE IS NOW ON FULL ALERT! TO YOUR POSITIONS!
BRING UP THE RADAR! I WANT US TRACKING HIM ON THE MAIN SCREEN.
AND GET A SQUAD OUT TO MEET HIM!
DISTANCE IS CLOSING RAPIDLY!
BEEP!
50 FEET!
BEEP!
40 FEET!
BEEP!
30 FEET!
BEEP!
20 FEET!
BEEP! BEEP! BEEP!
I'VE NEVER SEEN ANYTHING MOVE SO FAST!
UM... FRIENDS OF YOURS?
WE DIDN'T.
OH YEAH... I FORGOT ABOUT THIS.
YOU KNOW THE RULES. NOW COME WITH ME, HAWK.
TARGET INTERCEPTED.

ow, I had always had big plans for the Apple Corps, but nothing ever happened with them. Sometimes thes tunities don't end up presenting themselves. I try to keep a list of open threads so I can tackle them all a point, but these guys just never made it onto my list. I think it actually had a lot to do with Eve being the poin

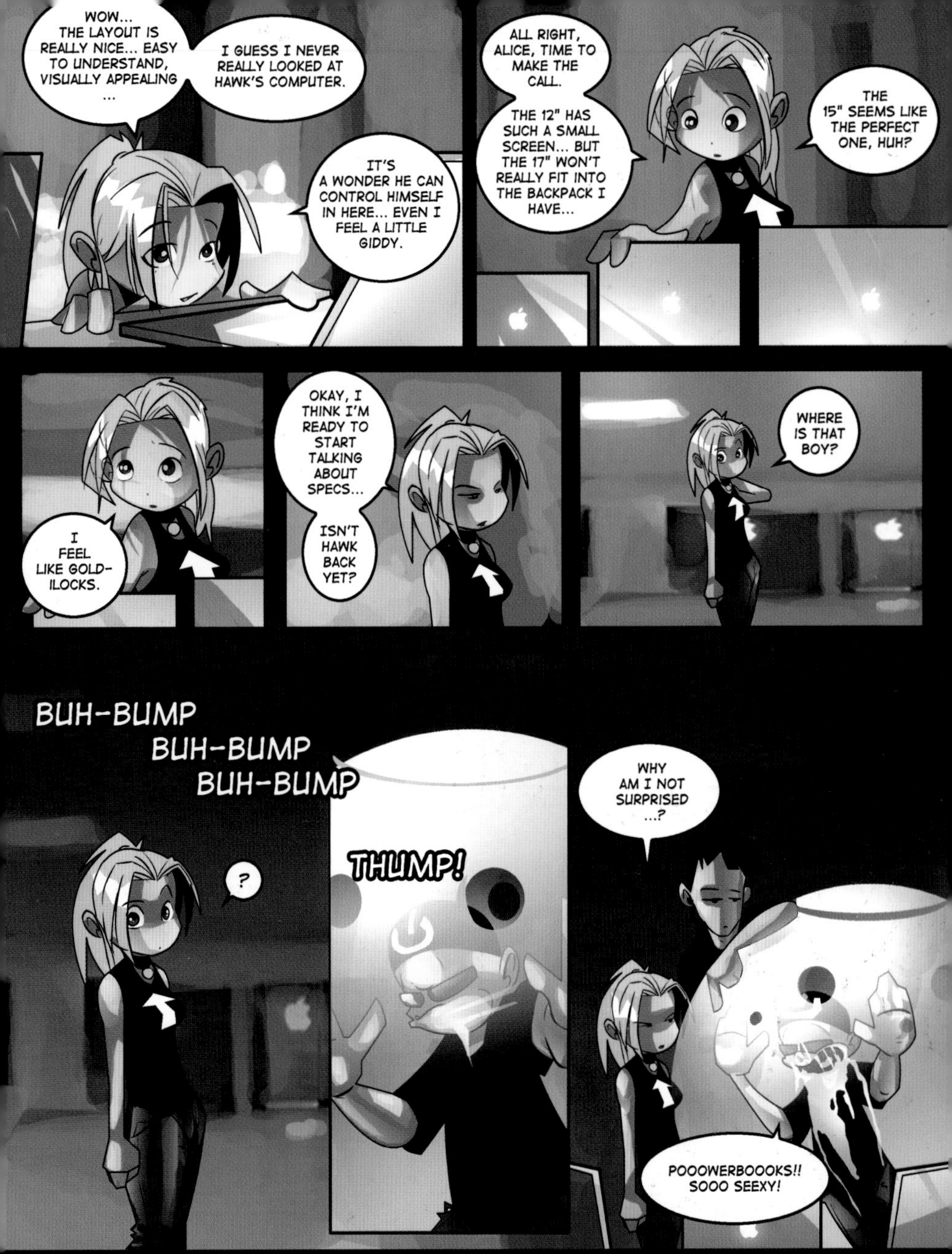
WOW... THE LAYOUT IS REALLY NICE... EASY TO UNDERSTAND, VISUALLY APPEALING ...
I GUESS I NEVER REALLY LOOKED AT HAWK'S COMPUTER.
IT'S A WONDER HE CAN CONTROL HIMSELF IN HERE... EVEN I FEEL A LITTLE GIDDY.
ALL RIGHT, ALICE, TIME TO MAKE THE CALL.
THE 12" HAS SUCH A SMALL SCREEN... BUT THE 17" WON'T REALLY FIT INTO THE BACKPACK I HAVE...
THE 15" SEEMS LIKE THE PERFECT ONE, HUH?
I FEEL LIKE GOLD-ILOCKS.
OKAY, I THINK I'M READY TO START TALKING ABOUT SPECS...
ISN'T HAWK BACK YET?
WHERE IS THAT BOY?
BUH-BUMP
BUH-BUMP
BUH-BUMP
?
THUMP!
WHY AM I NOT SURPRISED ...?
POOOWERBOOOKS!! SOOO SEEXY!

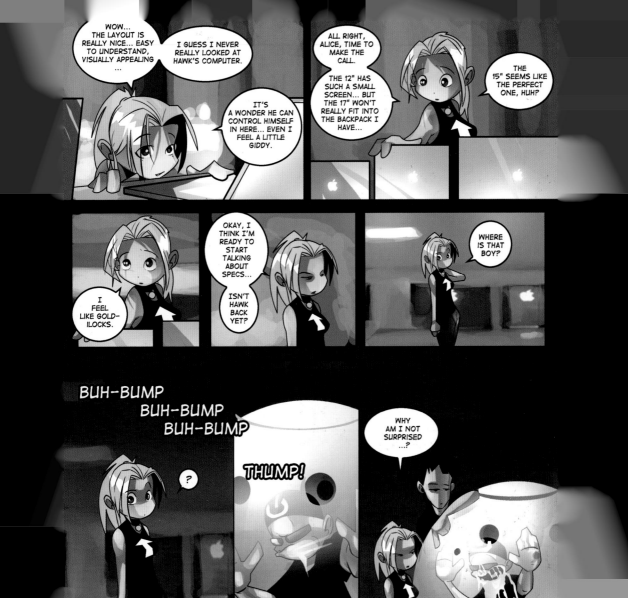

Man, the Powerbooks really date this comic, huh? This was our introduction to the hamster ball, something tha we've used quite often since. I remember staying up late and waiting for Hawk to finish illustrating this one, onl o get totally grossed out by the inhuman amount of drool on the inside of the hamster ball in the last panel

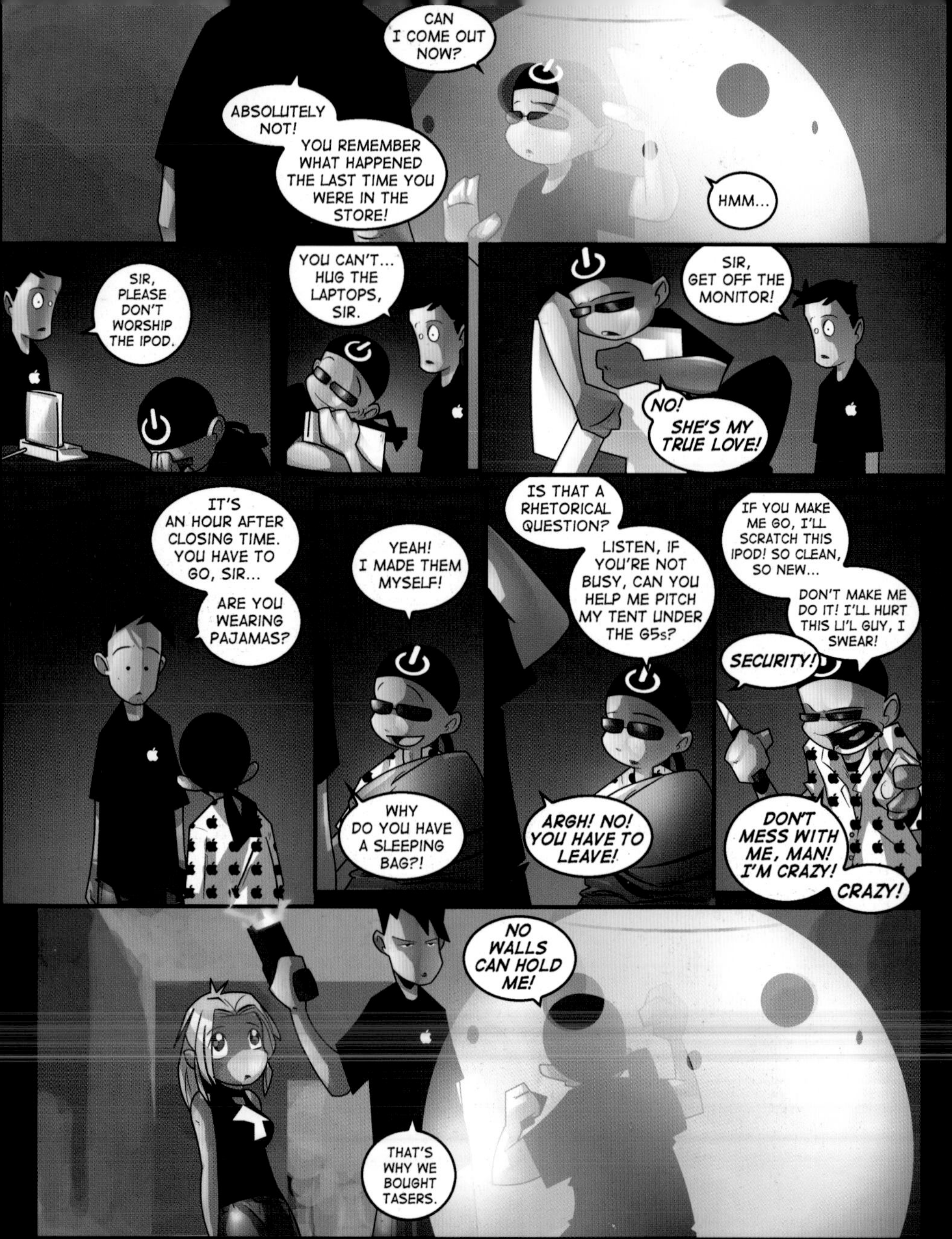
CAN I COME OUT NOW?
ABSOLUTELY NOT!
YOU REMEMBER WHAT HAPPENED THE LAST TIME YOU WERE IN THE STORE!
HMM...
SIR, PLEASE DON'T WORSHIP THE IPOD.
YOU CAN'T... HUG THE LAPTOPS, SIR.
SIR, GET OFF THE MONITOR!
NO! SHE'S MY TRUE LOVE!
IT'S AN HOUR AFTER CLOSING TIME. YOU HAVE TO GO, SIR...
ARE YOU WEARING PAJAMAS?
YEAH! I MADE THEM MYSELF!
WHY DO YOU HAVE A SLEEPING BAG?!
IS THAT A RHETORICAL QUESTION?
LISTEN, IF YOU'RE NOT BUSY, CAN YOU HELP ME PITCH MY TENT UNDER THE G5s?
ARGH! NO! YOU HAVE TO LEAVE!
IF YOU MAKE ME GO, I'LL SCRATCH THIS IPOD! SO CLEAN, SO NEW...
DON'T MAKE ME DO IT! I'LL HURT THIS LI'L GUY, I SWEAR!
SECURITY!
DON'T MESS WITH ME, MAN! I'M CRAZY!
CRAZY!
NO WALLS CAN HOLD ME!
THAT'S WHY WE BOUGHT TASERS.

He *is* crazy, and if he sets his sights on your electronics and shiny things, the best advice I can give you is to just give up. Incredibly, we did this comic before "Don't tase me, bro," but I feel that it can retroactively be applied here.

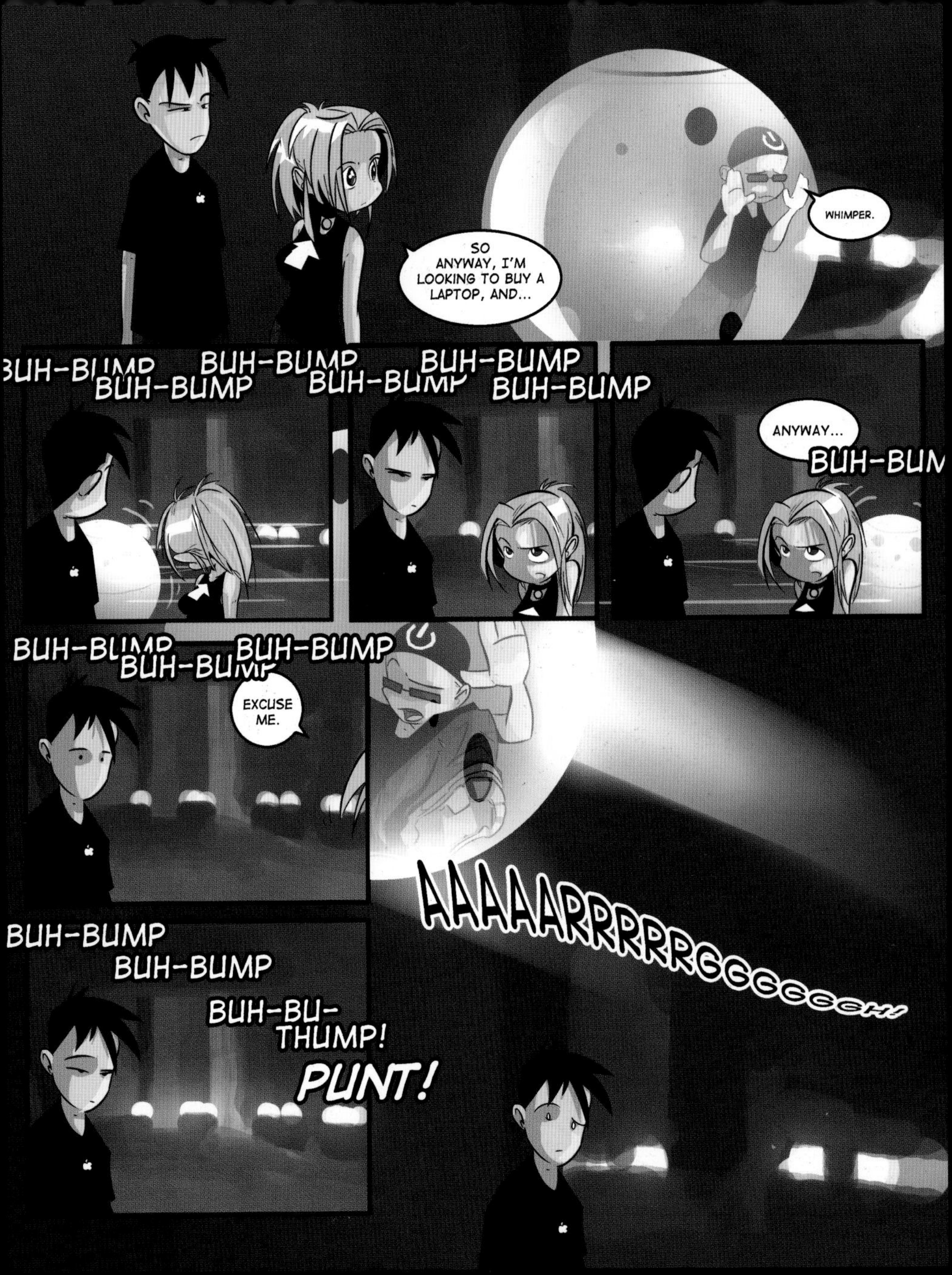
WHIMPER.
SO ANYWAY, I'M LOOKING TO BUY A LAPTOP, AND...
BUH-BUMP
BUH-BUMP
BUH-BUMP
BUH-BUMP
BUH-BUMP
BUH-BUMP
ANYWAY...
BUH-BUM
BUH-BUMP
BUH-BUMP
BUH-BUMP
EXCUSE ME.
AAAAARRRRRGGGGGGH!
BUH-BUMP
BUH-BUMP
BUH-BU-THUMP!
PUNT!

We don't do sound gags very often, but this was one of those comics where I thought we managed to do it to good effect. I also like how Hawk is leaning against the inside of the bubble in the first panel, as though on the brink of rolling

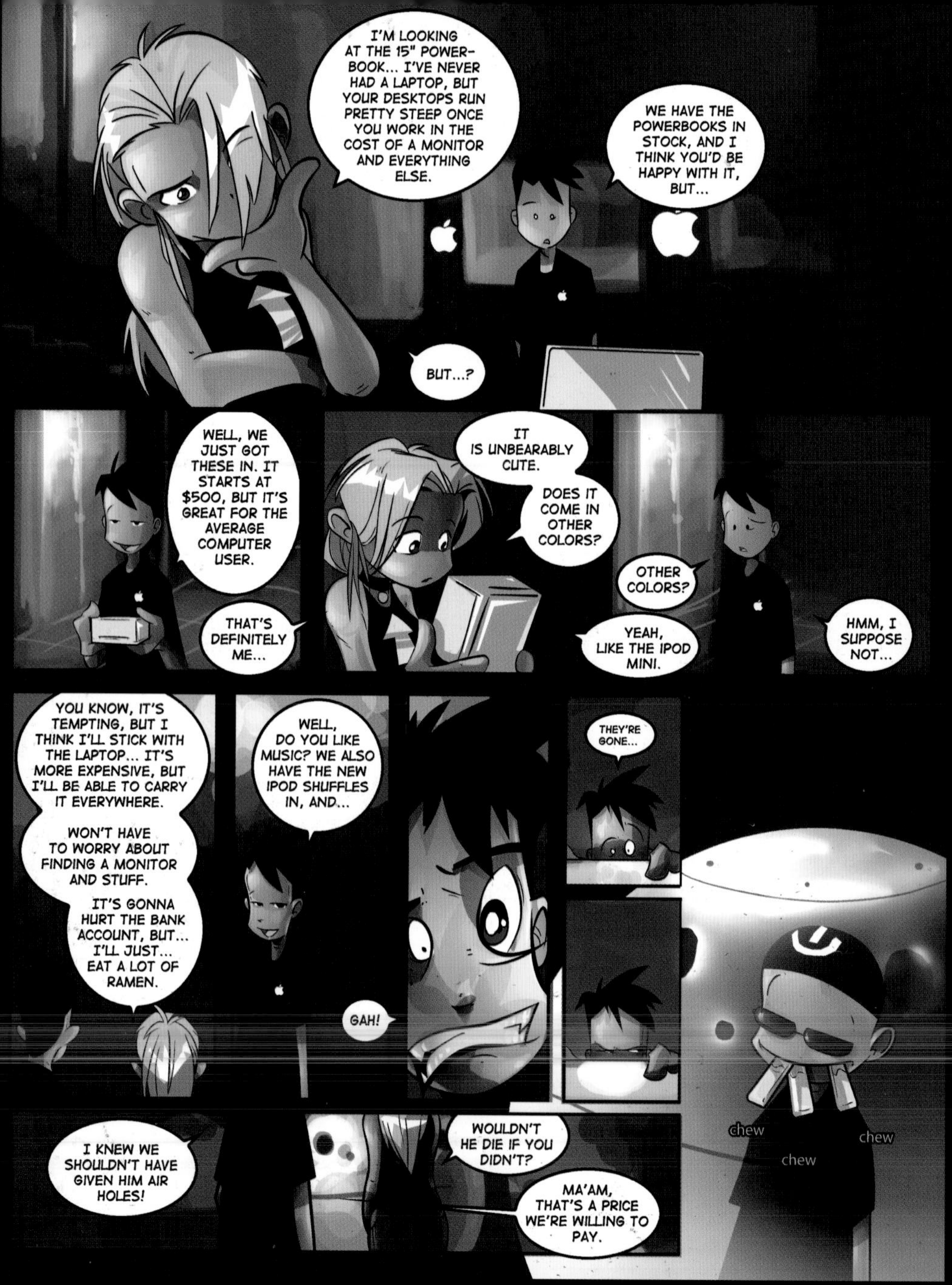
I'M LOOKING AT THE 15" POWER-BOOK... I'VE NEVER HAD A LAPTOP, BUT YOUR DESKTOPS RUN PRETTY STEEP ONCE YOU WORK IN THE COST OF A MONITOR AND EVERYTHING ELSE.
WE HAVE THE POWERBOOKS IN STOCK, AND I THINK YOU'D BE HAPPY WITH IT, BUT...
BUT...?
WELL, WE JUST GOT THESE IN. IT STARTS AT $500, BUT IT'S GREAT FOR THE AVERAGE COMPUTER USER.
THAT'S DEFINITELY ME...
IT IS UNBEARABLY CUTE.
DOES IT COME IN OTHER COLORS?
OTHER COLORS?
YEAH, LIKE THE IPOD MINI.
HMM, I SUPPOSE NOT...
YOU KNOW, IT'S TEMPTING, BUT I THINK I'LL STICK WITH THE LAPTOP... IT'S MORE EXPENSIVE, BUT I'LL BE ABLE TO CARRY IT EVERYWHERE.
WON'T HAVE TO WORRY ABOUT FINDING A MONITOR AND STUFF.
IT'S GONNA HURT THE BANK ACCOUNT, BUT... I'LL JUST... EAT A LOT OF RAMEN.
WELL, DO YOU LIKE MUSIC? WE ALSO HAVE THE NEW IPOD SHUFFLES IN, AND...
GAH!
THEY'RE GONE...
chew
chew
chew
I KNEW WE SHOULDN'T HAVE GIVEN HIM AIR HOLES!
WOULDN'T HE DIE IF YOU DIDN'T?
MA'AM, THAT'S A PRICE WE'RE WILLING TO PAY.

That's a price I'm *also* willing to pay, for the record. Sorry, Hawk. This mini story arc was a way for us to convert a member of the household into a Mac user, and it was a way for me to describe my switch as well—I didn't pick up a Mac laptop till my last year of college. I thought I'd keep my desktop around for the heavy stuff, but no! In

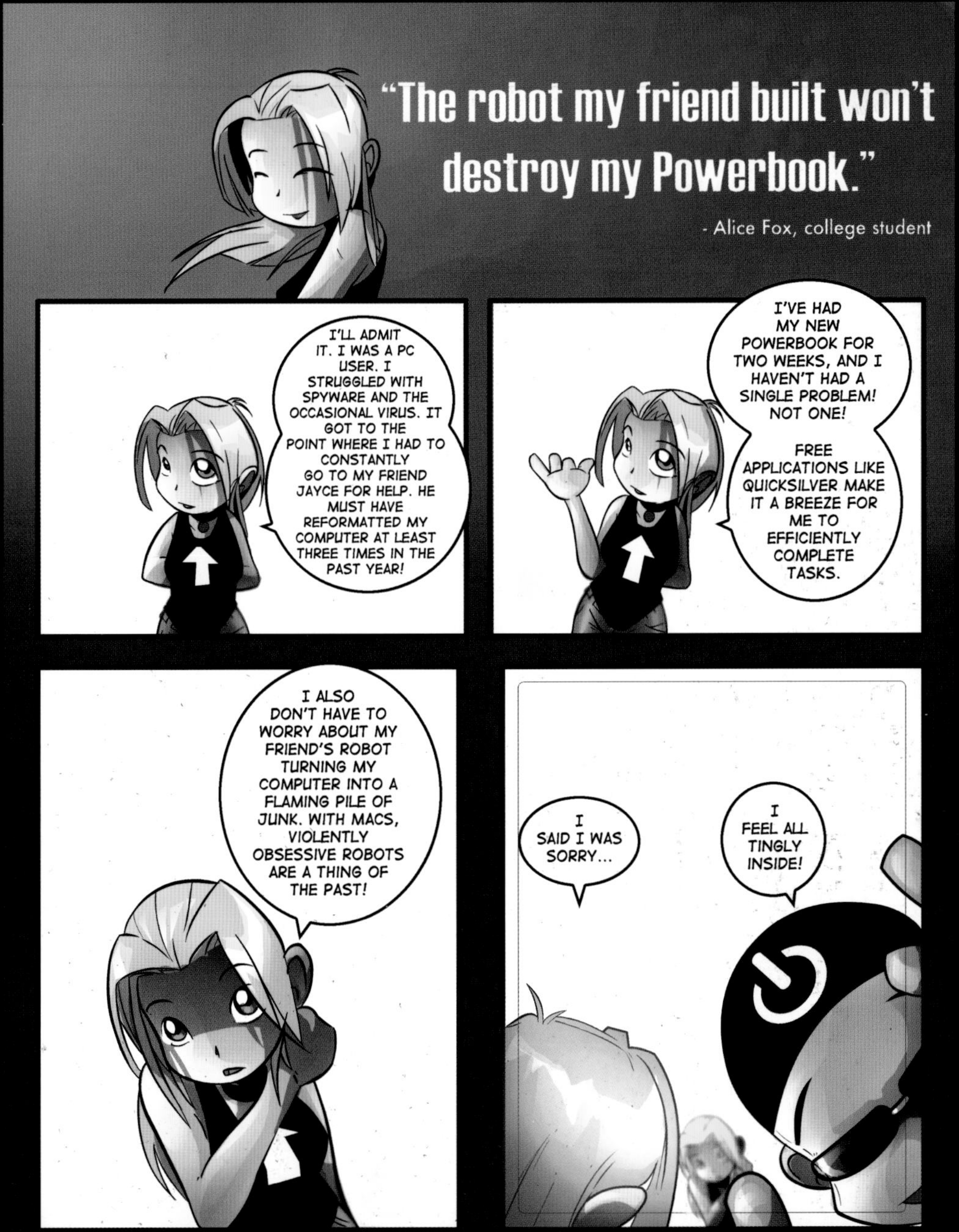
"The robot my friend built won't destroy my Powerbook."
- Alice Fox, college student
I'LL ADMIT IT. I WAS A PC USER. I STRUGGLED WITH SPYWARE AND THE OCCASIONAL VIRUS. IT GOT TO THE POINT WHERE I HAD TO CONSTANTLY GO TO MY FRIEND JAYCE FOR HELP. HE MUST HAVE REFORMATTED MY COMPUTER AT LEAST THREE TIMES IN THE PAST YEAR!
I'VE HAD MY NEW POWERBOOK FOR TWO WEEKS, AND I HAVEN'T HAD A SINGLE PROBLEM! NOT ONE!
FREE APPLICATIONS LIKE QUICKSILVER MAKE IT A BREEZE FOR ME TO EFFICIENTLY COMPLETE TASKS.
I ALSO DON'T HAVE TO WORRY ABOUT MY FRIEND'S ROBOT TURNING MY COMPUTER INTO A FLAMING PILE OF JUNK. WITH MACS, VIOLENTLY OBSESSIVE ROBOTS ARE A THING OF THE PAST!
I SAID I WAS SORRY...
I FEEL ALL TINGLY INSIDE!

We were parodying an old Apple commercial, which should date this comic sufficiently. I believe the format of the original commercial had various users describing their switch from PC to Mac platforms. Apple's ad campaigns have always been pretty fun, if occasionally a little too snarky for my taste.

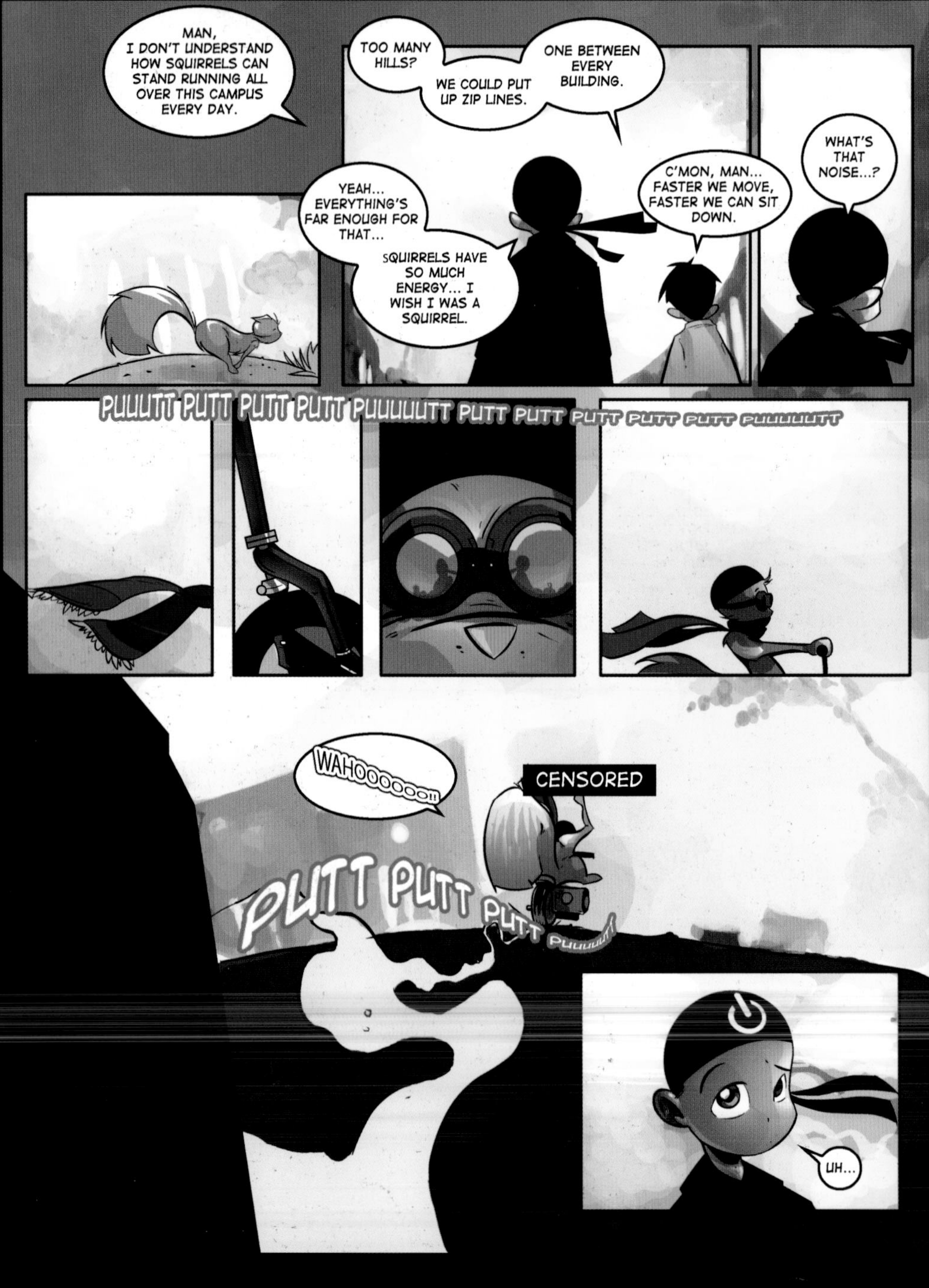
MAN, I DON'T UNDERSTAND HOW SQUIRRELS CAN STAND RUNNING ALL OVER THIS CAMPUS EVERY DAY.
TOO MANY HILLS?
WE COULD PUT UP ZIP LINES.
ONE BETWEEN EVERY BUILDING.
YEAH... EVERYTHING'S FAR ENOUGH FOR THAT...
SQUIRRELS HAVE SO MUCH ENERGY... I WISH I WAS A SQUIRREL.
C'MON, MAN... FASTER WE MOVE, FASTER WE CAN SIT DOWN.
WHAT'S THAT NOISE...?
PUUUTT PUTT PUTT PUTT PUUUUUTT PUTT PUTT PUTT PUTT PUTT PUUUUUUTT
WAHOOOOOOO!!
CENSORED
PUTT PUTT PUTT PUTT Puuuuutt
UH...

I always rather liked the colors in this comic. Squirrels run rampant on the University of Maryland campus, to the point that you're practically tripping over them. We were complaining about how huge our campus was, and the running joke became that even the wildlife had to find quick ways to get around. Oh, and the little scooter . . . It was actually inspired by a girl on campus. She used a Vespa to get to class, and was this total, unbelievable mod knockout.

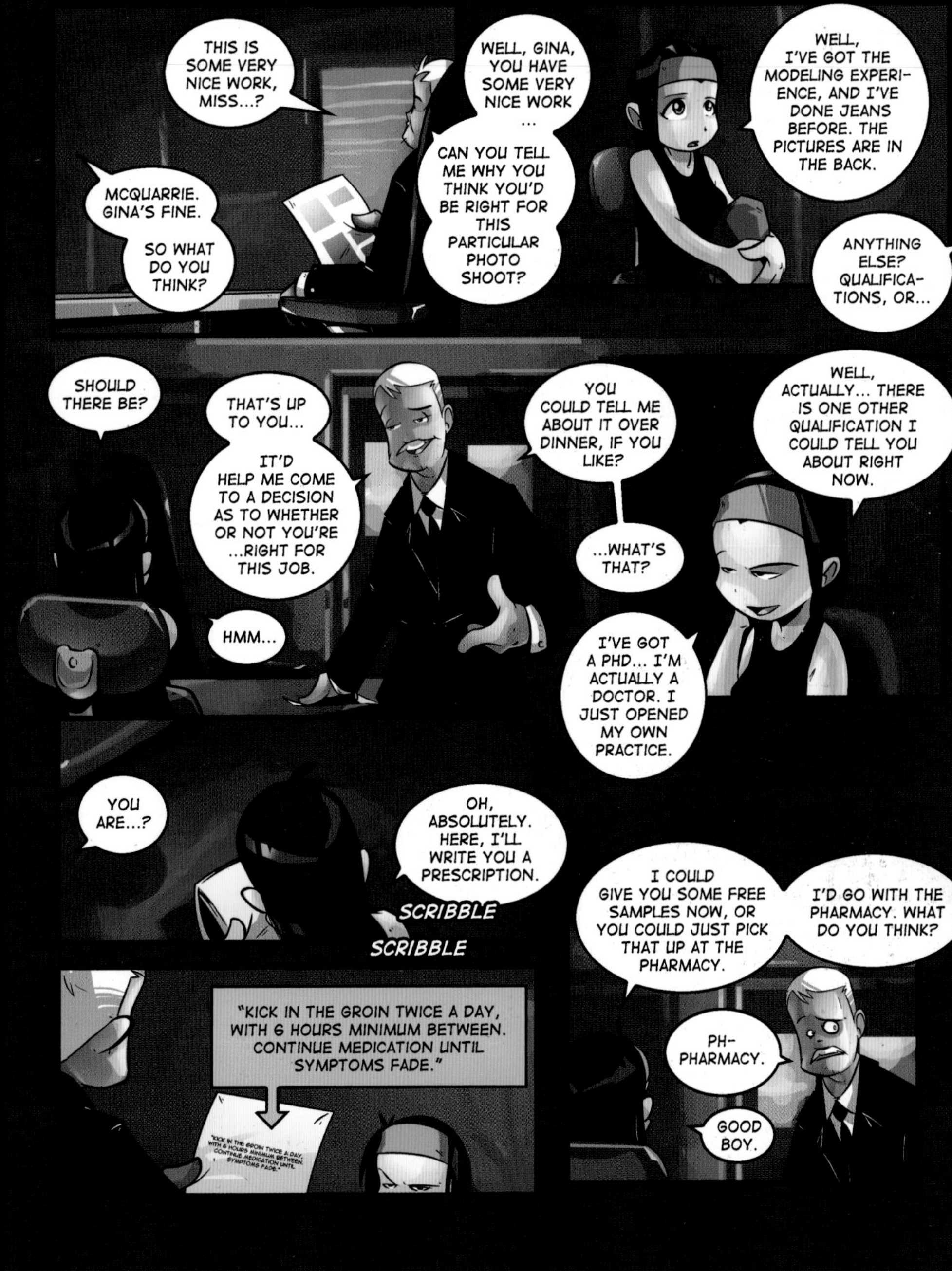
THIS IS SOME VERY NICE WORK, MISS...?
MCQUARRIE. GINA'S FINE.
SO WHAT DO YOU THINK?
WELL, GINA, YOU HAVE SOME VERY NICE WORK ...
CAN YOU TELL ME WHY YOU THINK YOU'D BE RIGHT FOR THIS PARTICULAR PHOTO SHOOT?
WELL, I'VE GOT THE MODELING EXPERI-ENCE, AND I'VE DONE JEANS BEFORE. THE PICTURES ARE IN THE BACK.
ANYTHING ELSE? QUALIFICA-TIONS, OR...
SHOULD THERE BE?
THAT'S UP TO YOU...
IT'D HELP ME COME TO A DECISION AS TO WHETHER OR NOT YOU'RE ...RIGHT FOR THIS JOB.
HMM...
YOU COULD TELL ME ABOUT IT OVER DINNER, IF YOU LIKE?
...WHAT'S THAT?
WELL, ACTUALLY... THERE IS ONE OTHER QUALIFICATION I COULD TELL YOU ABOUT RIGHT NOW.
I'VE GOT A PHD... I'M ACTUALLY A DOCTOR. I JUST OPENED MY OWN PRACTICE.
YOU ARE...?
OH, ABSOLUTELY. HERE, I'LL WRITE YOU A PRESCRIPTION.
SCRIBBLE
SCRIBBLE
"KICK IN THE GROIN TWICE A DAY, WITH 6 HOURS MINIMUM BETWEEN. CONTINUE MEDICATION UNTIL SYMPTOMS FADE."
I COULD GIVE YOU SOME FREE SAMPLES NOW, OR YOU COULD JUST PICK THAT UP AT THE PHARMACY.
I'D GO WITH THE PHARMACY. WHAT DO YOU THINK?
PH-PHARMACY.
GOOD BOY.

I like the colors here as well, and the line work is very crisp. Nice work, Hawk! I heard a friend of mine lament about some of the difficulties she'd had getting into modeling, and it lined up with some things I'd been knocking around for Gina, so this comic happened. Ladies, I salute you. You put up with a lot of crap.

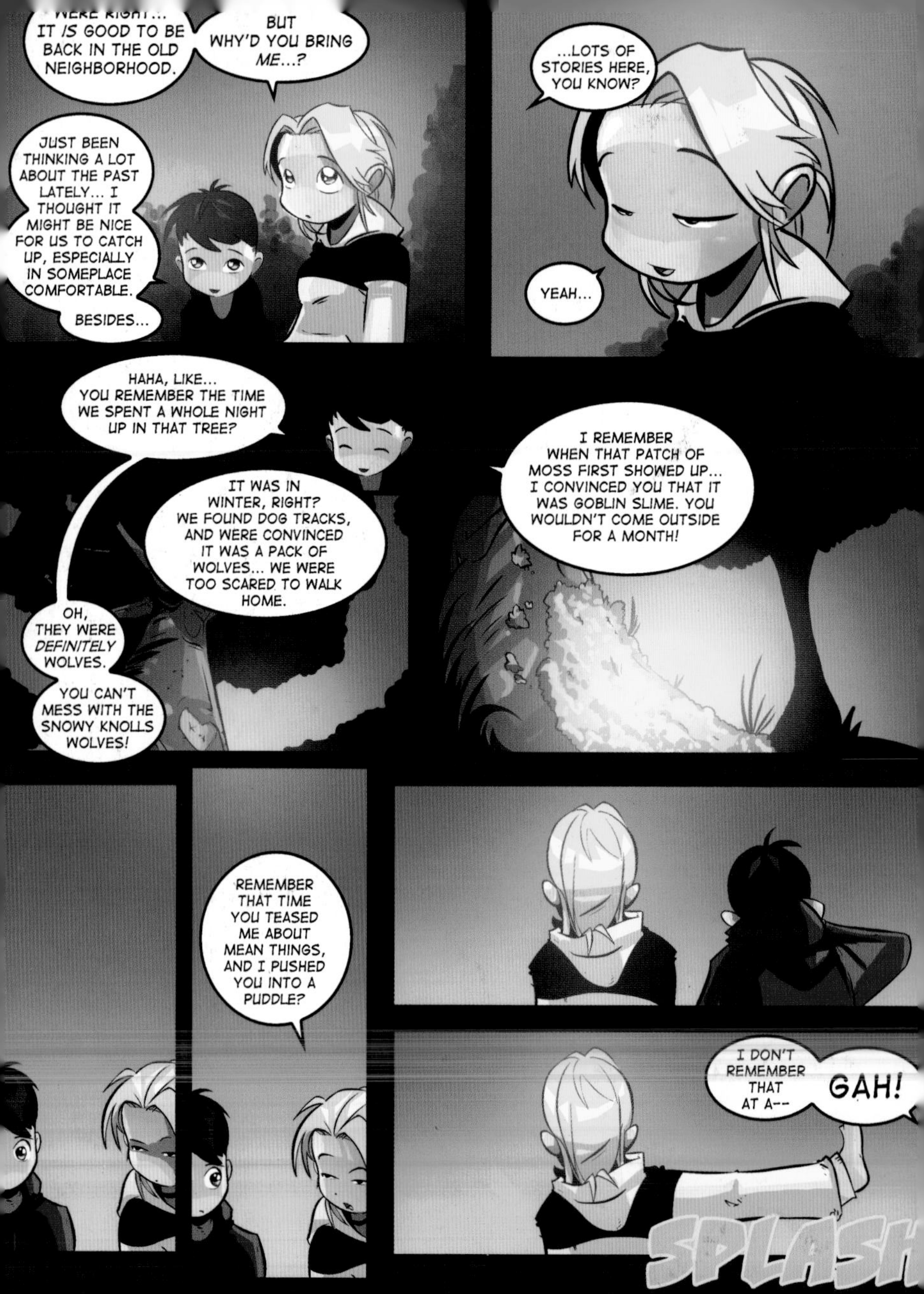
WERE RIGHT... IT *IS* GOOD TO BE BACK IN THE OLD NEIGHBORHOOD.
BUT WHY'D YOU BRING *ME*...?
JUST BEEN THINKING A LOT ABOUT THE PAST LATELY... I THOUGHT IT MIGHT BE NICE FOR US TO CATCH UP, ESPECIALLY IN SOMEPLACE COMFORTABLE.
BESIDES...
...LOTS OF STORIES HERE, YOU KNOW?
YEAH...
HAHA, LIKE... YOU REMEMBER THE TIME WE SPENT A WHOLE NIGHT UP IN THAT TREE?
IT WAS IN WINTER, RIGHT? WE FOUND DOG TRACKS, AND WERE CONVINCED IT WAS A PACK OF WOLVES... WE WERE TOO SCARED TO WALK HOME.
OH, THEY WERE *DEFINITELY* WOLVES.
YOU CAN'T MESS WITH THE SNOWY KNOLLS WOLVES!
I REMEMBER WHEN THAT PATCH OF MOSS FIRST SHOWED UP... I CONVINCED YOU THAT IT WAS GOBLIN SLIME. YOU WOULDN'T COME OUTSIDE FOR A MONTH!
REMEMBER THAT TIME YOU TEASED ME ABOUT MEAN THINGS, AND I PUSHED YOU INTO A PUDDLE?
I DON'T REMEMBER THAT AT A--
GAH!
SPLASH

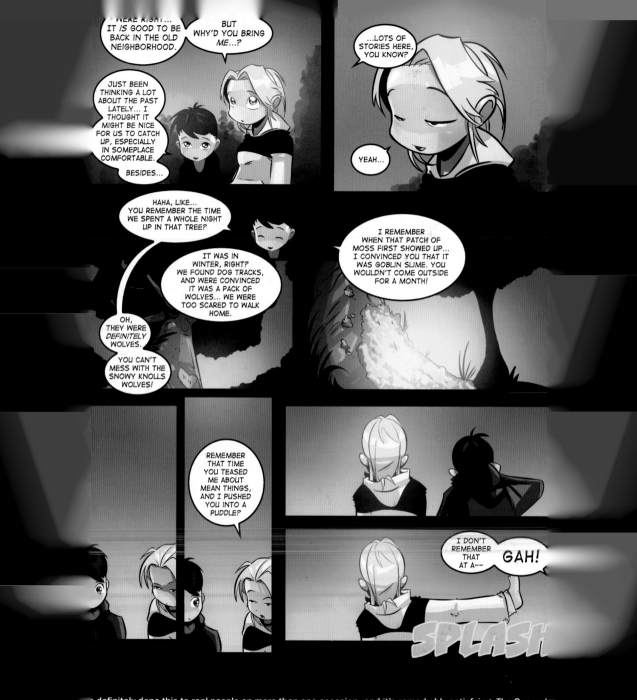

e definitely done this to real people on more than one occasion, and it's remarkably satisfying. The Snowy K es are actually based on a local legend from the neighborhood of my childhood. The story went that there wolves that roamed the neighborhood when a blizzard was at its thickest. Every time there were dog t

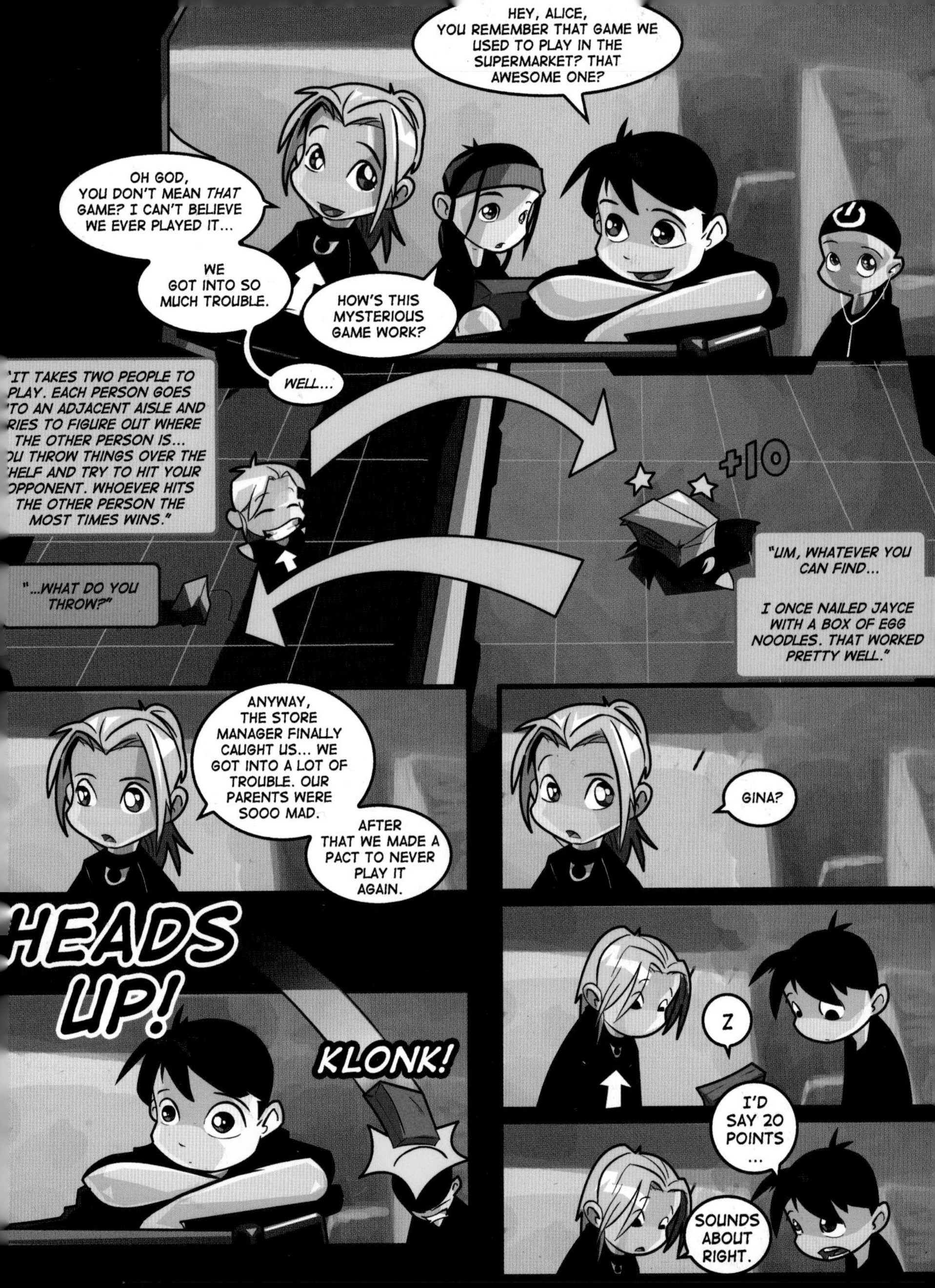
HEY, ALICE, YOU REMEMBER THAT GAME WE USED TO PLAY IN THE SUPERMARKET? THAT AWESOME ONE?
OH GOD, YOU DON'T MEAN *THAT* GAME? I CAN'T BELIEVE WE EVER PLAYED IT...
WE GOT INTO SO MUCH TROUBLE.
HOW'S THIS MYSTERIOUS GAME WORK?
WELL...
"IT TAKES TWO PEOPLE TO PLAY. EACH PERSON GOES TO AN ADJACENT AISLE AND RIES TO FIGURE OUT WHERE THE OTHER PERSON IS... OU THROW THINGS OVER THE HELF AND TRY TO HIT YOUR OPPONENT. WHOEVER HITS THE OTHER PERSON THE MOST TIMES WINS."
+10
"...WHAT DO YOU THROW?"
"UM, WHATEVER YOU CAN FIND...
I ONCE NAILED JAYCE WITH A BOX OF EGG NOODLES. THAT WORKED PRETTY WELL."
ANYWAY, THE STORE MANAGER FINALLY CAUGHT US... WE GOT INTO A LOT OF TROUBLE. OUR PARENTS WERE SOOO MAD.
AFTER THAT WE MADE A PACT TO NEVER PLAY IT AGAIN.
GINA?
HEADS UP!
KLONK!
Z
I'D SAY 20 POINTS ...
SOUNDS ABOUT RIGHT.

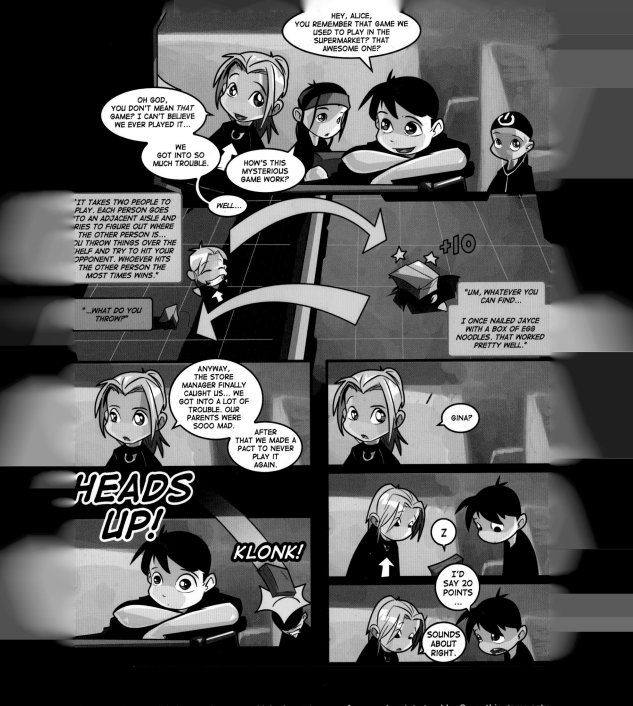

ther one of our terrible invented games, which also got some of our readers into trouble. Guys, this game actu
ates a lot of extra work for supermarket staff, so play it at your own risk (you really shouldn't). Then again,

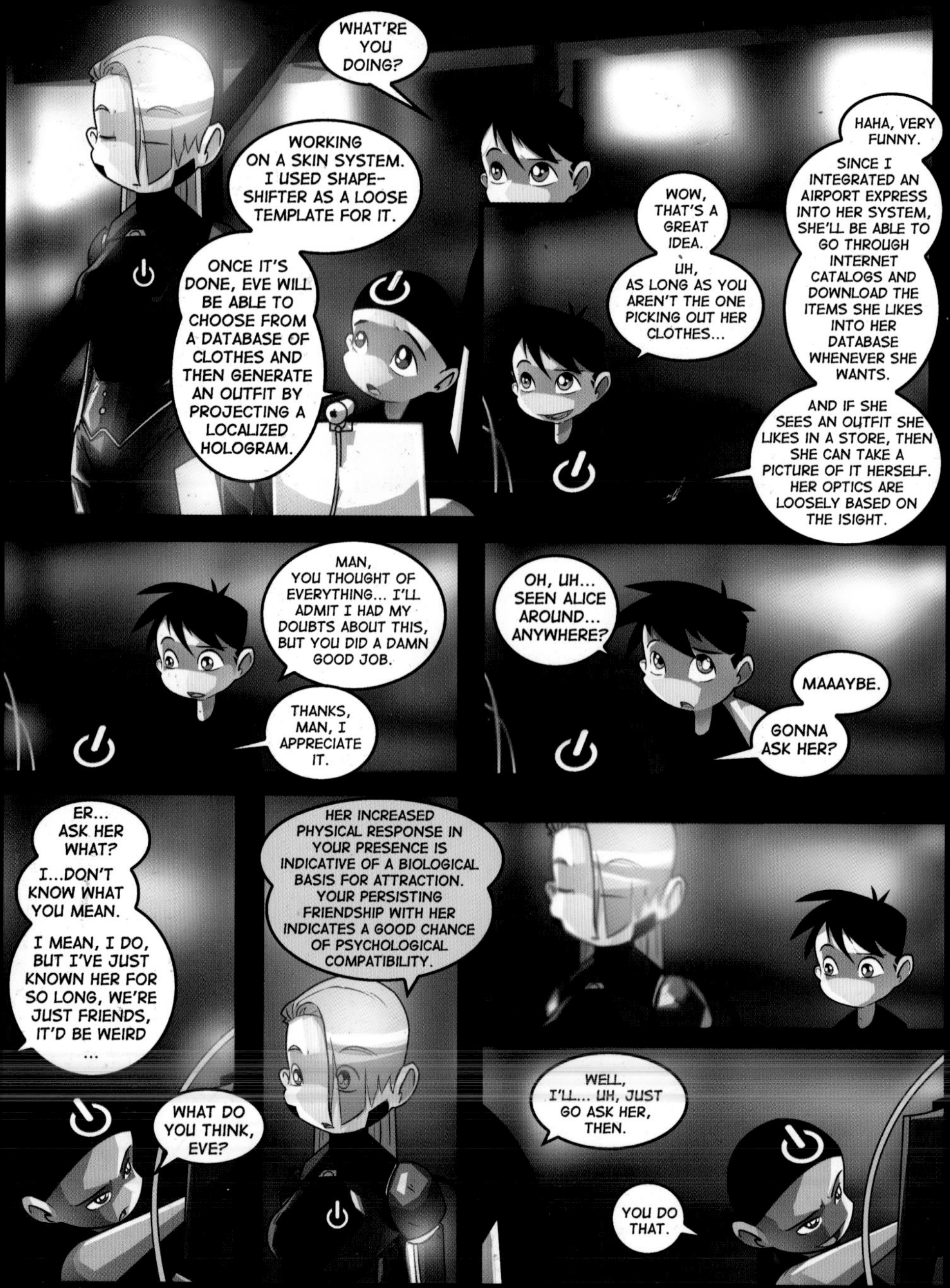
WHAT'RE YOU DOING?
WORKING ON A SKIN SYSTEM. I USED SHAPE-SHIFTER AS A LOOSE TEMPLATE FOR IT.
ONCE IT'S DONE, EVE WILL BE ABLE TO CHOOSE FROM A DATABASE OF CLOTHES AND THEN GENERATE AN OUTFIT BY PROJECTING A LOCALIZED HOLOGRAM.
WOW, THAT'S A GREAT IDEA.
UH, AS LONG AS YOU AREN'T THE ONE PICKING OUT HER CLOTHES...
HAHA, VERY FUNNY.
SINCE I INTEGRATED AN AIRPORT EXPRESS INTO HER SYSTEM, SHE'LL BE ABLE TO GO THROUGH INTERNET CATALOGS AND DOWNLOAD THE ITEMS SHE LIKES INTO HER DATABASE WHENEVER SHE WANTS.
AND IF SHE SEES AN OUTFIT SHE LIKES IN A STORE, THEN SHE CAN TAKE A PICTURE OF IT HERSELF. HER OPTICS ARE LOOSELY BASED ON THE ISIGHT.
MAN, YOU THOUGHT OF EVERYTHING... I'LL ADMIT I HAD MY DOUBTS ABOUT THIS, BUT YOU DID A DAMN GOOD JOB.
THANKS, MAN, I APPRECIATE IT.
OH, UH... SEEN ALICE AROUND... ANYWHERE?
MAAAYBE.
GONNA ASK HER?
ER... ASK HER WHAT?
I...DON'T KNOW WHAT YOU MEAN.
I MEAN, I DO, BUT I'VE JUST KNOWN HER FOR SO LONG, WE'RE JUST FRIENDS, IT'D BE WEIRD ...
WHAT DO YOU THINK, EVE?
HER INCREASED PHYSICAL RESPONSE IN YOUR PRESENCE IS INDICATIVE OF A BIOLOGICAL BASIS FOR ATTRACTION. YOUR PERSISTING FRIENDSHIP WITH HER INDICATES A GOOD CHANCE OF PSYCHOLOGICAL COMPATIBILITY.
WELL, I'LL... UH, JUST GO ASK HER, THEN.
YOU DO THAT.

Whoaaa, that's a wall of text. I was really into puzzling out all the details of how Eve works, and I think that led me to suffer from Shirow Masamune-esque moments (what I've dubbed "Shirowments") from time to time. Also, this began the quiet culmination of our substory about Jayce and Alice's burgeoning relationship.

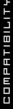

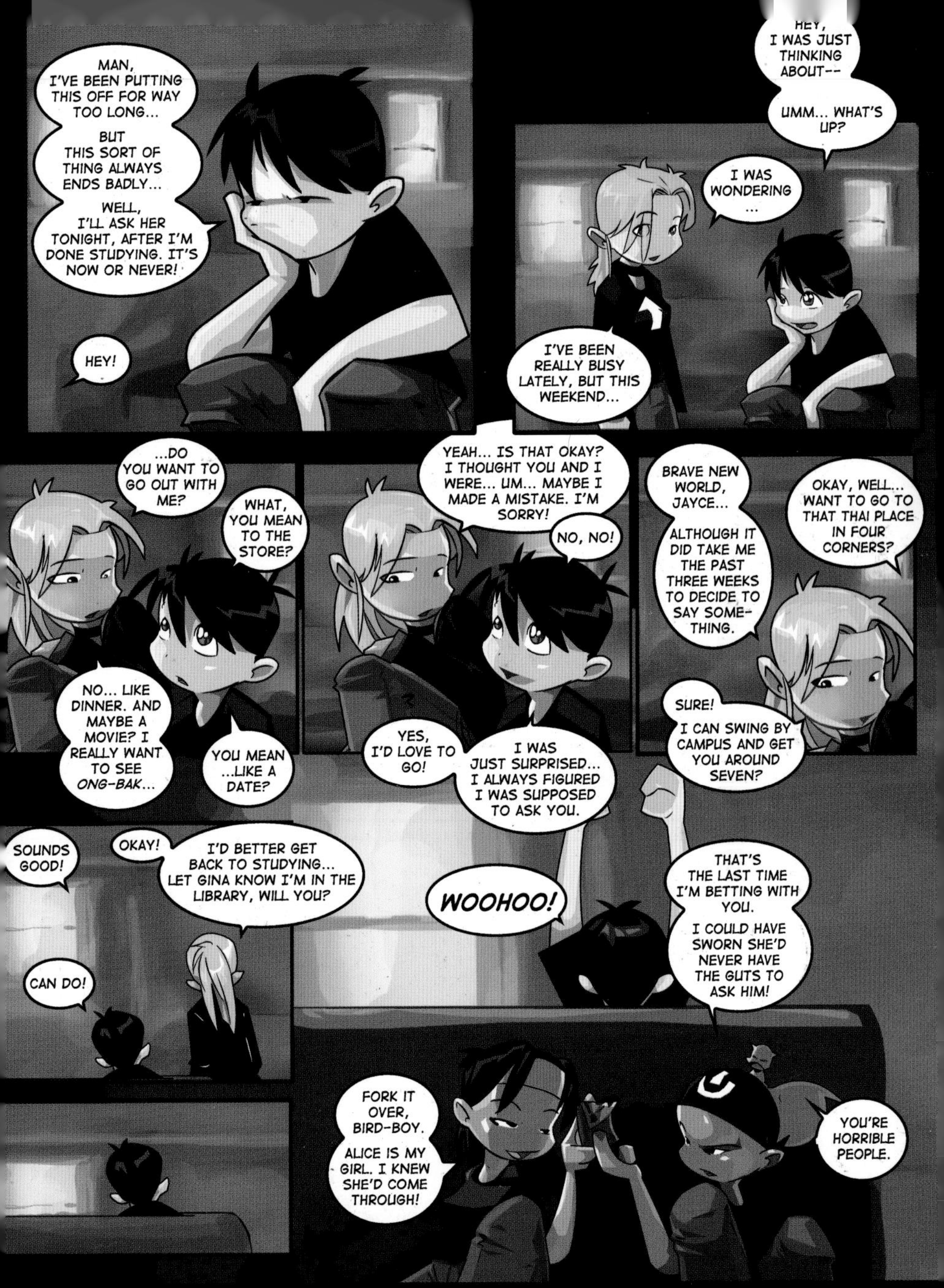
MAN, I'VE BEEN PUTTING THIS OFF FOR WAY TOO LONG...
BUT THIS SORT OF THING ALWAYS ENDS BADLY...
WELL, I'LL ASK HER TONIGHT, AFTER I'M DONE STUDYING. IT'S NOW OR NEVER!
HEY!
HEY, I WAS JUST THINKING ABOUT--
UMM... WHAT'S UP?
I WAS WONDERING ...
I'VE BEEN REALLY BUSY LATELY, BUT THIS WEEKEND...
...DO YOU WANT TO GO OUT WITH ME?
WHAT, YOU MEAN TO THE STORE?
NO... LIKE DINNER. AND MAYBE A MOVIE? I REALLY WANT TO SEE *ONG-BAK*...
YOU MEAN ...LIKE A DATE?
YEAH... IS THAT OKAY? I THOUGHT YOU AND I WERE... UM... MAYBE I MADE A MISTAKE. I'M SORRY!
NO, NO!
YES, I'D LOVE TO GO!
I WAS JUST SURPRISED... I ALWAYS FIGURED I WAS SUPPOSED TO ASK YOU.
BRAVE NEW WORLD, JAYCE...
ALTHOUGH IT DID TAKE ME THE PAST THREE WEEKS TO DECIDE TO SAY SOME-THING.
OKAY, WELL... WANT TO GO TO THAT THAI PLACE IN FOUR CORNERS?
SURE! I CAN SWING BY CAMPUS AND GET YOU AROUND SEVEN?
SOUNDS GOOD!
OKAY!
I'D BETTER GET BACK TO STUDYING... LET GINA KNOW I'M IN THE LIBRARY, WILL YOU?
CAN DO!
WOOHOO!
THAT'S THE LAST TIME I'M BETTING WITH YOU.
I COULD HAVE SWORN SHE'D NEVER HAVE THE GUTS TO ASK HIM!
FORK IT OVER, BIRD-BOY.
ALICE IS MY GIRL. I KNEW SHE'D COME THROUGH!
YOU'RE HORRIBLE PEOPLE.

ccurred to me somewhere along the way that Alice would probably be the one to take the initiative. It seems tc that way a lot of the time when it comes to geek guys. They're just too shy. (I'm often told this is an endearing occasionally infuriating quality.) Actually, let me take this opportunity to say: You guy, you girl... ASK 'EM! It's r

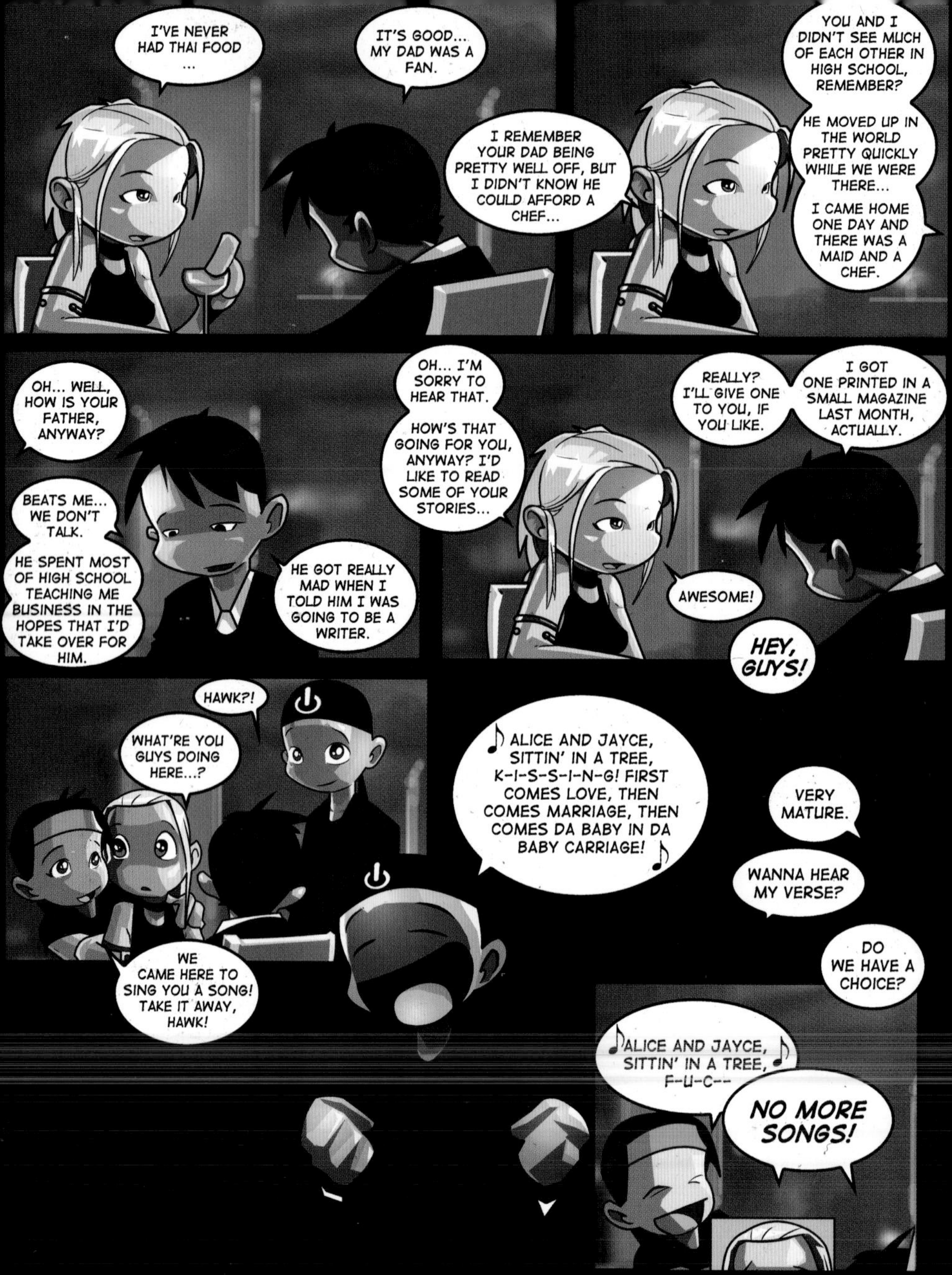
I'VE NEVER HAD THAI FOOD ...
IT'S GOOD... MY DAD WAS A FAN.
I REMEMBER YOUR DAD BEING PRETTY WELL OFF, BUT I DIDN'T KNOW HE COULD AFFORD A CHEF...
YOU AND I DIDN'T SEE MUCH OF EACH OTHER IN HIGH SCHOOL, REMEMBER?
HE MOVED UP IN THE WORLD PRETTY QUICKLY WHILE WE WERE THERE...
I CAME HOME ONE DAY AND THERE WAS A MAID AND A CHEF.
OH... WELL, HOW IS YOUR FATHER, ANYWAY?
BEATS ME... WE DON'T TALK.
HE SPENT MOST OF HIGH SCHOOL TEACHING ME BUSINESS IN THE HOPES THAT I'D TAKE OVER FOR HIM.
HE GOT REALLY MAD WHEN I TOLD HIM I WAS GOING TO BE A WRITER.
OH... I'M SORRY TO HEAR THAT.
HOW'S THAT GOING FOR YOU, ANYWAY? I'D LIKE TO READ SOME OF YOUR STORIES...
I GOT ONE PRINTED IN A SMALL MAGAZINE LAST MONTH, ACTUALLY.
REALLY? I'LL GIVE ONE TO YOU, IF YOU LIKE.
AWESOME!
HEY, GUYS!
HAWK?!
WHAT'RE YOU GUYS DOING HERE...?
WE CAME HERE TO SING YOU A SONG! TAKE IT AWAY, HAWK!
ALICE AND JAYCE, SITTIN' IN A TREE, K-I-S-S-I-N-G! FIRST COMES LOVE, THEN COMES MARRIAGE, THEN COMES DA BABY IN DA BABY CARRIAGE!
VERY MATURE.
WANNA HEAR MY VERSE?
DO WE HAVE A CHOICE?
ALICE AND JAYCE, SITTIN' IN A TREE, F-U-C--
NO MORE SONGS!

. . . and their first date ruined in record time! You know, as far as ruiners go, Hawk and Gina actually make a remarkably effective team. Also, the thing on Alice's arm reminds me of Demona from *Gargoyles*—remember that show?

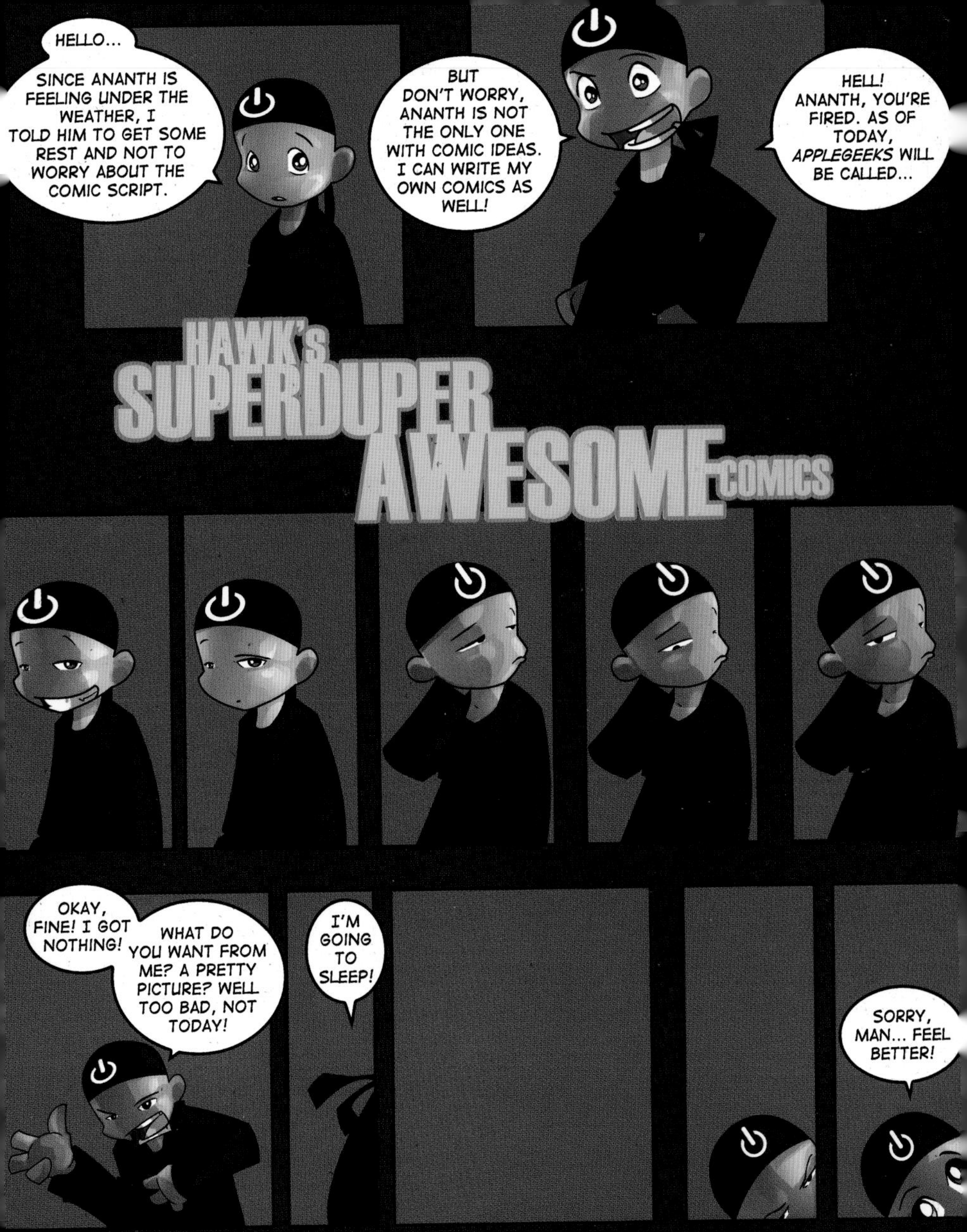
HELLO...
SINCE ANANTH IS FEELING UNDER THE WEATHER, I TOLD HIM TO GET SOME REST AND NOT TO WORRY ABOUT THE COMIC SCRIPT.
BUT DON'T WORRY, ANANTH IS NOT THE ONLY ONE WITH COMIC IDEAS. I CAN WRITE MY OWN COMICS AS WELL!
HELL! ANANTH, YOU'RE FIRED. AS OF TODAY, *APPLEGEEKS* WILL BE CALLED...
HAWK's SUPERDUPER AWESOME COMICS
OKAY, FINE! I GOT NOTHING!
WHAT DO YOU WANT FROM ME? A PRETTY PICTURE? WELL TOO BAD, NOT TODAY!
I'M GOING TO SLEEP!
SORRY, MAN... FEEL BETTER!

is was something really nice that Hawk did for me when I was really sick. Thanks, buddy, I still really apprecia

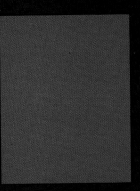

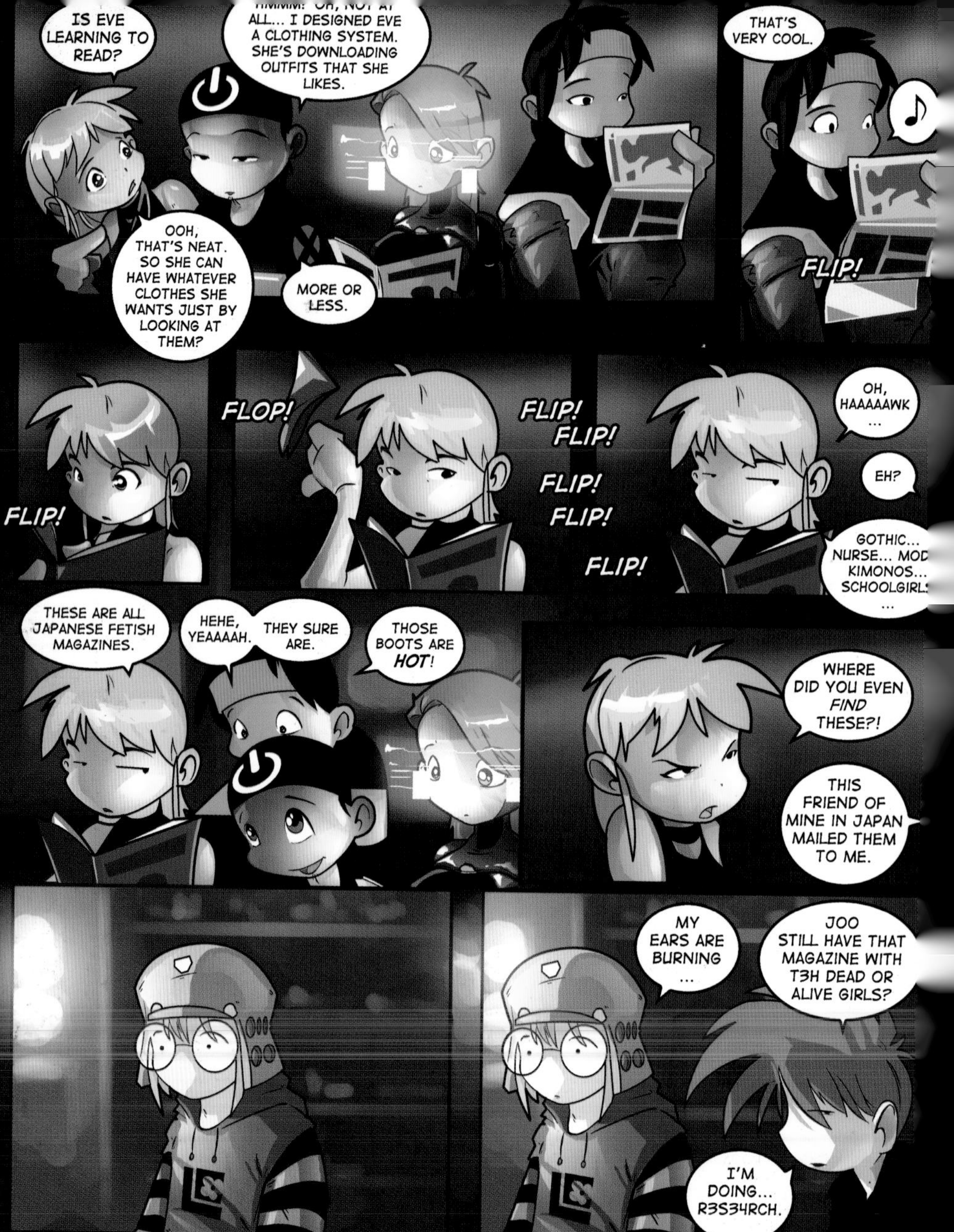
IS EVE LEARNING TO READ?
ALL... I DESIGNED EVE A CLOTHING SYSTEM. SHE'S DOWNLOADING OUTFITS THAT SHE LIKES.
OOH, THAT'S NEAT. SO SHE CAN HAVE WHATEVER CLOTHES SHE WANTS JUST BY LOOKING AT THEM?
MORE OR LESS.
THAT'S VERY COOL.
♪
FLIP!
FLIP!
FLOP!
FLIP!
FLIP!
FLIP!
FLIP!
FLIP!
OH, HAAAAAWK ...
EH?
GOTHIC... NURSE... MOD KIMONOS... SCHOOLGIRLS ...
THESE ARE ALL JAPANESE FETISH MAGAZINES.
HEHE, YEAAAAH.
THEY SURE ARE.
THOSE BOOTS ARE *HOT*!
WHERE DID YOU EVEN *FIND* THESE?!
THIS FRIEND OF MINE IN JAPAN MAILED THEM TO ME.
MY EARS ARE BURNING ...
JOO STILL HAVE THAT MAGAZINE WITH T3H DEAD OR ALIVE GIRLS?
I'M DOING... R3S34RCH.

I always thought this cameo went smoothly. It's also the first time we ever crossed over with Fred Gallagher's *Mega*
but it certainly isn't the last! Just keep on reading

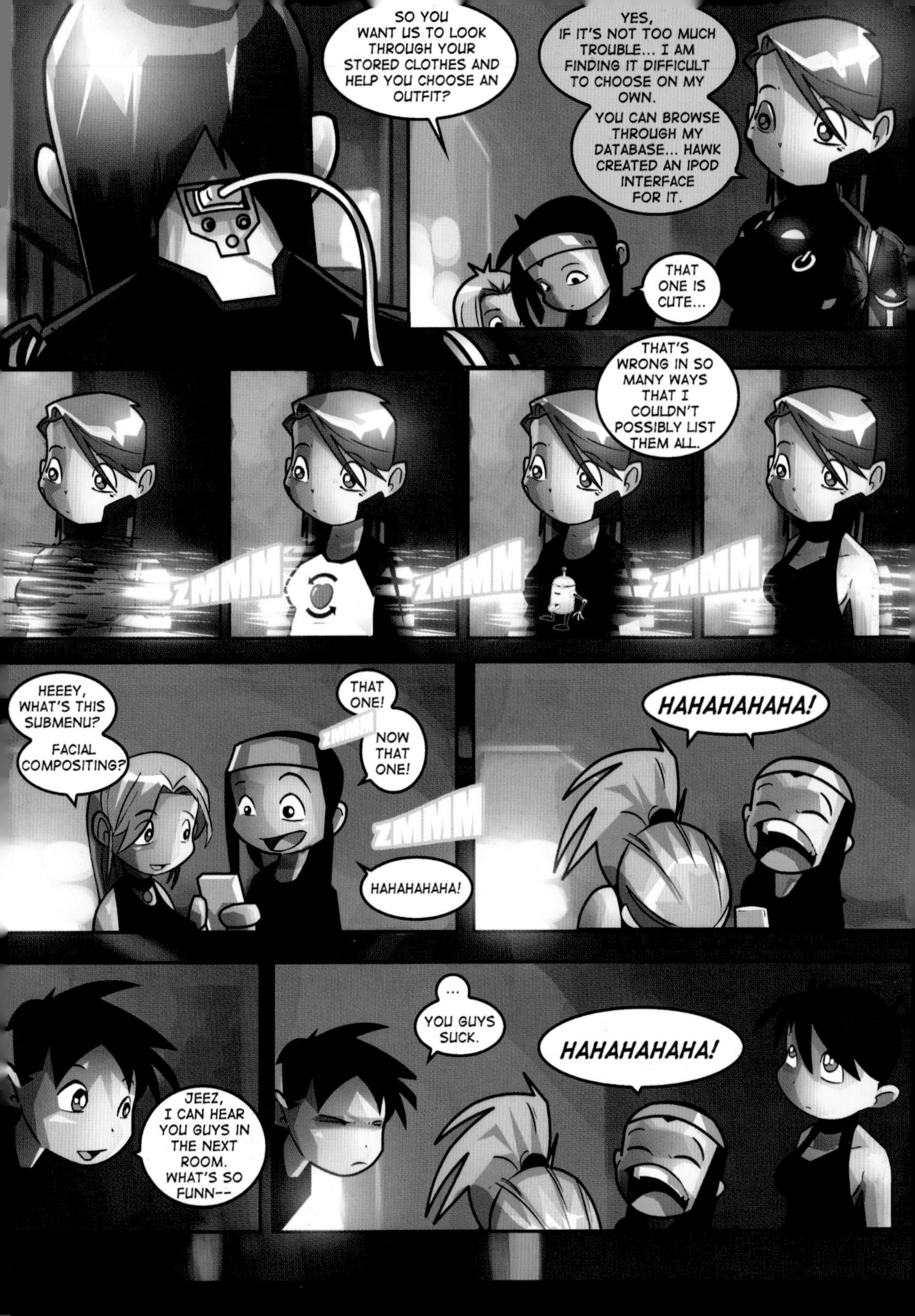
SO YOU WANT US TO LOOK THROUGH YOUR STORED CLOTHES AND HELP YOU CHOOSE AN OUTFIT?
YES, IF IT'S NOT TOO MUCH TROUBLE... I AM FINDING IT DIFFICULT TO CHOOSE ON MY OWN.
YOU CAN BROWSE THROUGH MY DATABASE... HAWK CREATED AN IPOD INTERFACE FOR IT.
THAT ONE IS CUTE...
THAT'S WRONG IN SO MANY WAYS THAT I COULDN'T POSSIBLY LIST THEM ALL.
ZMMM
ZMMM
ZMMM
HEEEY, WHAT'S THIS SUBMENU?
FACIAL COMPOSITING?
THAT ONE!
ZMMM
NOW THAT ONE!
ZMMM
HAHAHAHAHA!
HAHAHAHAHA!
JEEZ, I CAN HEAR YOU GUYS IN THE NEXT ROOM. WHAT'S SO FUNN--
...
YOU GUYS SUCK.
HAHAHAHAHA!

been tossing around ideas about how to make Eve less conspicuous when she inevitably went outside . . . I re
the holoclothing-catalog concept that we came up with to address that. I kind of wish we had that sort of thing in
ut that would mean that everyone would actually be walking around naked. That seems too easy to abuse. If you

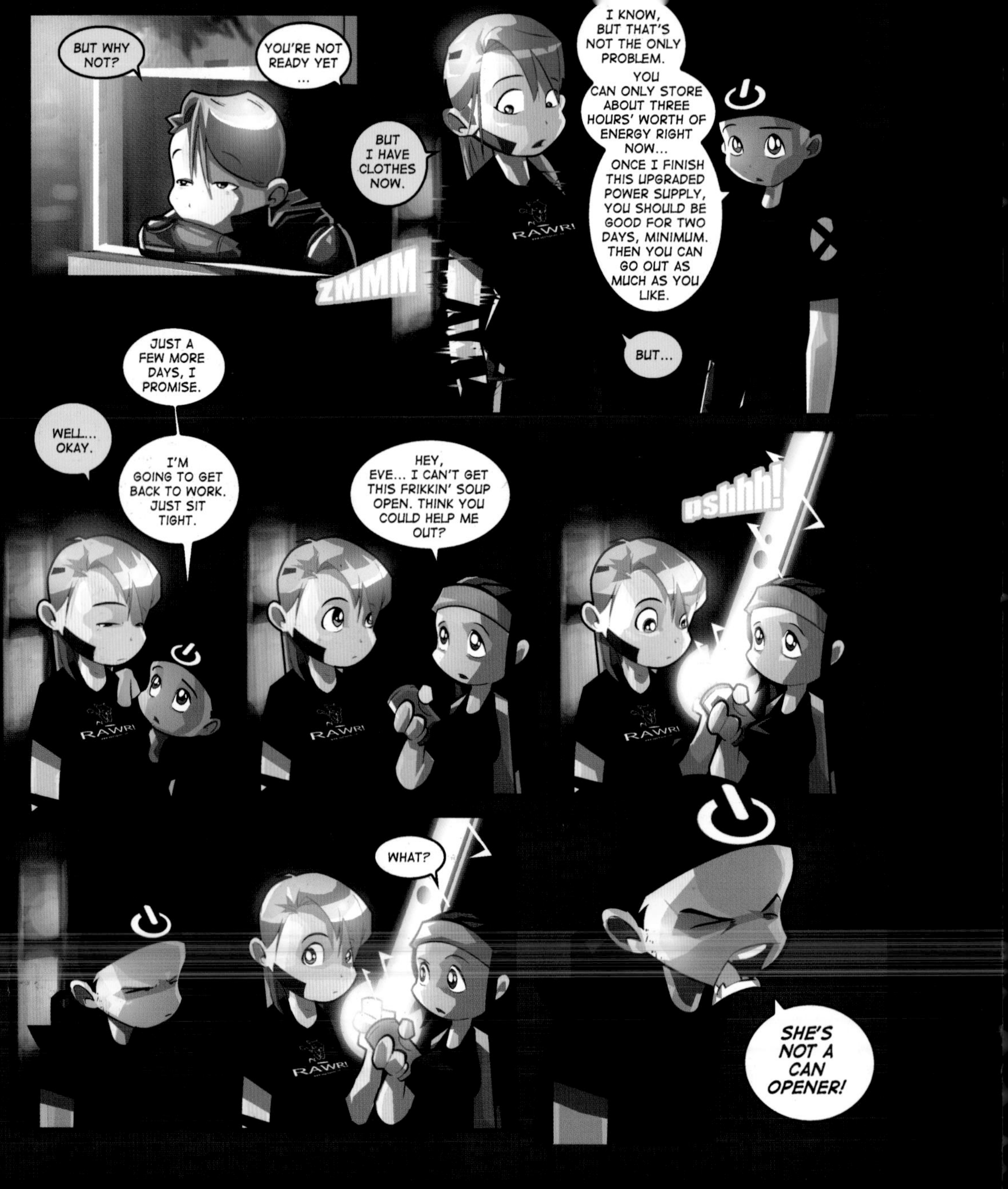
BUT WHY NOT?
YOU'RE NOT READY YET ...
BUT I HAVE CLOTHES NOW.
I KNOW, BUT THAT'S NOT THE ONLY PROBLEM.
YOU CAN ONLY STORE ABOUT THREE HOURS' WORTH OF ENERGY RIGHT NOW...
ONCE I FINISH THIS UPGRADED POWER SUPPLY, YOU SHOULD BE GOOD FOR TWO DAYS, MINIMUM. THEN YOU CAN GO OUT AS MUCH AS YOU LIKE.
ZMMM
BUT...
JUST A FEW MORE DAYS, I PROMISE.
WELL... OKAY.
I'M GOING TO GET BACK TO WORK. JUST SIT TIGHT.
HEY, EVE... I CAN'T GET THIS FRIKKIN' SOUP OPEN. THINK YOU COULD HELP ME OUT?
pshhh!
WHAT?
SHE'S NOT A CAN OPENER!

If someone can abuse technology to make their life easier, they'll probably do that too.

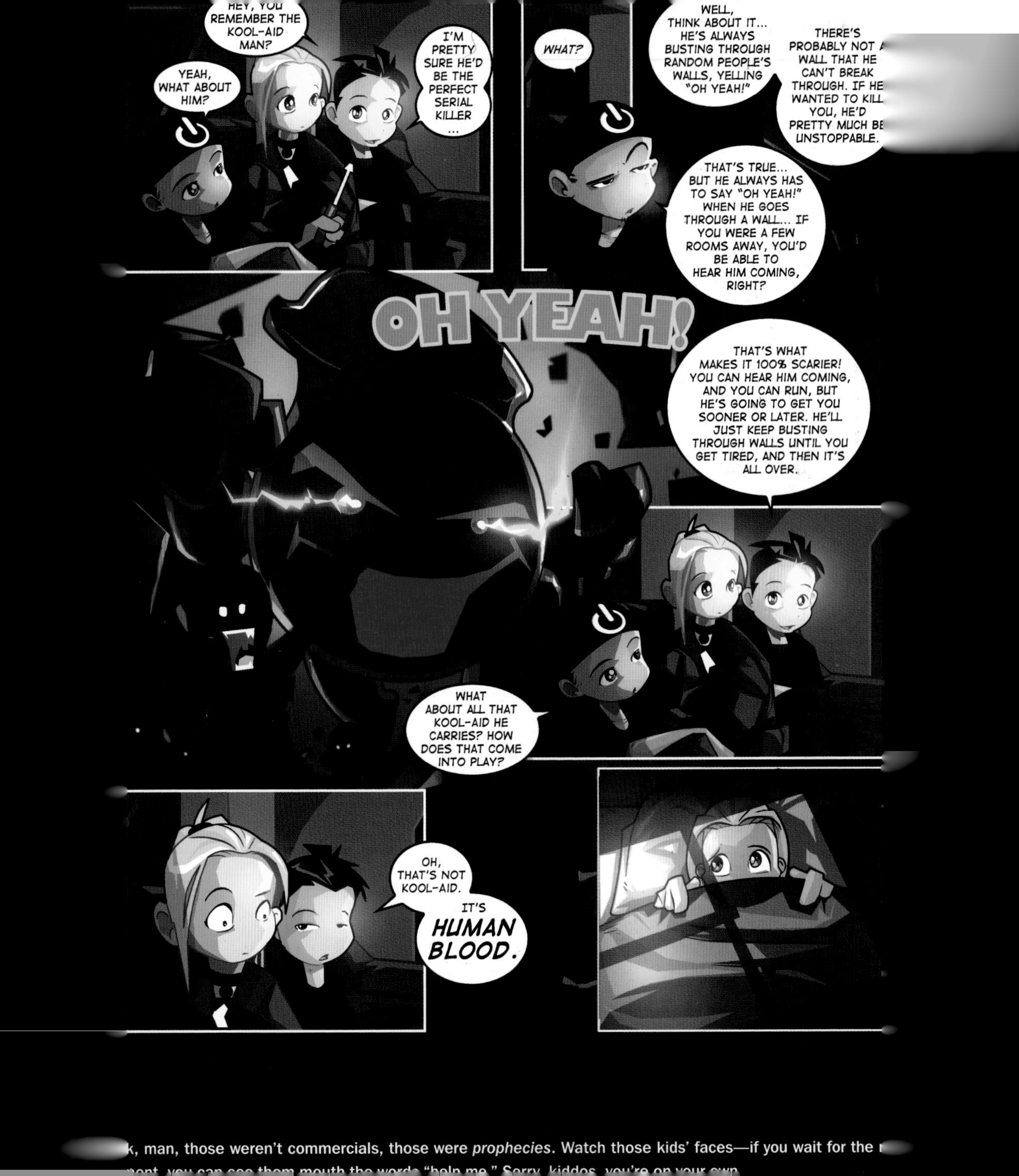
HEY, YOU REMEMBER THE KOOL-AID MAN?
YEAH, WHAT ABOUT HIM?
I'M PRETTY SURE HE'D BE THE PERFECT SERIAL KILLER ...
WHAT?
WELL, THINK ABOUT IT... HE'S ALWAYS BUSTING THROUGH RANDOM PEOPLE'S WALLS, YELLING "OH YEAH!"
THERE'S PROBABLY NOT A WALL THAT HE CAN'T BREAK THROUGH. IF HE WANTED TO KILL YOU, HE'D PRETTY MUCH BE UNSTOPPABLE.
THAT'S TRUE... BUT HE ALWAYS HAS TO SAY "OH YEAH!" WHEN HE GOES THROUGH A WALL... IF YOU WERE A FEW ROOMS AWAY, YOU'D BE ABLE TO HEAR HIM COMING, RIGHT?
OH YEAH!
THAT'S WHAT MAKES IT 100% SCARIER! YOU CAN HEAR HIM COMING, AND YOU CAN RUN, BUT HE'S GOING TO GET YOU SOONER OR LATER. HE'LL JUST KEEP BUSTING THROUGH WALLS UNTIL YOU GET TIRED, AND THEN IT'S ALL OVER.
WHAT ABOUT ALL THAT KOOL-AID HE CARRIES? HOW DOES THAT COME INTO PLAY?
OH, THAT'S NOT KOOL-AID.
IT'S *HUMAN BLOOD.*

k, man, those weren't commercials, those were *prophecies*. Watch those kids' faces—if you wait for the m
ment, you can see them mouth the words "help me." Sorry, kiddos, you're on your own.

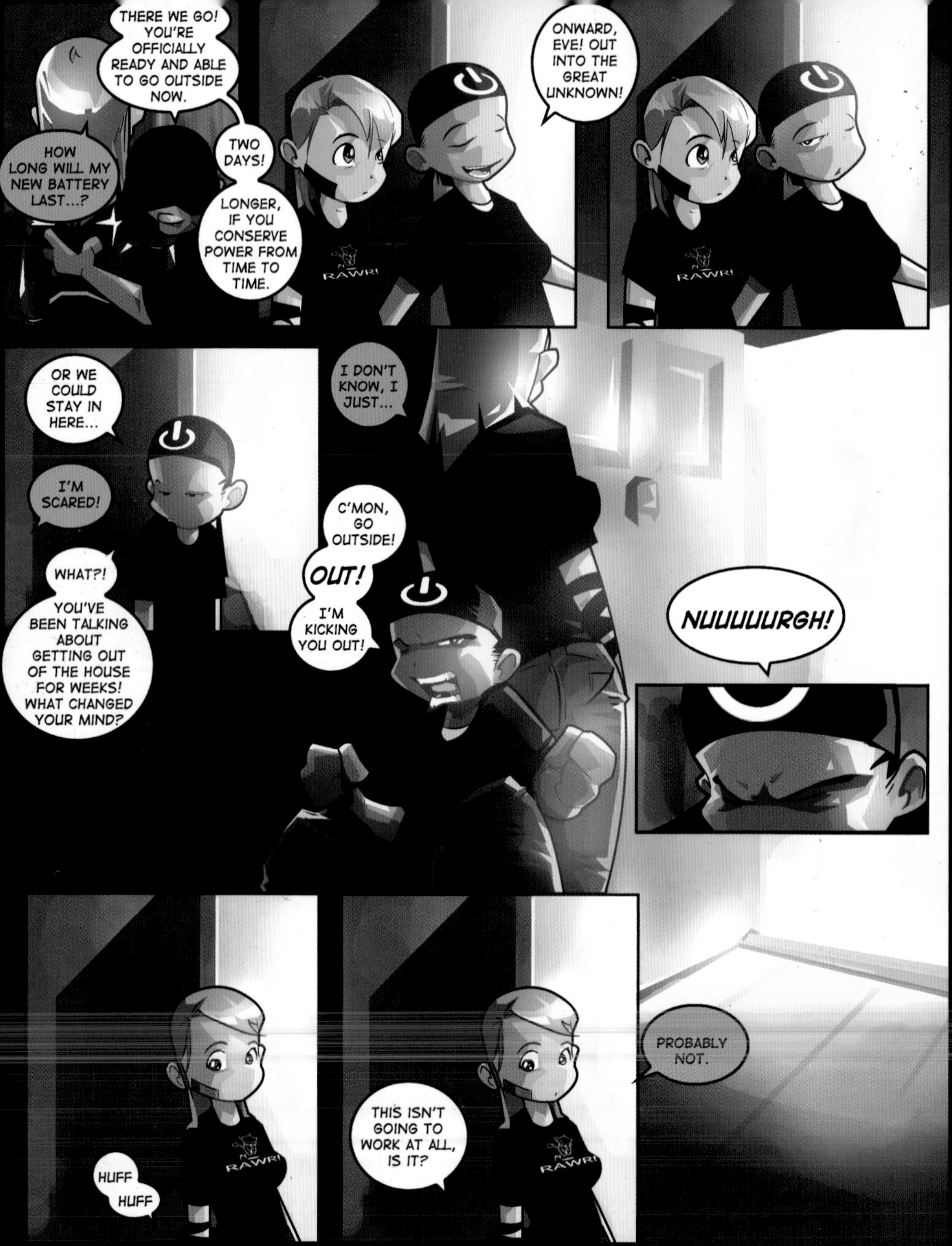
THERE WE GO! YOU'RE OFFICIALLY READY AND ABLE TO GO OUTSIDE NOW.
HOW LONG WILL MY NEW BATTERY LAST...?
TWO DAYS!
LONGER, IF YOU CONSERVE POWER FROM TIME TO TIME.
RAWR!
ONWARD, EVE! OUT INTO THE GREAT UNKNOWN!
RAWR!
OR WE COULD STAY IN HERE...
I'M SCARED!
WHAT?!
YOU'VE BEEN TALKING ABOUT GETTING OUT OF THE HOUSE FOR WEEKS! WHAT CHANGED YOUR MIND?
I DON'T KNOW, I JUST...
C'MON, GO OUTSIDE!
OUT!
I'M KICKING YOU OUT!
NUUUUURGH!
HUFF
HUFF
RAWR!
THIS ISN'T GOING TO WORK AT ALL, IS IT?
RAWR!
PROBABLY NOT.

Here we learn that although Hawk may be quite the inventor, he's not particularly strong. Eve was a little timid about going out into the big wide world in the beginning. Baby steps, baby steps.

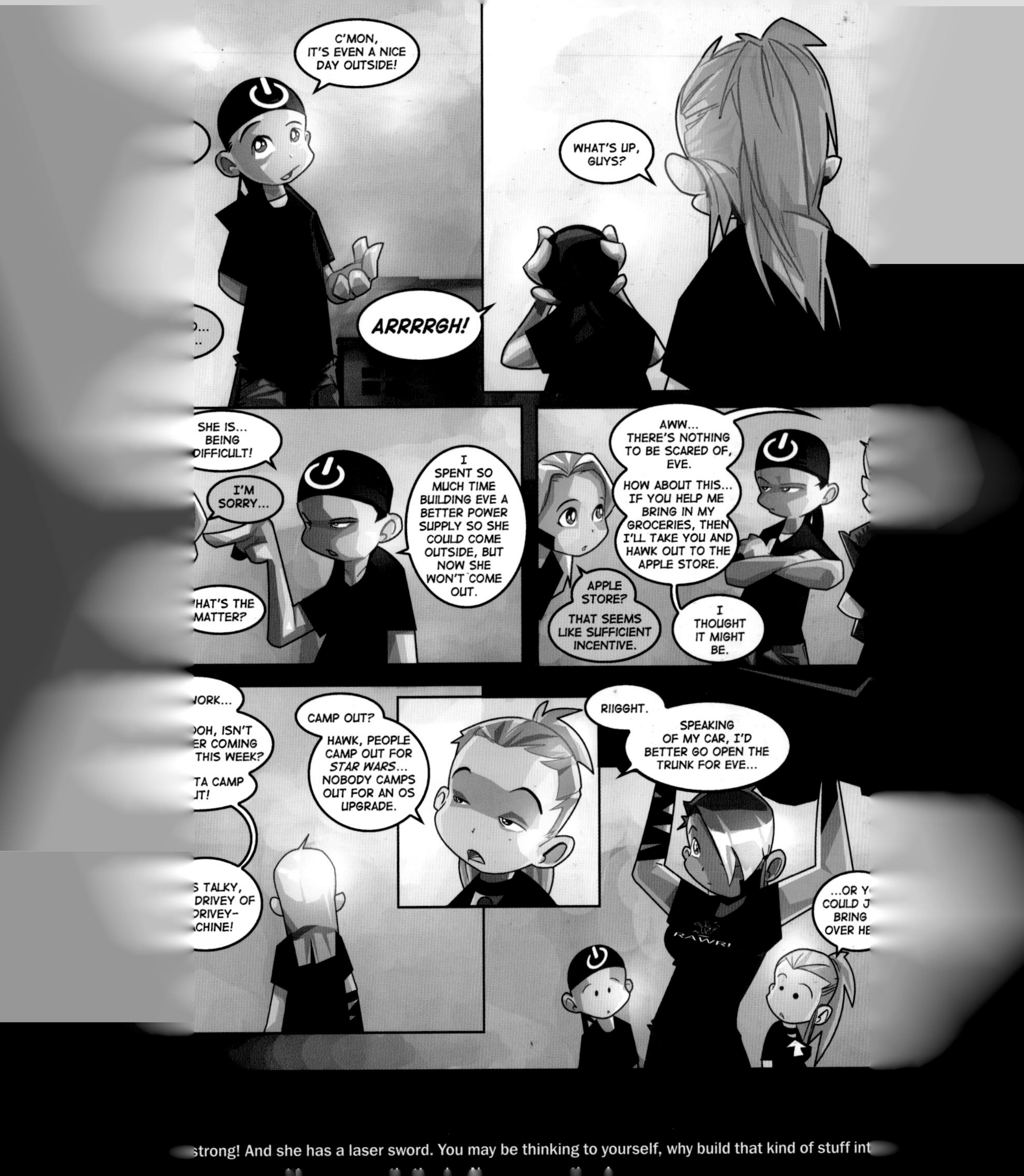
C'MON, IT'S EVEN A NICE DAY OUTSIDE!
ARRRRGH!
WHAT'S UP, GUYS?
SHE IS... BEING DIFFICULT!
I'M SORRY...
I SPENT SO MUCH TIME BUILDING EVE A BETTER POWER SUPPLY SO SHE COULD COME OUTSIDE, BUT NOW SHE WON'T COME OUT.
HAT'S THE MATTER?
AWW... THERE'S NOTHING TO BE SCARED OF, EVE.
HOW ABOUT THIS... IF YOU HELP ME BRING IN MY GROCERIES, THEN I'LL TAKE YOU AND HAWK OUT TO THE APPLE STORE.
APPLE STORE?
THAT SEEMS LIKE SUFFICIENT INCENTIVE.
I THOUGHT IT MIGHT BE.
ORK...
OOH, ISN'T ER COMING THIS WEEK?
TA CAMP UT!
S TALKY, DRIVEY OF RIVEY- CHINE!
CAMP OUT?
HAWK, PEOPLE CAMP OUT FOR *STAR WARS*... NOBODY CAMPS OUT FOR AN OS UPGRADE.
RIIGGHT.
SPEAKING OF MY CAR, I'D BETTER GO OPEN THE TRUNK FOR EVE...
...OR Y COULD J BRING OVER HE

strong! And she has a laser sword. You may be thinking to yourself, why build that kind of stuff int

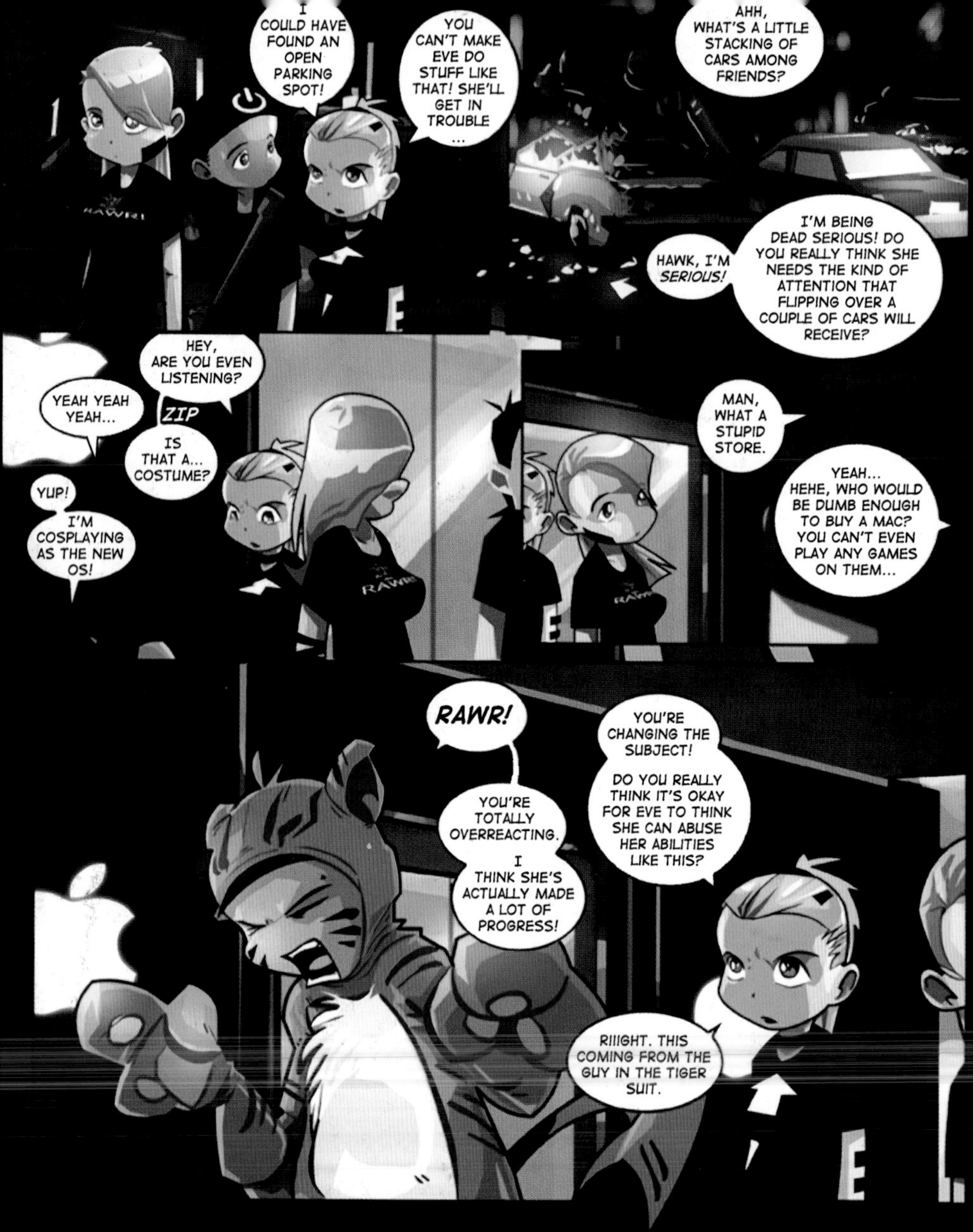
I COULD HAVE FOUND AN OPEN PARKING SPOT!
YOU CAN'T MAKE EVE DO STUFF LIKE THAT! SHE'LL GET IN TROUBLE ...
AHH, WHAT'S A LITTLE STACKING OF CARS AMONG FRIENDS?
HAWK, I'M *SERIOUS!*
I'M BEING DEAD SERIOUS! DO YOU REALLY THINK SHE NEEDS THE KIND OF ATTENTION THAT FLIPPING OVER A COUPLE OF CARS WILL RECEIVE?
HEY, ARE YOU EVEN LISTENING?
YEAH YEAH YEAH...
ZIP
IS THAT A... COSTUME?
YUP! I'M COSPLAYING AS THE NEW OS!
MAN, WHAT A STUPID STORE.
YEAH... HEHE, WHO WOULD BE DUMB ENOUGH TO BUY A MAC? YOU CAN'T EVEN PLAY ANY GAMES ON THEM...
RAWR!
YOU'RE TOTALLY OVERREACTING. I THINK SHE'S ACTUALLY MADE A LOT OF PROGRESS!
YOU'RE CHANGING THE SUBJECT! DO YOU REALLY THINK IT'S OKAY FOR EVE TO THINK SHE CAN ABUSE HER ABILITIES LIKE THIS?
RIIIGHT. THIS COMING FROM THE GUY IN THE TIGER SUIT.

Look closely at what color everyone is wearing in this comic. Okay, now take a wild guess as to what color Hawk's entire closet is. Did you guess black? You win! Next page!

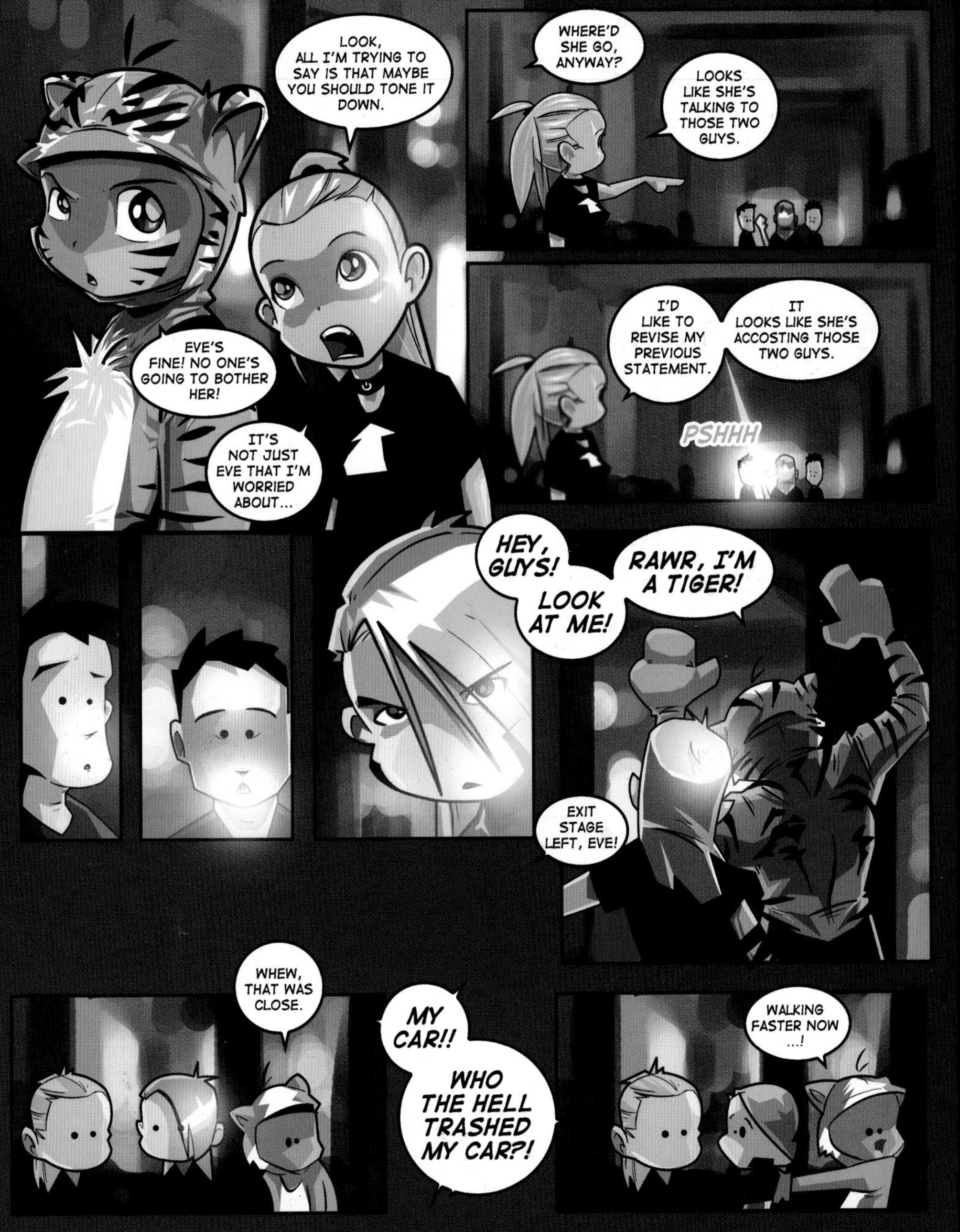
LOOK, ALL I'M TRYING TO SAY IS THAT MAYBE YOU SHOULD TONE IT DOWN.
EVE'S FINE! NO ONE'S GOING TO BOTHER HER!
IT'S NOT JUST EVE THAT I'M WORRIED ABOUT...
WHERE'D SHE GO, ANYWAY?
LOOKS LIKE SHE'S TALKING TO THOSE TWO GUYS.
I'D LIKE TO REVISE MY PREVIOUS STATEMENT.
IT LOOKS LIKE SHE'S ACCOSTING THOSE TWO GUYS.
PSHHH
HEY, GUYS!
LOOK AT ME!
RAWR, I'M A TIGER!
EXIT STAGE LEFT, EVE!
WHEW, THAT WAS CLOSE.
MY CAR!!
WHO THE HELL TRASHED MY CAR?!
WALKING FASTER NOW ...!

Man, Eve's first excursion into public doesn't seem to be going too smoothly, huh? She is sort of temperamental . . . Good thing there's that guy in a tiger suit to distract everyone. What compels a man to put on a tiger suit, anyway? Is it fame? Fortune? Brain damage?

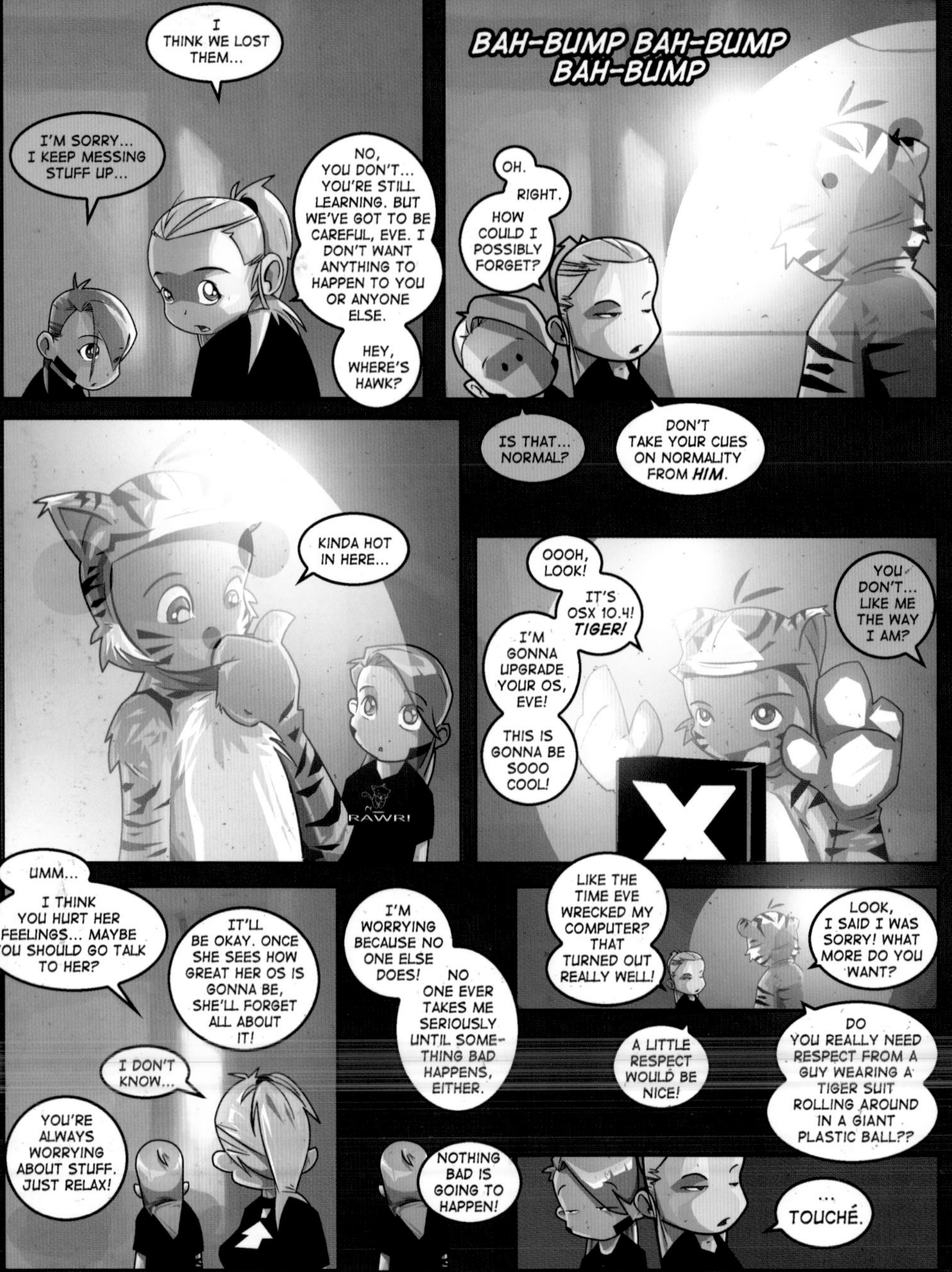

I THINK WE LOST THEM...
I'M SORRY... I KEEP MESSING STUFF UP...
NO, YOU DON'T... YOU'RE STILL LEARNING. BUT WE'VE GOT TO BE CAREFUL, EVE. I DON'T WANT ANYTHING TO HAPPEN TO YOU OR ANYONE ELSE.
HEY, WHERE'S HAWK?
BAH-BUMP BAH-BUMP BAH-BUMP
OH.
RIGHT.
HOW COULD I POSSIBLY FORGET?
KINDA HOT IN HERE...
RAWR!
IS THAT... NORMAL?
DON'T TAKE YOUR CUES ON NORMALITY FROM *HIM*.
OOOH, LOOK!
IT'S OSX 10.4! *TIGER!*
I'M GONNA UPGRADE YOUR OS, EVE!
THIS IS GONNA BE SOOO COOL!
YOU DON'T... LIKE ME THE WAY I AM?
UMM...
I THINK YOU HURT HER FEELINGS... MAYBE YOU SHOULD GO TALK TO HER?
IT'LL BE OKAY. ONCE SHE SEES HOW GREAT HER OS IS GONNA BE, SHE'LL FORGET ALL ABOUT IT!
I DON'T KNOW...
YOU'RE ALWAYS WORRYING ABOUT STUFF. JUST RELAX!
NOTHING BAD IS GOING TO HAPPEN!
I'M WORRYING BECAUSE NO ONE ELSE DOES!
NO ONE EVER TAKES ME SERIOUSLY UNTIL SOME-THING BAD HAPPENS, EITHER.
LIKE THE TIME EVE WRECKED MY COMPUTER? THAT TURNED OUT REALLY WELL!
LOOK, I SAID I WAS SORRY! WHAT MORE DO YOU WANT?
A LITTLE RESPECT WOULD BE NICE!
DO YOU REALLY NEED RESPECT FROM A GUY WEARING A TIGER SUIT ROLLING AROUND IN A GIANT PLASTIC BALL??
... TOUCHÉ.

Everyone is acclimating themselves to the idea that Eve has feelings too. Hawk clearly hasn't caught on quite yet; he's a little cavalier with the idea of simply tromping around inside Eve's head, changing things willy-nilly.

Oh, *he'll* learn . . . They'll *all* learn . . . Cue the villainous laughter, please!

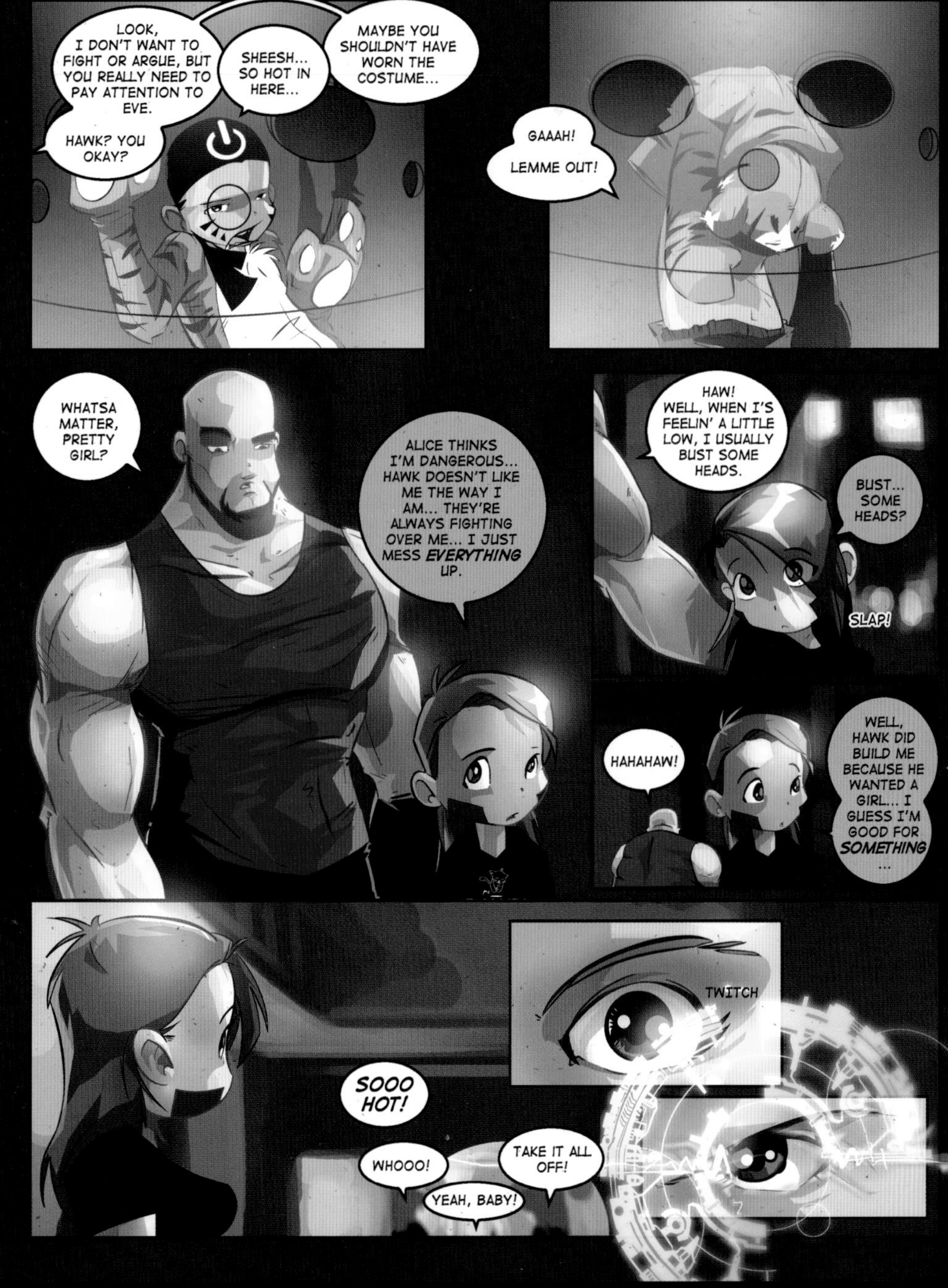

LOOK, I DON'T WANT TO FIGHT OR ARGUE, BUT YOU REALLY NEED TO PAY ATTENTION TO EVE.
SHEESH... SO HOT IN HERE...
MAYBE YOU SHOULDN'T HAVE WORN THE COSTUME...
HAWK? YOU OKAY?
GAAAH!
LEMME OUT!
WHATSA MATTER, PRETTY GIRL?
ALICE THINKS I'M DANGEROUS... HAWK DOESN'T LIKE ME THE WAY I AM... THEY'RE ALWAYS FIGHTING OVER ME... I JUST MESS *EVERYTHING* UP.
HAW! WELL, WHEN I'S FEELIN' A LITTLE LOW, I USUALLY BUST SOME HEADS.
BUST... SOME HEADS?
SLAP!
HAHAHAW!
WELL, HAWK DID BUILD ME BECAUSE HE WANTED A GIRL... I GUESS I'M GOOD FOR *SOMETHING*...
SOOO HOT!
WHOOO!
YEAH, BABY!
TAKE IT ALL OFF!
TWITCH

We're introduced to Eve's built-in low self-esteem. I was so glad people didn't take her dialogue the wrong way in this comic; it was meant to sound uncomfortable. If someone built you so they'd have a girlfriend who was easy to date, you'd have a complex too.

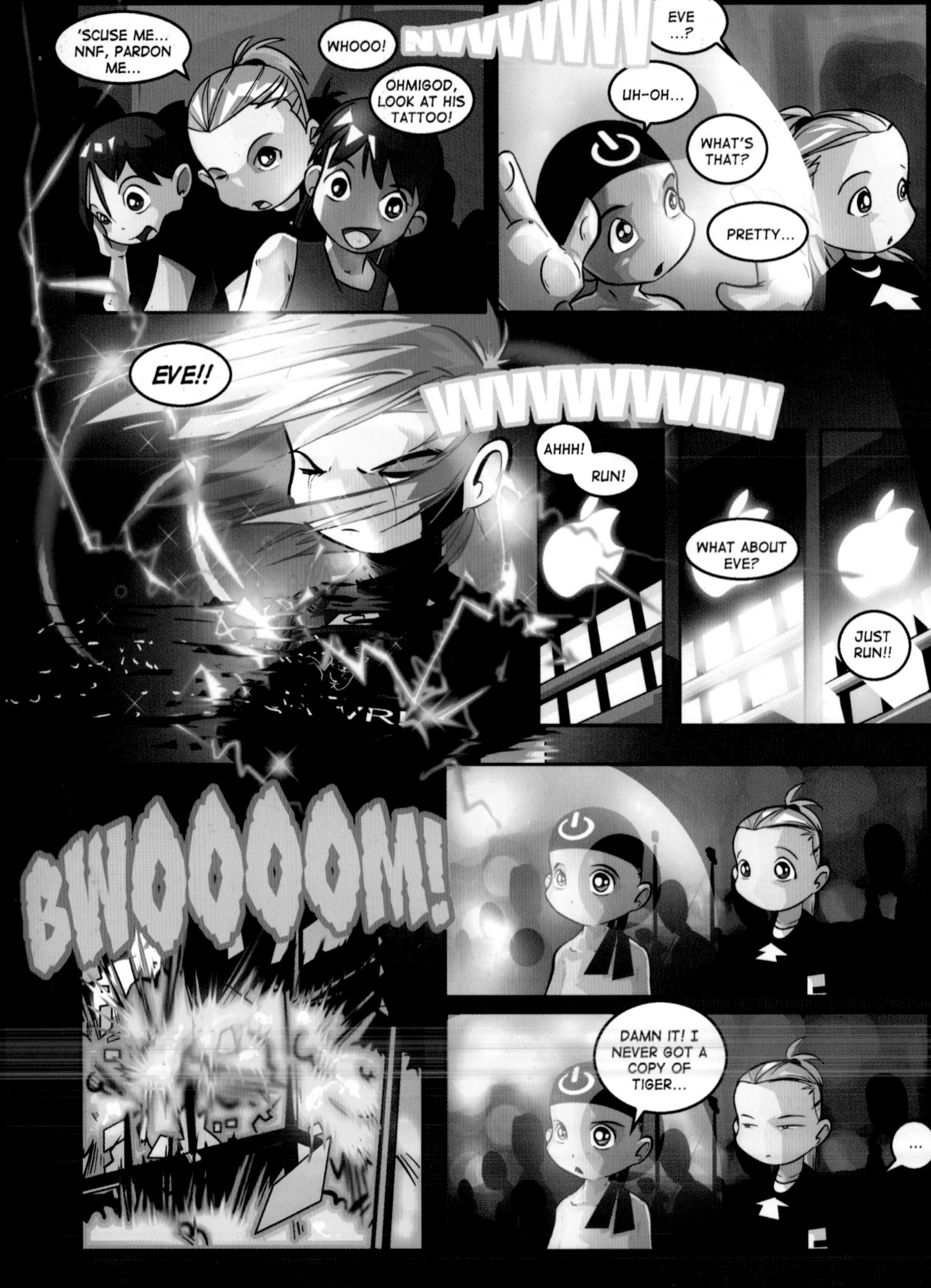
'SCUSE ME... NNF, PARDON ME...
WHOOO!
OHMIGOD, LOOK AT HIS TATTOO!
NVVVVVV
EVE ...?
UH-OH...
WHAT'S THAT?
PRETTY...
EVE!!
VVVVVVVVVMN
AHHH!
RUN!
WHAT ABOUT EVE?
JUST RUN!!
BWOOOOM!
DAMN IT! I NEVER GOT A COPY OF TIGER...
...

The next couple of pages mark a departure in the style of the comics. Here is the background: Hawk and I had been doing *Applegeeks* a certain way for a while, and we decided it was time to try something new. Neither of us had attempted to write or draw something more serious, so we said, "What the hell, we'll give it a shot."

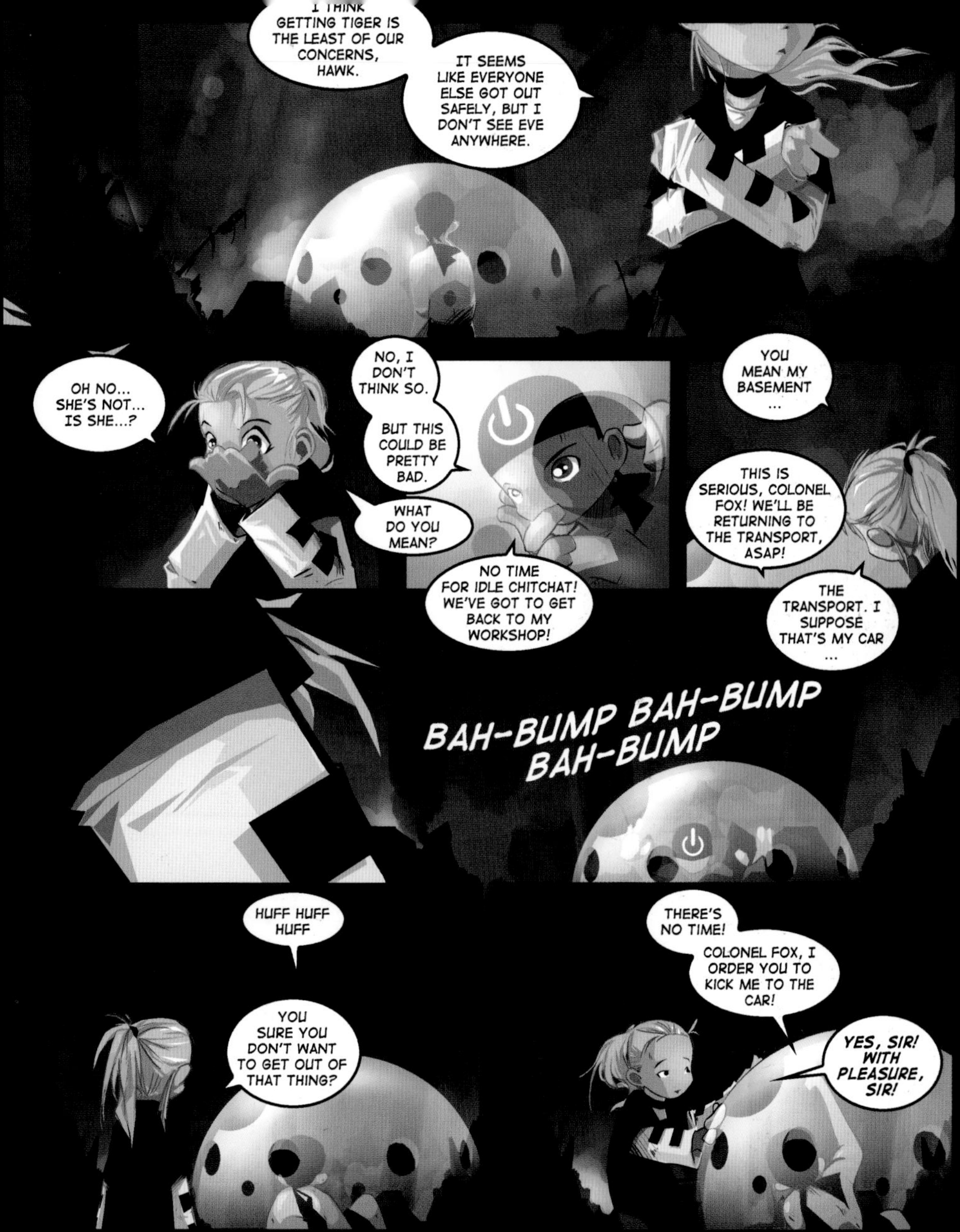
I THINK GETTING TIGER IS THE LEAST OF OUR CONCERNS, HAWK.
IT SEEMS LIKE EVERYONE ELSE GOT OUT SAFELY, BUT I DON'T SEE EVE ANYWHERE.
OH NO... SHE'S NOT... IS SHE...?
NO, I DON'T THINK SO.
BUT THIS COULD BE PRETTY BAD.
WHAT DO YOU MEAN?
NO TIME FOR IDLE CHITCHAT! WE'VE GOT TO GET BACK TO MY WORKSHOP!
YOU MEAN MY BASEMENT ...
THIS IS SERIOUS, COLONEL FOX! WE'LL BE RETURNING TO THE TRANSPORT, ASAP!
THE TRANSPORT. I SUPPOSE THAT'S MY CAR ...
BAH-BUMP BAH-BUMP BAH-BUMP
HUFF HUFF HUFF
YOU SURE YOU DON'T WANT TO GET OUT OF THAT THING?
THERE'S NO TIME!
COLONEL FOX, I ORDER YOU TO KICK ME TO THE CAR!
YES, SIR! WITH PLEASURE, SIR!

I was doing my best here to balance seriousness with humor, to create a proper transition over to the serious art

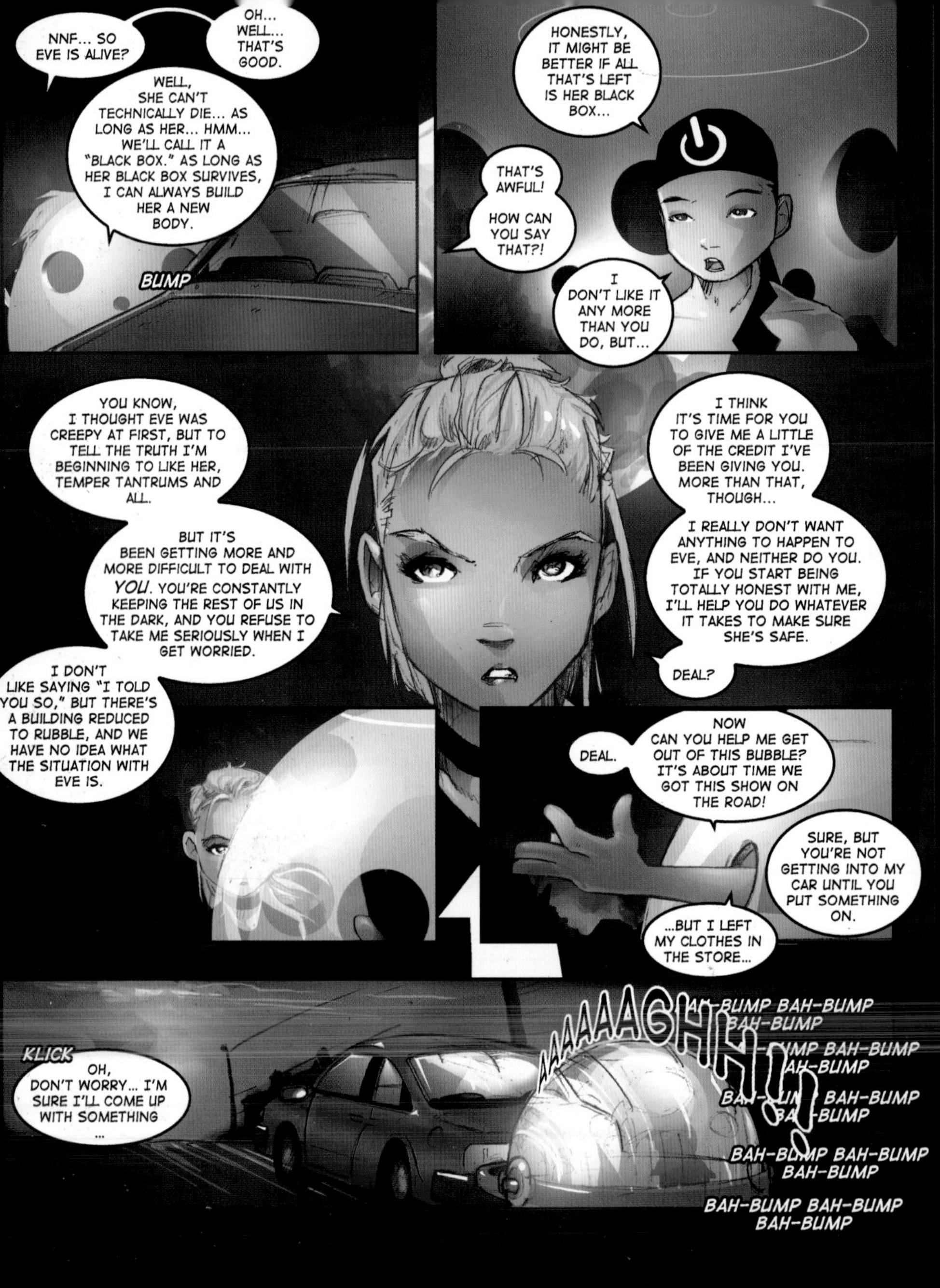
NNF... SO EVE IS ALIVE?
OH... WELL... THAT'S GOOD.
WELL, SHE CAN'T TECHNICALLY DIE... AS LONG AS HER... HMM... WE'LL CALL IT A "BLACK BOX." AS LONG AS HER BLACK BOX SURVIVES, I CAN ALWAYS BUILD HER A NEW BODY.
BUMP
HONESTLY, IT MIGHT BE BETTER IF ALL THAT'S LEFT IS HER BLACK BOX...
THAT'S AWFUL!
HOW CAN YOU SAY THAT?!
I DON'T LIKE IT ANY MORE THAN YOU DO, BUT...
YOU KNOW, I THOUGHT EVE WAS CREEPY AT FIRST, BUT TO TELL THE TRUTH I'M BEGINNING TO LIKE HER, TEMPER TANTRUMS AND ALL.
BUT IT'S BEEN GETTING MORE AND MORE DIFFICULT TO DEAL WITH *YOU*. YOU'RE CONSTANTLY KEEPING THE REST OF US IN THE DARK, AND YOU REFUSE TO TAKE ME SERIOUSLY WHEN I GET WORRIED.
I DON'T LIKE SAYING "I TOLD YOU SO," BUT THERE'S A BUILDING REDUCED TO RUBBLE, AND WE HAVE NO IDEA WHAT THE SITUATION WITH EVE IS.
I THINK IT'S TIME FOR YOU TO GIVE ME A LITTLE OF THE CREDIT I'VE BEEN GIVING YOU. MORE THAN THAT, THOUGH...
I REALLY DON'T WANT ANYTHING TO HAPPEN TO EVE, AND NEITHER DO YOU. IF YOU START BEING TOTALLY HONEST WITH ME, I'LL HELP YOU DO WHATEVER IT TAKES TO MAKE SURE SHE'S SAFE.
DEAL?
DEAL.
NOW CAN YOU HELP ME GET OUT OF THIS BUBBLE? IT'S ABOUT TIME WE GOT THIS SHOW ON THE ROAD!
SURE, BUT YOU'RE NOT GETTING INTO MY CAR UNTIL YOU PUT SOMETHING ON.
...BUT I LEFT MY CLOTHES IN THE STORE...
KLICK
OH, DON'T WORRY... I'M SURE I'LL COME UP WITH SOMETHING ...
AAAAAAGHH!!
BAH-BUMP BAH-BUMP
BAH-BUMP BAH-BUMP BAH-BUMP
BAH-BUMP BAH-BUMP BAH-BUMP

I think Hawk was channeling a bit of Jim Lee and especially Michael Turner when he drew this. He grew up reading

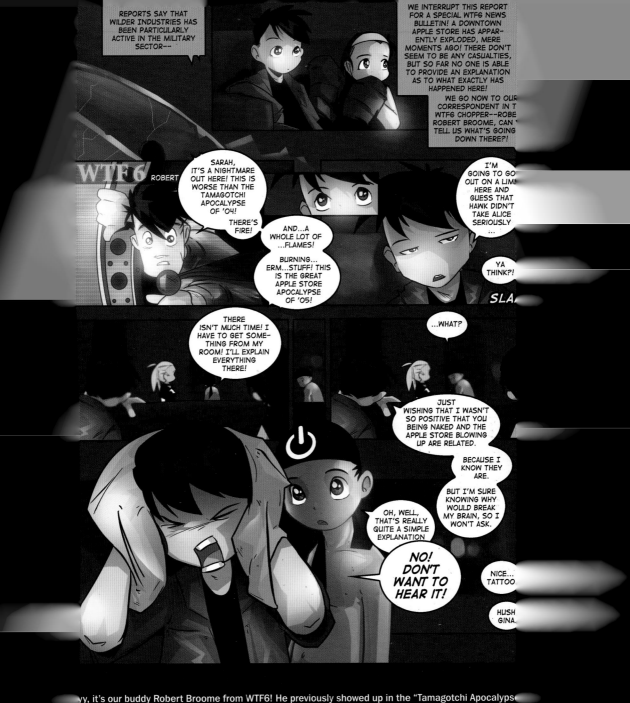

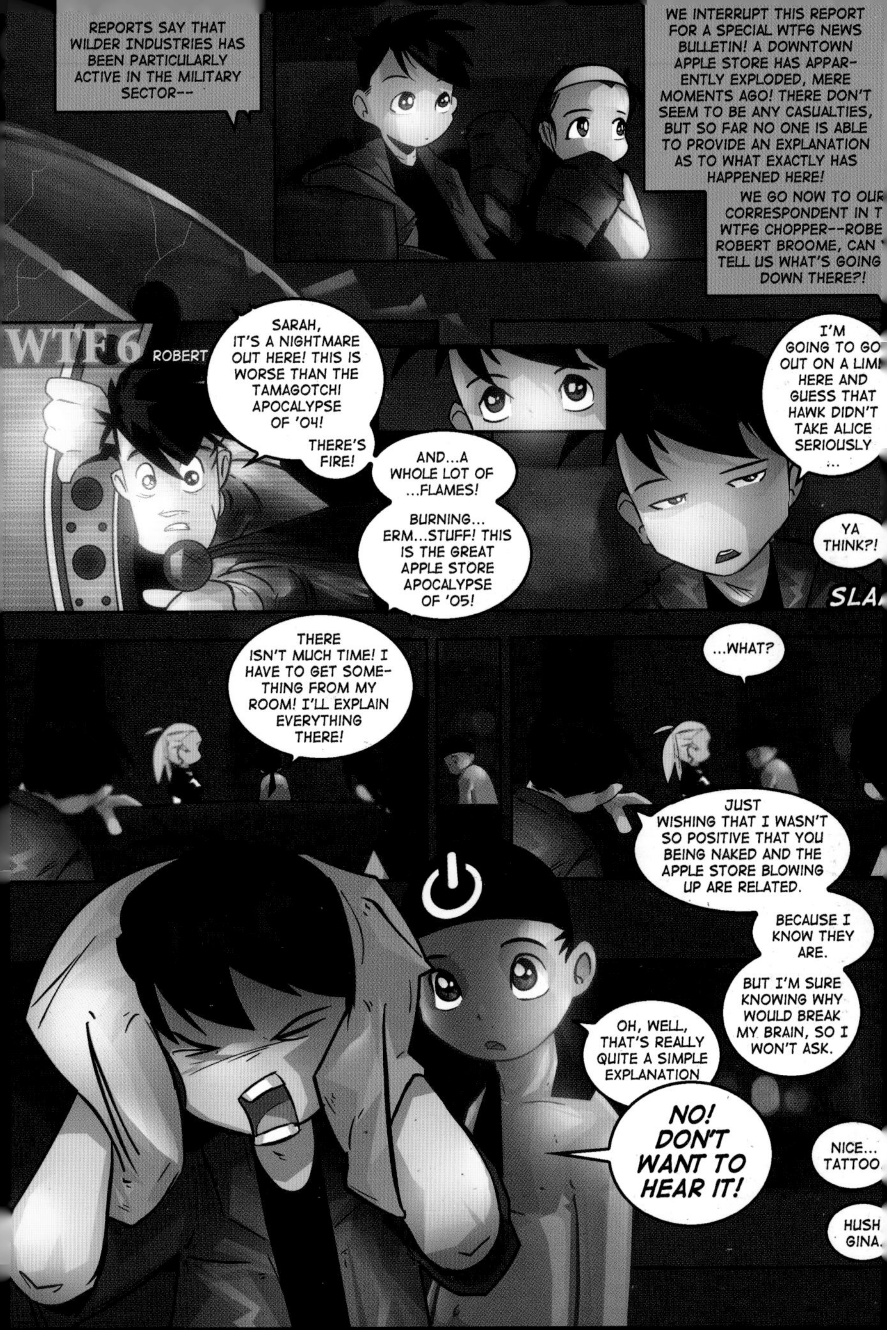
REPORTS SAY THAT WILDER INDUSTRIES HAS BEEN PARTICULARLY ACTIVE IN THE MILITARY SECTOR--
WE INTERRUPT THIS REPORT FOR A SPECIAL WTF6 NEWS BULLETIN! A DOWNTOWN APPLE STORE HAS APPARENTLY EXPLODED, MERE MOMENTS AGO! THERE DON'T SEEM TO BE ANY CASUALTIES, BUT SO FAR NO ONE IS ABLE TO PROVIDE AN EXPLANATION AS TO WHAT EXACTLY HAS HAPPENED HERE!
WE GO NOW TO OUR CORRESPONDENT IN T WTF6 CHOPPER--ROBE ROBERT BROOME, CAN TELL US WHAT'S GOING DOWN THERE?!
WTF 6
ROBERT
SARAH, IT'S A NIGHTMARE OUT HERE! THIS IS WORSE THAN THE TAMAGOTCHI APOCALYPSE OF '04!
THERE'S FIRE!
AND...A WHOLE LOT OF ...FLAMES!
BURNING... ERM...STUFF! THIS IS THE GREAT APPLE STORE APOCALYPSE OF '05!
I'M GOING TO GO OUT ON A LIM HERE AND GUESS THAT HAWK DIDN'T TAKE ALICE SERIOUSLY ...
YA THINK?!
SLA
THERE ISN'T MUCH TIME! I HAVE TO GET SOMETHING FROM MY ROOM! I'LL EXPLAIN EVERYTHING THERE!
...WHAT?
JUST WISHING THAT I WASN'T SO POSITIVE THAT YOU BEING NAKED AND THE APPLE STORE BLOWING UP ARE RELATED.
BECAUSE I KNOW THEY ARE.
BUT I'M SURE KNOWING WHY WOULD BREAK MY BRAIN, SO I WON'T ASK.
OH, WELL, THAT'S REALLY QUITE A SIMPLE EXPLANATION
NO! DON'T WANT TO HEAR IT!
NICE... TATTOO
HUSH GINA.

yy, it's our buddy Robert Broome from WTF6! He previously showed up in the "Tamagotchi Apocalyps olume 1 (page 64). Also, Alice is remarkably calm about the fact that Hawk is naked. I'll chalk it

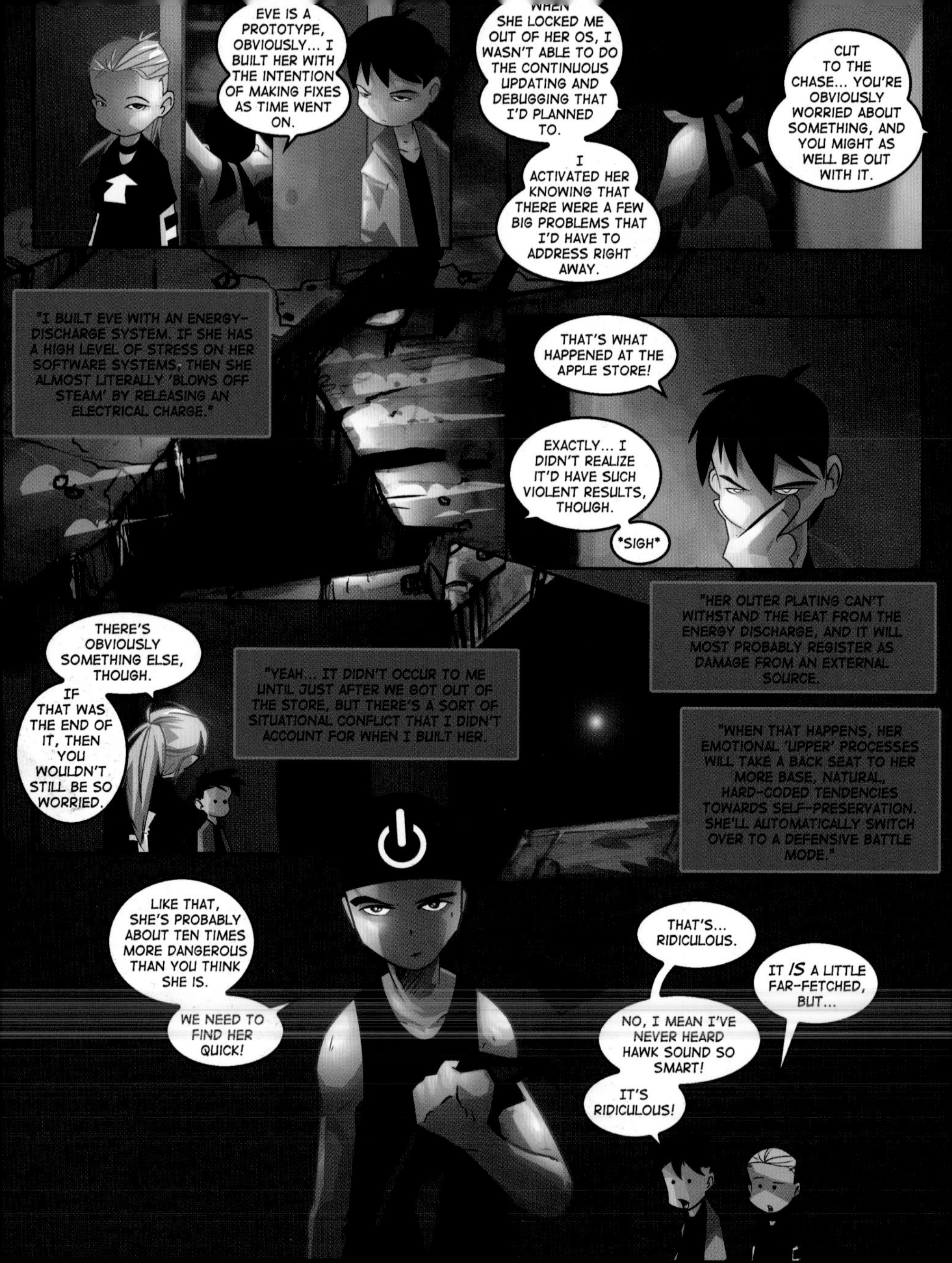
EVE IS A PROTOTYPE, OBVIOUSLY... I BUILT HER WITH THE INTENTION OF MAKING FIXES AS TIME WENT ON.
WHEN SHE LOCKED ME OUT OF HER OS, I WASN'T ABLE TO DO THE CONTINUOUS UPDATING AND DEBUGGING THAT I'D PLANNED TO.
I ACTIVATED HER KNOWING THAT THERE WERE A FEW BIG PROBLEMS THAT I'D HAVE TO ADDRESS RIGHT AWAY.
CUT TO THE CHASE... YOU'RE OBVIOUSLY WORRIED ABOUT SOMETHING, AND YOU MIGHT AS WELL BE OUT WITH IT.
"I BUILT EVE WITH AN ENERGY-DISCHARGE SYSTEM. IF SHE HAS A HIGH LEVEL OF STRESS ON HER SOFTWARE SYSTEMS, THEN SHE ALMOST LITERALLY 'BLOWS OFF STEAM' BY RELEASING AN ELECTRICAL CHARGE."
THAT'S WHAT HAPPENED AT THE APPLE STORE!
EXACTLY... I DIDN'T REALIZE IT'D HAVE SUCH VIOLENT RESULTS, THOUGH.
SIGH
THERE'S OBVIOUSLY SOMETHING ELSE, THOUGH.
IF THAT WAS THE END OF IT, THEN YOU WOULDN'T STILL BE SO WORRIED.
"YEAH... IT DIDN'T OCCUR TO ME UNTIL JUST AFTER WE GOT OUT OF THE STORE, BUT THERE'S A SORT OF SITUATIONAL CONFLICT THAT I DIDN'T ACCOUNT FOR WHEN I BUILT HER.
"HER OUTER PLATING CAN'T WITHSTAND THE HEAT FROM THE ENERGY DISCHARGE, AND IT WILL MOST PROBABLY REGISTER AS DAMAGE FROM AN EXTERNAL SOURCE.
"WHEN THAT HAPPENS, HER EMOTIONAL 'UPPER' PROCESSES WILL TAKE A BACK SEAT TO HER MORE BASE, NATURAL, HARD-CODED TENDENCIES TOWARDS SELF-PRESERVATION. SHE'LL AUTOMATICALLY SWITCH OVER TO A DEFENSIVE BATTLE MODE."
LIKE THAT, SHE'S PROBABLY ABOUT TEN TIMES MORE DANGEROUS THAN YOU THINK SHE IS.
WE NEED TO FIND HER QUICK!
THAT'S... RIDICULOUS.
IT *IS* A LITTLE FAR-FETCHED, BUT...
NO, I MEAN I'VE NEVER HEARD HAWK SOUND SO SMART!
IT'S RIDICULOUS!

I like the contrast of serious Hawk and silly Jayce and Alice in the last panel. Details like that helped keep the mood balanced, which is exactly where we wanted to be. Oh, and in case people were wondering why Hawk chose that particular effect for Eve's glowing eye inside the rubble, think *Terminator*! I always loved how inhuman the Terminator's

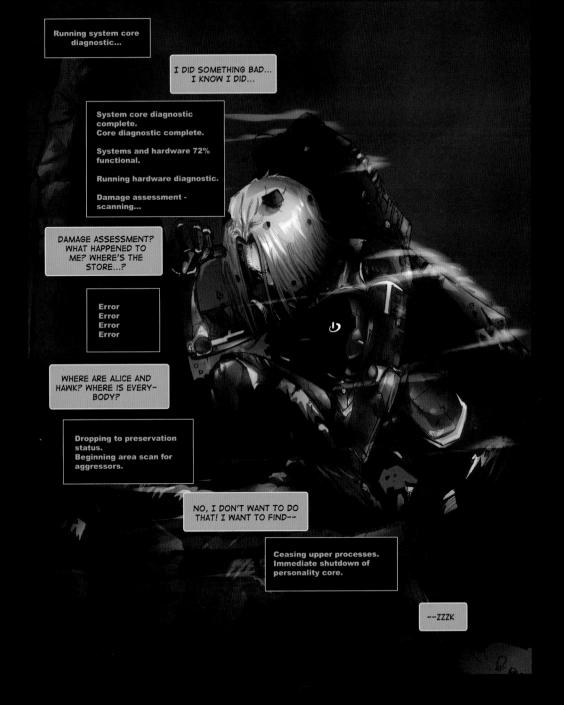

Running system core diagnostic...

I DID SOMETHING BAD... I KNOW I DID...

System core diagnostic complete.
Core diagnostic complete.

Systems and hardware 72% functional.

Running hardware diagnostic.

Damage assessment - scanning...

DAMAGE ASSESSMENT? WHAT HAPPENED TO ME? WHERE'S THE STORE...?

Error
Error
Error
Error

WHERE ARE ALICE AND HAWK? WHERE IS EVERY-BODY?

Dropping to preservation status.
Beginning area scan for aggressors.

NO, I DON'T WANT TO DO THAT! I WANT TO FIND--

Ceasing upper processes.
Immediate shutdown of personality core.

--ZZZK

ERROR

Instinct wins out over intelligence. Poor Eve!

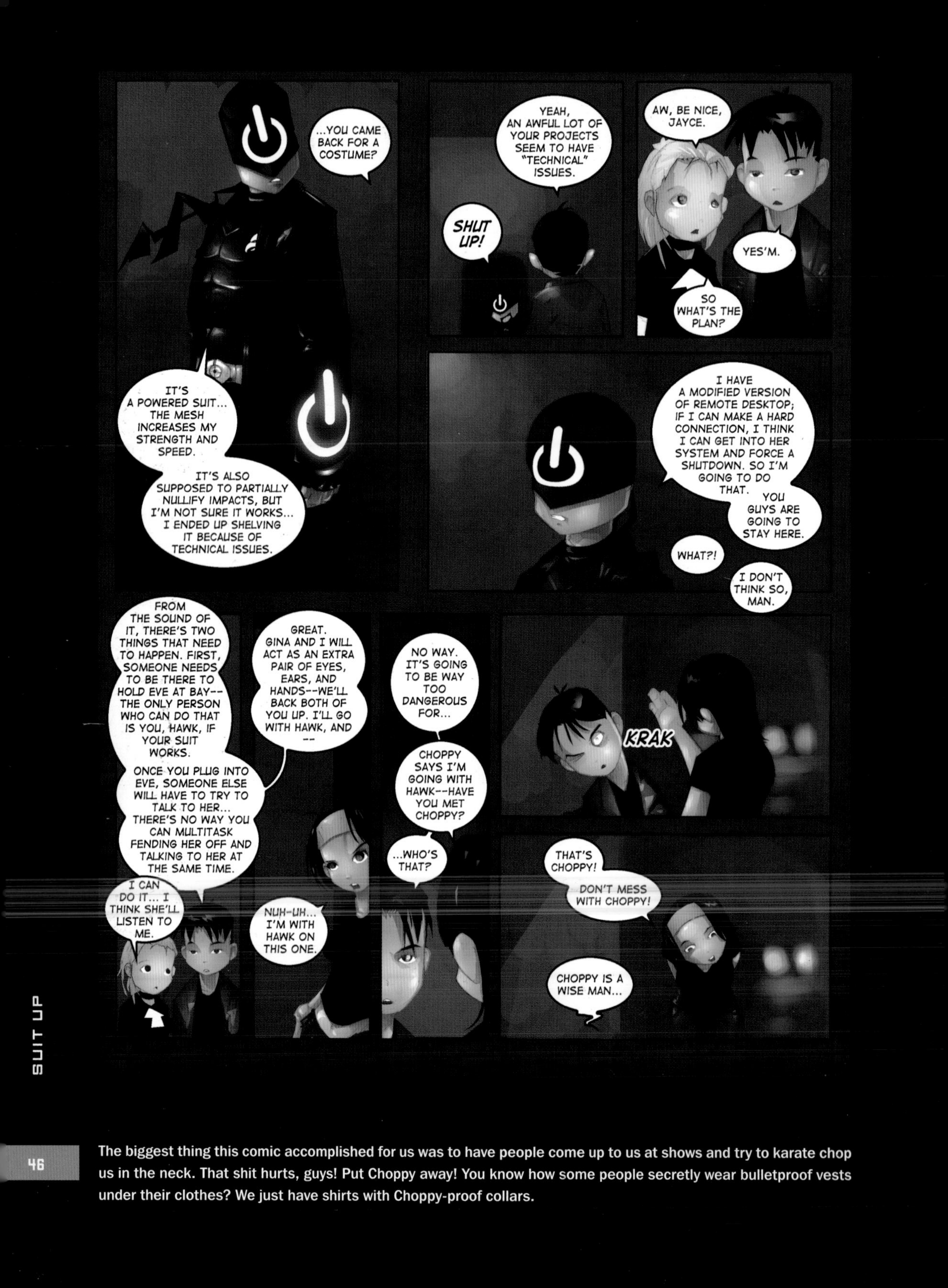
...YOU CAME BACK FOR A COSTUME?
YEAH, AN AWFUL LOT OF YOUR PROJECTS SEEM TO HAVE "TECHNICAL" ISSUES.
SHUT UP!
AW, BE NICE, JAYCE.
YES'M.
SO WHAT'S THE PLAN?
IT'S A POWERED SUIT... THE MESH INCREASES MY STRENGTH AND SPEED.
IT'S ALSO SUPPOSED TO PARTIALLY NULLIFY IMPACTS, BUT I'M NOT SURE IT WORKS... I ENDED UP SHELVING IT BECAUSE OF TECHNICAL ISSUES.
I HAVE A MODIFIED VERSION OF REMOTE DESKTOP; IF I CAN MAKE A HARD CONNECTION, I THINK I CAN GET INTO HER SYSTEM AND FORCE A SHUTDOWN. SO I'M GOING TO DO THAT.
YOU GUYS ARE GOING TO STAY HERE.
WHAT?!
I DON'T THINK SO, MAN.
FROM THE SOUND OF IT, THERE'S TWO THINGS THAT NEED TO HAPPEN. FIRST, SOMEONE NEEDS TO BE THERE TO HOLD EVE AT BAY--THE ONLY PERSON WHO CAN DO THAT IS YOU, HAWK, IF YOUR SUIT WORKS.
ONCE YOU PLUG INTO EVE, SOMEONE ELSE WILL HAVE TO TRY TO TALK TO HER... THERE'S NO WAY YOU CAN MULTITASK FENDING HER OFF AND TALKING TO HER AT THE SAME TIME.
I CAN DO IT... I THINK SHE'LL LISTEN TO ME.
GREAT. GINA AND I WILL ACT AS AN EXTRA PAIR OF EYES, EARS, AND HANDS--WE'LL BACK BOTH OF YOU UP. I'LL GO WITH HAWK, AND --
NUH-UH... I'M WITH HAWK ON THIS ONE.
NO WAY. IT'S GOING TO BE WAY TOO DANGEROUS FOR...
CHOPPY SAYS I'M GOING WITH HAWK--HAVE YOU MET CHOPPY?
...WHO'S THAT?
KRAK
THAT'S CHOPPY!
DON'T MESS WITH CHOPPY!
CHOPPY IS A WISE MAN...

The biggest thing this comic accomplished for us was to have people come up to us at shows and try to karate chop us in the neck. That shit hurts, guys! Put Choppy away! You know how some people secretly wear bulletproof vests under their clothes? We just have shirts with Choppy-proof collars.

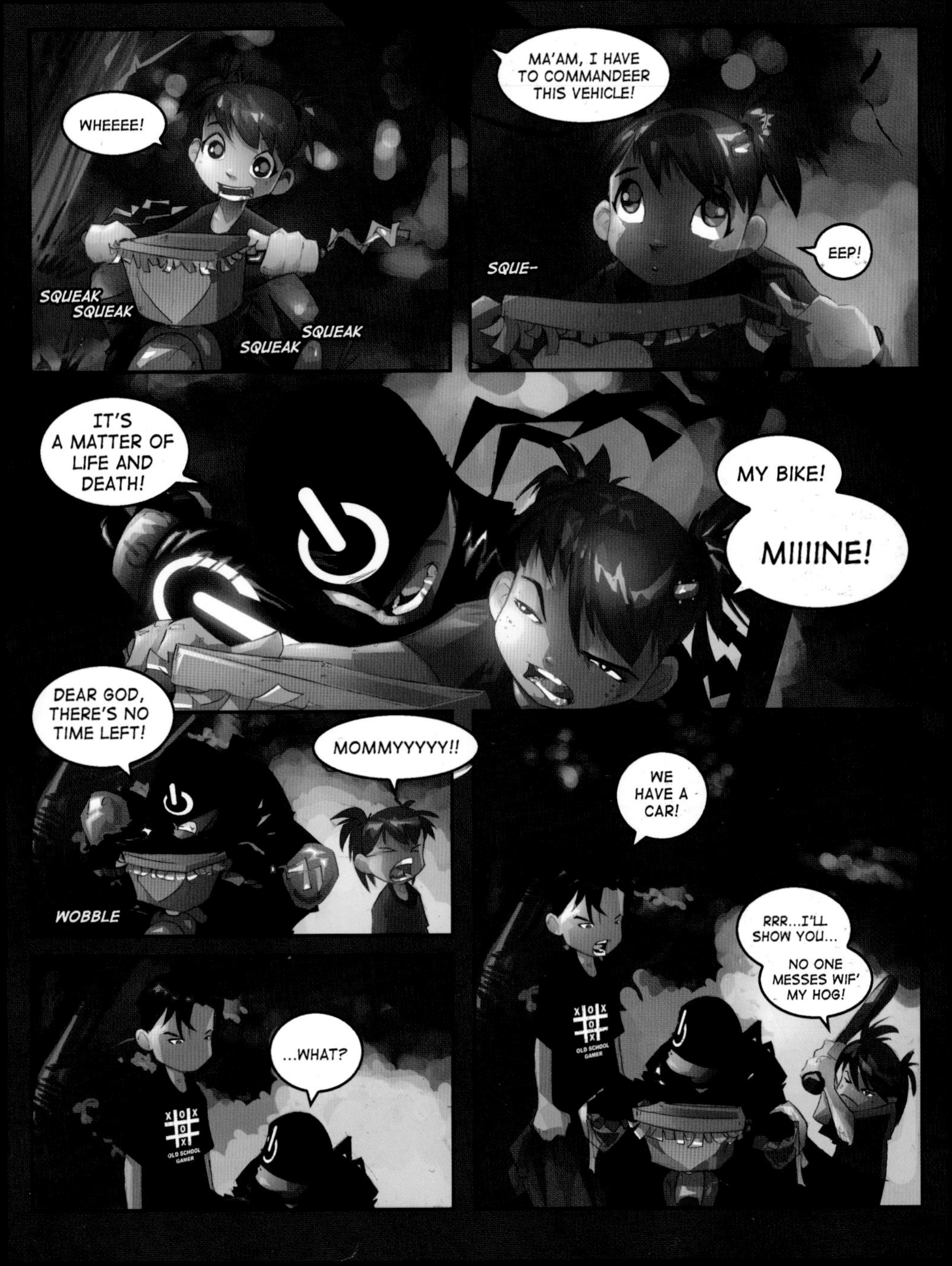
WHEEEE!
SQUEAK
SQUEAK
SQUEAK
SQUEAK
MA'AM, I HAVE TO COMMANDEER THIS VEHICLE!
SQUE-
EEP!
IT'S A MATTER OF LIFE AND DEATH!
MY BIKE!
MIIIINE!
DEAR GOD, THERE'S NO TIME LEFT!
MOMMYYYYY!!
WOBBLE
WE HAVE A CAR!
RRR...I'LL SHOW YOU...
NO ONE MESSES WIF' MY HOG!
...WHAT?

It's ASHLEY! Much like the squirrel back in volume 1, we had no idea she'd return further down the line, but she does! We also didn't realize how much people would like her, but now I am revealing too much too early on. It is pretty clear here that she's got a good deal of pluck, though. I'll leave it at that!

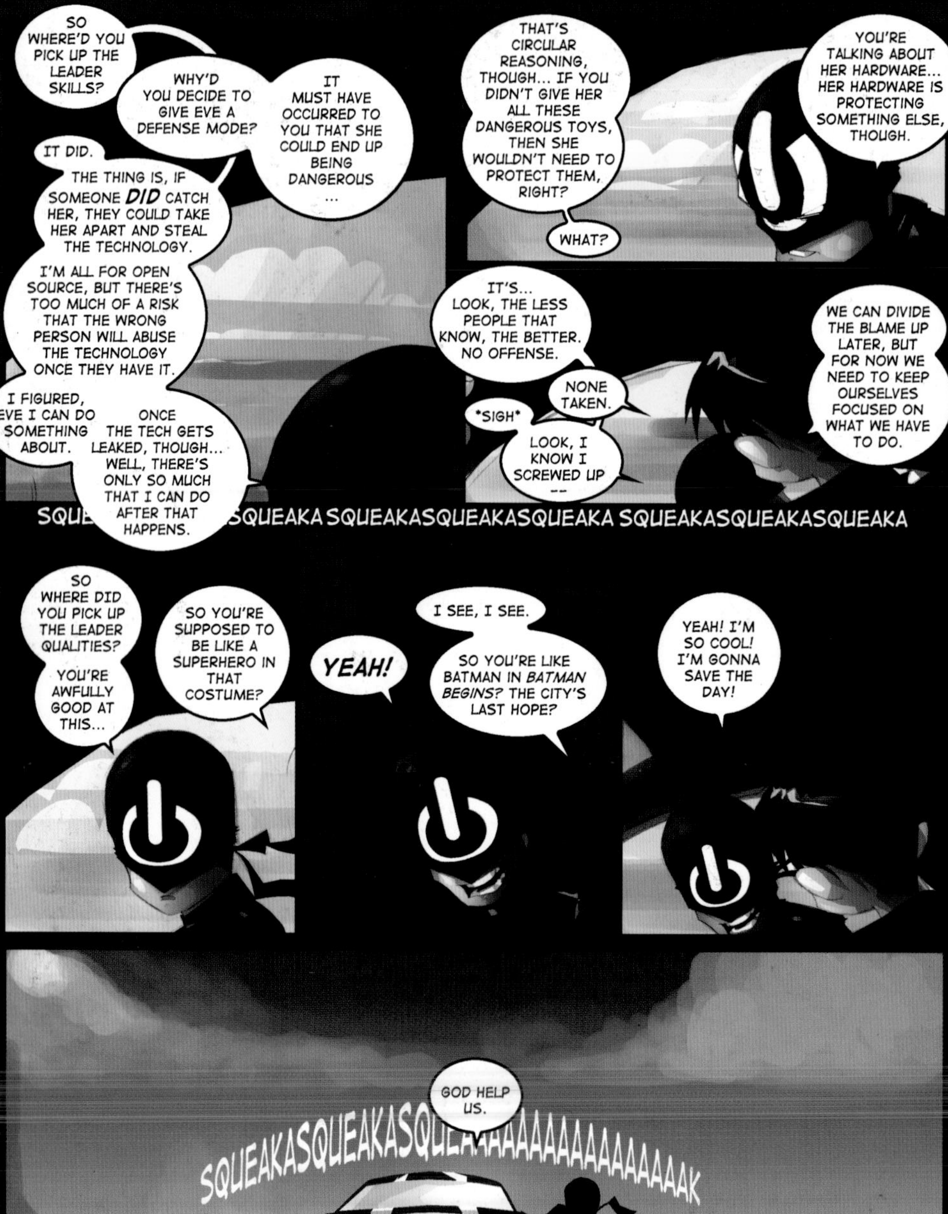
SO WHERE'D YOU PICK UP THE LEADER SKILLS?
WHY'D YOU DECIDE TO GIVE EVE A DEFENSE MODE?
IT MUST HAVE OCCURRED TO YOU THAT SHE COULD END UP BEING DANGEROUS ...
IT DID.
THE THING IS, IF SOMEONE *DID* CATCH HER, THEY COULD TAKE HER APART AND STEAL THE TECHNOLOGY.
I'M ALL FOR OPEN SOURCE, BUT THERE'S TOO MUCH OF A RISK THAT THE WRONG PERSON WILL ABUSE THE TECHNOLOGY ONCE THEY HAVE IT.
I FIGURED, EVE I CAN DO SOMETHING ABOUT.
ONCE THE TECH GETS LEAKED, THOUGH... WELL, THERE'S ONLY SO MUCH THAT I CAN DO AFTER THAT HAPPENS.
THAT'S CIRCULAR REASONING, THOUGH... IF YOU DIDN'T GIVE HER ALL THESE DANGEROUS TOYS, THEN SHE WOULDN'T NEED TO PROTECT THEM, RIGHT?
YOU'RE TALKING ABOUT HER HARDWARE... HER HARDWARE IS PROTECTING SOMETHING ELSE, THOUGH.
WHAT?
IT'S... LOOK, THE LESS PEOPLE THAT KNOW, THE BETTER. NO OFFENSE.
NONE TAKEN.
SIGH
LOOK, I KNOW I SCREWED UP --
WE CAN DIVIDE THE BLAME UP LATER, BUT FOR NOW WE NEED TO KEEP OURSELVES FOCUSED ON WHAT WE HAVE TO DO.
SQUE SQUEAKA SQUEAKASQUEAKASQUEAKA SQUEAKASQUEAKASQUEAKA
SO WHERE DID YOU PICK UP THE LEADER QUALITIES?
YOU'RE AWFULLY GOOD AT THIS...
SO YOU'RE SUPPOSED TO BE LIKE A SUPERHERO IN THAT COSTUME?
YEAH!
I SEE, I SEE.
SO YOU'RE LIKE BATMAN IN *BATMAN BEGINS?* THE CITY'S LAST HOPE?
YEAH! I'M SO COOL! I'M GONNA SAVE THE DAY!
GOD HELP US.
SQUEAKASQUEAKASQUEAAAAAAAAAAAAAAAAK

Jayce and Hawk are having a serious conversation here, so I'm going to take this opportunity to indulge myself and do some shout-outs to my friends from the FKNoP! (It's not a gang—think *The Sandlot*.) Ajay! Archer! Ryan! Marcus! Sam! Fil! Bowl! Wang! Christian! Charles! Jon! Joe! Other Joe! Mike! Hayley! Justin!

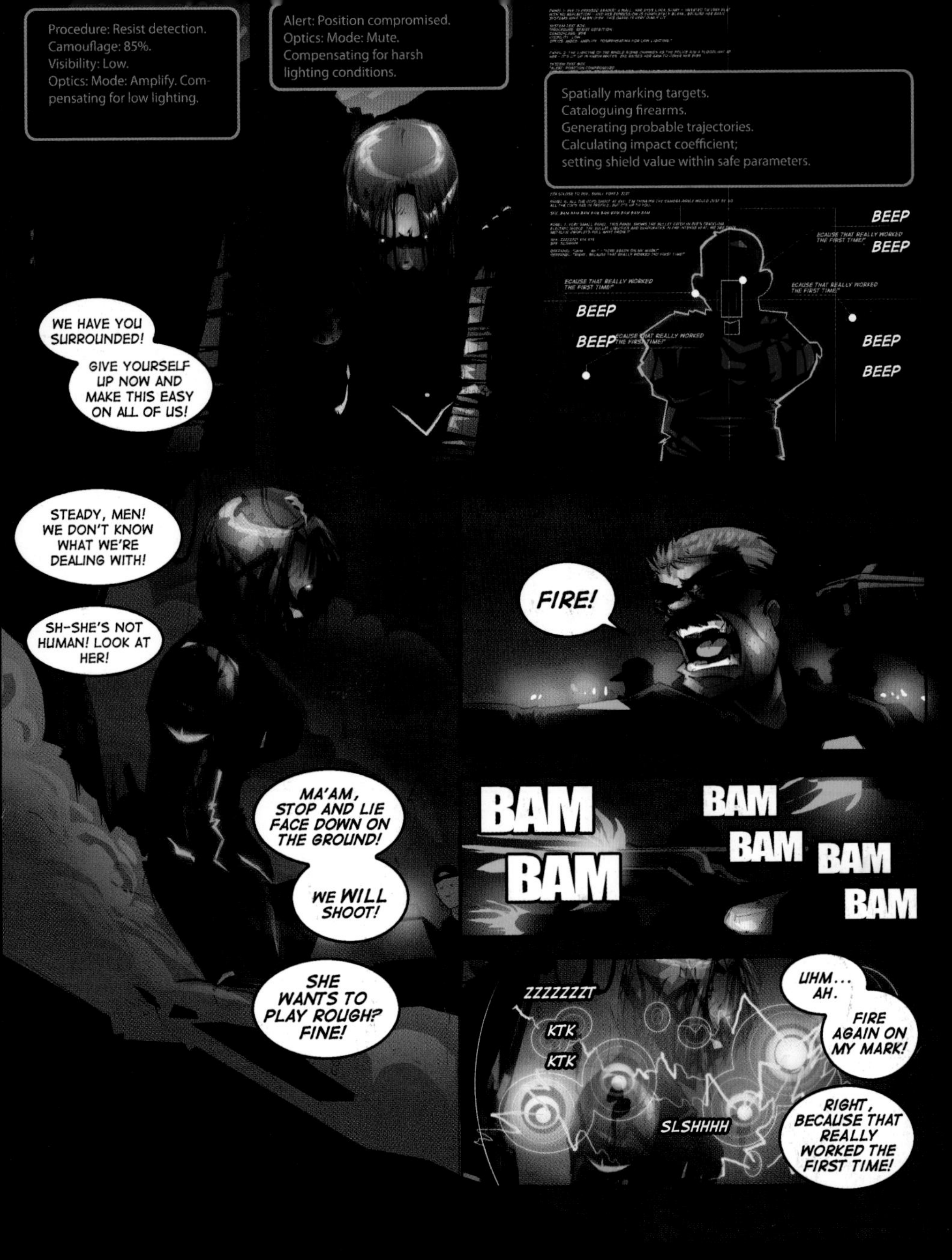

Procedure: Resist detection.
Camouflage: 85%.
Visibility: Low.
Optics: Mode: Amplify. Compensating for low lighting.
Alert: Position compromised.
Optics: Mode: Mute.
Compensating for harsh lighting conditions.
WE HAVE YOU SURROUNDED!
GIVE YOURSELF UP NOW AND MAKE THIS EASY ON ALL OF US!
Spatially marking targets.
Cataloguing firearms.
Generating probable trajectories.
Calculating impact coefficient;
setting shield value within safe parameters.
BEEP
BEEP
BEEP
BEEP
BEEP
BEEP
STEADY, MEN! WE DON'T KNOW WHAT WE'RE DEALING WITH!
SH-SHE'S NOT HUMAN! LOOK AT HER!
MA'AM, STOP AND LIE FACE DOWN ON THE GROUND!
WE WILL SHOOT!
SHE WANTS TO PLAY ROUGH? FINE!
FIRE!
BAM
BAM
BAM
BAM
BAM
BAM
ZZZZZZZT
KTK
KTK
SLSHHHH
UHM... AH.
FIRE AGAIN ON MY MARK!
RIGHT, BECAUSE THAT REALLY WORKED THE FIRST TIME!

I'm not quite sure why that police captain looks like J. Jonah Jameson, but hey, sometimes times are tough and you have to find a new line of work. Eve's firearm tracking and shields are two new features we haven't seen before. Also, I really like the pixel font that Hawk picked for the technical readouts. Here's a secret: in panel three, the "process code"

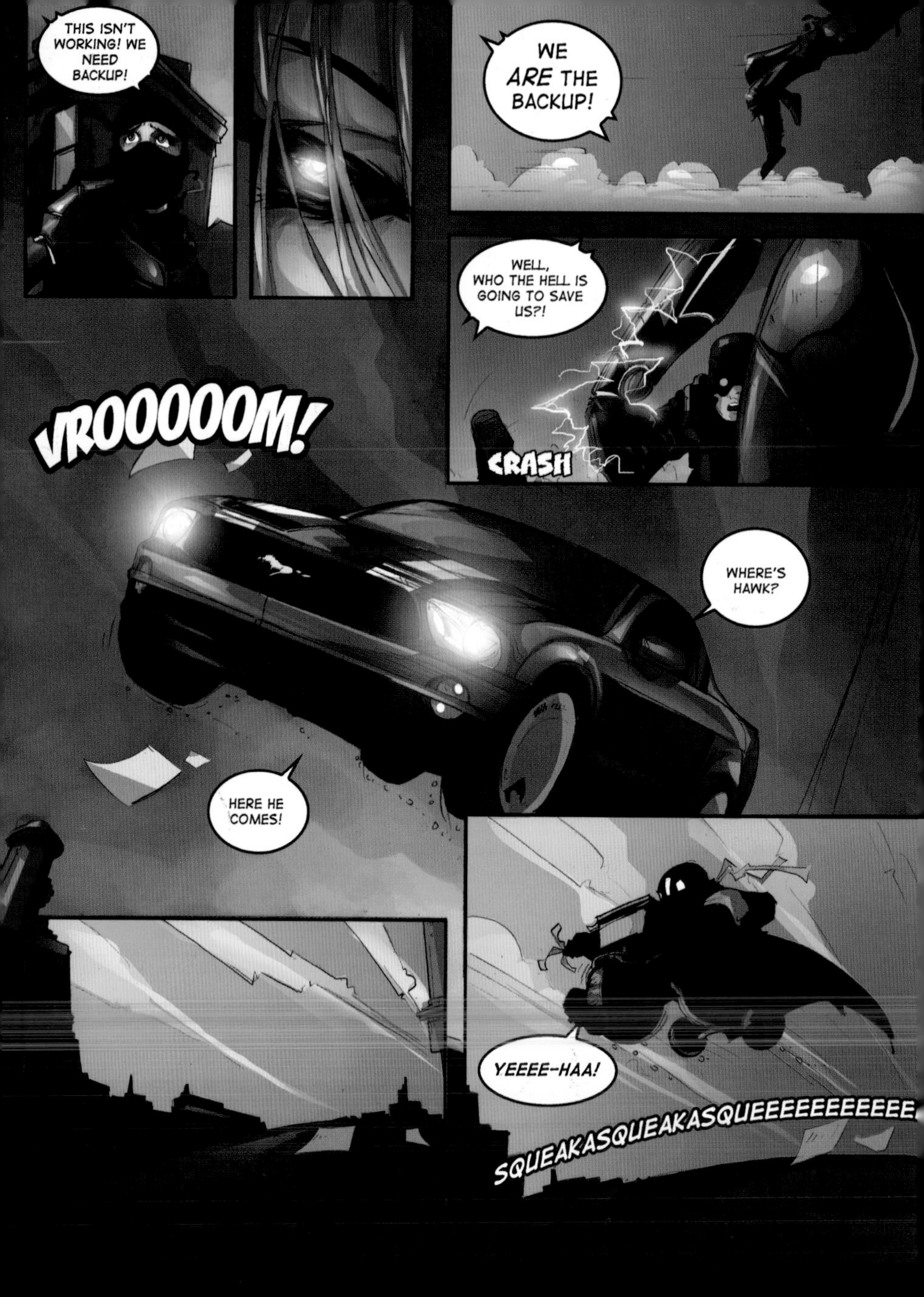
THIS ISN'T WORKING! WE NEED BACKUP!
WE ARE THE BACKUP!
WELL, WHO THE HELL IS GOING TO SAVE US?!
CRASH
VROOOOOM!
WHERE'S HAWK?
HERE HE COMES!
YEEEE-HAA!
SQUEAKASQUEAKASQUEEEEEEEEEEE

This, for me, was one of the most satisfying e-mail-generating moments of the comic. People loved the tricycle co
over the hill. I dunno... it's those pink streamers that really do it for me (those were my idea. I'm happy to say

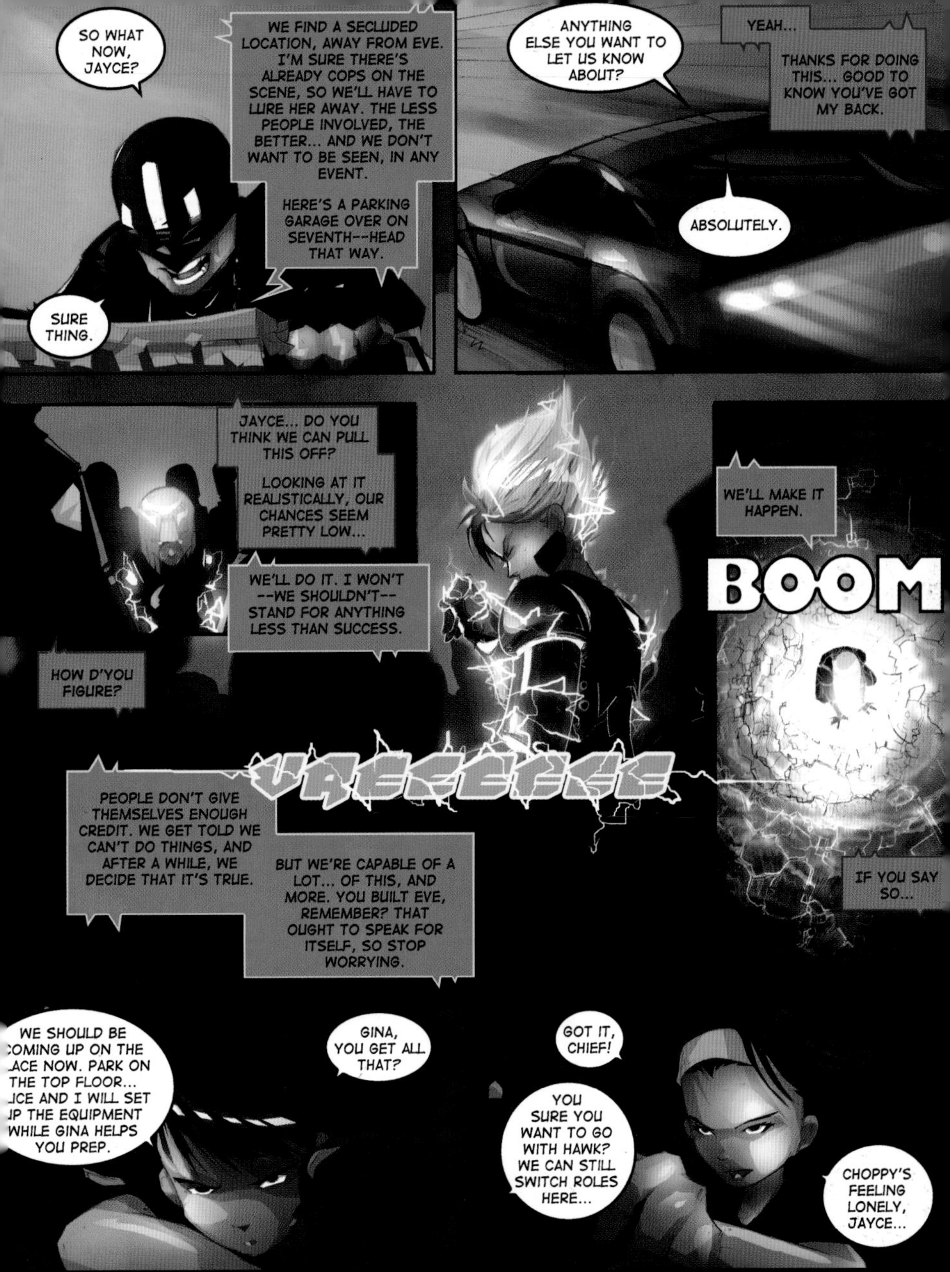
SO WHAT NOW, JAYCE?
WE FIND A SECLUDED LOCATION, AWAY FROM EVE. I'M SURE THERE'S ALREADY COPS ON THE SCENE, SO WE'LL HAVE TO LURE HER AWAY. THE LESS PEOPLE INVOLVED, THE BETTER... AND WE DON'T WANT TO BE SEEN, IN ANY EVENT.
HERE'S A PARKING GARAGE OVER ON SEVENTH--HEAD THAT WAY.
SURE THING.
ANYTHING ELSE YOU WANT TO LET US KNOW ABOUT?
YEAH...
THANKS FOR DOING THIS... GOOD TO KNOW YOU'VE GOT MY BACK.
ABSOLUTELY.
JAYCE... DO YOU THINK WE CAN PULL THIS OFF?
LOOKING AT IT REALISTICALLY, OUR CHANCES SEEM PRETTY LOW...
WE'LL DO IT. I WON'T --WE SHOULDN'T-- STAND FOR ANYTHING LESS THAN SUCCESS.
HOW D'YOU FIGURE?
PEOPLE DON'T GIVE THEMSELVES ENOUGH CREDIT. WE GET TOLD WE CAN'T DO THINGS, AND AFTER A WHILE, WE DECIDE THAT IT'S TRUE.
BUT WE'RE CAPABLE OF A LOT... OF THIS, AND MORE. YOU BUILT EVE, REMEMBER? THAT OUGHT TO SPEAK FOR ITSELF, SO STOP WORRYING.
WE'LL MAKE IT HAPPEN.
BOOM
IF YOU SAY SO...
WE SHOULD BE COMING UP ON THE LACE NOW. PARK ON THE TOP FLOOR... LICE AND I WILL SET UP THE EQUIPMENT WHILE GINA HELPS YOU PREP.
GINA, YOU GET ALL THAT?
GOT IT, CHIEF!
YOU SURE YOU WANT TO GO WITH HAWK? WE CAN STILL SWITCH ROLES HERE...
CHOPPY'S FEELING LONELY, JAYCE...

e is the man with the plan! It seems strange seeing him take charge of the situation, but it gets explainec

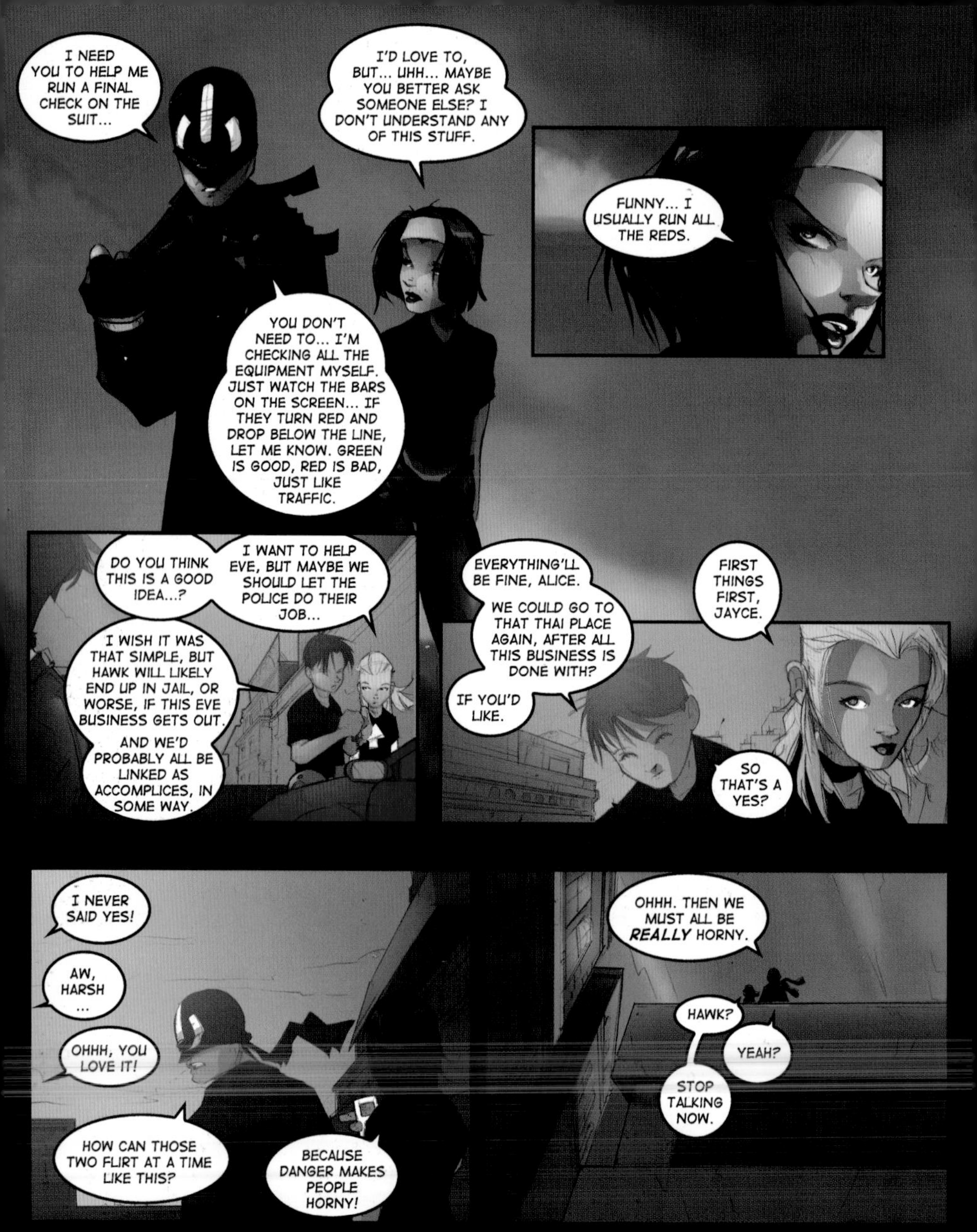
I NEED YOU TO HELP ME RUN A FINAL CHECK ON THE SUIT...
I'D LOVE TO, BUT... UHH... MAYBE YOU BETTER ASK SOMEONE ELSE? I DON'T UNDERSTAND ANY OF THIS STUFF.
YOU DON'T NEED TO... I'M CHECKING ALL THE EQUIPMENT MYSELF. JUST WATCH THE BARS ON THE SCREEN... IF THEY TURN RED AND DROP BELOW THE LINE, LET ME KNOW. GREEN IS GOOD, RED IS BAD, JUST LIKE TRAFFIC.
FUNNY... I USUALLY RUN ALL THE REDS.
DO YOU THINK THIS IS A GOOD IDEA...?
I WANT TO HELP EVE, BUT MAYBE WE SHOULD LET THE POLICE DO THEIR JOB...
I WISH IT WAS THAT SIMPLE, BUT HAWK WILL LIKELY END UP IN JAIL, OR WORSE, IF THIS EVE BUSINESS GETS OUT.
AND WE'D PROBABLY ALL BE LINKED AS ACCOMPLICES, IN SOME WAY.
EVERYTHING'LL BE FINE, ALICE.
WE COULD GO TO THAT THAI PLACE AGAIN, AFTER ALL THIS BUSINESS IS DONE WITH?
IF YOU'D LIKE.
FIRST THINGS FIRST, JAYCE.
SO THAT'S A YES?
I NEVER SAID YES!
AW, HARSH ...
OHHH, YOU LOVE IT!
HOW CAN THOSE TWO FLIRT AT A TIME LIKE THIS?
BECAUSE DANGER MAKES PEOPLE HORNY!
OHHH. THEN WE MUST ALL BE *REALLY* HORNY.
HAWK?
YEAH?
STOP TALKING NOW.

Hawk messes with a new style. This comic was actually colored especially for the book—the original in the archive on the website is still in pencil. Although there was ultimately a lot of mixed reaction to these pages, I really think

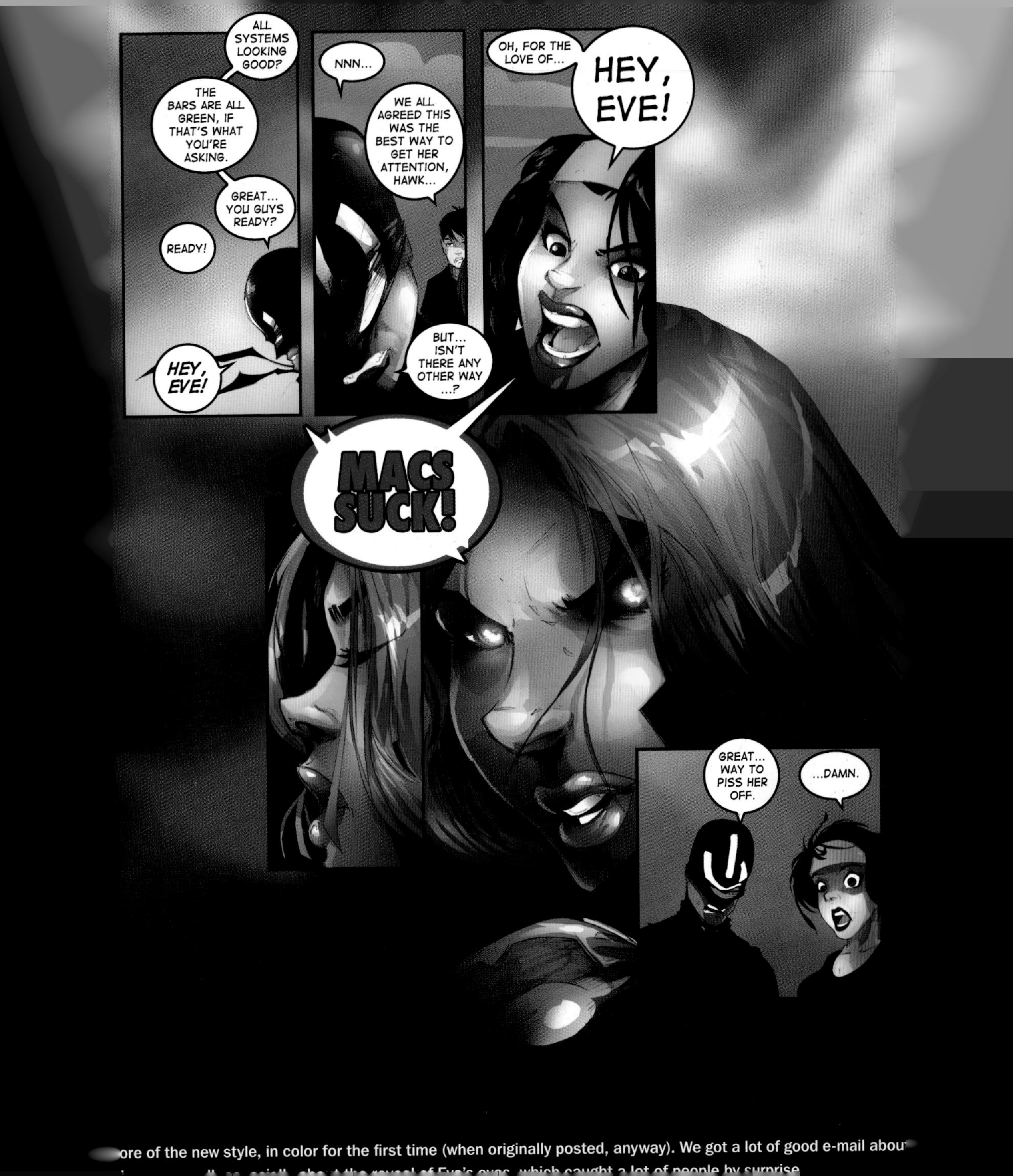
ALL SYSTEMS LOOKING GOOD?
THE BARS ARE ALL GREEN, IF THAT'S WHAT YOU'RE ASKING.
GREAT... YOU GUYS READY?
READY!
HEY, EVE!
NNN...
WE ALL AGREED THIS WAS THE BEST WAY TO GET HER ATTENTION, HAWK...
BUT... ISN'T THERE ANY OTHER WAY ...?
OH, FOR THE LOVE OF...
HEY, EVE!
MACS SUCK!
GREAT... WAY TO PISS HER OFF.
...DAMN.

ore of the new style, in color for the first time (when originally posted, anyway). We got a lot of good e-mail abou

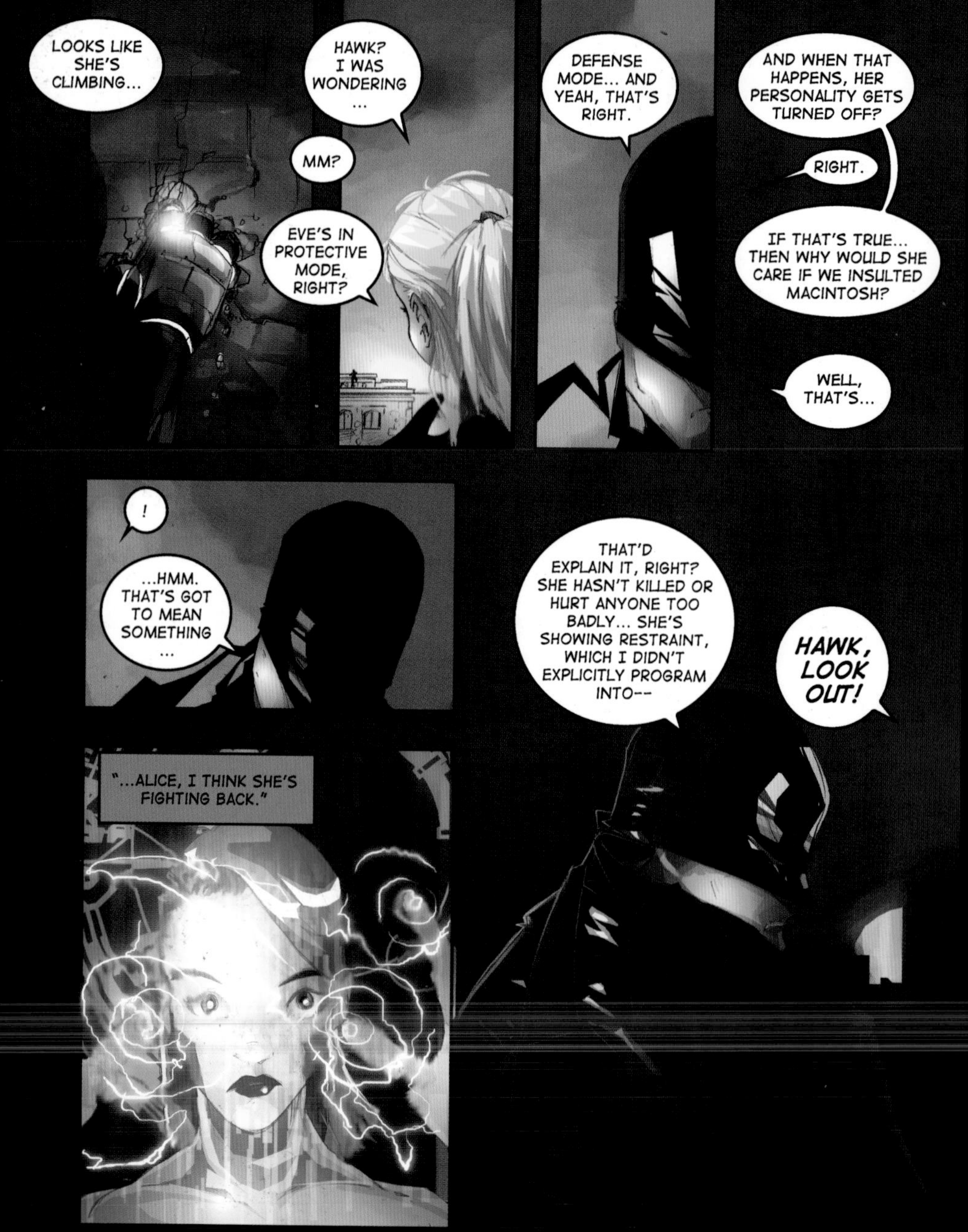
LOOKS LIKE SHE'S CLIMBING...
HAWK? I WAS WONDERING ...
MM?
EVE'S IN PROTECTIVE MODE, RIGHT?
DEFENSE MODE... AND YEAH, THAT'S RIGHT.
AND WHEN THAT HAPPENS, HER PERSONALITY GETS TURNED OFF?
RIGHT.
IF THAT'S TRUE... THEN WHY WOULD SHE CARE IF WE INSULTED MACINTOSH?
WELL, THAT'S...
!
...HMM. THAT'S GOT TO MEAN SOMETHING ...
"...ALICE, I THINK SHE'S FIGHTING BACK."
THAT'D EXPLAIN IT, RIGHT? SHE HASN'T KILLED OR HURT ANYONE TOO BADLY... SHE'S SHOWING RESTRAINT, WHICH I DIDN'T EXPLICITLY PROGRAM INTO--
HAWK, LOOK OUT!

Hawk suddenly gets pretty stocky! Ironically enough, this is possibly the closest to Hawk's actual build that we've seen cartoon Hawk have in the comic. That second-to-last panel with Eve is more or less inspired by the

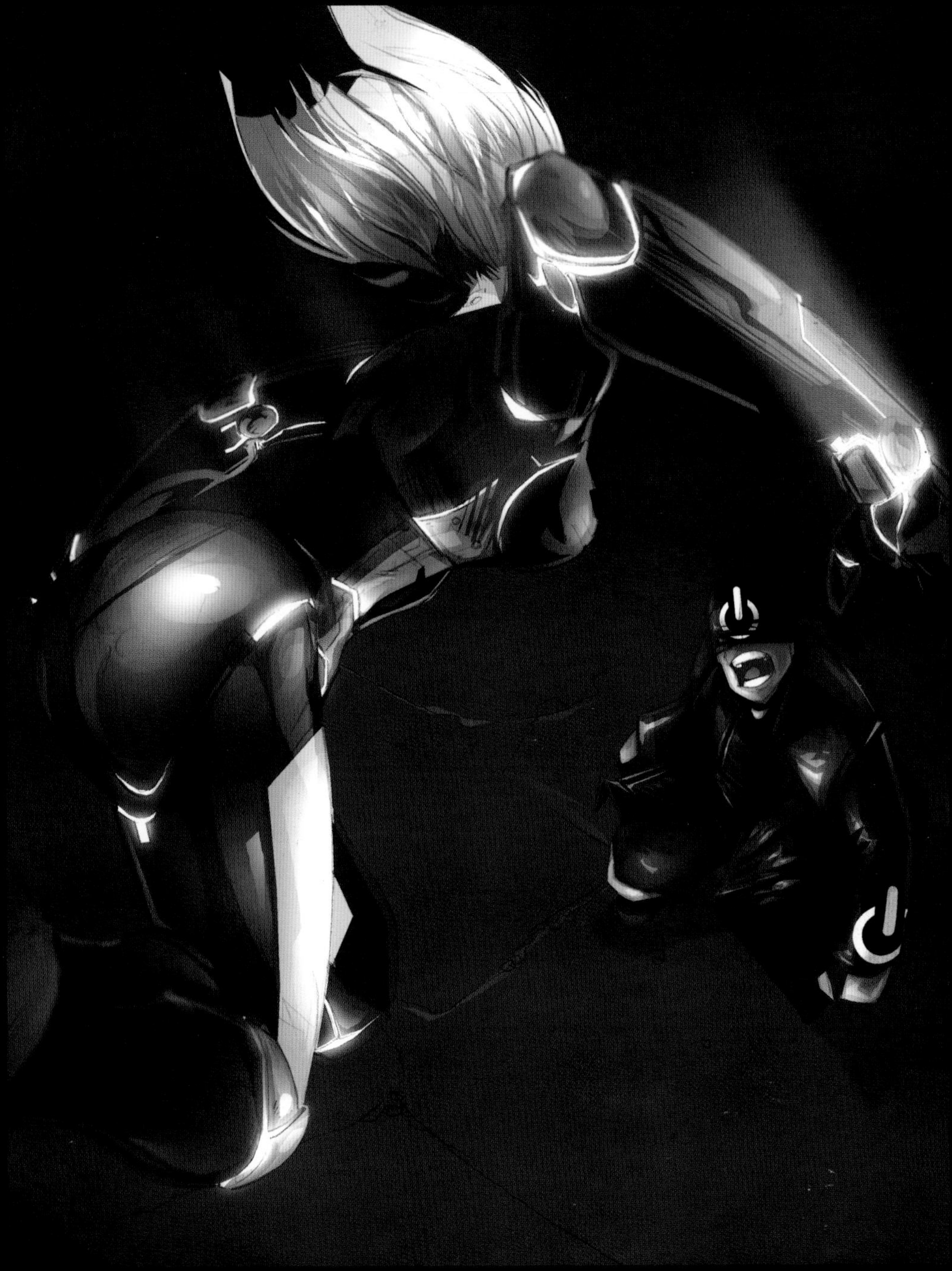

This image actually appeared as a limited-edition print packaged with the Eve figurine. More on that in the back of the book—there's a section there all about the development of the figurine! They're all sold out now, but we're talking about doing a new one, maybe . . .

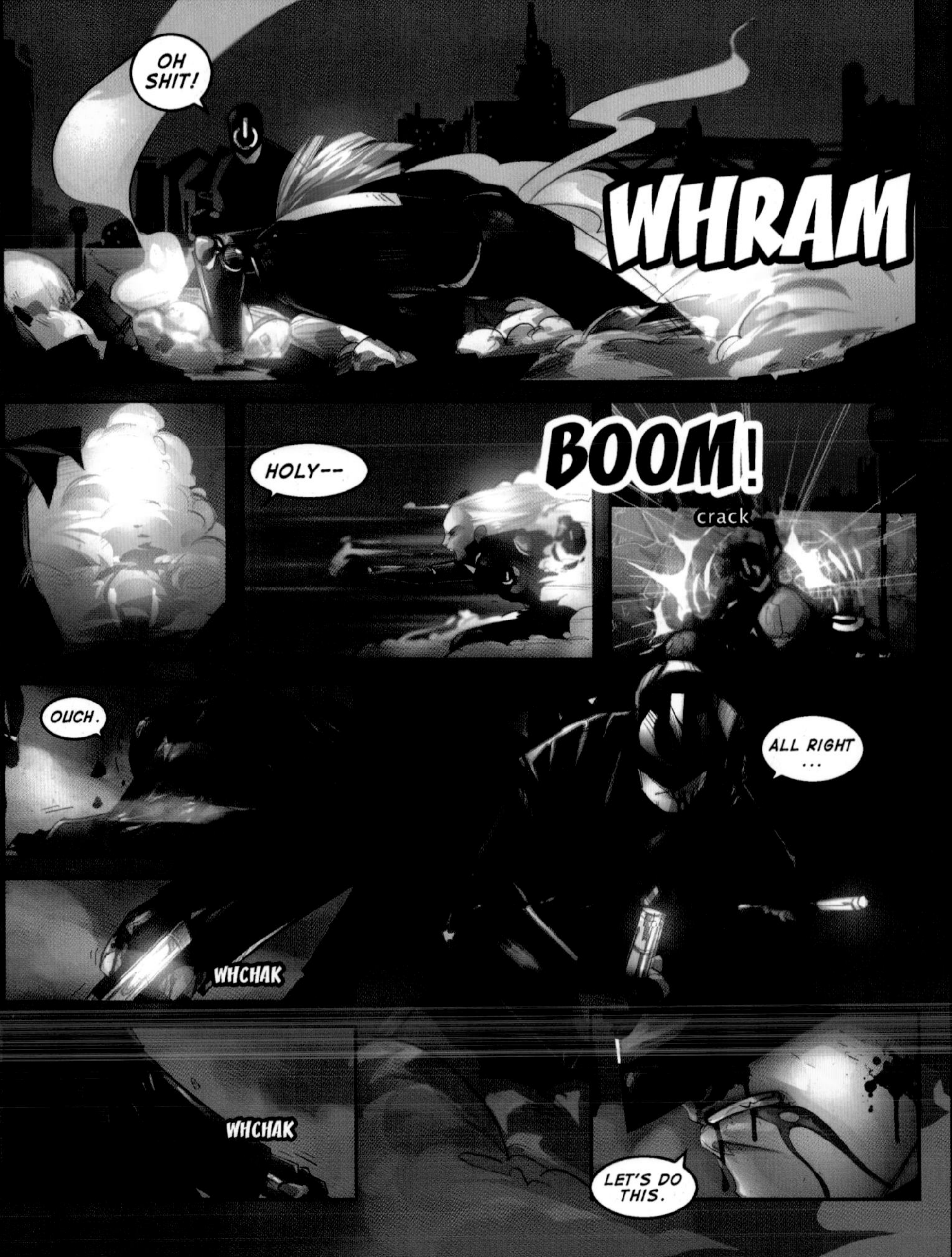
OH SHIT!
WHRAM
HOLY--
BOOM!
crack
OUCH.
ALL RIGHT ...
WHCHAK
WHCHAK
LET'S DO THIS.

That looks like it hurt! Back when we came up with the concept of Eve, we didn't really design her with the idea in mind that she'd end up fighting people. I guess it was a natural transition, though, since *Ghost in the Shell* and *Battle Angel Alita* influenced her design so heavily.

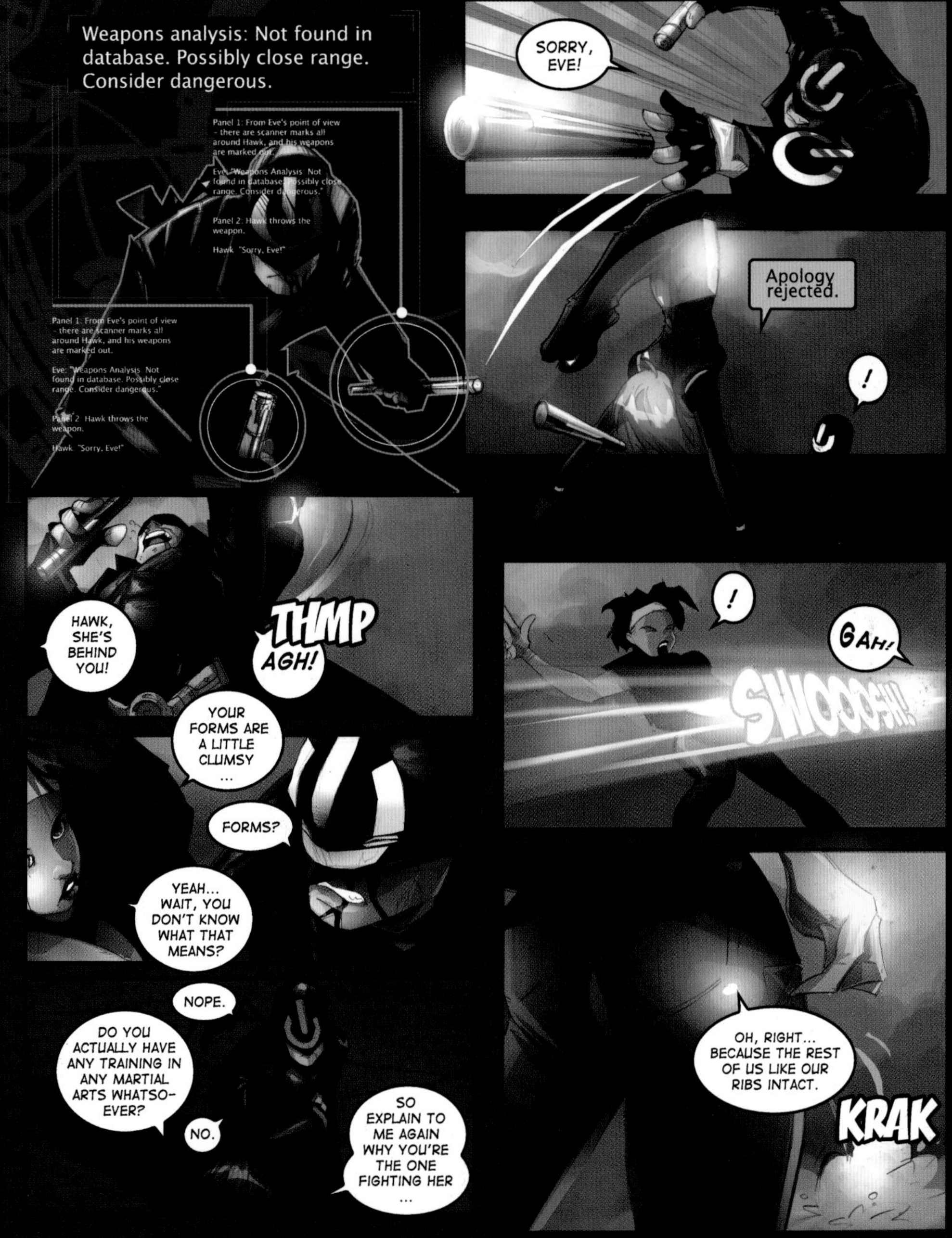
Weapons analysis: Not found in database. Possibly close range. Consider dangerous.
Panel 1: From Eve's point of view - there are scanner marks all around Hawk, and his weapons are marked out.
Eve: "Weapons Analysis: Not found in database. Possibly close range. Consider dangerous."
Panel 2: Hawk throws the weapon.
Hawk: "Sorry, Eve!"
SORRY, EVE!
Apology rejected.
!
HAWK, SHE'S BEHIND YOU!
THMP
AGH!
YOUR FORMS ARE A LITTLE CLUMSY ...
FORMS?
YEAH... WAIT, YOU DON'T KNOW WHAT THAT MEANS?
NOPE.
DO YOU ACTUALLY HAVE ANY TRAINING IN ANY MARTIAL ARTS WHATSO-EVER?
NO.
SO EXPLAIN TO ME AGAIN WHY YOU'RE THE ONE FIGHTING HER ...
!
GAH!
SWOOOSH!
OH, RIGHT... BECAUSE THE REST OF US LIKE OUR RIBS INTACT.
KRAK

Hawk was never meant to be a fighter, and I thought it was important to acknowledge that. He's sort of stumbling through this whole ordeal, putting on a good show of it, but ultimately the only reason he's not being made into paste on the pavement is his fancy combat suit.

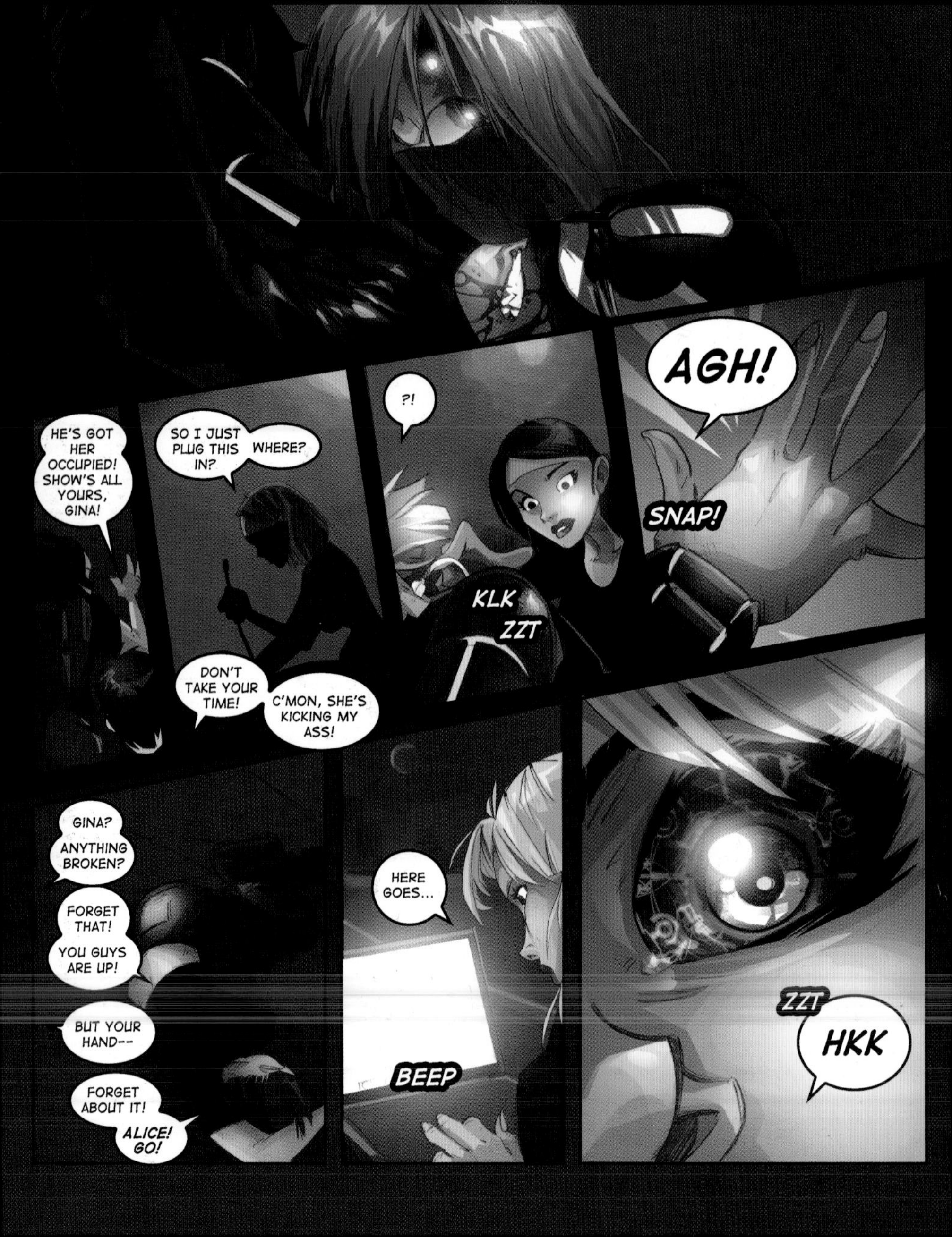
HE'S GOT HER OCCUPIED! SHOW'S ALL YOURS, GINA!
SO I JUST PLUG THIS IN?
WHERE?
DON'T TAKE YOUR TIME!
C'MON, SHE'S KICKING MY ASS!
?!
KLK
ZZT
AGH!
SNAP!
GINA?
ANYTHING BROKEN?
FORGET THAT!
YOU GUYS ARE UP!
BUT YOUR HAND--
FORGET ABOUT IT!
ALICE! GO!
HERE GOES...
BEEP
ZZT
HKK

I always thought that, given the change in direction that this story arc took us, the art style complemented it pretty well. It's somewhere between our normal cartoony look and a more serious approach. We had a lot of mixed reaction to the style change, but on the whole people were pretty open to it. By the end of this arc we were receiving mail from a lot of new readers, and that's always a good gauge for us.

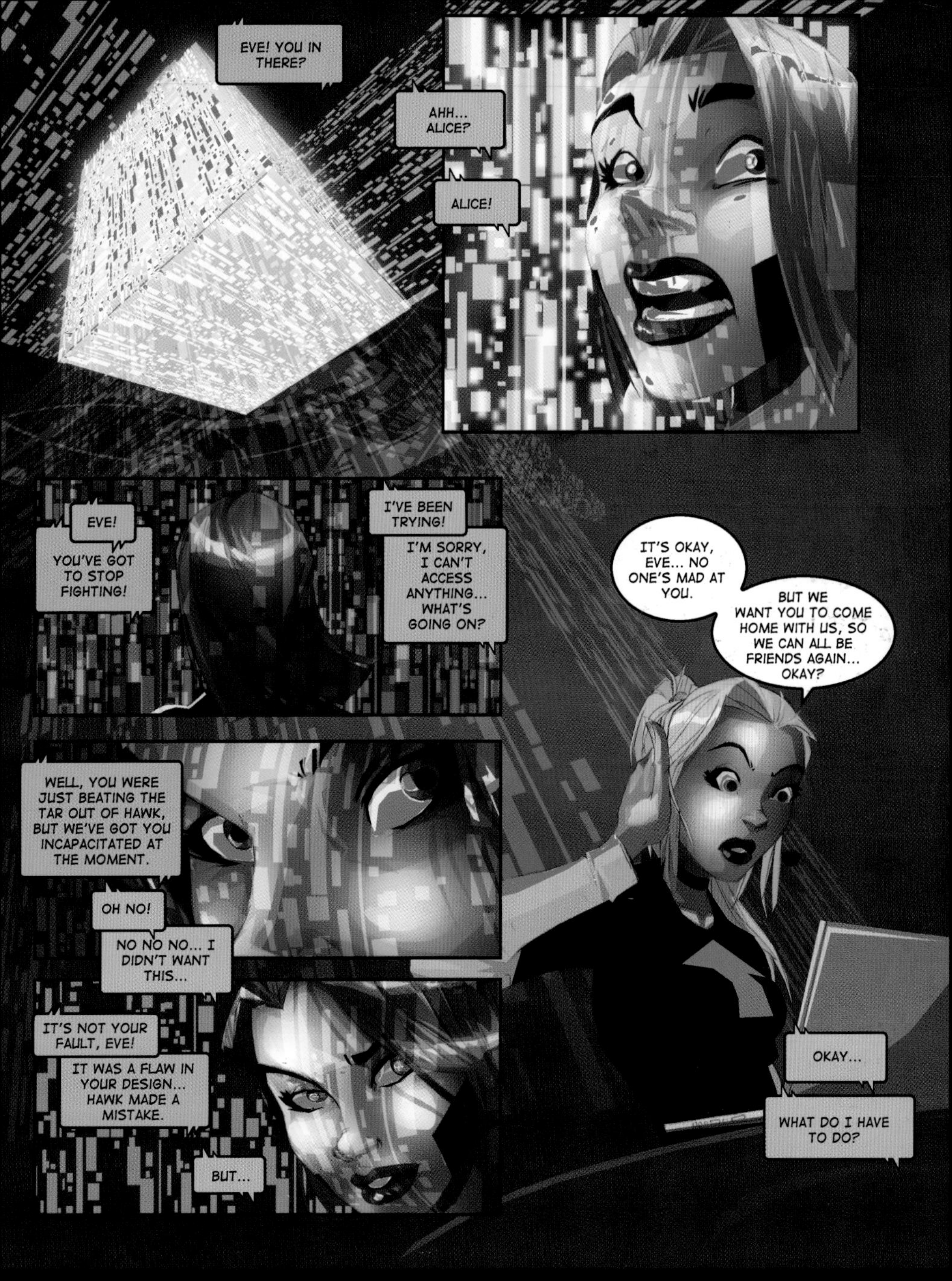
EVE! YOU IN THERE?
AHH... ALICE?
ALICE!
EVE!
YOU'VE GOT TO STOP FIGHTING!
I'VE BEEN TRYING!
I'M SORRY, I CAN'T ACCESS ANYTHING... WHAT'S GOING ON?
WELL, YOU WERE JUST BEATING THE TAR OUT OF HAWK, BUT WE'VE GOT YOU INCAPACITATED AT THE MOMENT.
OH NO!
NO NO NO... I DIDN'T WANT THIS...
IT'S NOT YOUR FAULT, EVE!
IT WAS A FLAW IN YOUR DESIGN... HAWK MADE A MISTAKE.
BUT...
IT'S OKAY, EVE... NO ONE'S MAD AT YOU.
BUT WE WANT YOU TO COME HOME WITH US, SO WE CAN ALL BE FRIENDS AGAIN... OKAY?
OKAY...
WHAT DO I HAVE TO DO?

The way Hawk drew this reminds me of a scene from an old anime they used to air on the Sci Fi channel . . . I can't seem to recall the name of it. They were in space, and there was this robot and this hotshot pilot, and this girl got trapped in a weird space prison. I can't remember. It wasn't as weird as *Roujin Z*, though.

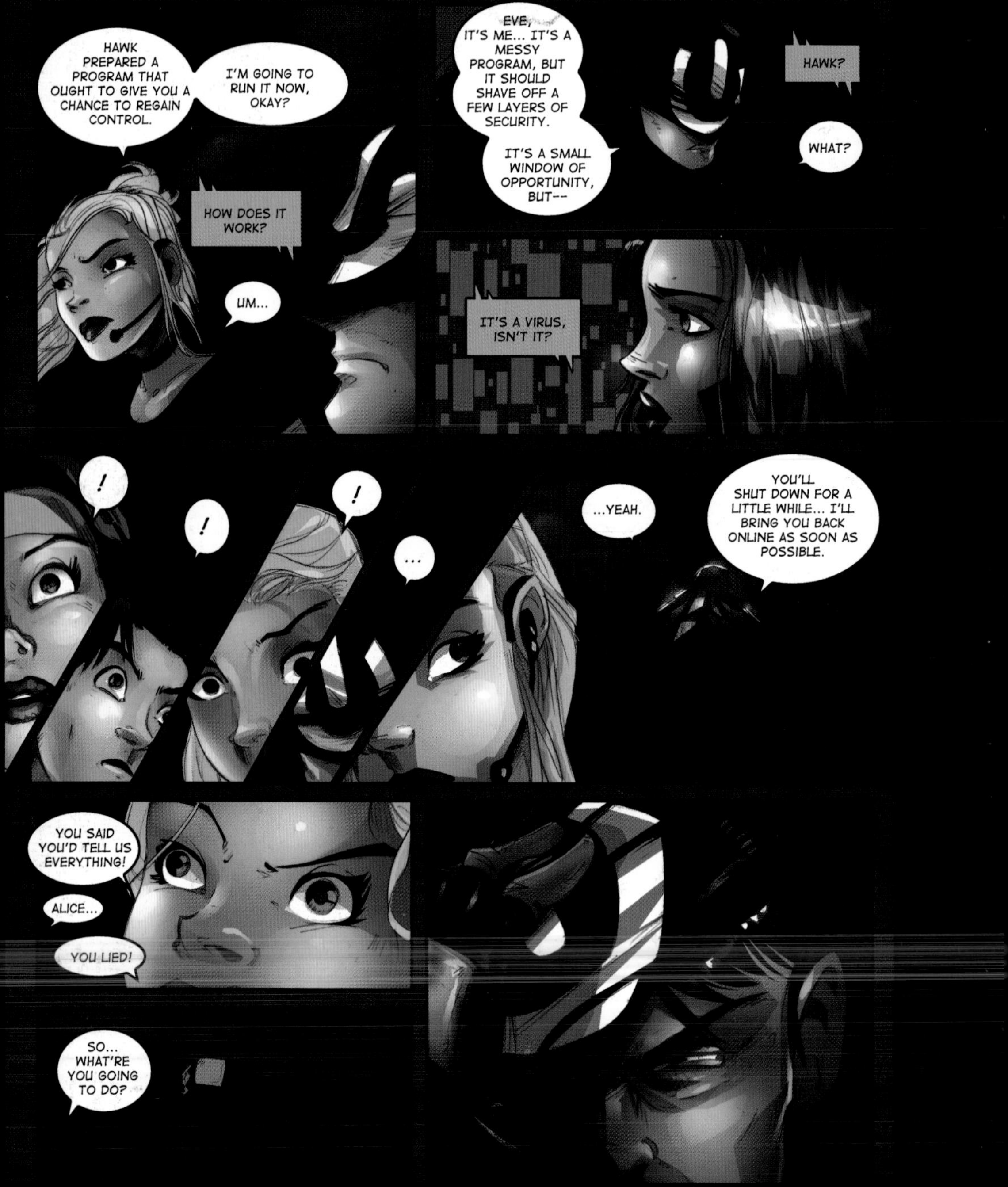

HAWK PREPARED A PROGRAM THAT OUGHT TO GIVE YOU A CHANCE TO REGAIN CONTROL.
I'M GOING TO RUN IT NOW, OKAY?
HOW DOES IT WORK?
UM...
EVE, IT'S ME... IT'S A MESSY PROGRAM, BUT IT SHOULD SHAVE OFF A FEW LAYERS OF SECURITY.
IT'S A SMALL WINDOW OF OPPORTUNITY, BUT--
HAWK?
WHAT?
IT'S A VIRUS, ISN'T IT?
!
!
!
...
...YEAH.
YOU'LL SHUT DOWN FOR A LITTLE WHILE... I'LL BRING YOU BACK ONLINE AS SOON AS POSSIBLE.
YOU SAID YOU'D TELL US EVERYTHING!
ALICE...
YOU LIED!
SO... WHAT'RE YOU GOING TO DO?

Hawk's been keeping secrets! Not cool! There's a saying about desperate times that certainly applies . . .

(Oh, and *Roujin Z* was about this computerized hospital bed that ran amuck with its patient onboard. It was this strange morality tale that had a pretty black sense of humor. Totally weird and totally worth a watch.)

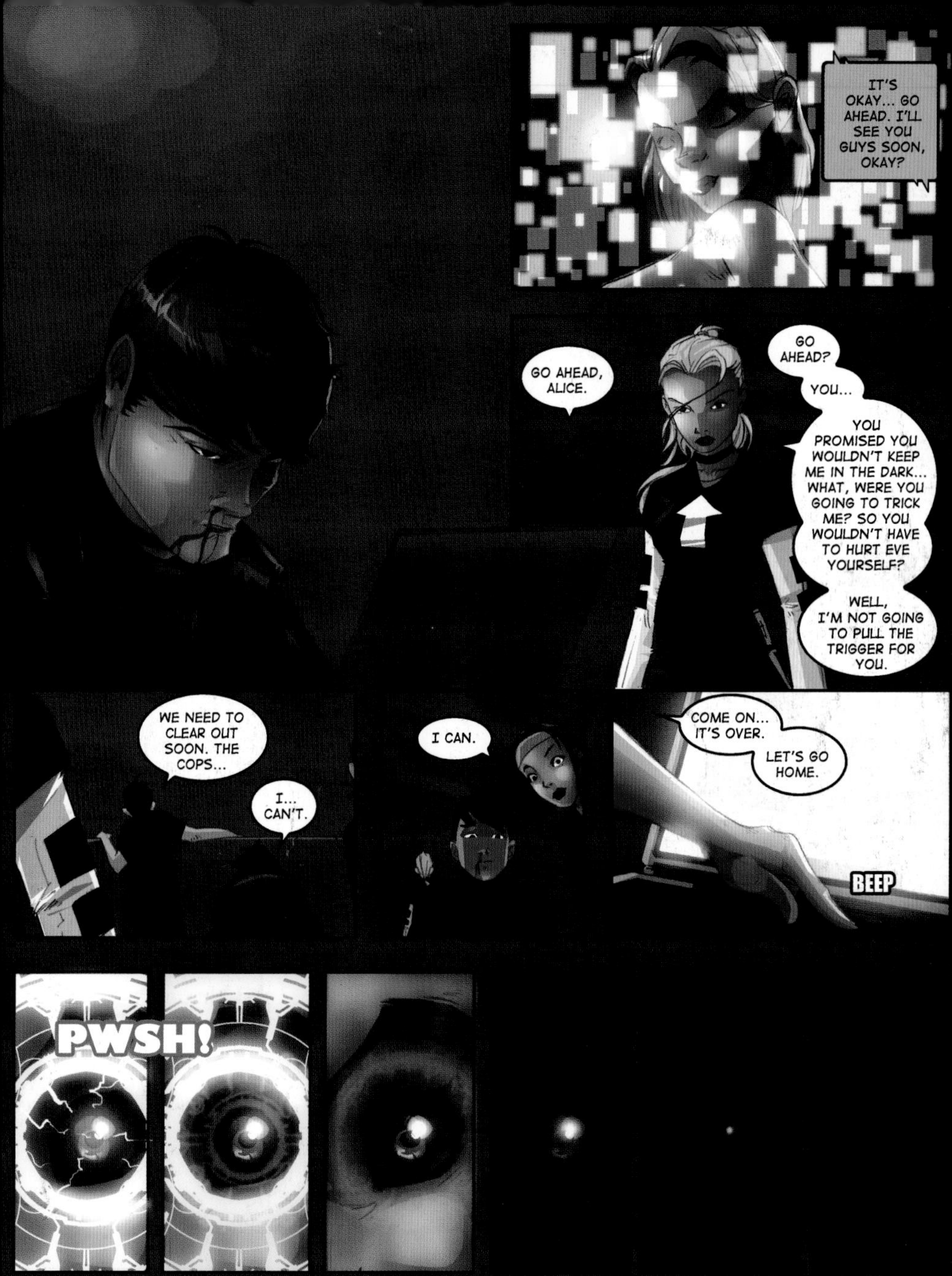
IT'S OKAY... GO AHEAD. I'LL SEE YOU GUYS SOON, OKAY?
GO AHEAD, ALICE.
GO AHEAD?
YOU...
YOU PROMISED YOU WOULDN'T KEEP ME IN THE DARK... WHAT, WERE YOU GOING TO TRICK ME? SO YOU WOULDN'T HAVE TO HURT EVE YOURSELF?
WELL, I'M NOT GOING TO PULL THE TRIGGER FOR YOU.
WE NEED TO CLEAR OUT SOON. THE COPS...
I... CAN'T.
I CAN.
COME ON... IT'S OVER.
LET'S GO HOME.
BEEP
PWSH!

And that, as they say, is that. I always feel bad for Eve at the end of this story arc, and truth be told, I always feel a

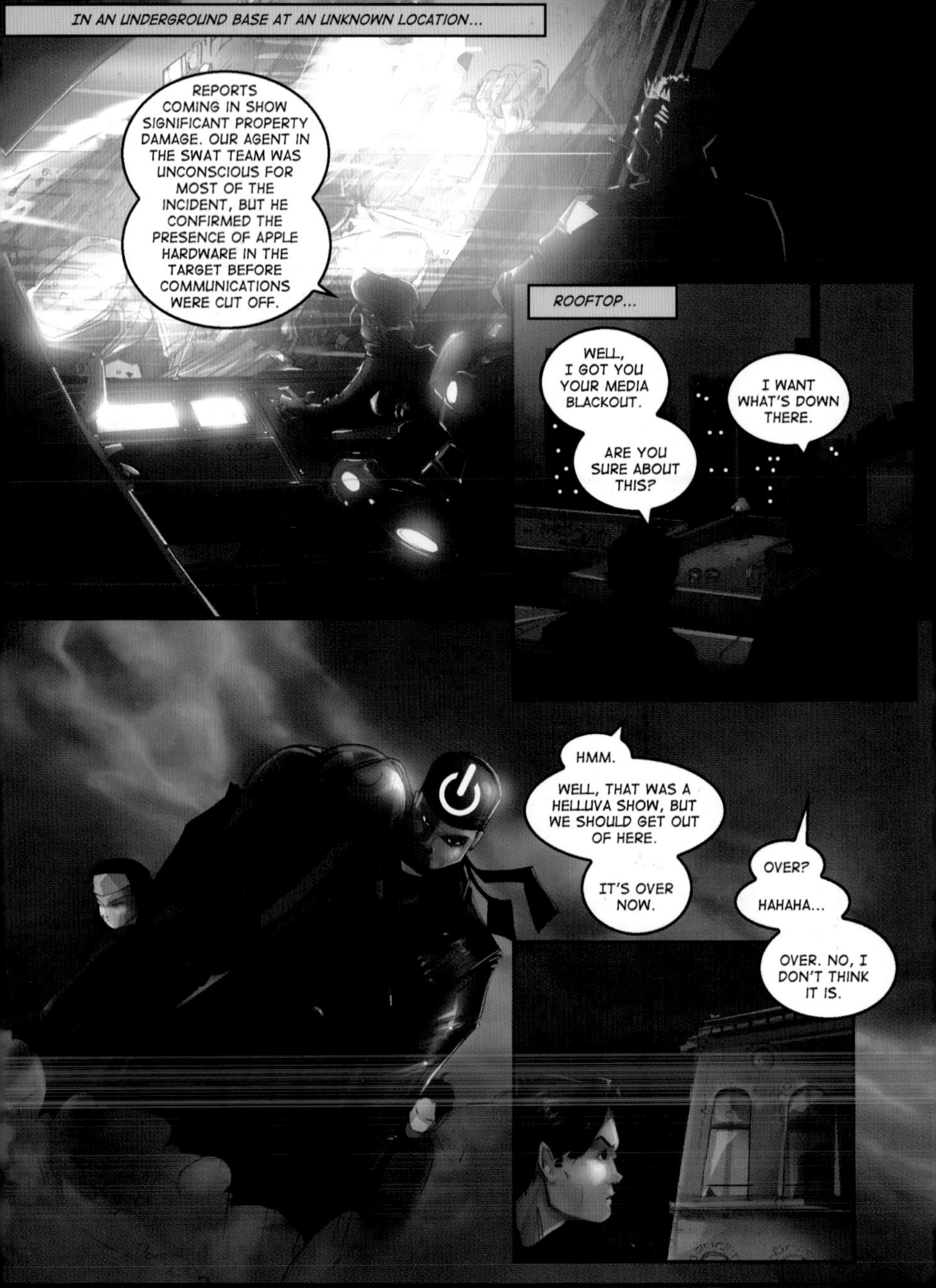
IN AN UNDERGROUND BASE AT AN UNKNOWN LOCATION...
REPORTS COMING IN SHOW SIGNIFICANT PROPERTY DAMAGE. OUR AGENT IN THE SWAT TEAM WAS UNCONSCIOUS FOR MOST OF THE INCIDENT, BUT HE CONFIRMED THE PRESENCE OF APPLE HARDWARE IN THE TARGET BEFORE COMMUNICATIONS WERE CUT OFF.
ROOFTOP...
WELL, I GOT YOU YOUR MEDIA BLACKOUT.
ARE YOU SURE ABOUT THIS?
I WANT WHAT'S DOWN THERE.
HMM.
WELL, THAT WAS A HELLUVA SHOW, BUT WE SHOULD GET OUT OF HERE.
IT'S OVER NOW.
OVER?
HAHAHA...
OVER. NO, I DON'T THINK IT IS.

ks like it's not over! We were flying by the seat of our pants during most of this story arc . . . At this point I

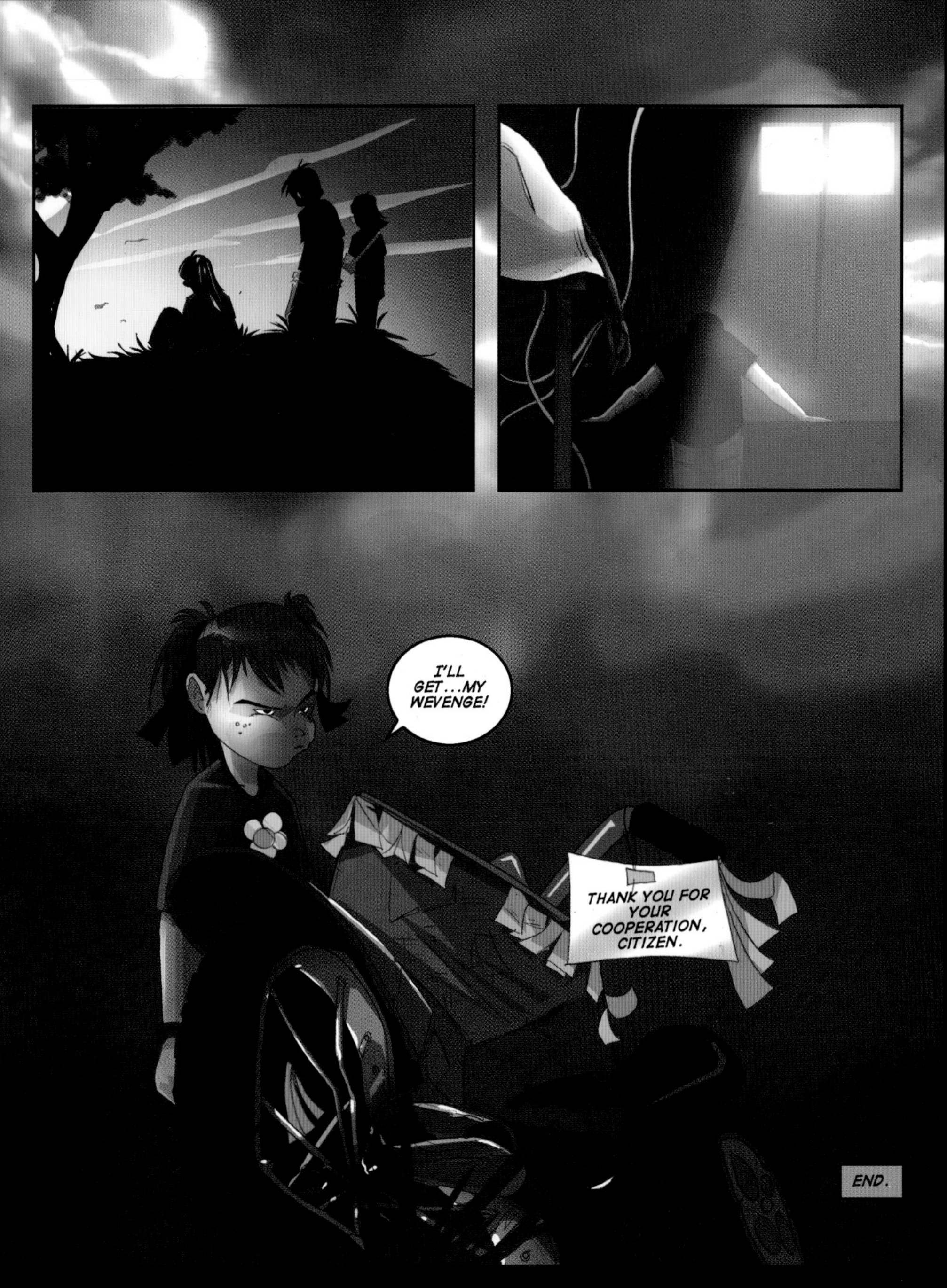
I'LL GET...MY WEVENGE!
THANK YOU FOR YOUR COOPERATION, CITIZEN.
END.

Ashley swears her undying revenge in this issue, and she makes good on it quite a few times over. Sadly, it is Hawk's friends who bear the brunt of this grudge.

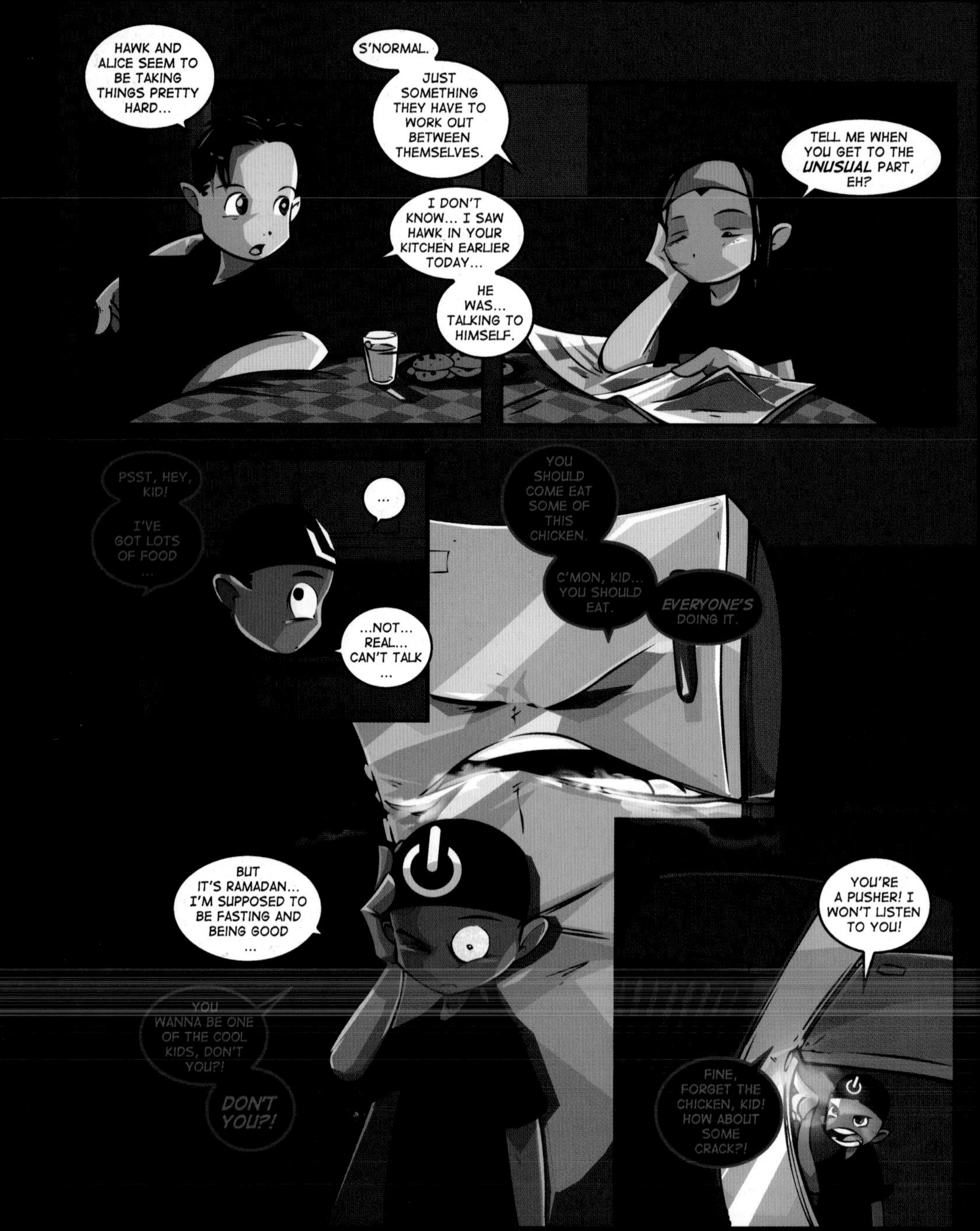
HAWK AND ALICE SEEM TO BE TAKING THINGS PRETTY HARD...
S'NORMAL.
JUST SOMETHING THEY HAVE TO WORK OUT BETWEEN THEMSELVES.
I DON'T KNOW... I SAW HAWK IN YOUR KITCHEN EARLIER TODAY...
HE WAS... TALKING TO HIMSELF.
TELL ME WHEN YOU GET TO THE *UNUSUAL* PART, EH?
PSST, HEY, KID!
I'VE GOT LOTS OF FOOD ...
...
YOU SHOULD COME EAT SOME OF THIS CHICKEN.
C'MON, KID... YOU SHOULD EAT.
EVERYONE'S DOING IT.
...NOT... REAL... CAN'T TALK ...
BUT IT'S RAMADAN... I'M SUPPOSED TO BE FASTING AND BEING GOOD ...
YOU WANNA BE ONE OF THE COOL KIDS, DON'T YOU?!
DON'T YOU?!
YOU'RE A PUSHER! I WON'T LISTEN TO YOU!
FINE, FORGET THE CHICKEN, KID! HOW ABOUT SOME CRACK?!

The end of our first major story arc lined up with the beginning of Ramadan, so the topic of the next comic was pretty clear. This was the second year we did Ramadan comics . . . Hawk always gets a little crazy when he can't eat, but we decided to up the ante with the talking refrigerator.

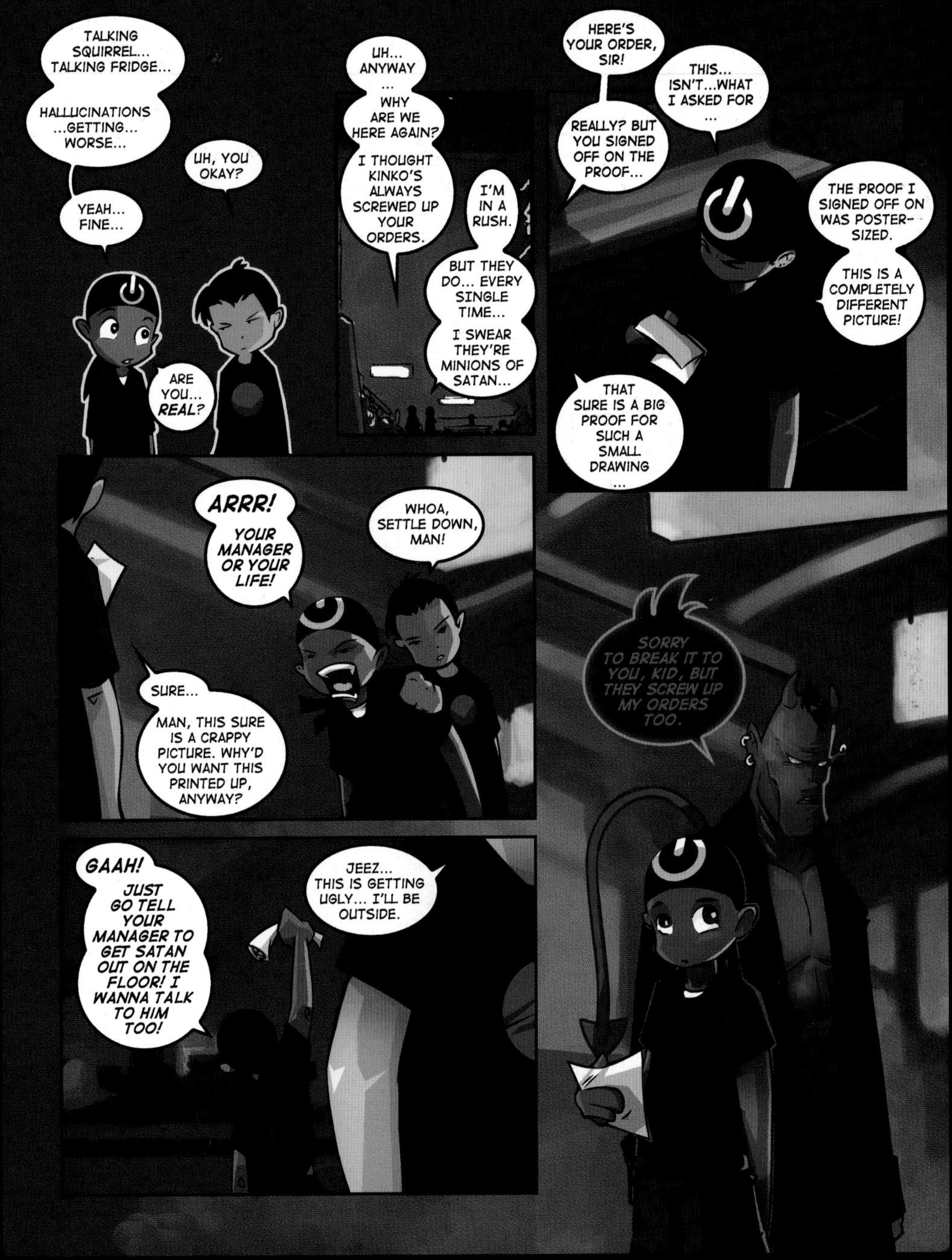
TALKING SQUIRREL... TALKING FRIDGE...
HALLUCINATIONS ...GETTING... WORSE...
UH, YOU OKAY?
YEAH... FINE...
ARE YOU... REAL?
UH... ANYWAY ... WHY ARE WE HERE AGAIN?
I THOUGHT KINKO'S ALWAYS SCREWED UP YOUR ORDERS.
I'M IN A RUSH.
BUT THEY DO... EVERY SINGLE TIME...
I SWEAR THEY'RE MINIONS OF SATAN...
HERE'S YOUR ORDER, SIR!
THIS... ISN'T...WHAT I ASKED FOR ...
REALLY? BUT YOU SIGNED OFF ON THE PROOF...
THE PROOF I SIGNED OFF ON WAS POSTER-SIZED.
THIS IS A COMPLETELY DIFFERENT PICTURE!
THAT SURE IS A BIG PROOF FOR SUCH A SMALL DRAWING ...
ARRR!
YOUR MANAGER OR YOUR LIFE!
WHOA, SETTLE DOWN, MAN!
SURE...
MAN, THIS SURE IS A CRAPPY PICTURE. WHY'D YOU WANT THIS PRINTED UP, ANYWAY?
GAAH!
JUST GO TELL YOUR MANAGER TO GET SATAN OUT ON THE FLOOR! I WANNA TALK TO HIM TOO!
JEEZ... THIS IS GETTING UGLY... I'LL BE OUTSIDE.
SORRY TO BREAK IT TO YOU, KID, BUT THEY SCREW UP MY ORDERS TOO.

I can't properly describe the rage that fills me when I think about going to Kinko's. I used Kinko's in college to print up my large-format projects, and it didn't matter whether I went to the one by campus or any other Kinko's in the area—they just, summarily, don't get their orders right. We got e-mails back from Kinko's employees saying they had a good laugh at the comic, and that some of them had printed it out and put it up in the office.

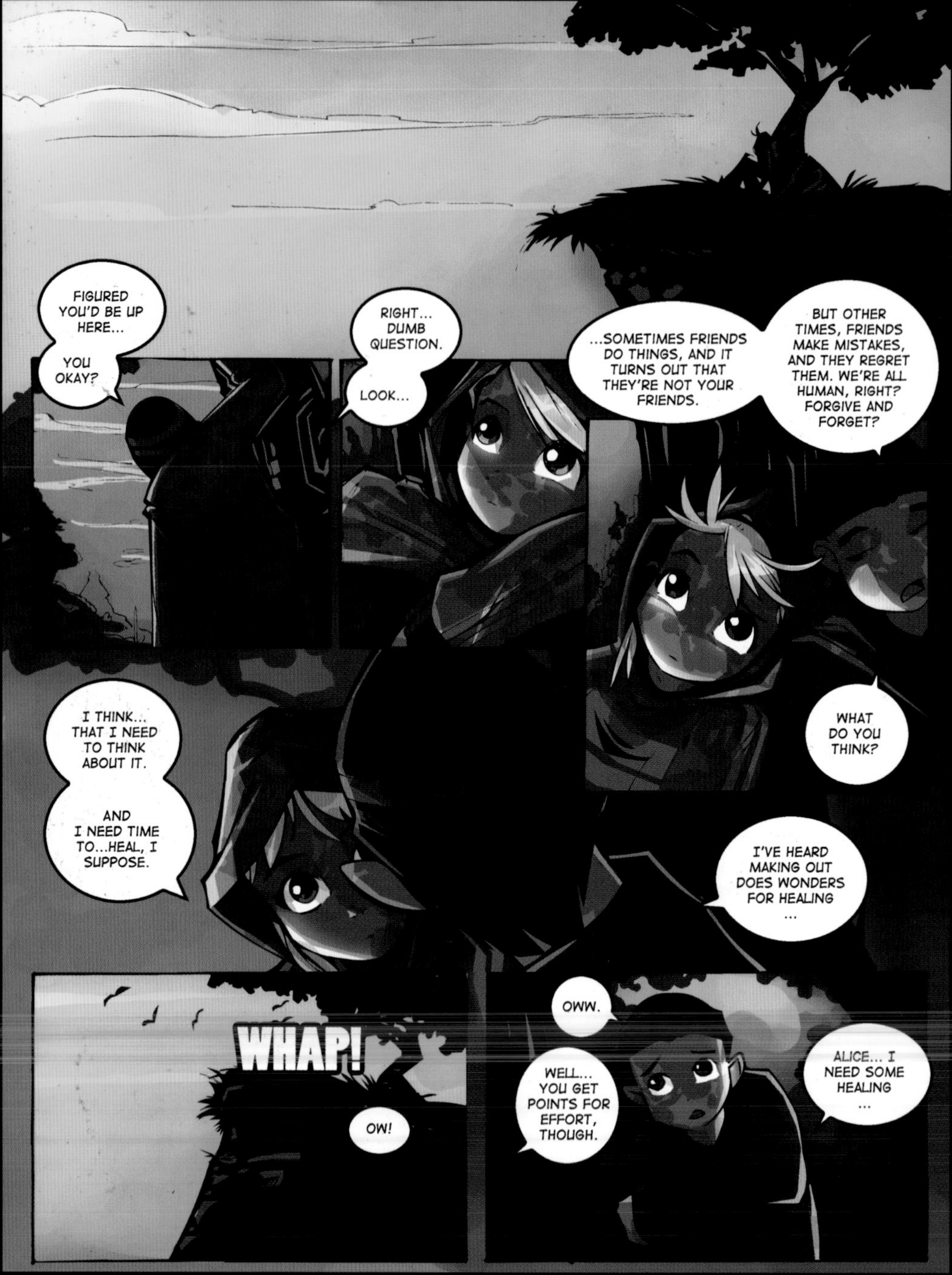

FIGURED YOU'D BE UP HERE...
YOU OKAY?
RIGHT... DUMB QUESTION.
LOOK...
...SOMETIMES FRIENDS DO THINGS, AND IT TURNS OUT THAT THEY'RE NOT YOUR FRIENDS.
BUT OTHER TIMES, FRIENDS MAKE MISTAKES, AND THEY REGRET THEM. WE'RE ALL HUMAN, RIGHT? FORGIVE AND FORGET?
WHAT DO YOU THINK?
I THINK... THAT I NEED TO THINK ABOUT IT.
AND I NEED TIME TO...HEAL, I SUPPOSE.
I'VE HEARD MAKING OUT DOES WONDERS FOR HEALING ...
WHAP!
OW!
OWW.
WELL... YOU GET POINTS FOR EFFORT, THOUGH.
ALICE... I NEED SOME HEALING ...

Jayce is just not that smooth. Actually, Jayce's line here reminds me of johnnywander.com artist Yuko's mock slogan for the new *Battlestar Galactica*: "SPACE MAKEOUTS FOR A BRIGHTER FUTURE!" Yeah, dude, everyone makes out on that show. It is pretty ridiculous. Everyone. No, *EVERYONE*.

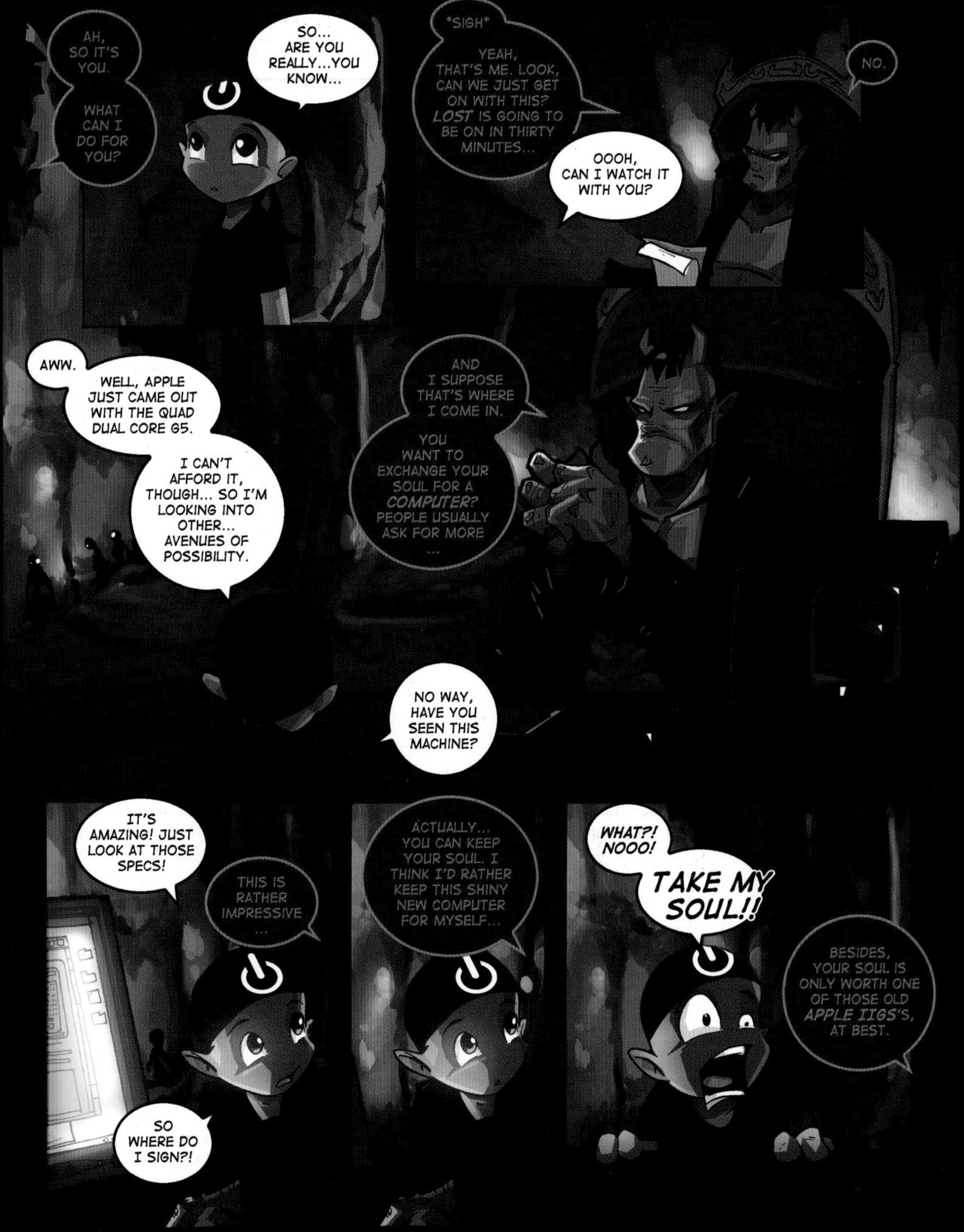

AH, SO IT'S YOU.
WHAT CAN I DO FOR YOU?
SO... ARE YOU REALLY...YOU KNOW...
SIGH
YEAH, THAT'S ME. LOOK, CAN WE JUST GET ON WITH THIS? *LOST* IS GOING TO BE ON IN THIRTY MINUTES...
OOOH, CAN I WATCH IT WITH YOU?
NO.
AWW.
WELL, APPLE JUST CAME OUT WITH THE QUAD DUAL CORE G5.
I CAN'T AFFORD IT, THOUGH... SO I'M LOOKING INTO OTHER... AVENUES OF POSSIBILITY.
AND I SUPPOSE THAT'S WHERE I COME IN.
YOU WANT TO EXCHANGE YOUR SOUL FOR A *COMPUTER?* PEOPLE USUALLY ASK FOR MORE ...
NO WAY, HAVE YOU SEEN THIS MACHINE?
IT'S AMAZING! JUST LOOK AT THOSE SPECS!
THIS IS RATHER IMPRESSIVE ...
SO WHERE DO I SIGN?!
ACTUALLY... YOU CAN KEEP YOUR SOUL. I THINK I'D RATHER KEEP THIS SHINY NEW COMPUTER FOR MYSELF...
WHAT?! NOOO!
TAKE MY SOUL!!
BESIDES, YOUR SOUL IS ONLY WORTH ONE OF THOSE OLD *APPLE IIGS*'S, AT BEST.

222 is a third of 666, which is sort of appropriate for this comic, because the Devil (who has made appearances a couple of times before) never really comes across as particularly evil. He just likes to mess with Hawk, which, really, isn't any different from what Jayce likes to do. Hmmm . . . CONNECTION?? (Hint: There is no connection.)

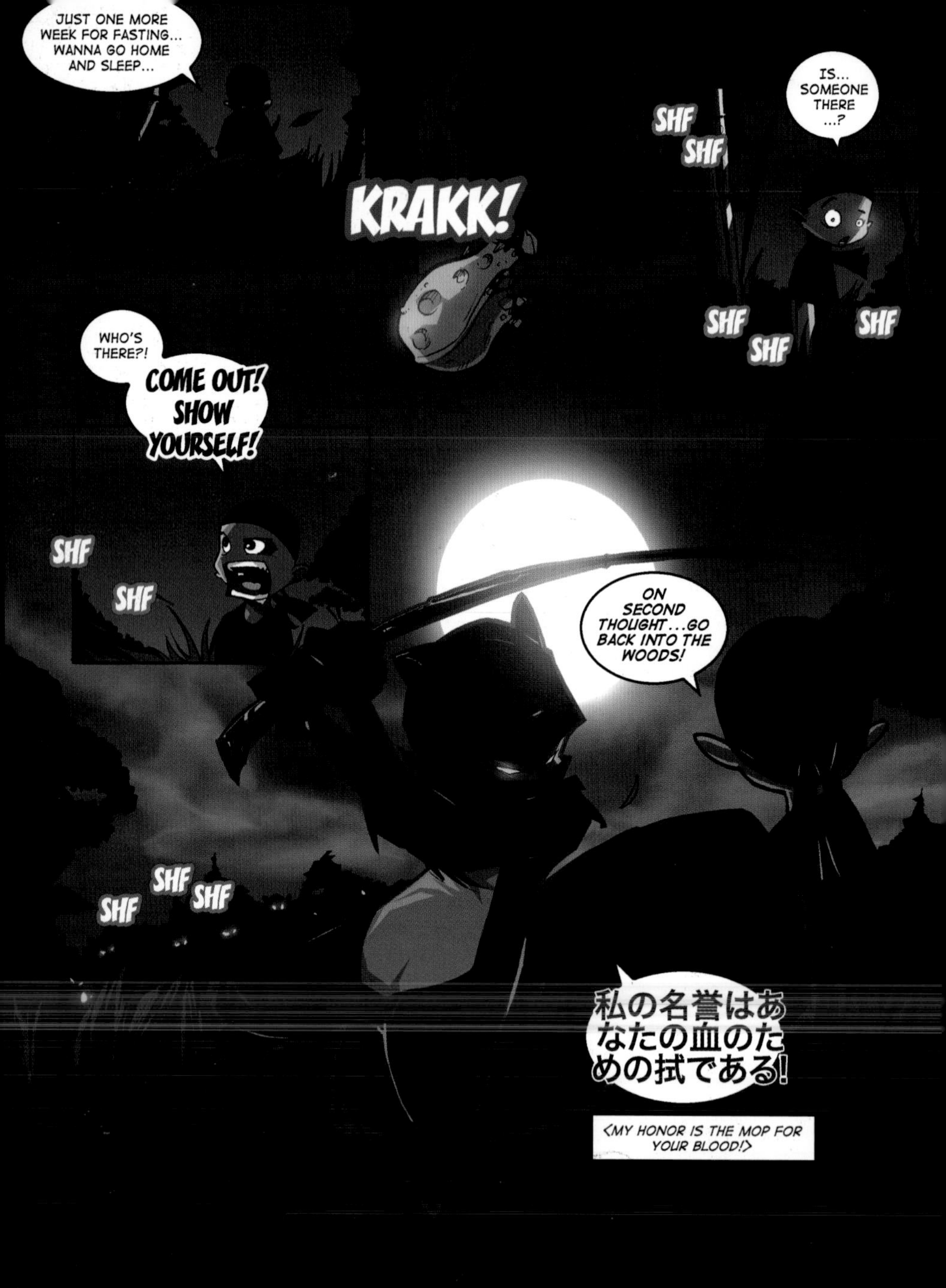
JUST ONE MORE WEEK FOR FASTING... WANNA GO HOME AND SLEEP...
SHF
SHF
IS... SOMEONE THERE ...?
KRAKK!
SHF
SHF
SHF
WHO'S THERE?!
COME OUT! SHOW YOURSELF!
SHF
SHF
ON SECOND THOUGHT...GO BACK INTO THE WOODS!
SHF
SHF
SHF
私の名誉はあなたの血のための拭である!
<MY HONOR IS THE MOP FOR YOUR BLOOD!>

And so Ramadan continues. Actually, this spawned one of our T-shirts, coyly dubbed "Silent Nut Attack." It features the squirrel from the bottom panel leaping off of an asphalt-gray shirt. I think there's also a mug . . . We have two mugs up for sale on megagear.com, but did you know that Hawk and I have never seen them in person? Sometimes

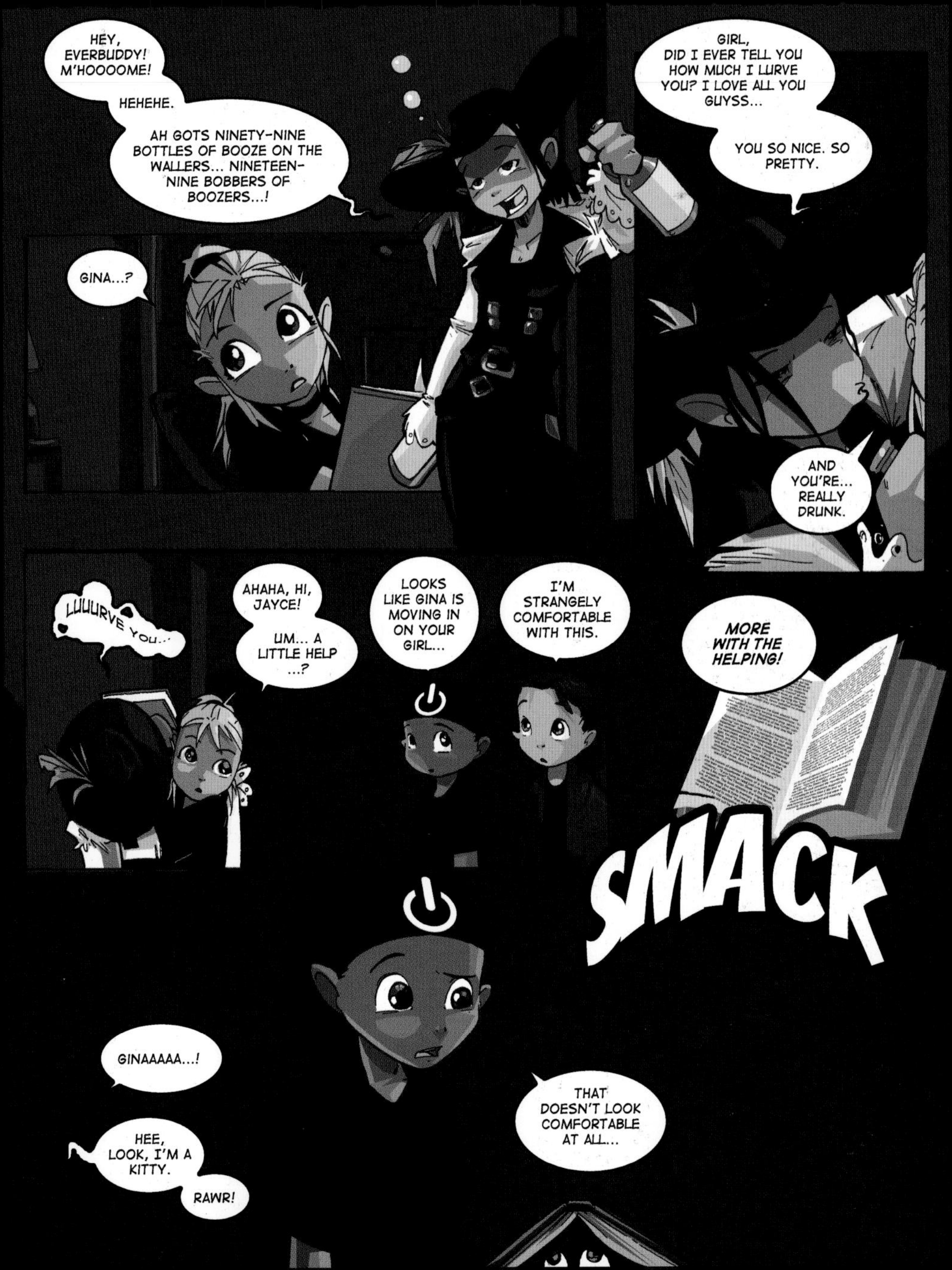
HEY, EVERBUDDY! M'HOOOOME!
HEHEHE.
AH GOTS NINETY-NINE BOTTLES OF BOOZE ON THE WALLERS... NINETEEN-NINE BOBBERS OF BOOZERS...!
GIRL, DID I EVER TELL YOU HOW MUCH I LURVE YOU? I LOVE ALL YOU GUYSS...
YOU SO NICE. SO PRETTY.
GINA...?
AND YOU'RE... REALLY DRUNK.
LUUURVE YOU...
AHAHA, HI, JAYCE!
UM... A LITTLE HELP ...?
LOOKS LIKE GINA IS MOVING IN ON YOUR GIRL...
I'M STRANGELY COMFORTABLE WITH THIS.
MORE WITH THE HELPING!
SMACK
GINAAAAA...!
HEE, LOOK, I'M A KITTY.
RAWR!
THAT DOESN'T LOOK COMFORTABLE AT ALL...

Sometimes you just want to do a comic about the drunk friend. But listen, Gina's not an alcoholic or anything. She's drunk because it makes her *costume* more authentic. She's drinking rum. Pirates drink rum, right? Answer: Pirates drink anything.

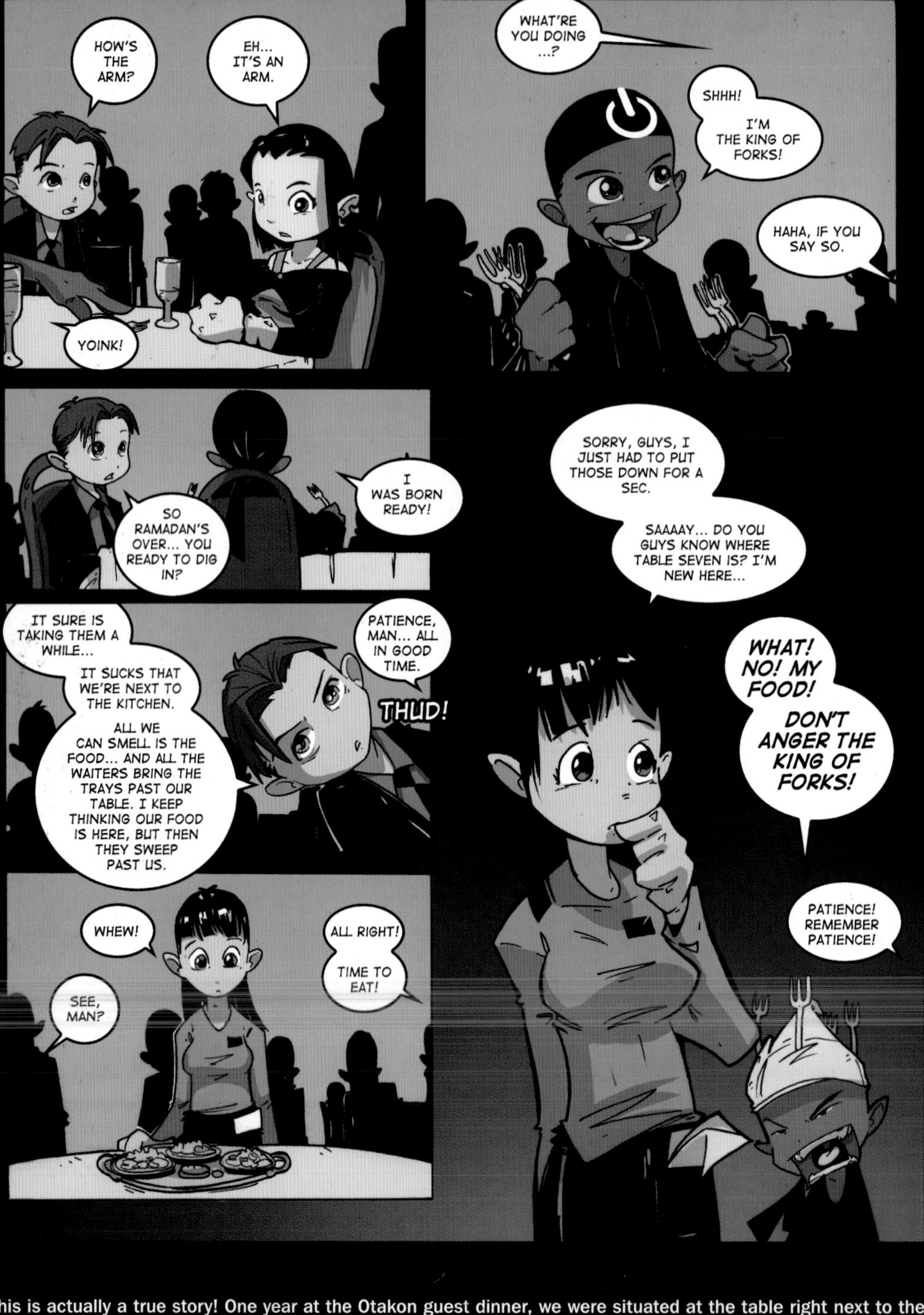
HOW'S THE ARM?
EH... IT'S AN ARM.
YOINK!
WHAT'RE YOU DOING ...?
SHHH!
I'M THE KING OF FORKS!
HAHA, IF YOU SAY SO.
SO RAMADAN'S OVER... YOU READY TO DIG IN?
I WAS BORN READY!
IT SURE IS TAKING THEM A WHILE...
IT SUCKS THAT WE'RE NEXT TO THE KITCHEN.
ALL WE CAN SMELL IS THE FOOD... AND ALL THE WAITERS BRING THE TRAYS PAST OUR TABLE. I KEEP THINKING OUR FOOD IS HERE, BUT THEN THEY SWEEP PAST US.
PATIENCE, MAN... ALL IN GOOD TIME.
THUD!
WHEW!
SEE, MAN?
ALL RIGHT!
TIME TO EAT!
SORRY, GUYS, I JUST HAD TO PUT THOSE DOWN FOR A SEC.
SAAAAY... DO YOU GUYS KNOW WHERE TABLE SEVEN IS? I'M NEW HERE...
WHAT! NO! MY FOOD!
DON'T ANGER THE KING OF FORKS!
PATIENCE! REMEMBER PATIENCE!

This is actually a true story! One year at the Otakon guest dinner, we were situated at the table right next to the kitchen. Every time a waiter or waitress came out, they'd look at our table, and then walk past to some far corner of the restaurant. It's not quite clear how it happened, but Hawk slowly accumulated all of the forks on the table and started muttering crazy shit to himself.

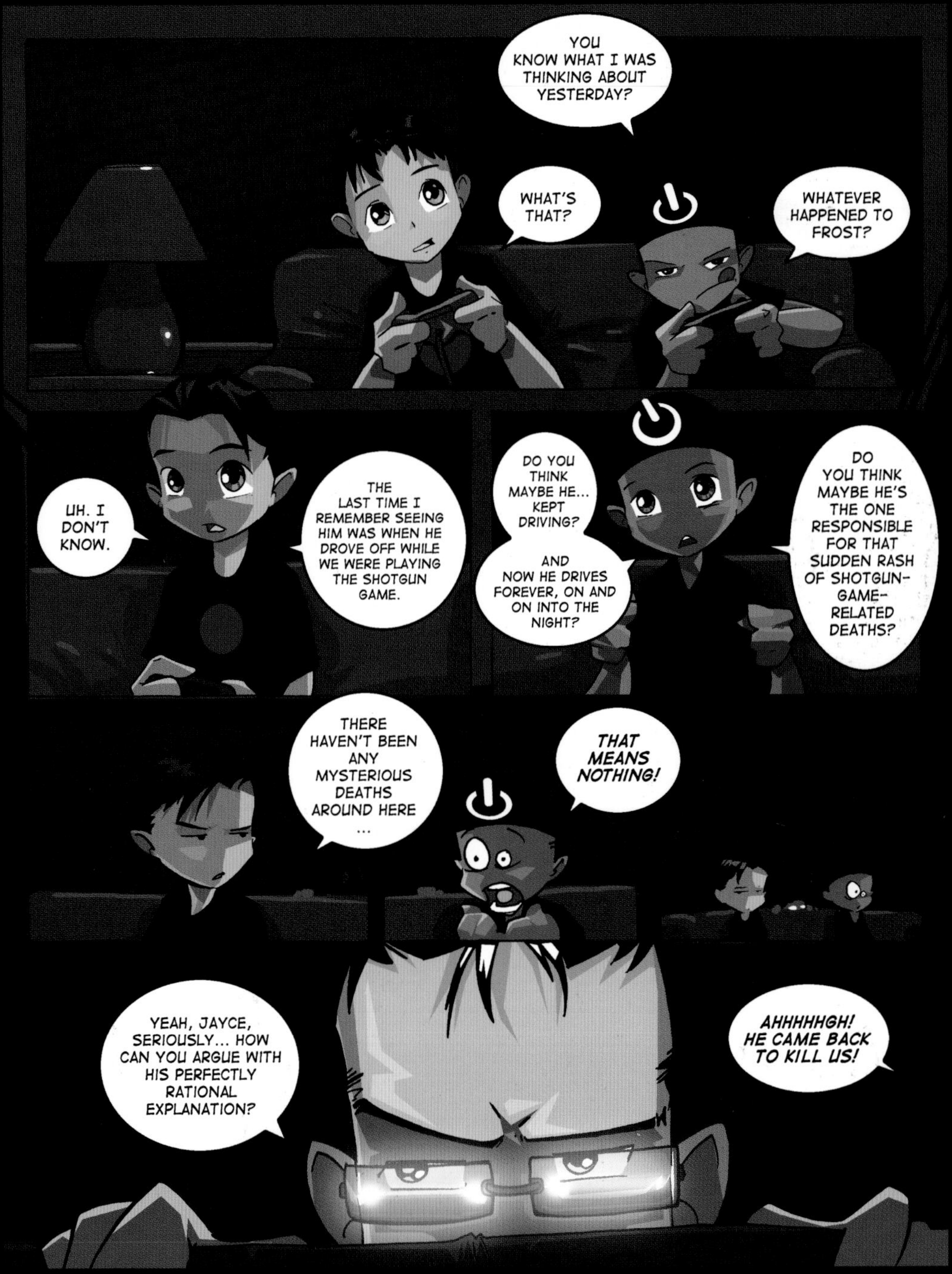
YOU KNOW WHAT I WAS THINKING ABOUT YESTERDAY?
WHAT'S THAT?
WHATEVER HAPPENED TO FROST?
UH. I DON'T KNOW.
THE LAST TIME I REMEMBER SEEING HIM WAS WHEN HE DROVE OFF WHILE WE WERE PLAYING THE SHOTGUN GAME.
DO YOU THINK MAYBE HE... KEPT DRIVING?
AND NOW HE DRIVES FOREVER, ON AND ON INTO THE NIGHT?
DO YOU THINK MAYBE HE'S THE ONE RESPONSIBLE FOR THAT SUDDEN RASH OF SHOTGUN-GAME-RELATED DEATHS?
THERE HAVEN'T BEEN ANY MYSTERIOUS DEATHS AROUND HERE ...
THAT MEANS NOTHING!
YEAH, JAYCE, SERIOUSLY... HOW CAN YOU ARGUE WITH HIS PERFECTLY RATIONAL EXPLANATION?
AHHHHHGH! HE CAME BACK TO KILL US!

Well, well, well, look who it is! We intermittently got e-mails asking us where Frost went off to, but I wanted to hold off on bringing him back until there was a good punch line involved. The opportunity finally presented itself here. Poor Hawk has an overactive imagination, but I guess that's where all them thar inventin' smarts comes from.

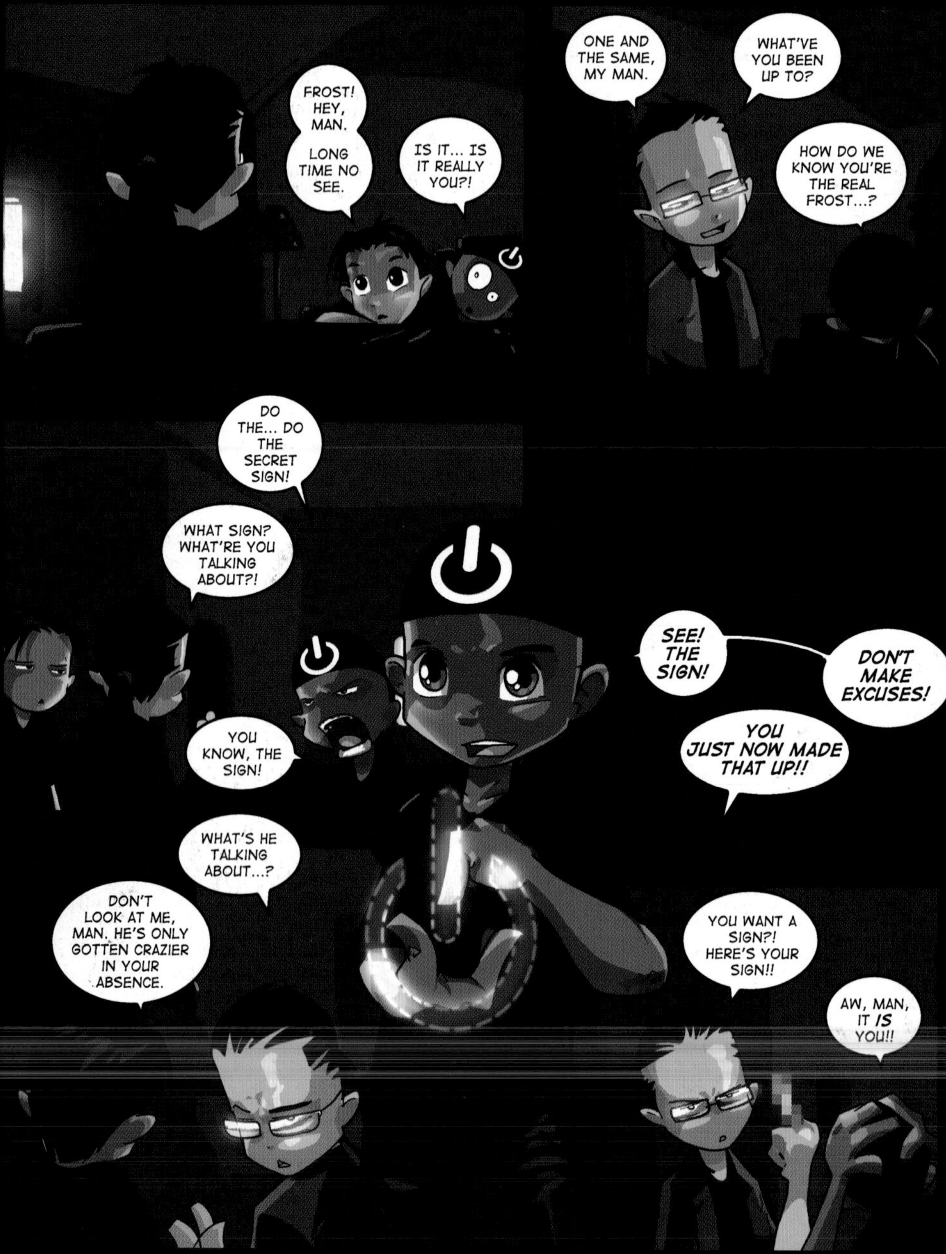
FROST! HEY, MAN.
LONG TIME NO SEE.
IS IT... IS IT REALLY YOU?!
ONE AND THE SAME, MY MAN.
WHAT'VE YOU BEEN UP TO?
HOW DO WE KNOW YOU'RE THE REAL FROST...?
DO THE... DO THE SECRET SIGN!
WHAT SIGN? WHAT'RE YOU TALKING ABOUT?!
YOU KNOW, THE SIGN!
SEE! THE SIGN!
DON'T MAKE EXCUSES!
YOU JUST NOW MADE THAT UP!!
WHAT'S HE TALKING ABOUT...?
DON'T LOOK AT ME, MAN. HE'S ONLY GOTTEN CRAZIER IN YOUR ABSENCE.
YOU WANT A SIGN?! HERE'S YOUR SIGN!!
AW, MAN, IT *IS* YOU!!

I'm not big on using the middle finger, but if there's a way to make it work in the larger context of a joke, I'm happy to do so. If I had to verify my friend's identity and he flipped me off, I'd be convinced. Also, nerdiest gang sign ever?

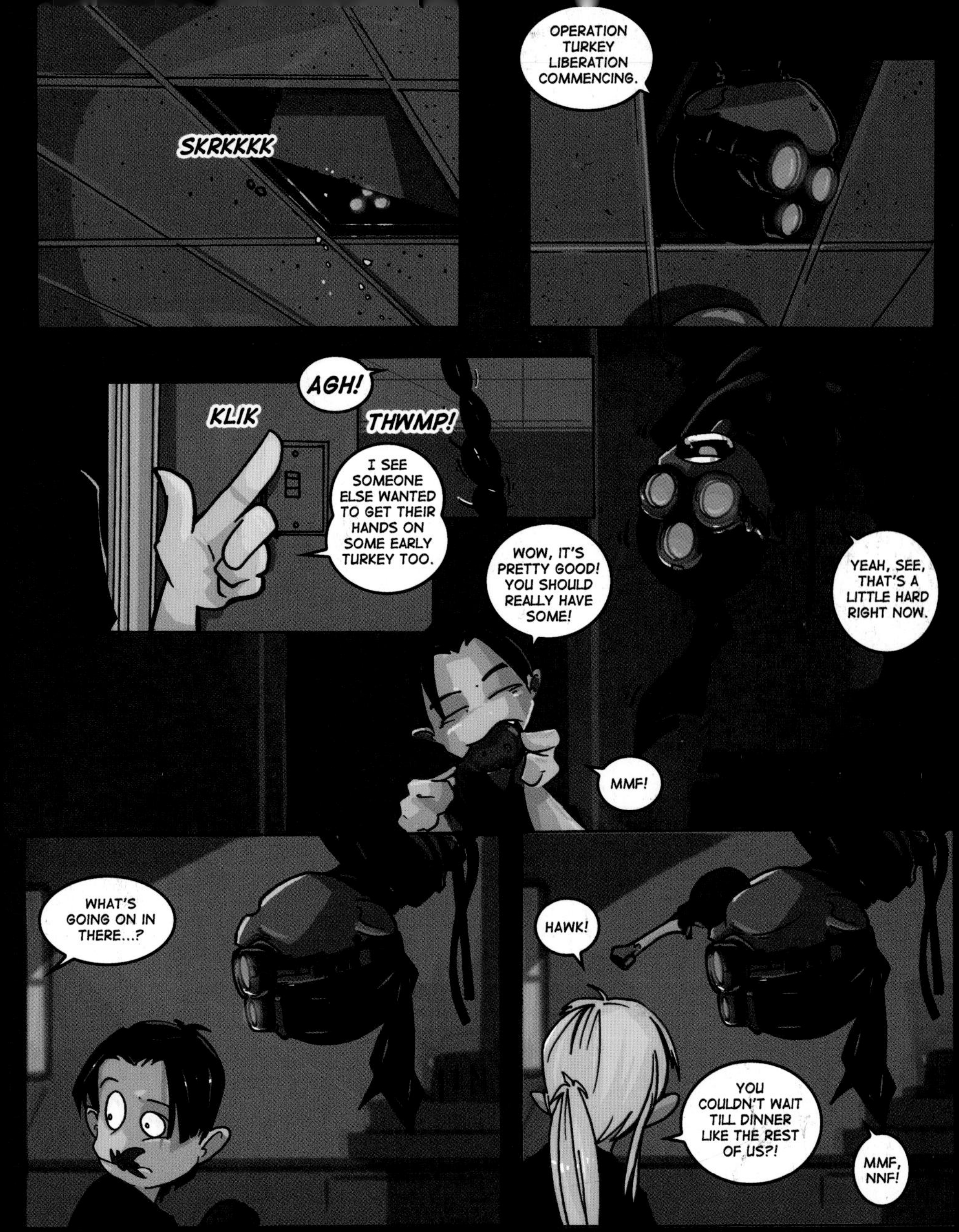
SKRKKKK
OPERATION TURKEY LIBERATION COMMENCING.
KLIK
AGH!
THWMP!
I SEE SOMEONE ELSE WANTED TO GET THEIR HANDS ON SOME EARLY TURKEY TOO.
WOW, IT'S PRETTY GOOD! YOU SHOULD REALLY HAVE SOME!
YEAH, SEE, THAT'S A LITTLE HARD RIGHT NOW.
MMF!
WHAT'S GOING ON IN THERE...?
HAWK!
YOU COULDN'T WAIT TILL DINNER LIKE THE REST OF US?!
MMF, NNF!

If you saw the goggles and thought *Splinter Cell*, good job! Occasionally the high-tech approach is a little too much . . . Sometimes it is the prerogative of the geek to overthink what ought to be a fairly simple solution. Hawk would probably be good at building Rube Goldberg machines.

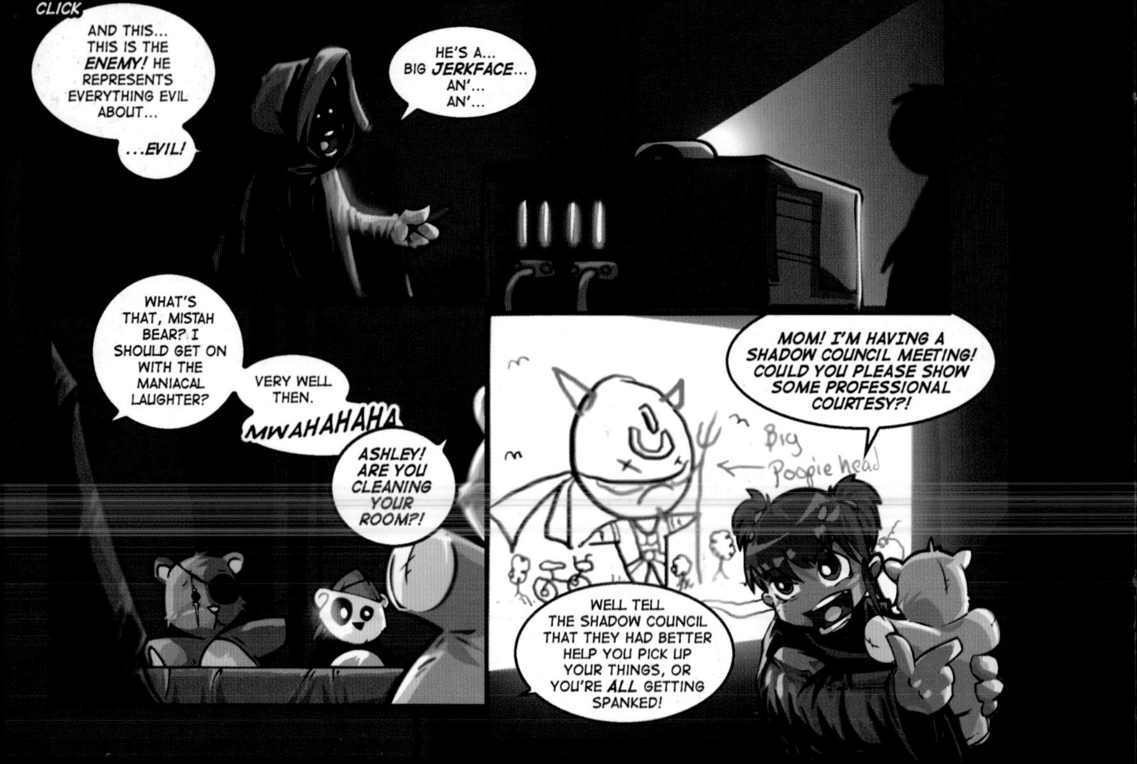
CLICK
AND THIS... THIS IS THE ENEMY! HE REPRESENTS EVERYTHING EVIL ABOUT...
...EVIL!
HE'S A... BIG JERKFACE... AN'... AN'...
WHAT'S THAT, MISTAH BEAR? I SHOULD GET ON WITH THE MANIACAL LAUGHTER?
VERY WELL THEN.
MWAHAHAHAHA
ASHLEY! ARE YOU CLEANING YOUR ROOM?!
Big Poopie head
MOM! I'M HAVING A SHADOW COUNCIL MEETING! COULD YOU PLEASE SHOW SOME PROFESSIONAL COURTESY?!
WELL TELL THE SHADOW COUNCIL THAT THEY HAD BETTER HELP YOU PICK UP YOUR THINGS, OR YOU'RE ALL GETTING SPANKED!

Hold on, I've always wanted to do this: She's *baaaaaack*. Ashley is one of our most beloved, if maniacal, characters. She and Mister Bear have quite a few things in store for our intrepid semiheroes! We've long talked about doing an *Applegeeks Lite*–style comic strip about Ashley and Mister Bear . . .

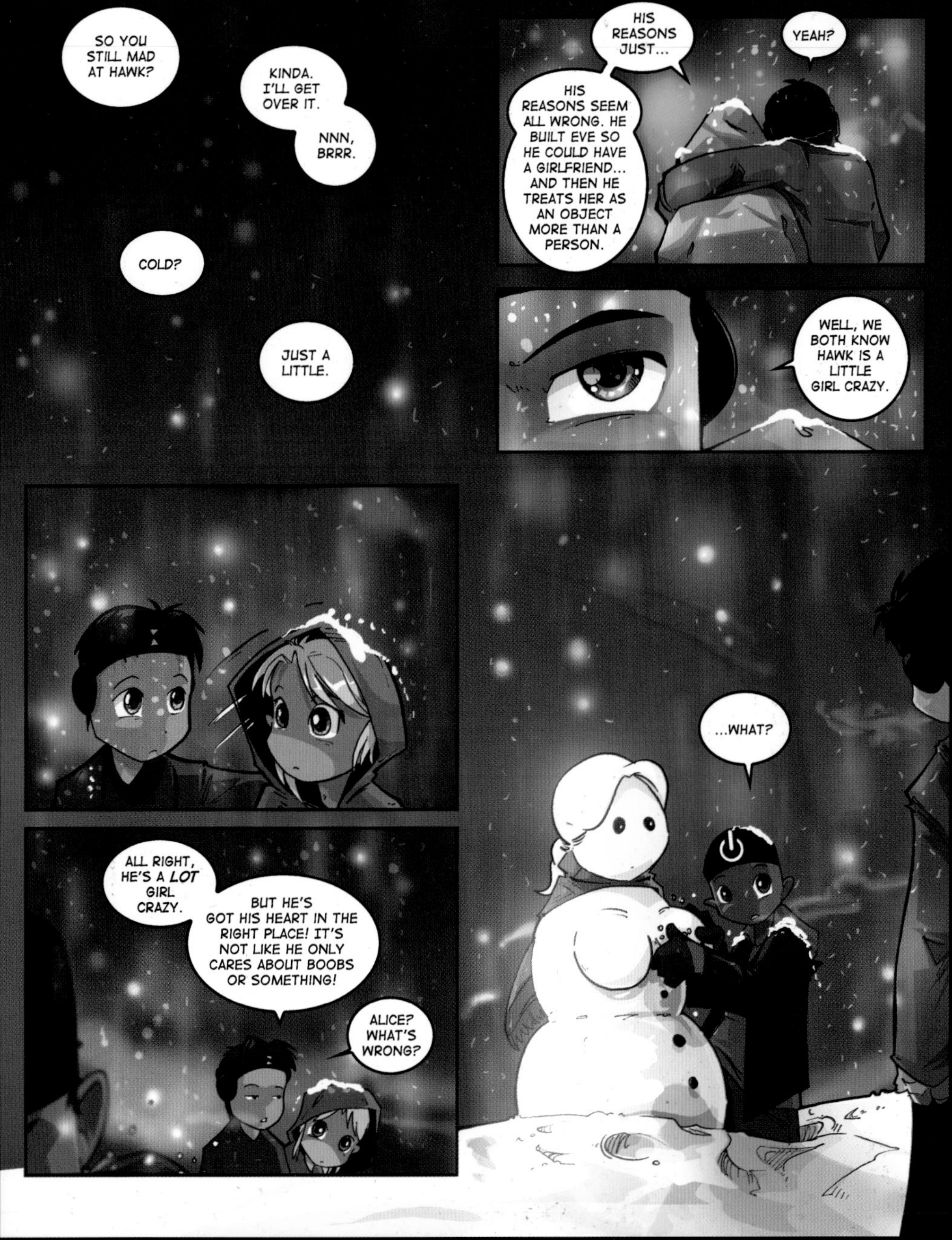
SO YOU STILL MAD AT HAWK?
KINDA. I'LL GET OVER IT.
NNN, BRRR.
COLD?
JUST A LITTLE.
HIS REASONS JUST...
YEAH?
HIS REASONS SEEM ALL WRONG. HE BUILT EVE SO HE COULD HAVE A GIRLFRIEND... AND THEN HE TREATS HER AS AN OBJECT MORE THAN A PERSON.
WELL, WE BOTH KNOW HAWK IS A LITTLE GIRL CRAZY.
ALL RIGHT, HE'S A *LOT* GIRL CRAZY.
BUT HE'S GOT HIS HEART IN THE RIGHT PLACE! IT'S NOT LIKE HE ONLY CARES ABOUT BOOBS OR SOMETHING!
ALICE? WHAT'S WRONG?
...WHAT?

Oh . . . Oh, Hawk. You've got problems.

The last panel got turned into a postcard for the Webcomic Holiday Postcard Fundraiser. It was part of a set, with all proceeds going to Penny Arcade's Child's Play charity.

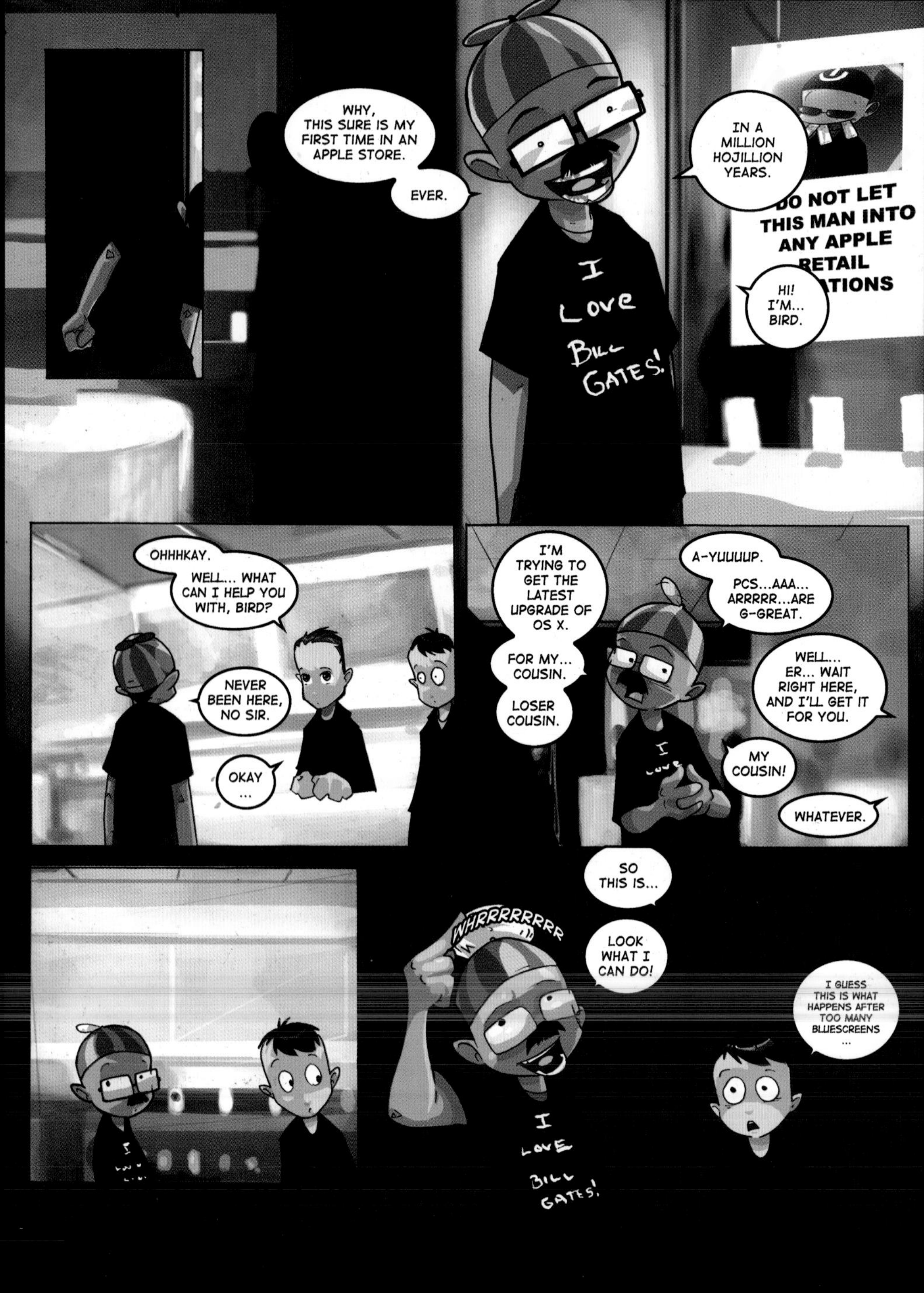
WHY, THIS SURE IS MY FIRST TIME IN AN APPLE STORE.
EVER.
I LOVE BILL GATES!
IN A MILLION HOJILLION YEARS.
DO NOT LET THIS MAN INTO ANY APPLE
HI! I'M... BIRD.
OHHHKAY.
WELL... WHAT CAN I HELP YOU WITH, BIRD?
NEVER BEEN HERE, NO SIR.
OKAY ...
I'M TRYING TO GET THE LATEST UPGRADE OF OS X.
FOR MY... COUSIN.
LOSER COUSIN.
A-YUUUUP.
PCS...AAA... ARRRRR...ARE G-GREAT.
WELL... ER... WAIT RIGHT HERE, AND I'LL GET IT FOR YOU.
MY COUSIN!
WHATEVER.
SO THIS IS...
WHRRRRRRRR
LOOK WHAT I CAN DO!
I LOVE BILL GATES!
I GUESS THIS IS WHAT HAPPENS AFTER TOO MANY BLUESCREENS ...

I actually think this is a good look for Hawk.

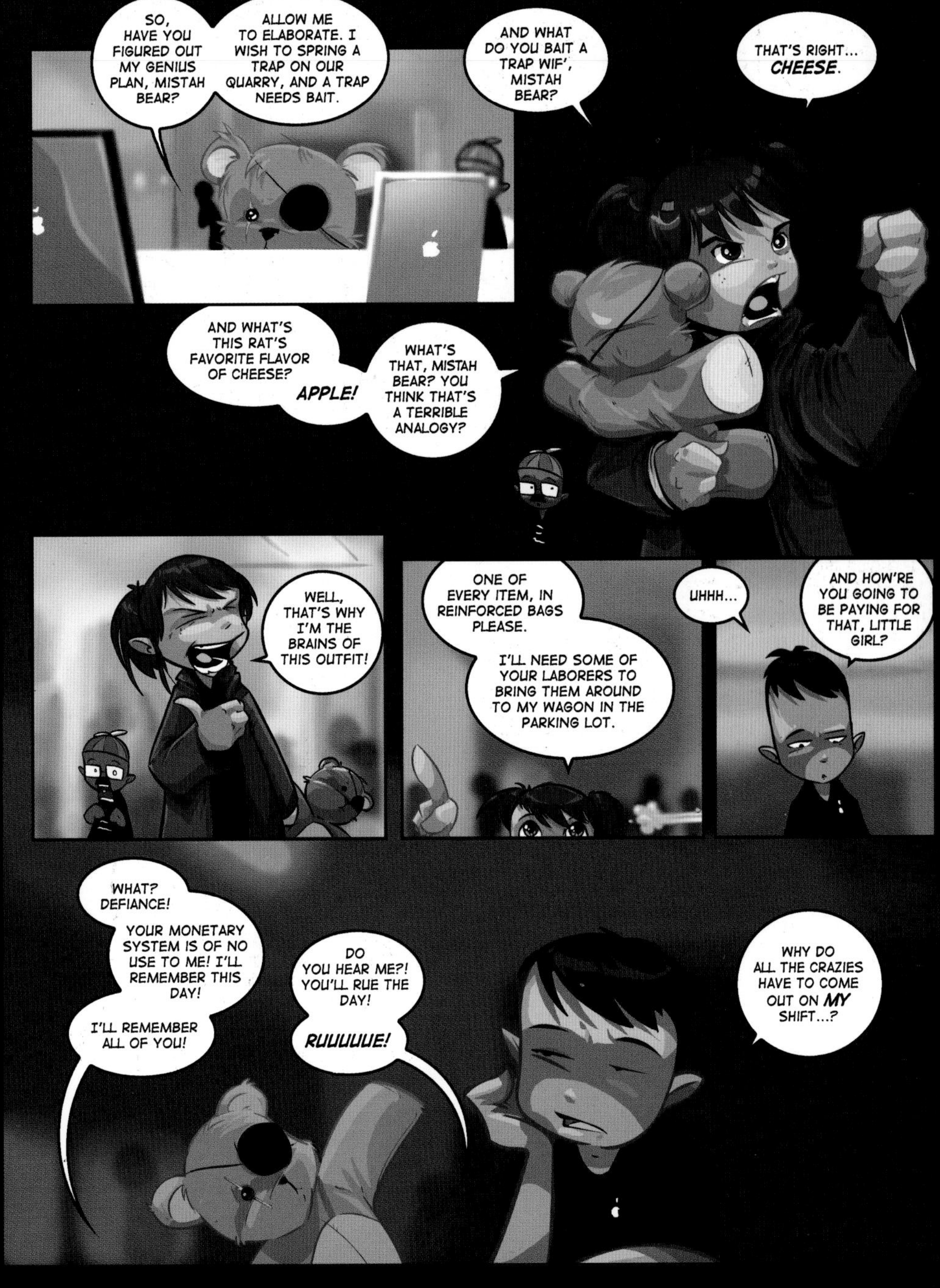
SO, HAVE YOU FIGURED OUT MY GENIUS PLAN, MISTAH BEAR?
ALLOW ME TO ELABORATE. I WISH TO SPRING A TRAP ON OUR QUARRY, AND A TRAP NEEDS BAIT.
AND WHAT DO YOU BAIT A TRAP WIF', MISTAH BEAR?
THAT'S RIGHT... CHEESE.
AND WHAT'S THIS RAT'S FAVORITE FLAVOR OF CHEESE?
APPLE!
WHAT'S THAT, MISTAH BEAR? YOU THINK THAT'S A TERRIBLE ANALOGY?
WELL, THAT'S WHY I'M THE BRAINS OF THIS OUTFIT!
ONE OF EVERY ITEM, IN REINFORCED BAGS PLEASE.
I'LL NEED SOME OF YOUR LABORERS TO BRING THEM AROUND TO MY WAGON IN THE PARKING LOT.
UHHH...
AND HOW'RE YOU GOING TO BE PAYING FOR THAT, LITTLE GIRL?
WHAT? DEFIANCE!
YOUR MONETARY SYSTEM IS OF NO USE TO ME! I'LL REMEMBER THIS DAY!
I'LL REMEMBER ALL OF YOU!
DO YOU HEAR ME?! YOU'LL RUE THE DAY!
RUUUUUE!
WHY DO ALL THE CRAZIES HAVE TO COME OUT ON MY SHIFT...?

She might be loonier than him. I don't know. It's too late for Hawk, but she still has time to straighten out! Although she could go either way. You just never know. Hm . . . Who am I kidding, she's already a regular tyrant. Someone open up an FBI file on this kid! Yeah, I'll testify, but I want protection!

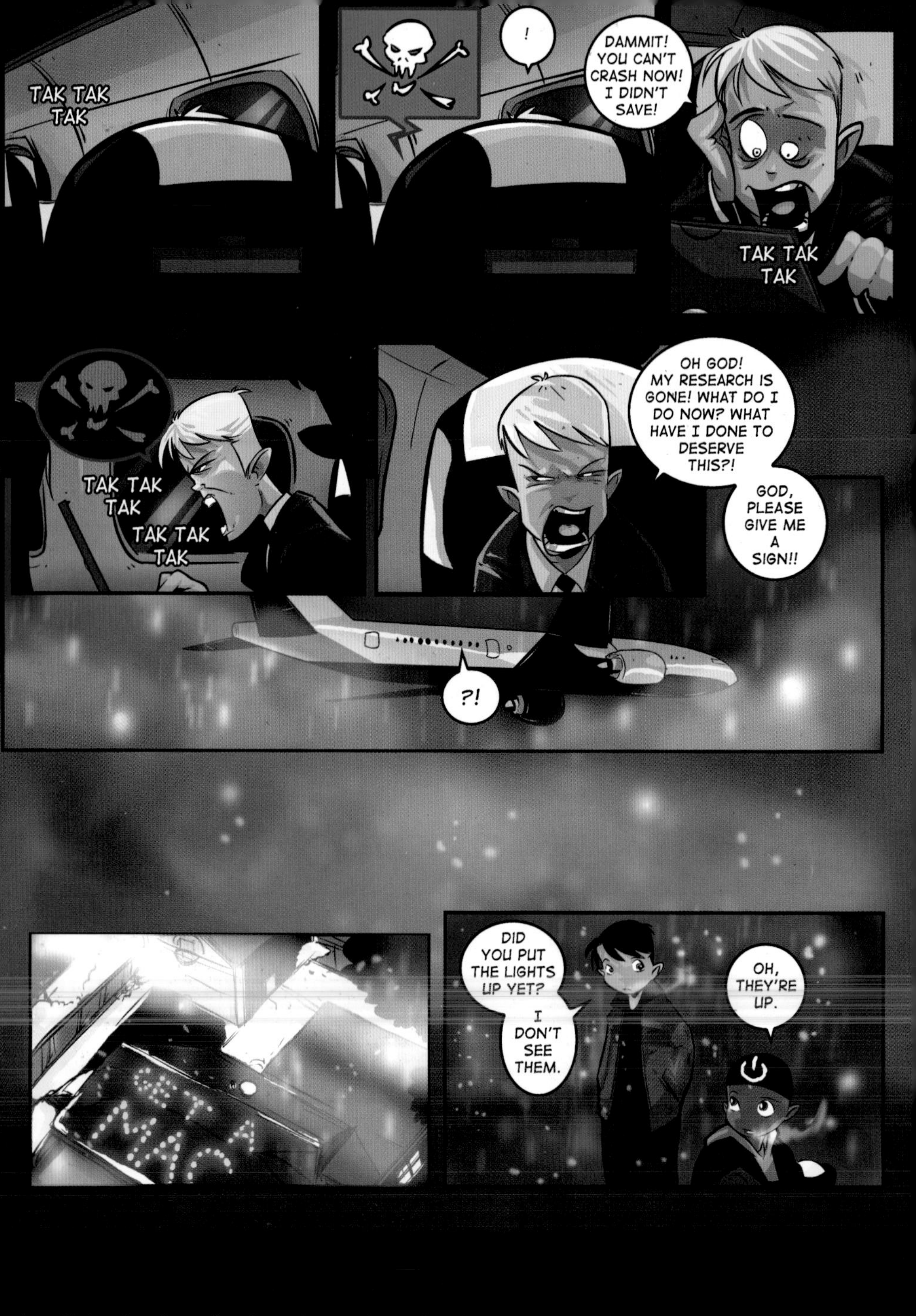

TAK TAK TAK
!
DAMMIT! YOU CAN'T CRASH NOW! I DIDN'T SAVE!
TAK TAK TAK
TAK TAK TAK
TAK TAK TAK
OH GOD! MY RESEARCH IS GONE! WHAT DO I DO NOW? WHAT HAVE I DONE TO DESERVE THIS?!
GOD, PLEASE GIVE ME A SIGN!!
?!
GET A MAC
DID YOU PUT THE LIGHTS UP YET?
I DON'T SEE THEM.
OH, THEY'RE UP.

awk and I do a lot of traveling these days, and one thing I never get tired of is the view from a plane as you fly i

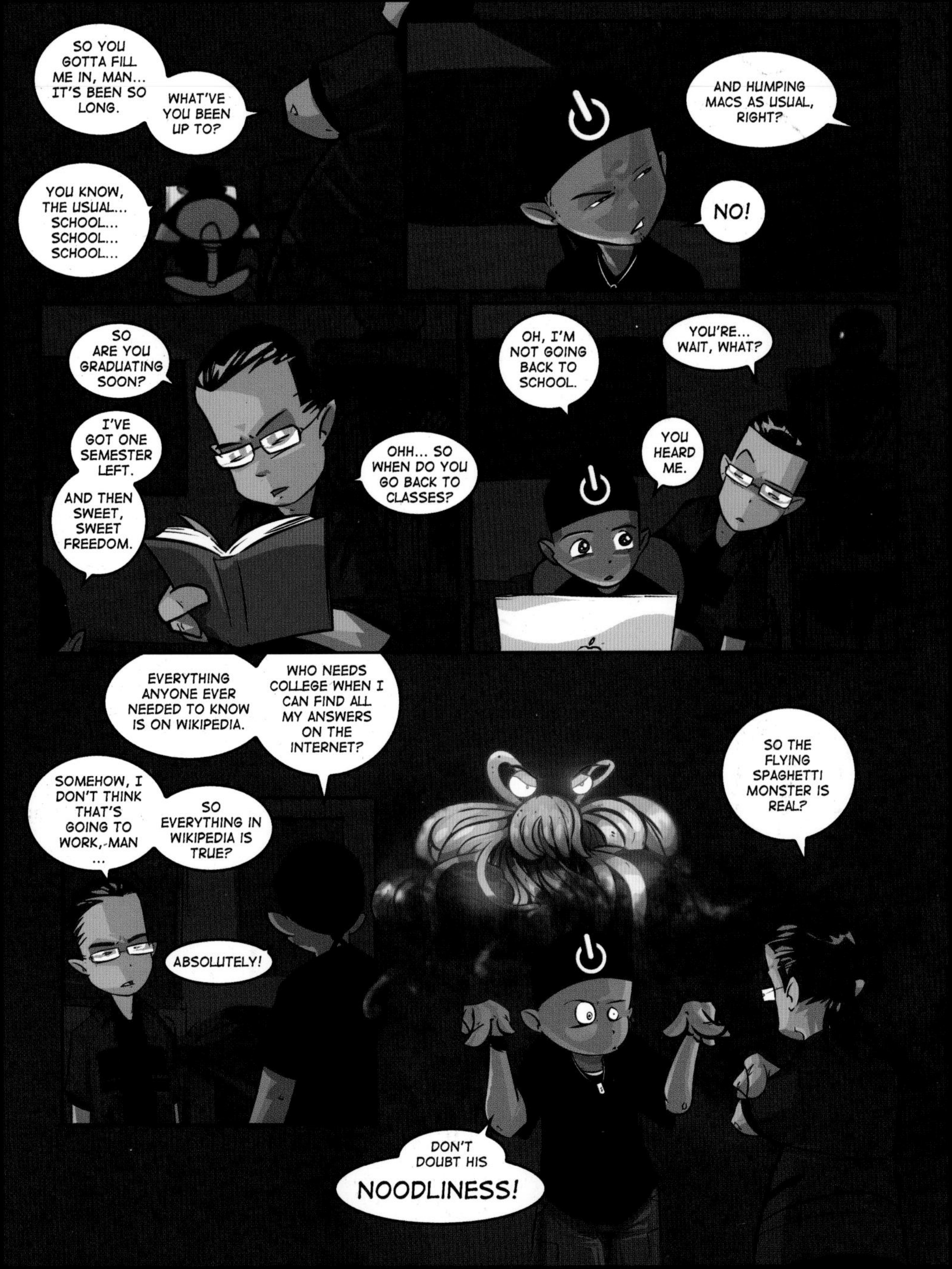
SO YOU GOTTA FILL ME IN, MAN... IT'S BEEN SO LONG.
WHAT'VE YOU BEEN UP TO?
YOU KNOW, THE USUAL... SCHOOL... SCHOOL... SCHOOL...
AND HUMPING MACS AS USUAL, RIGHT?
NO!
SO ARE YOU GRADUATING SOON?
I'VE GOT ONE SEMESTER LEFT.
AND THEN SWEET, SWEET FREEDOM.
OHH... SO WHEN DO YOU GO BACK TO CLASSES?
OH, I'M NOT GOING BACK TO SCHOOL.
YOU'RE... WAIT, WHAT?
YOU HEARD ME.
EVERYTHING ANYONE EVER NEEDED TO KNOW IS ON WIKIPEDIA.
WHO NEEDS COLLEGE WHEN I CAN FIND ALL MY ANSWERS ON THE INTERNET?
SOMEHOW, I DON'T THINK THAT'S GOING TO WORK, MAN ...
SO EVERYTHING IN WIKIPEDIA IS TRUE?
ABSOLUTELY!
SO THE FLYING SPAGHETTI MONSTER IS REAL?
DON'T DOUBT HIS NOODLINESS!

I'm going to level with you guys . . . I saw some "fan art" of the Flying Spaghetti Monster doing some unspeakable things, and ever since then I just haven't been able to look at it straight. The Flying Spaghetti Monster craze was at its peak a few years ago; I went to a costume party one Halloween and a girl had intricately woven foam pool noodles into a pretty accurate rendition. Cool costume, but sadly there was some trouble getting her noodliness through the door.

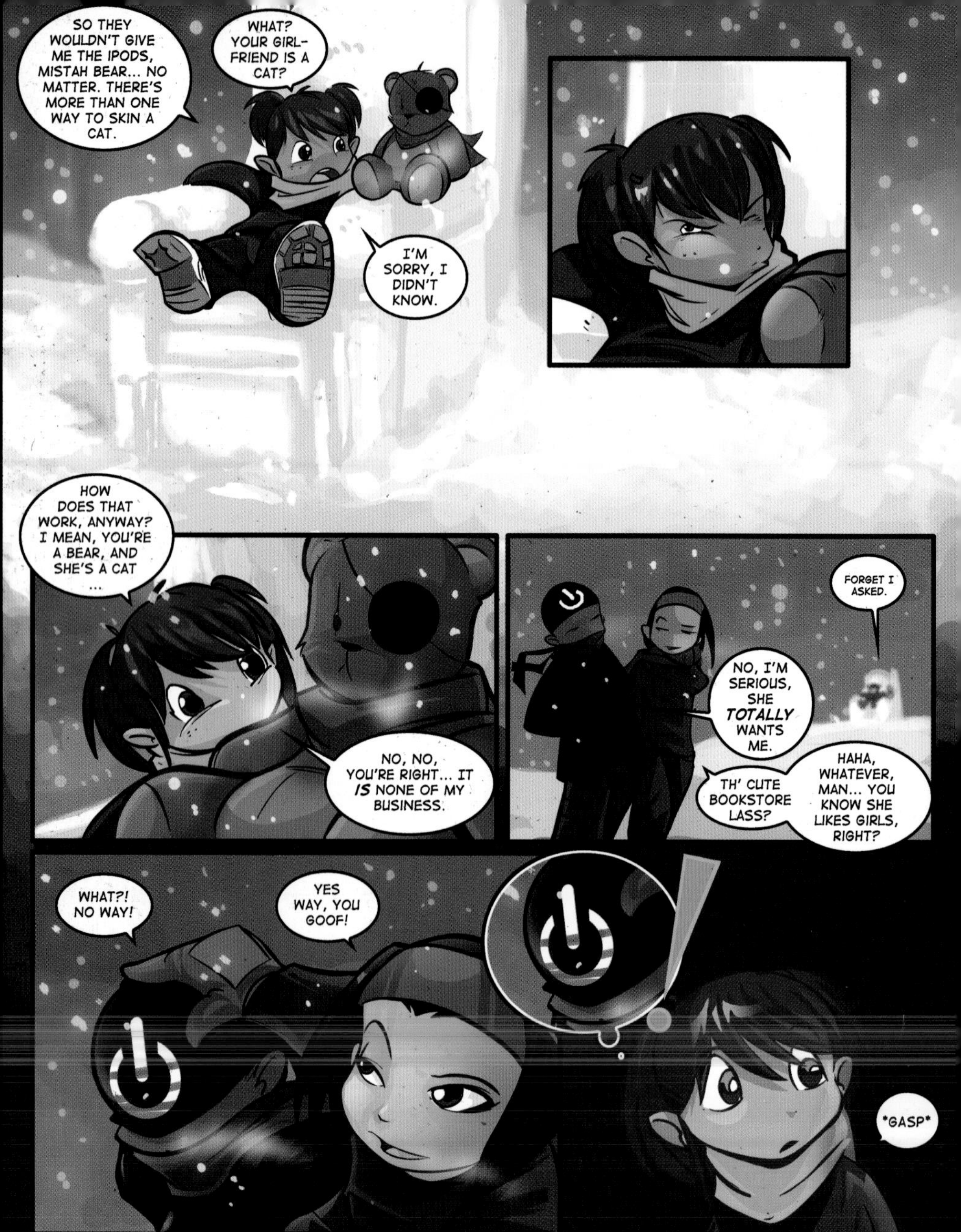
SO THEY WOULDN'T GIVE ME THE IPODS, MISTAH BEAR... NO MATTER. THERE'S MORE THAN ONE WAY TO SKIN A CAT.
WHAT? YOUR GIRL-FRIEND IS A CAT?
I'M SORRY, I DIDN'T KNOW.
HOW DOES THAT WORK, ANYWAY? I MEAN, YOU'RE A BEAR, AND SHE'S A CAT ...
NO, NO, YOU'RE RIGHT... IT *IS* NONE OF MY BUSINESS.
FORGET I ASKED.
NO, I'M SERIOUS, SHE *TOTALLY* WANTS ME.
TH' CUTE BOOKSTORE LASS?
HAHA, WHATEVER, MAN... YOU KNOW SHE LIKES GIRLS, RIGHT?
WHAT?! NO WAY!
YES WAY, YOU GOOF!
GASP

A discovery is made. The game is afoot.

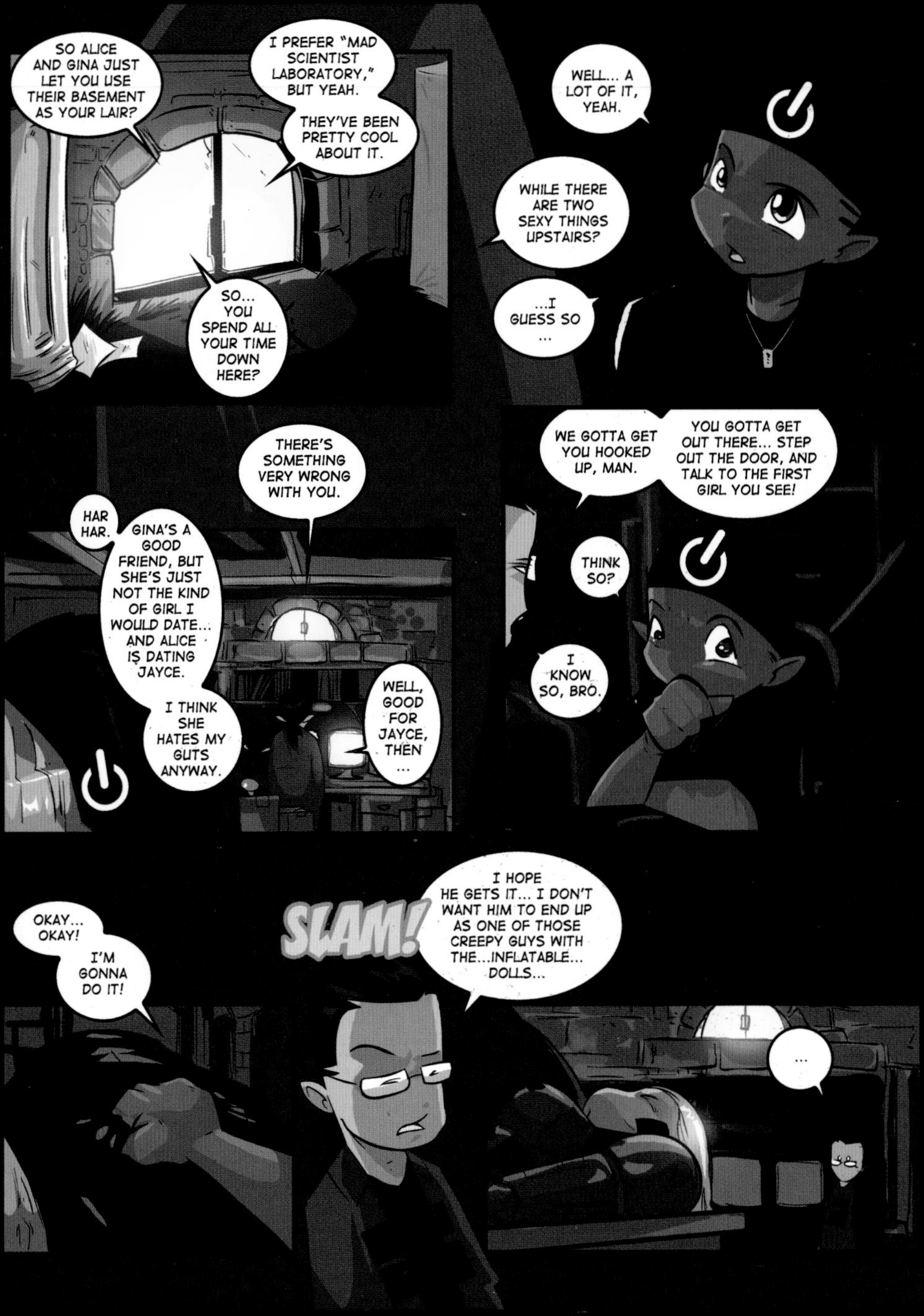
SO ALICE AND GINA JUST LET YOU USE THEIR BASEMENT AS YOUR LAIR?
I PREFER "MAD SCIENTIST LABORATORY," BUT YEAH.
THEY'VE BEEN PRETTY COOL ABOUT IT.
SO... YOU SPEND ALL YOUR TIME DOWN HERE?
WELL... A LOT OF IT, YEAH.
WHILE THERE ARE TWO SEXY THINGS UPSTAIRS?
...I GUESS SO ...
HAR HAR.
GINA'S A GOOD FRIEND, BUT SHE'S JUST NOT THE KIND OF GIRL I WOULD DATE... AND ALICE IS DATING JAYCE.
THERE'S SOMETHING VERY WRONG WITH YOU.
I THINK SHE HATES MY GUTS ANYWAY.
WELL, GOOD FOR JAYCE, THEN ...
WE GOTTA GET YOU HOOKED UP, MAN.
YOU GOTTA GET OUT THERE... STEP OUT THE DOOR, AND TALK TO THE FIRST GIRL YOU SEE!
THINK SO?
I KNOW SO, BRO.
OKAY... OKAY!
I'M GONNA DO IT!
SLAM!
I HOPE HE GETS IT... I DON'T WANT HIM TO END UP AS ONE OF THOSE CREEPY GUYS WITH THE...INFLATABLE... DOLLS...
...

I wrote this comic before I learned about Real Dolls . . . It's for the best. This strip could have ended much worse. Brrr.

What? You don't know what a Real Doll is? Look it up! (For the love of God, don't look it up.)

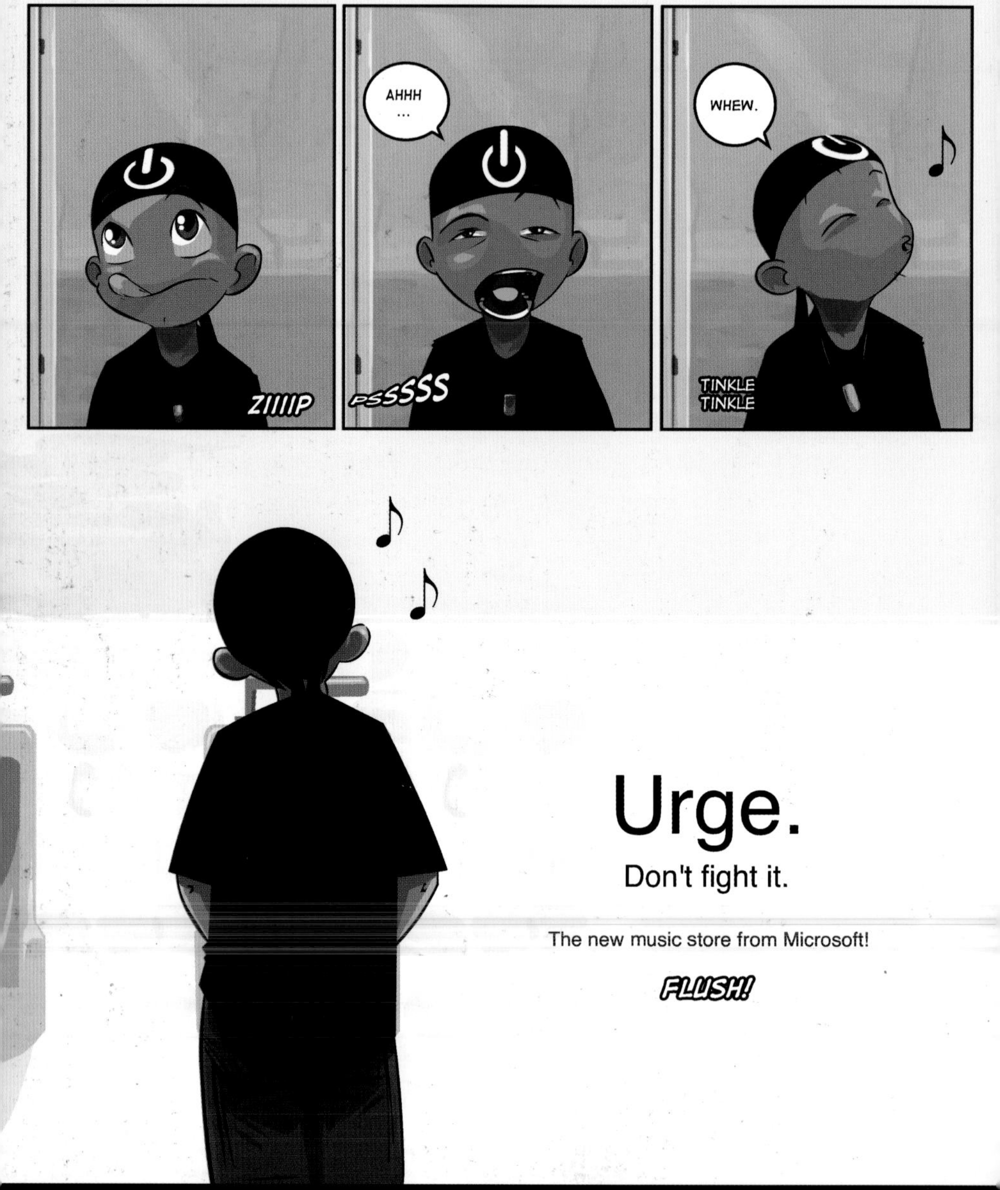
ZIIIIP
AHHH ...
PSSSSS
WHEW.
TINKLE TINKLE
Urge.
Don't fight it.
The new music store from Microsoft!
FLUSH!

URGE was a music store from Microsoft with some seriously weird rules. No one is going to take us seriously fo

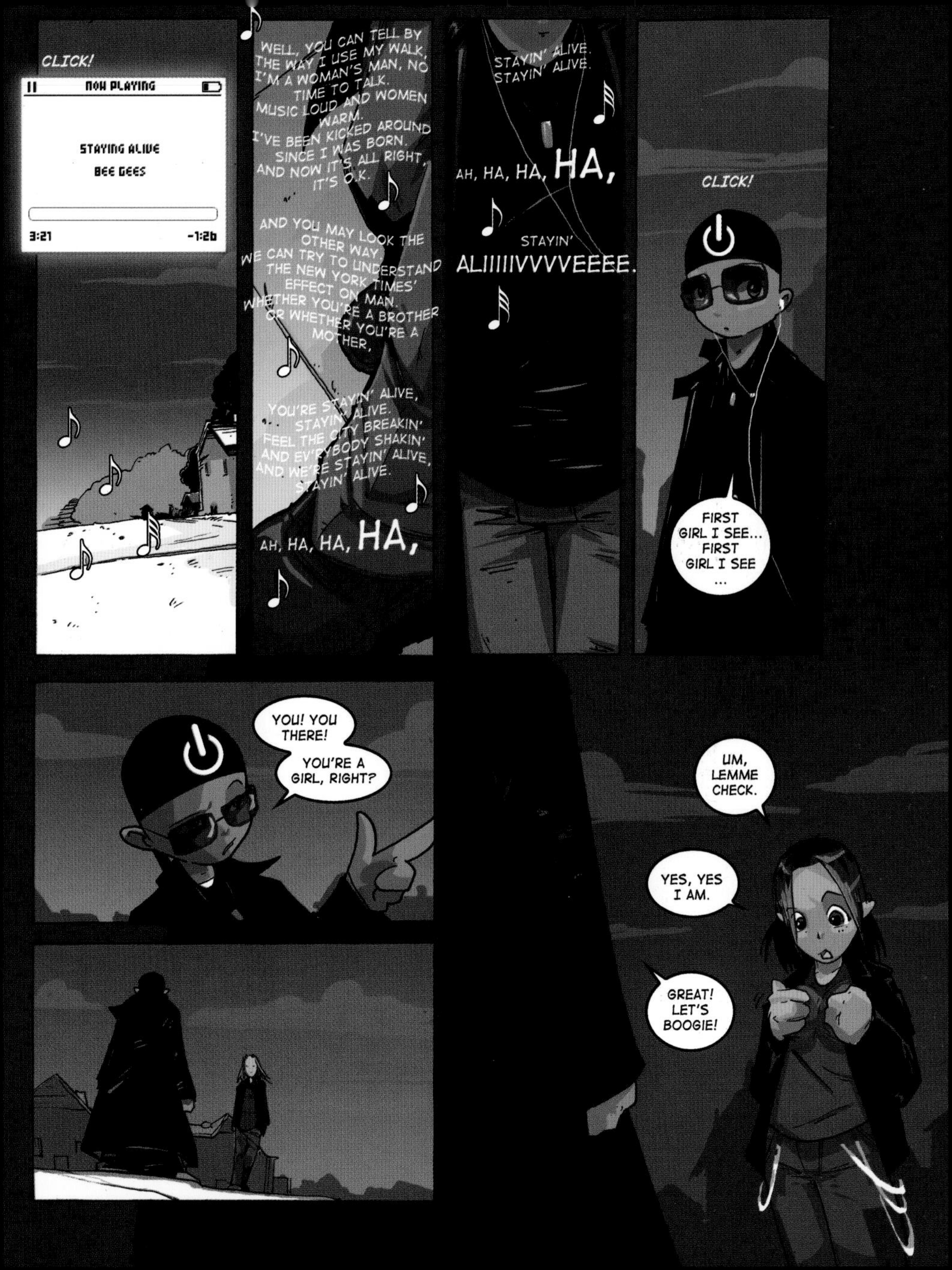
CLICK!
NOW PLAYING
STAYING ALIVE
BEE GEES
3:21
-1:26
WELL, YOU CAN TELL BY THE WAY I USE MY WALK, I'M A WOMAN'S MAN, NO TIME TO TALK. MUSIC LOUD AND WOMEN WARM. I'VE BEEN KICKED AROUND SINCE I WAS BORN. AND NOW IT'S ALL RIGHT, IT'S O.K.
AND YOU MAY LOOK THE OTHER WAY. WE CAN TRY TO UNDERSTAND THE NEW YORK TIMES' EFFECT ON MAN. WHETHER YOU'RE A BROTHER OR WHETHER YOU'RE A MOTHER,
YOU'RE STAYIN' ALIVE, STAYIN' ALIVE. FEEL THE CITY BREAKIN' AND EV'RYBODY SHAKIN' AND WE'RE STAYIN' ALIVE, STAYIN' ALIVE.
AH, HA, HA, HA,
STAYIN' ALIVE. STAYIN' ALIVE.
AH, HA, HA, HA,
STAYIN' ALIIIIIVVVVEEEE.
CLICK!
FIRST GIRL I SEE... FIRST GIRL I SEE ...
YOU! YOU THERE!
YOU'RE A GIRL, RIGHT?
UM, LEMME CHECK.
YES, YES I AM.
GREAT! LET'S BOOGIE!

He's off to a great start! It's a good thing she has a sense of humor. Her hair actually reminds me of Roxy from *Gen13*—I know some of you remember her! Adam Warren wrote my favorite runs of that book. He did a three-parter for *Gen13: Bootleg* that was about Grunge's crazy kung-fu exploitation flick, and then he wrote a knockout ending for the series that later got retconned (I think?). Anyway, he's one of the few guys who writes genuinely fun comics! He's doing *Empowered* now, which is also available for purchase from Dark Horse.

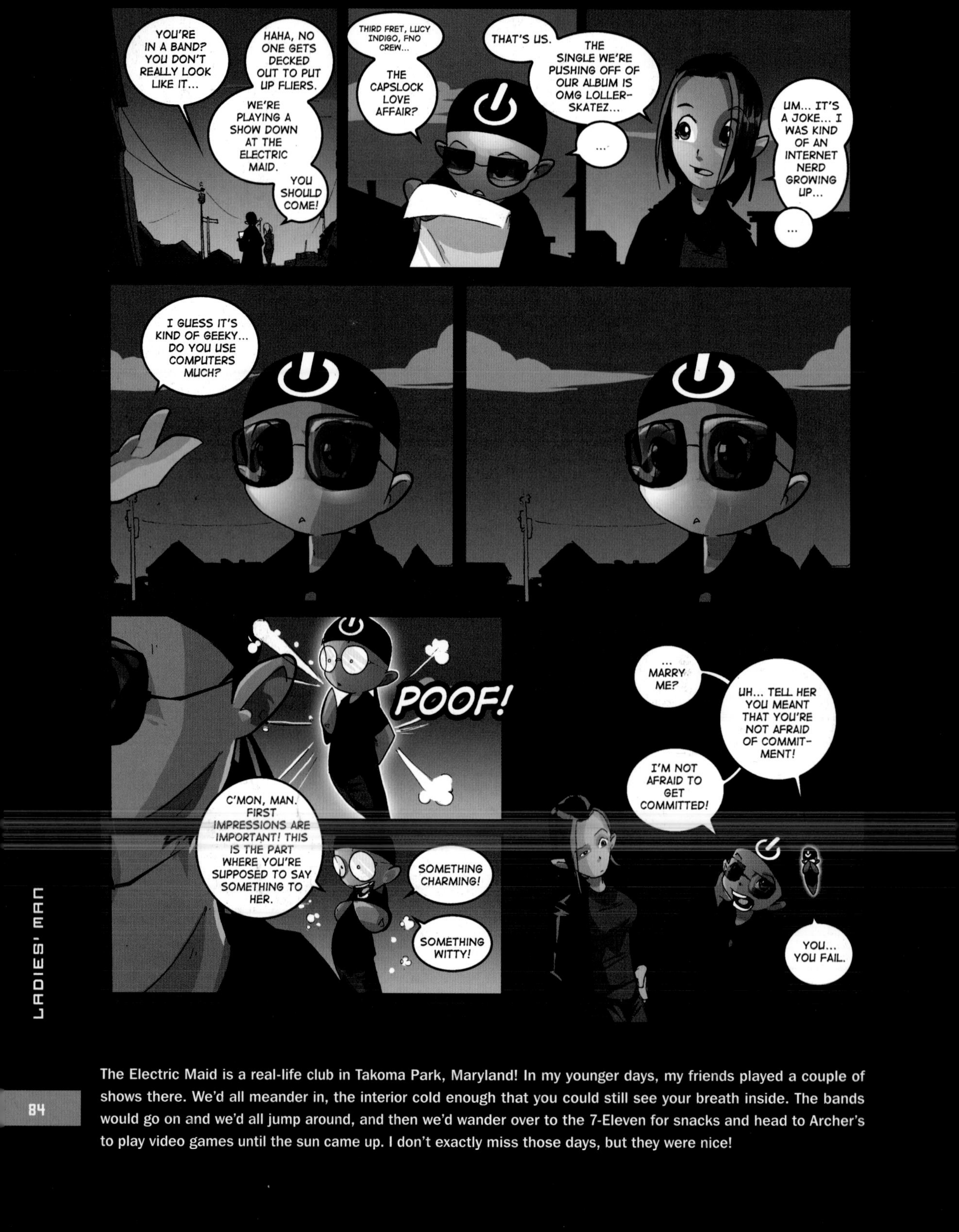
YOU'RE IN A BAND? YOU DON'T REALLY LOOK LIKE IT...
HAHA, NO ONE GETS DECKED OUT TO PUT UP FLIERS.
WE'RE PLAYING A SHOW DOWN AT THE ELECTRIC MAID.
YOU SHOULD COME!
THIRD FRET, LUCY INDIGO, FNO CREW...
THE CAPSLOCK LOVE AFFAIR?
THAT'S US.
THE SINGLE WE'RE PUSHING OFF OF OUR ALBUM IS OMG LOLLER-SKATEZ...
...
UM... IT'S A JOKE... I WAS KIND OF AN INTERNET NERD GROWING UP...
...
I GUESS IT'S KIND OF GEEKY... DO YOU USE COMPUTERS MUCH?
POOF!
C'MON, MAN. FIRST IMPRESSIONS ARE IMPORTANT! THIS IS THE PART WHERE YOU'RE SUPPOSED TO SAY SOMETHING TO HER.
SOMETHING CHARMING!
SOMETHING WITTY!
... MARRY ME?
UH... TELL HER YOU MEANT THAT YOU'RE NOT AFRAID OF COMMIT-MENT!
I'M NOT AFRAID TO GET COMMITTED!
YOU... YOU FAIL.

The Electric Maid is a real-life club in Takoma Park, Maryland! In my younger days, my friends played a couple of shows there. We'd all meander in, the interior cold enough that you could still see your breath inside. The bands would go on and we'd all jump around, and then we'd wander over to the 7-Eleven for snacks and head to Archer's to play video games until the sun came up. I don't exactly miss those days, but they were nice!

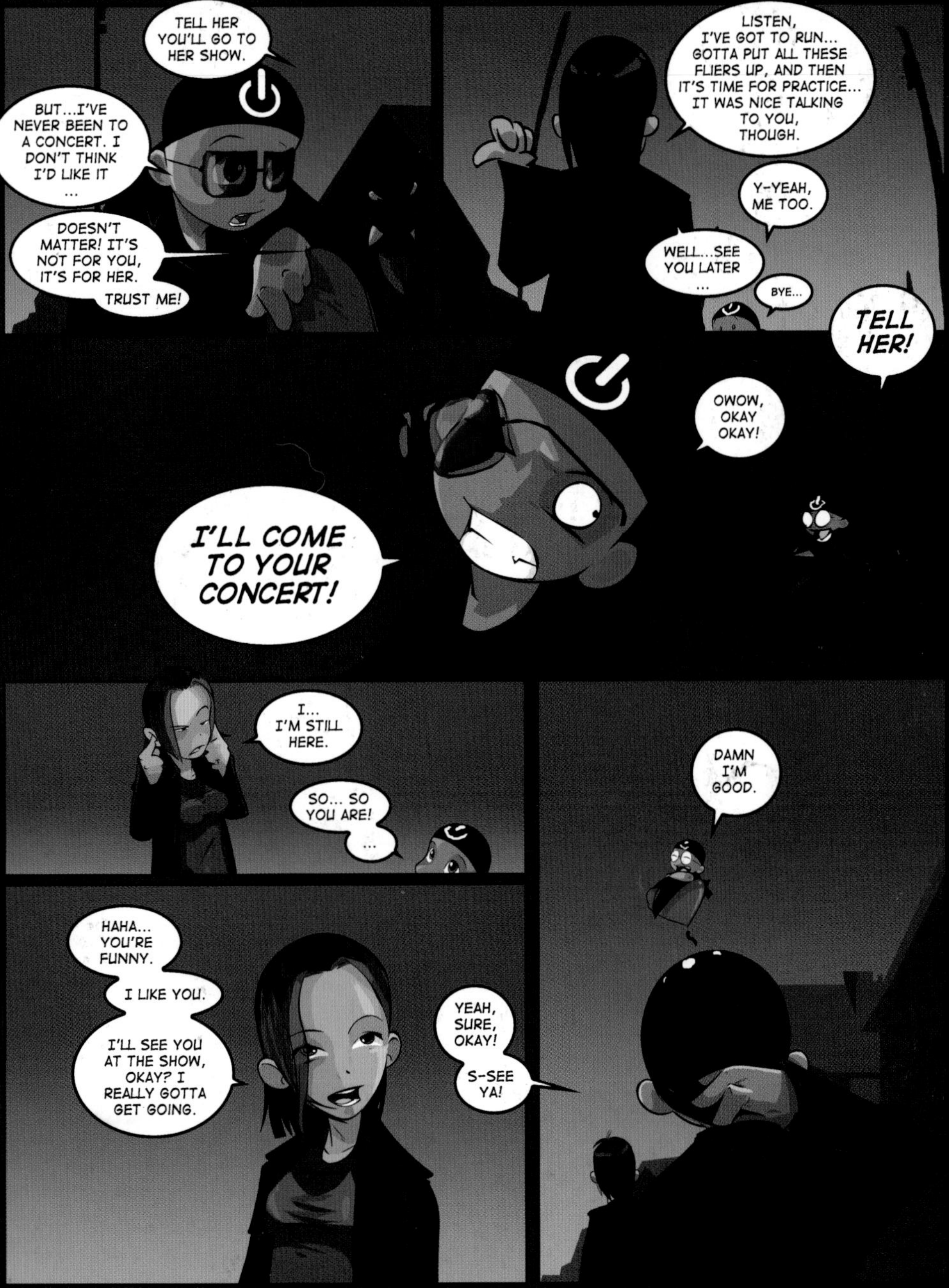
TELL HER YOU'LL GO TO HER SHOW.
BUT...I'VE NEVER BEEN TO A CONCERT. I DON'T THINK I'D LIKE IT ...
DOESN'T MATTER! IT'S NOT FOR YOU, IT'S FOR HER.
TRUST ME!
LISTEN, I'VE GOT TO RUN... GOTTA PUT ALL THESE FLIERS UP, AND THEN IT'S TIME FOR PRACTICE... IT WAS NICE TALKING TO YOU, THOUGH.
Y-YEAH, ME TOO.
WELL...SEE YOU LATER ...
BYE...
TELL HER!
OWOW, OKAY OKAY!
I'LL COME TO YOUR CONCERT!
I... I'M STILL HERE.
SO... SO YOU ARE!
...
HAHA... YOU'RE FUNNY.
I LIKE YOU.
I'LL SEE YOU AT THE SHOW, OKAY? I REALLY GOTTA GET GOING.
YEAH, SURE, OKAY!
S-SEE YA!
DAMN I'M GOOD.

I actually didn't have any idea whether or not cartoon Hawk would like going to concerts, so I turned to real-life Hawk for a cue on that. Also, the little Hawk floating up on the heart in the last panel wasn't in the script! It was a nice detail that real-life Hawk scribbled in on a whim. Nice!

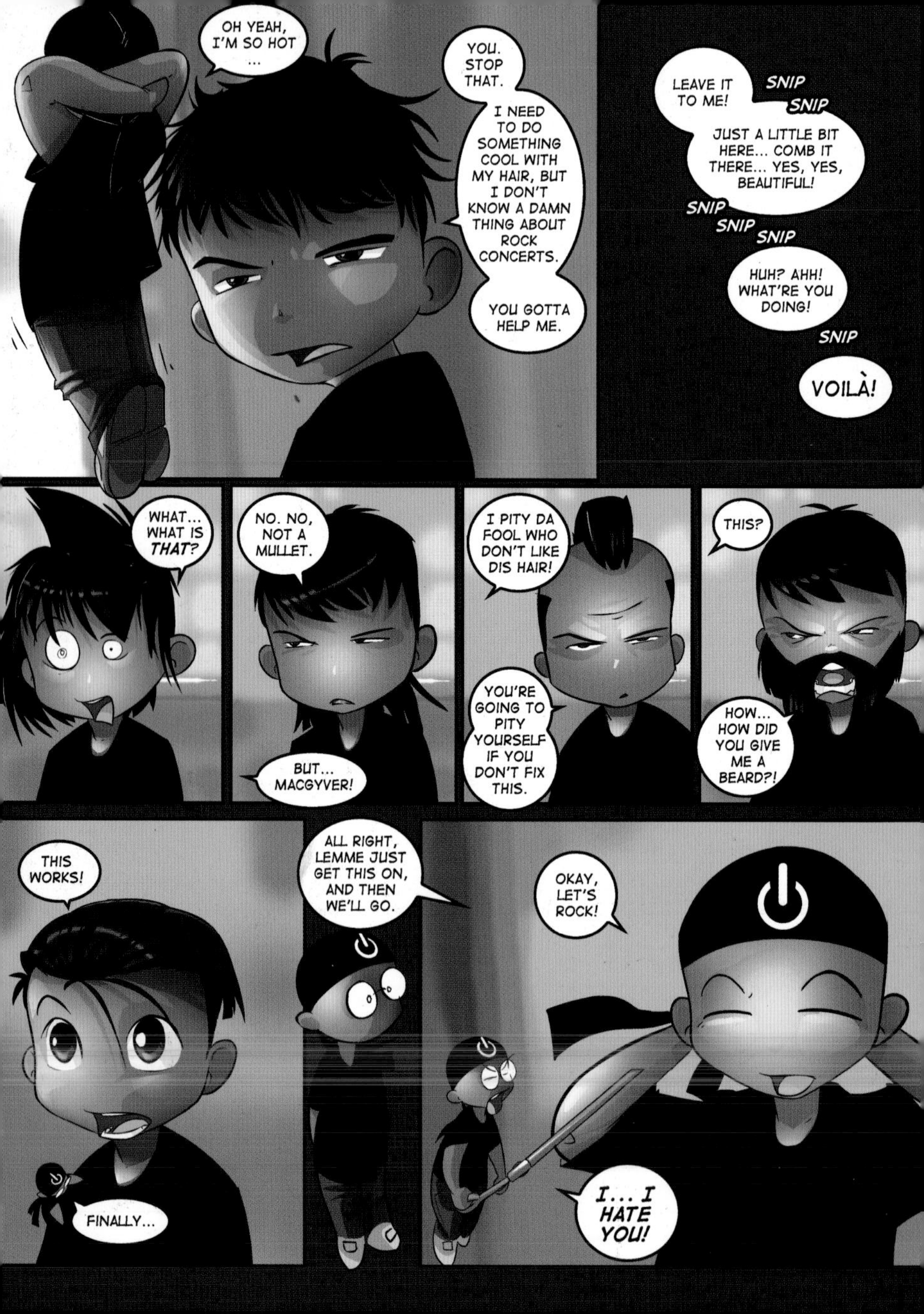
OH YEAH, I'M SO HOT ...
YOU. STOP THAT.
I NEED TO DO SOMETHING COOL WITH MY HAIR, BUT I DON'T KNOW A DAMN THING ABOUT ROCK CONCERTS.
YOU GOTTA HELP ME.
LEAVE IT TO ME!
SNIP
SNIP
JUST A LITTLE BIT HERE... COMB IT THERE... YES, YES, BEAUTIFUL!
SNIP
SNIP
SNIP
HUH? AHH! WHAT'RE YOU DOING!
SNIP
VOILÀ!
WHAT... WHAT IS *THAT*?
NO. NO, NOT A MULLET.
BUT... MACGYVER!
I PITY DA FOOL WHO DON'T LIKE DIS HAIR!
YOU'RE GOING TO PITY YOURSELF IF YOU DON'T FIX THIS.
THIS?
HOW... HOW DID YOU GIVE ME A BEARD?!
THIS WORKS!
FINALLY...
ALL RIGHT, LEMME JUST GET THIS ON, AND THEN WE'LL GO.
OKAY, LET'S ROCK!
I... I HATE YOU!

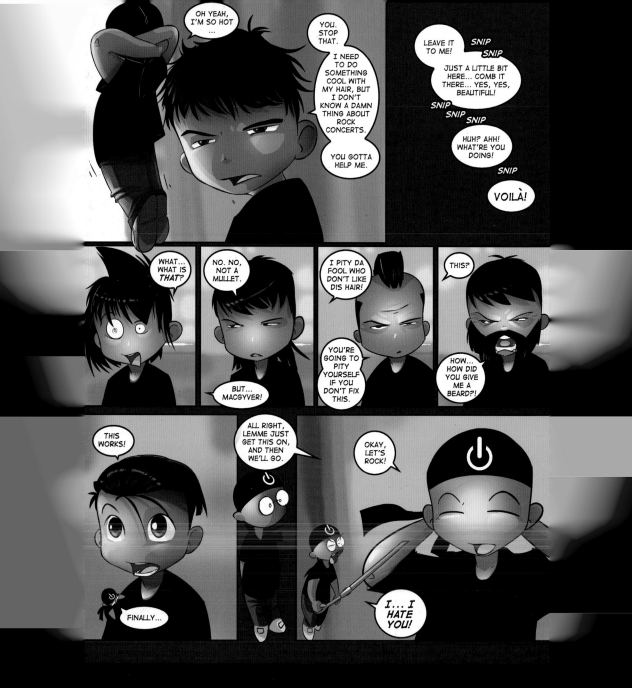

y, so a lot of people ask about that first haircut. I typed "scene haircut" into a Google image search and k the most bizarre photo I could find. Clearly I did a good job! Also, that beard: Epic? y/y

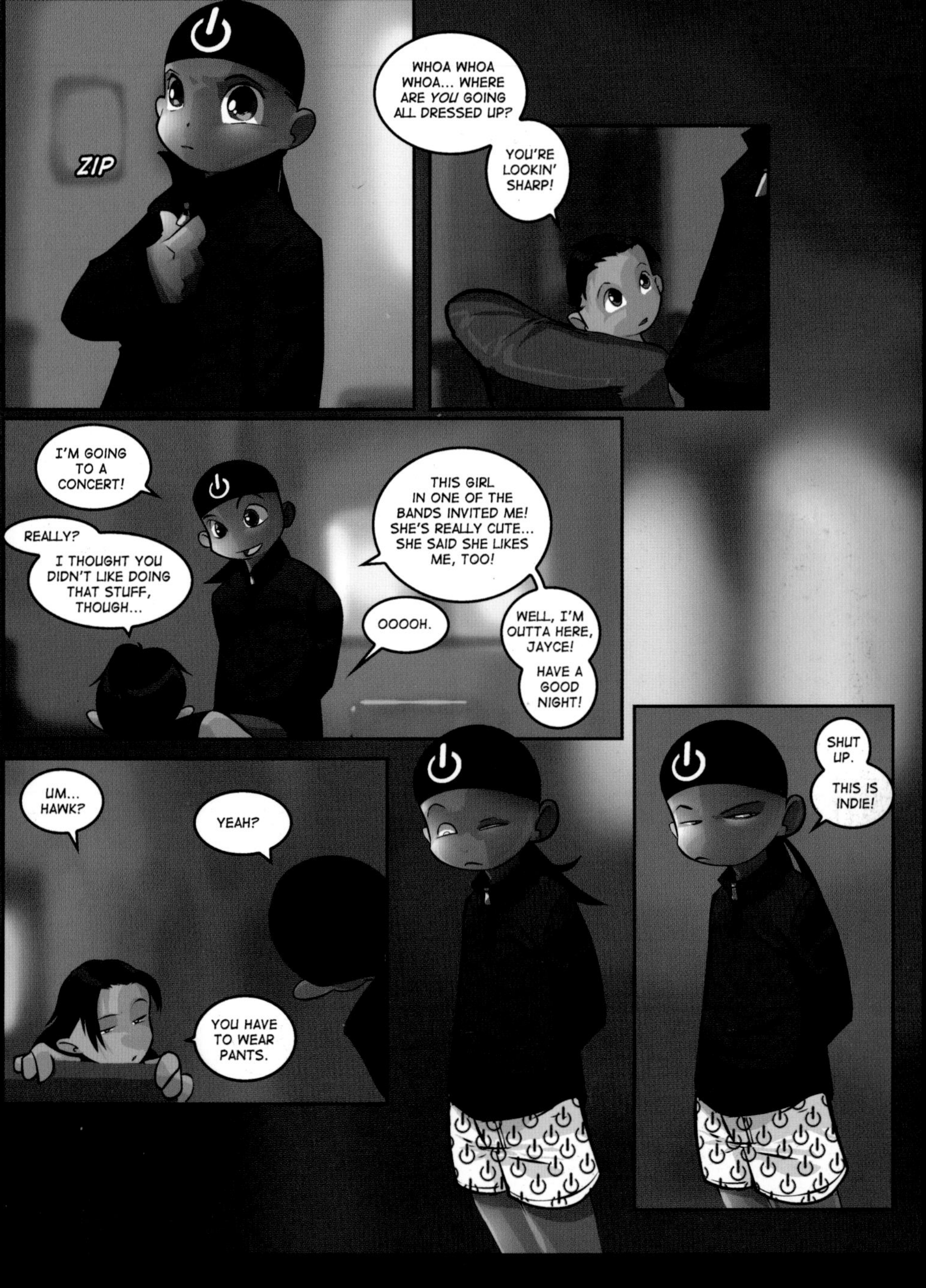
ZIP
WHOA WHOA WHOA... WHERE ARE *YOU* GOING ALL DRESSED UP?
YOU'RE LOOKIN' SHARP!
I'M GOING TO A CONCERT!
REALLY?
I THOUGHT YOU DIDN'T LIKE DOING THAT STUFF, THOUGH...
THIS GIRL IN ONE OF THE BANDS INVITED ME! SHE'S REALLY CUTE... SHE SAID SHE LIKES ME, TOO!
OOOOH.
WELL, I'M OUTTA HERE, JAYCE!
HAVE A GOOD NIGHT!
UM... HAWK?
YEAH?
YOU HAVE TO WEAR PANTS.
SHUT UP.
THIS IS INDIE!

Reading definitions for *indie* on urbandictionary.com is hilarious. Everyone's definition of *indie* tries to be indier than everyone else's.

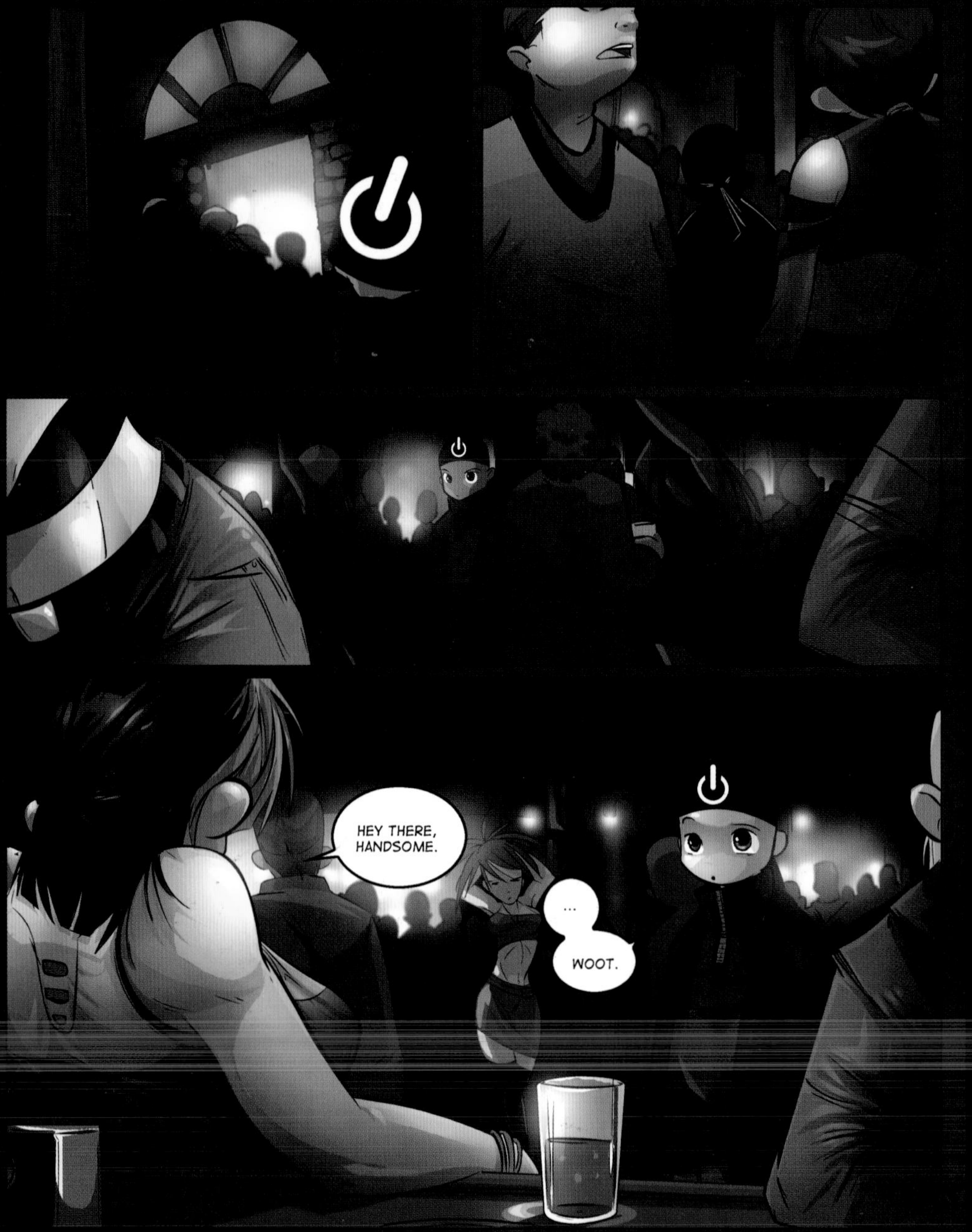
HEY THERE, HANDSOME.
...
WOOT.

Ever heard of photo bombing? It's the time-honored practice in which, at the last minute, someone leaps into the frame so as to ruin an otherwise perfectly planned photograph. I always thought that the girl in the red skirt and top in panel three was panel bombing. Er, Hawk's glaring at me . . . Moving on!

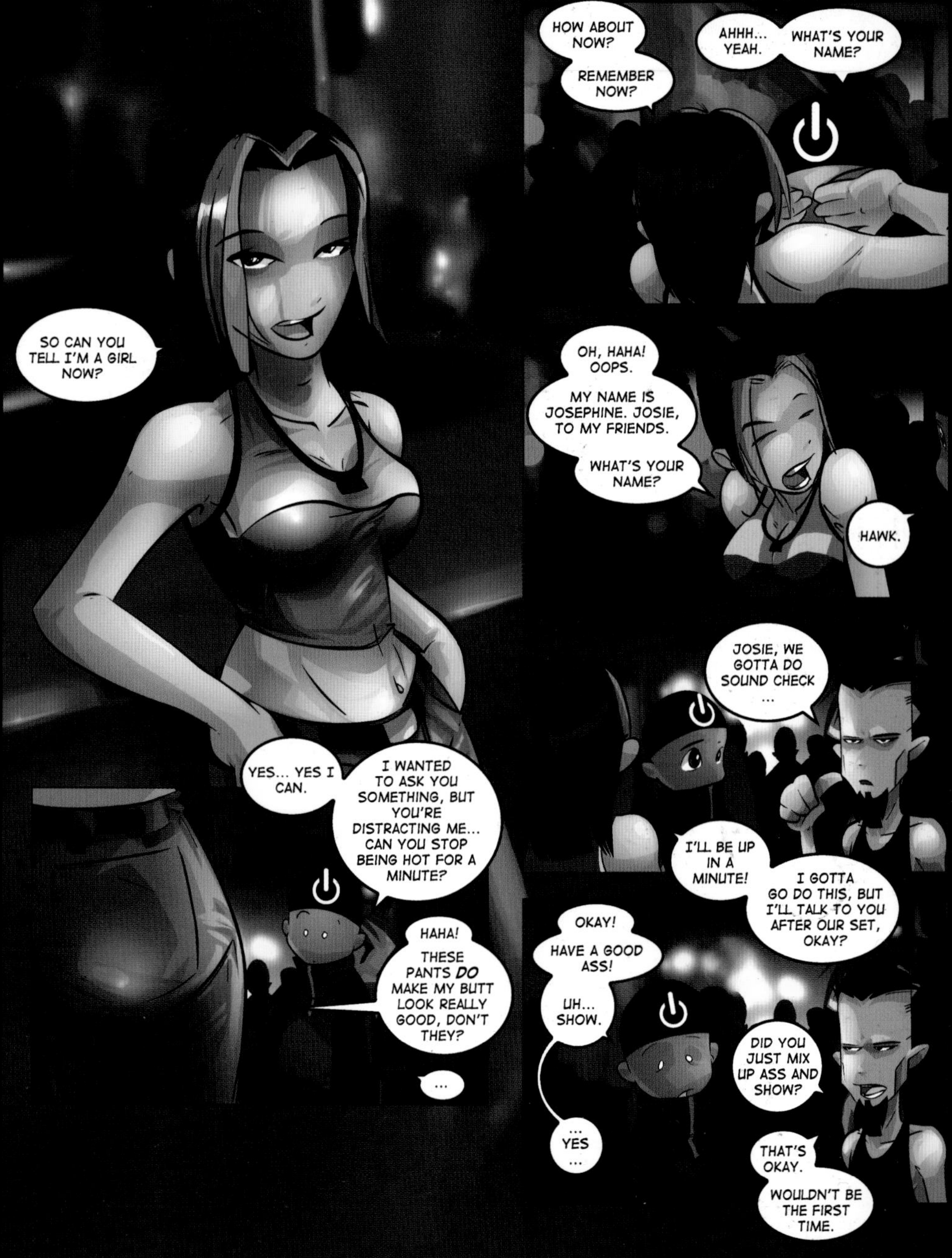
SO CAN YOU TELL I'M A GIRL NOW?
YES... YES I CAN.
I WANTED TO ASK YOU SOMETHING, BUT YOU'RE DISTRACTING ME... CAN YOU STOP BEING HOT FOR A MINUTE?
HAHA!
THESE PANTS *DO* MAKE MY BUTT LOOK REALLY GOOD, DON'T THEY?
...
HOW ABOUT NOW?
REMEMBER NOW?
AHHH... YEAH.
WHAT'S YOUR NAME?
OH, HAHA! OOPS.
MY NAME IS JOSEPHINE. JOSIE, TO MY FRIENDS.
WHAT'S YOUR NAME?
HAWK.
JOSIE, WE GOTTA DO SOUND CHECK ...
I'LL BE UP IN A MINUTE!
I GOTTA GO DO THIS, BUT I'LL TALK TO YOU AFTER OUR SET, OKAY?
OKAY!
HAVE A GOOD ASS!
UH... SHOW.
DID YOU JUST MIX UP ASS AND SHOW?
... YES ...
THAT'S OKAY.
WOULDN'T BE THE FIRST TIME.

I think the most embarrassing word mix-up I ever had in my life was when I was sitting down to dinner with a fairly conservative group of people. We were eating at this incredible Lebanese place, and I wanted to say, "Lebanese food is really good!" and instead I said, "Lesbian food is really good!" Sigh.

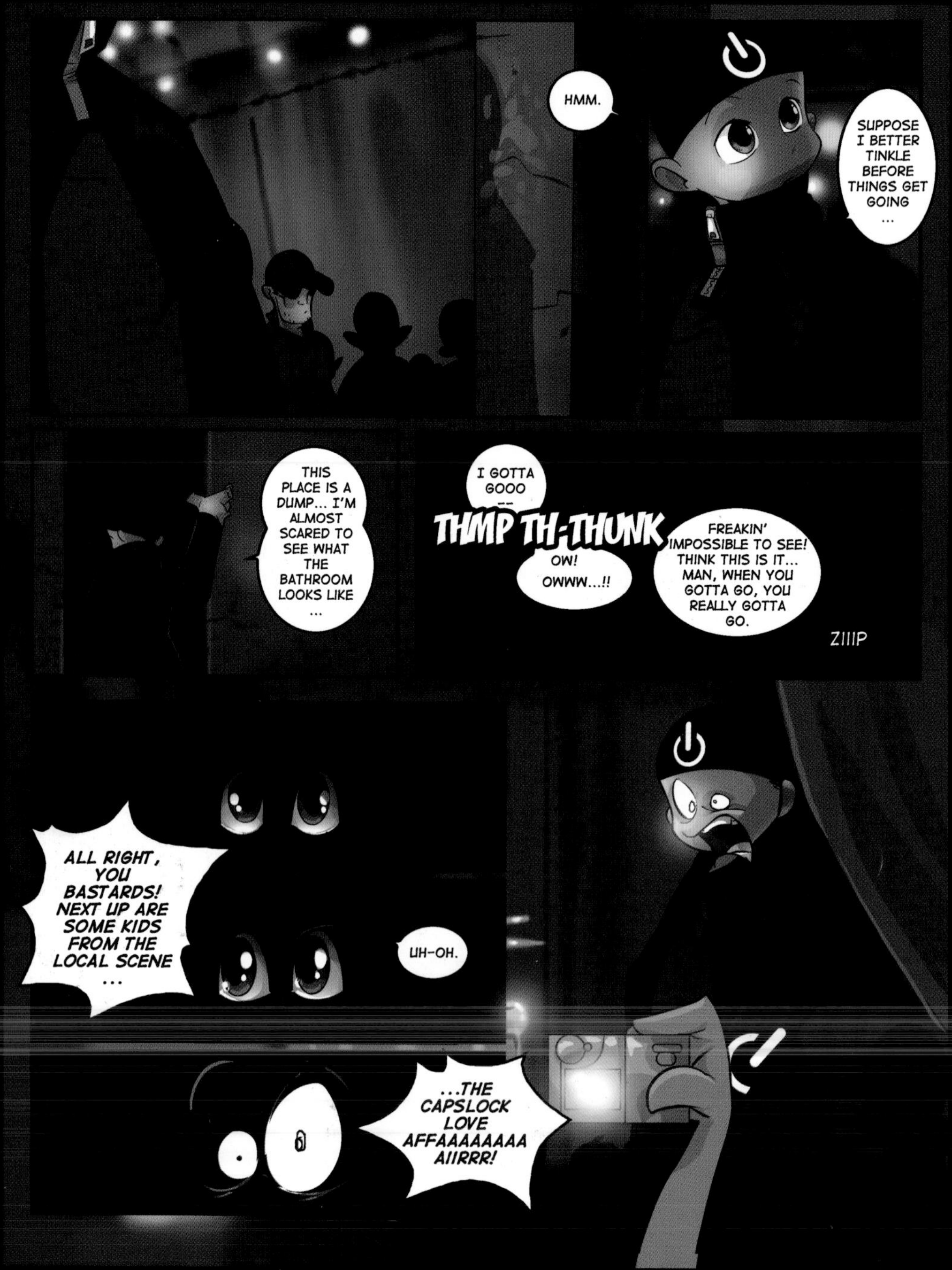
HMM.
SUPPOSE I BETTER TINKLE BEFORE THINGS GET GOING ...
THIS PLACE IS A DUMP... I'M ALMOST SCARED TO SEE WHAT THE BATHROOM LOOKS LIKE ...
I GOTTA GOOO --
THMP TH-THUNK
OW! OWWW...!!
FREAKIN' IMPOSSIBLE TO SEE! THINK THIS IS IT... MAN, WHEN YOU GOTTA GO, YOU REALLY GOTTA GO.
ZIIIP
ALL RIGHT, YOU BASTARDS! NEXT UP ARE SOME KIDS FROM THE LOCAL SCENE ...
UH-OH.
...THE CAPSLOCK LOVE AFFAAAAAAAAA AIIRRR!

I don't do drugs, but sometimes I wish I could say I did so I could explain away comics like this one.

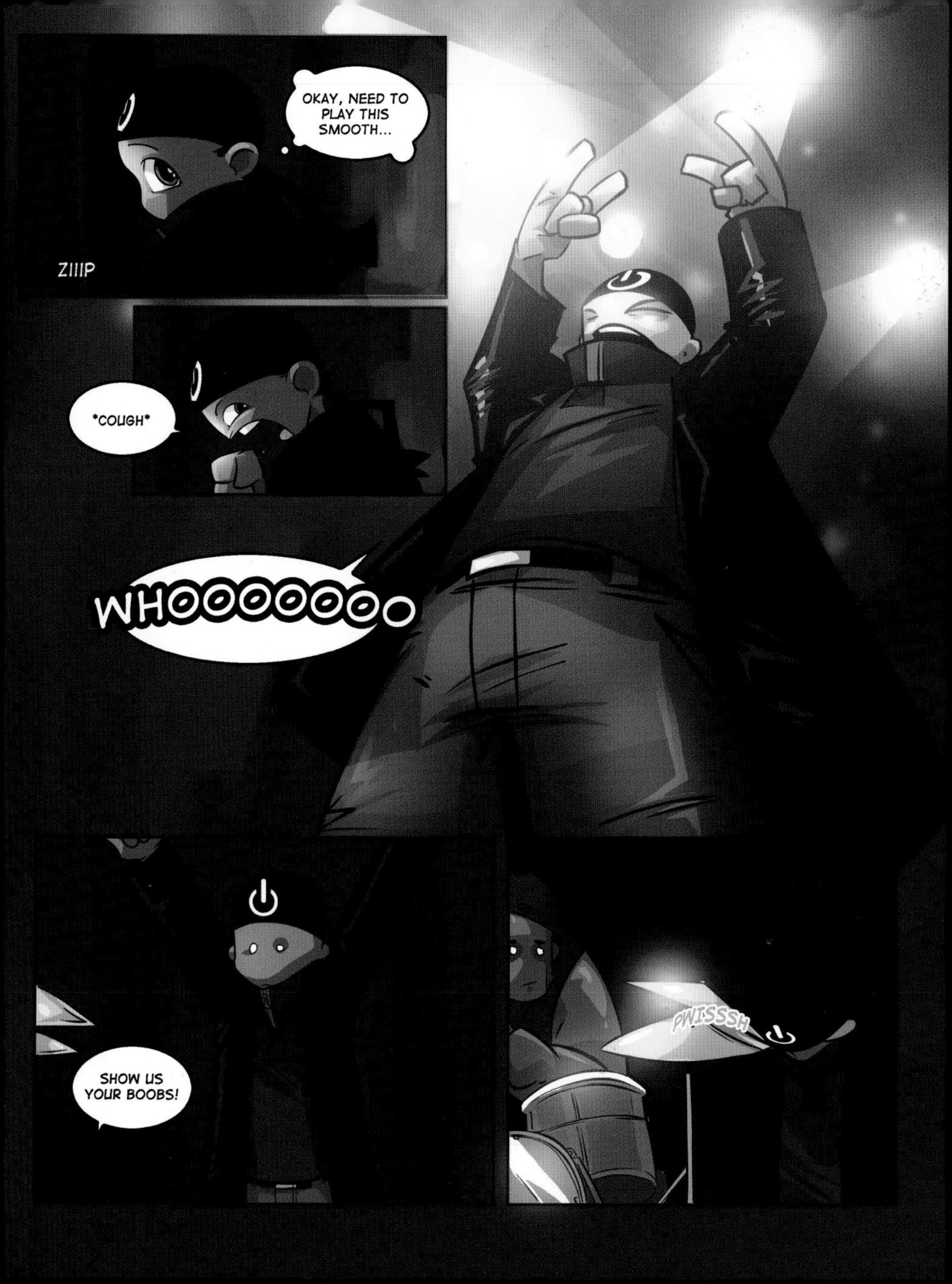
OKAY, NEED TO PLAY THIS SMOOTH...
ZIIIP
COUGH
WHOOOOOOOO
SHOW US YOUR BOOBS!
PWISSSH

at looks like Russel from the Gorillaz! This was before *Demon Days* came out, but Hawk and I were obsessed with em from the outset—the Gorillaz are like this glorified college art project. The music is great, but we're really inter- ted in the art end of things as well. Jamie Hewlett's art and animation are great. He was actually tap ed to do

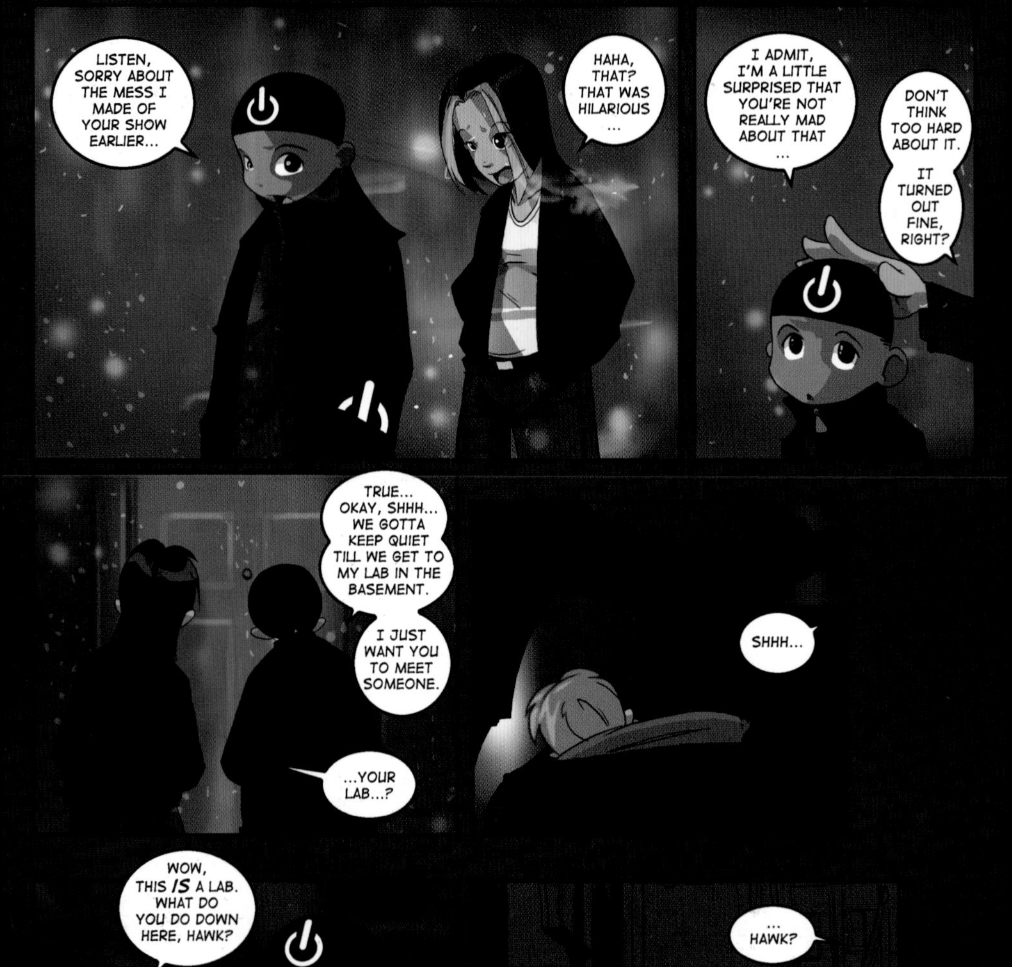
LISTEN, SORRY ABOUT THE MESS I MADE OF YOUR SHOW EARLIER...
HAHA, THAT? THAT WAS HILARIOUS ...
I ADMIT, I'M A LITTLE SURPRISED THAT YOU'RE NOT REALLY MAD ABOUT THAT ...
DON'T THINK TOO HARD ABOUT IT.
IT TURNED OUT FINE, RIGHT?
TRUE... OKAY, SHHH... WE GOTTA KEEP QUIET TILL WE GET TO MY LAB IN THE BASEMENT.
I JUST WANT YOU TO MEET SOMEONE.
...YOUR LAB...?
SHHH...
WOW, THIS *IS* A LAB. WHAT DO YOU DO DOWN HERE, HAWK?
HAWK?
... HAWK?
...SHE'S GONE.

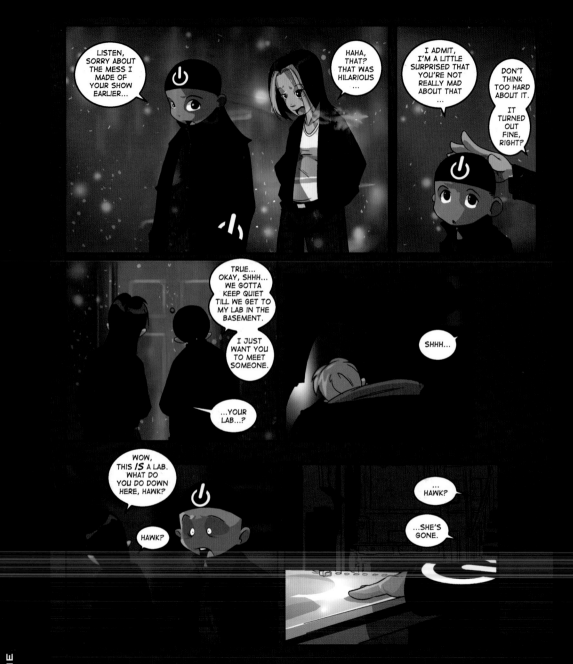

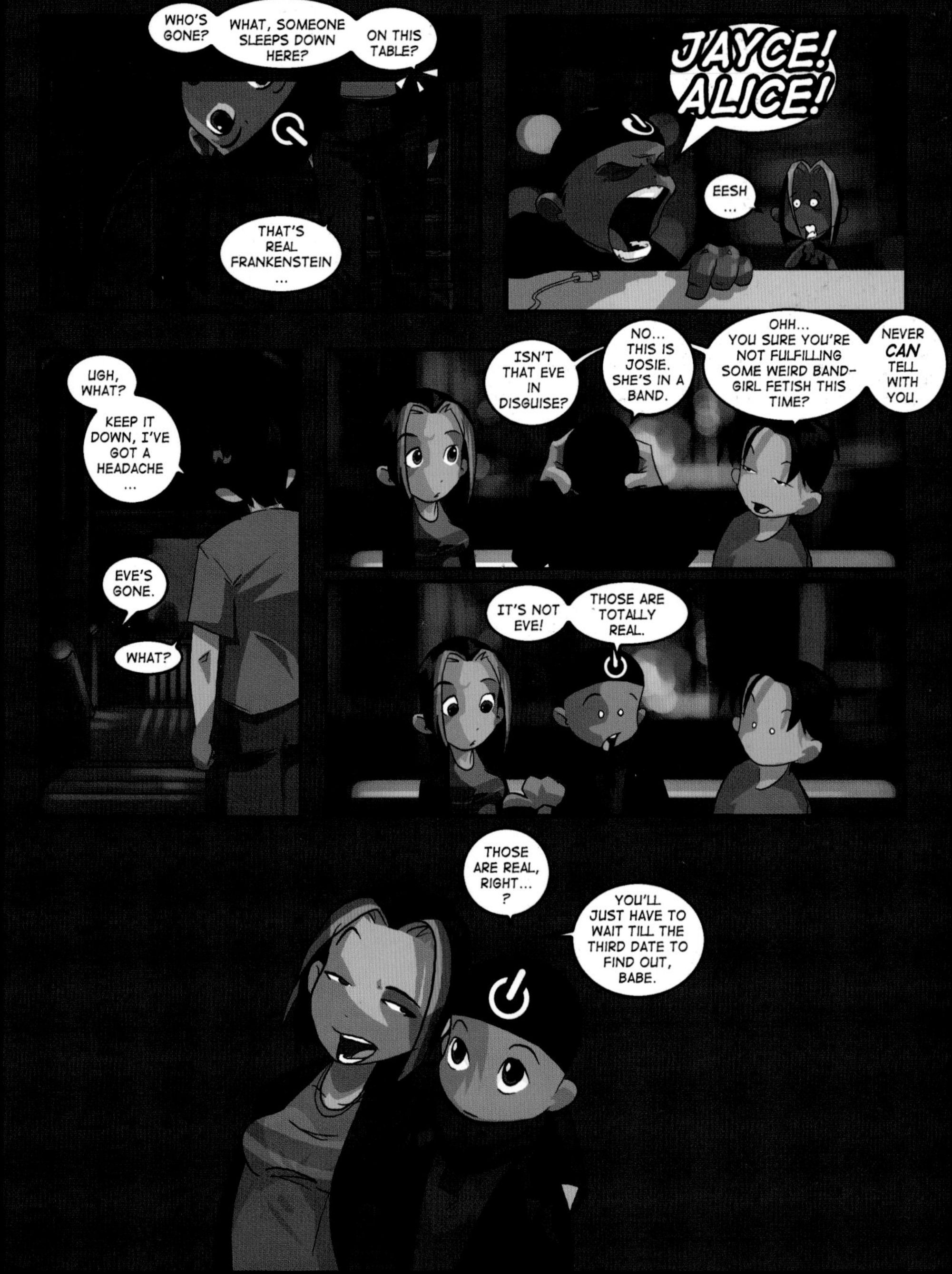
WHO'S GONE?
WHAT, SOMEONE SLEEPS DOWN HERE?
ON THIS TABLE?
THAT'S REAL FRANKENSTEIN . . .
JAYCE! ALICE!
EESH . . .
UGH, WHAT?
KEEP IT DOWN, I'VE GOT A HEADACHE . . .
EVE'S GONE.
WHAT?
ISN'T THAT EVE IN DISGUISE?
NO . . . THIS IS JOSIE. SHE'S IN A BAND.
OHH . . . YOU SURE YOU'RE NOT FULFILLING SOME WEIRD BAND-GIRL FETISH THIS TIME?
NEVER CAN TELL WITH YOU.
IT'S NOT EVE!
THOSE ARE TOTALLY REAL.
THOSE ARE REAL, RIGHT . . . ?
YOU'LL JUST HAVE TO WAIT TILL THE THIRD DATE TO FIND OUT, BABE.

Josie is the most forward female character I've written; in case you're wondering, yes, she's based on a real person! The one part that's fictional isn't her sense of humor, but her patience. Lucky for cartoon Hawk . . .

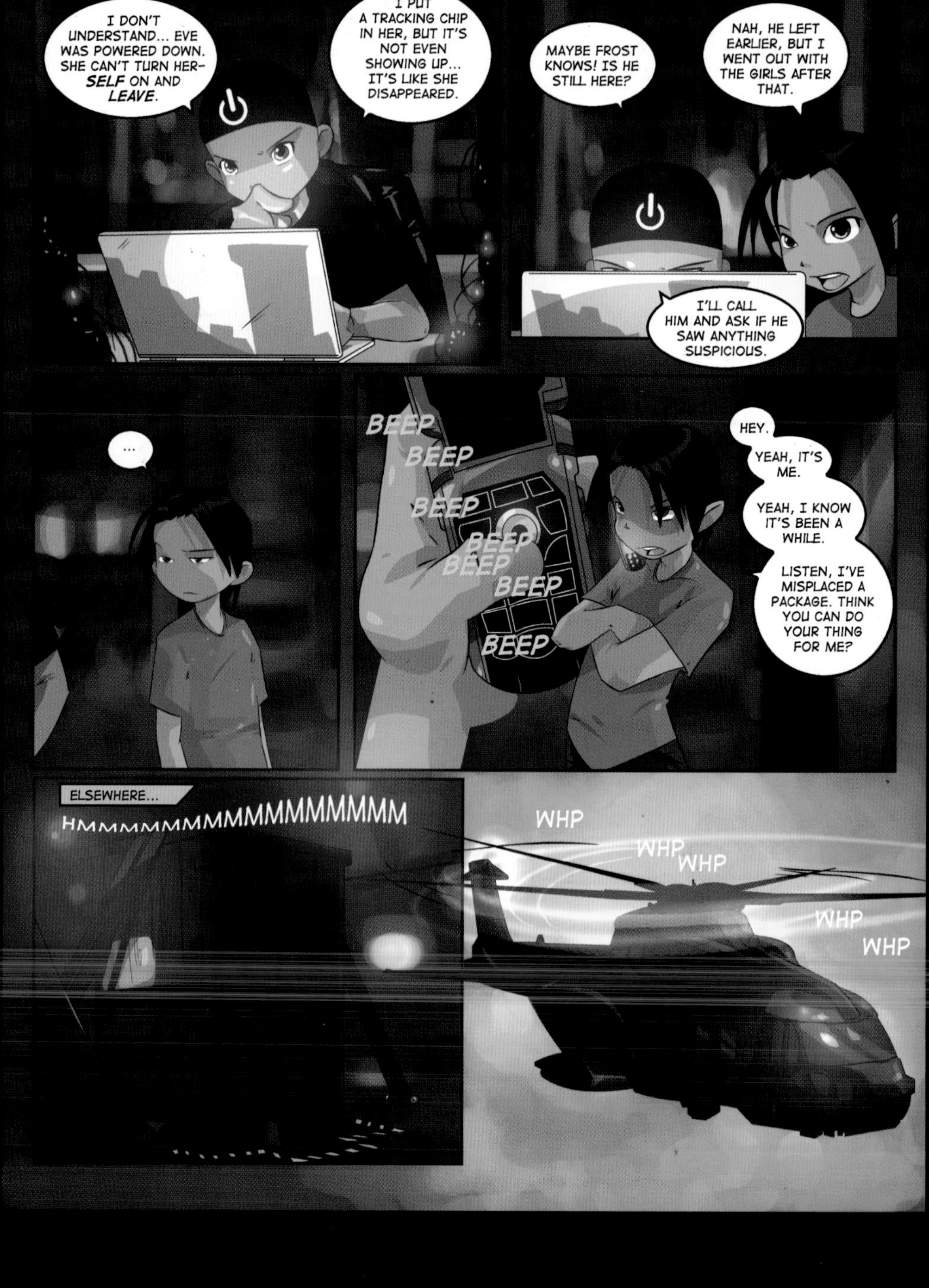
I DON'T UNDERSTAND... EVE WAS POWERED DOWN. SHE CAN'T TURN HER-SELF ON AND LEAVE.
I PUT A TRACKING CHIP IN HER, BUT IT'S NOT EVEN SHOWING UP... IT'S LIKE SHE DISAPPEARED.
MAYBE FROST KNOWS! IS HE STILL HERE?
NAH, HE LEFT EARLIER, BUT I WENT OUT WITH THE GIRLS AFTER THAT.
I'LL CALL HIM AND ASK IF HE SAW ANYTHING SUSPICIOUS.
...
BEEP
BEEP
BEEP
BEEP
BEEP
BEEP
BEEP
HEY.
YEAH, IT'S ME.
YEAH, I KNOW IT'S BEEN A WHILE.
LISTEN, I'VE MISPLACED A PACKAGE. THINK YOU CAN DO YOUR THING FOR ME?
ELSEWHERE...
HMMMMMMMMMMMMMMMMM
WHP
WHP WHP
WHP
WHP

TRACKING

Things happen! Jayce places a mystery call! A box is in a helicopter! I can't stop using exclamation marks!

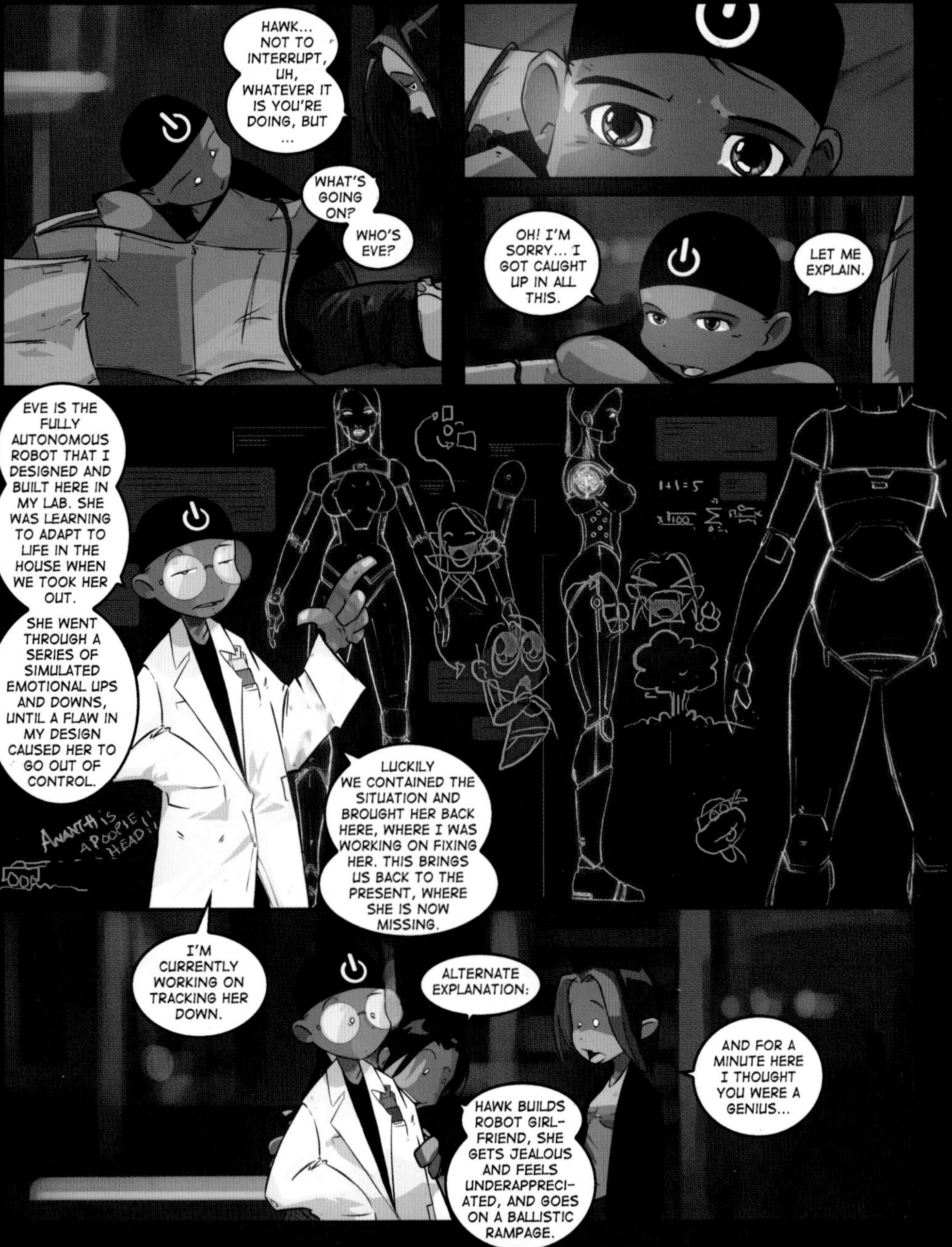
HAWK... NOT TO INTERRUPT, UH, WHATEVER IT IS YOU'RE DOING, BUT ...
WHAT'S GOING ON?
WHO'S EVE?
OH! I'M SORRY... I GOT CAUGHT UP IN ALL THIS.
LET ME EXPLAIN.
EVE IS THE FULLY AUTONOMOUS ROBOT THAT I DESIGNED AND BUILT HERE IN MY LAB. SHE WAS LEARNING TO ADAPT TO LIFE IN THE HOUSE WHEN WE TOOK HER OUT.
SHE WENT THROUGH A SERIES OF SIMULATED EMOTIONAL UPS AND DOWNS, UNTIL A FLAW IN MY DESIGN CAUSED HER TO GO OUT OF CONTROL.
LUCKILY WE CONTAINED THE SITUATION AND BROUGHT HER BACK HERE, WHERE I WAS WORKING ON FIXING HER. THIS BRINGS US BACK TO THE PRESENT, WHERE SHE IS NOW MISSING.
I'M CURRENTLY WORKING ON TRACKING HER DOWN.
ALTERNATE EXPLANATION:
HAWK BUILDS ROBOT GIRL-FRIEND, SHE GETS JEALOUS AND FEELS UNDERAPPRECI-ATED, AND GOES ON A BALLISTIC RAMPAGE.
AND FOR A MINUTE HERE I THOUGHT YOU WERE A GENIUS...

A lot of people make that mistake.

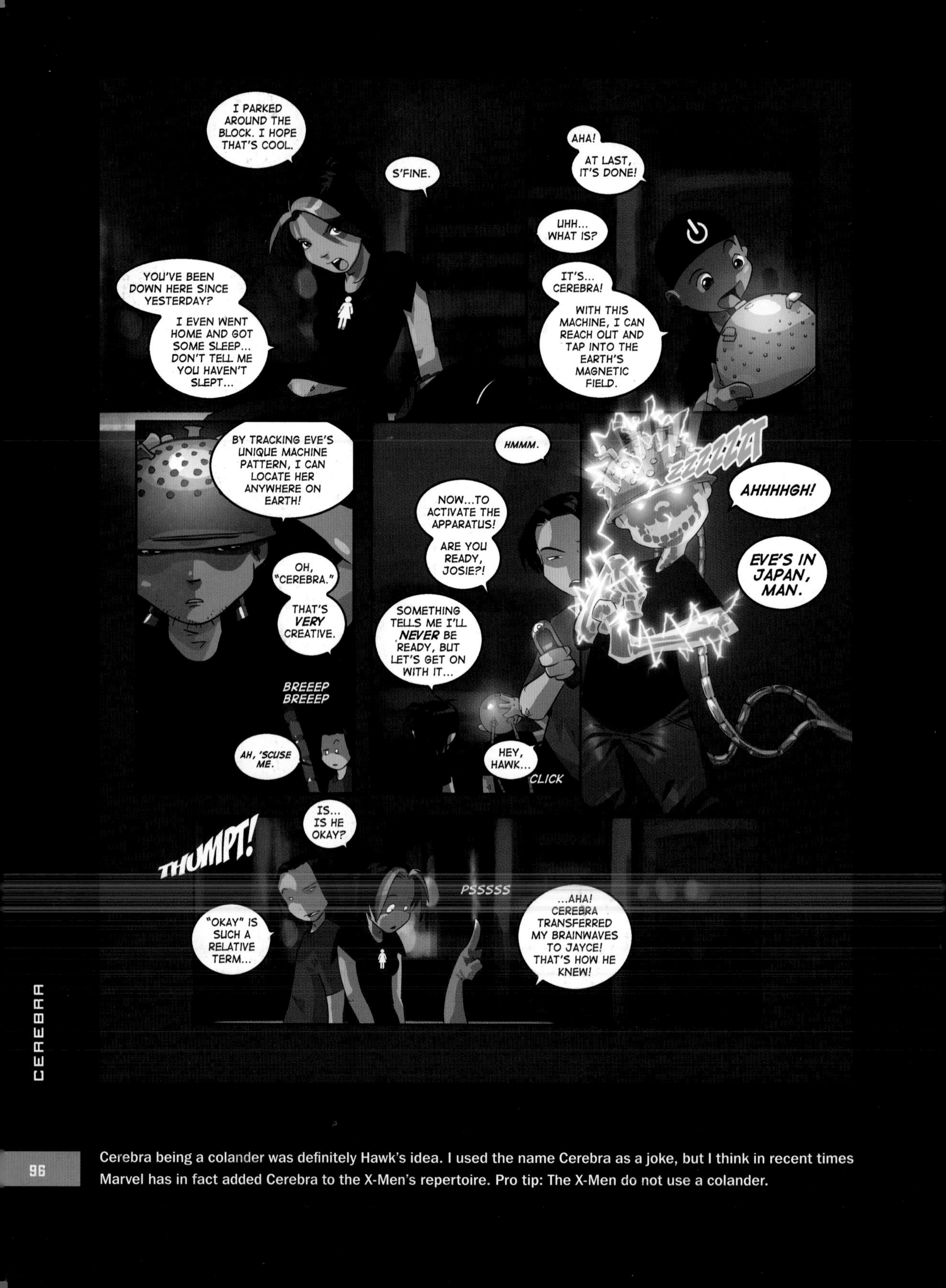
I PARKED AROUND THE BLOCK. I HOPE THAT'S COOL.
S'FINE.
YOU'VE BEEN DOWN HERE SINCE YESTERDAY?
I EVEN WENT HOME AND GOT SOME SLEEP... DON'T TELL ME YOU HAVEN'T SLEPT...
AHA!
AT LAST, IT'S DONE!
UHH... WHAT IS?
IT'S... CEREBRA!
WITH THIS MACHINE, I CAN REACH OUT AND TAP INTO THE EARTH'S MAGNETIC FIELD.
BY TRACKING EVE'S UNIQUE MACHINE PATTERN, I CAN LOCATE HER ANYWHERE ON EARTH!
OH, "CEREBRA."
THAT'S *VERY* CREATIVE.
BREEEP BREEEP
AH, 'SCUSE ME.
HMMM.
NOW...TO ACTIVATE THE APPARATUS!
ARE YOU READY, JOSIE?!
SOMETHING TELLS ME I'LL *NEVER* BE READY, BUT LET'S GET ON WITH IT...
HEY, HAWK...
CLICK
ZZZZZZZT
AHHHHGH!
EVE'S IN JAPAN, MAN.
THUMPT!
IS... IS HE OKAY?
PSSSSS
"OKAY" IS SUCH A RELATIVE TERM...
...AHA! CEREBRA TRANSFERRED MY BRAINWAVES TO JAYCE! THAT'S HOW HE KNEW!

Cerebra being a colander was definitely Hawk's idea. I used the name Cerebra as a joke, but I think in recent times Marvel has in fact added Cerebra to the X-Men's repertoire. Pro tip: The X-Men do not use a colander.

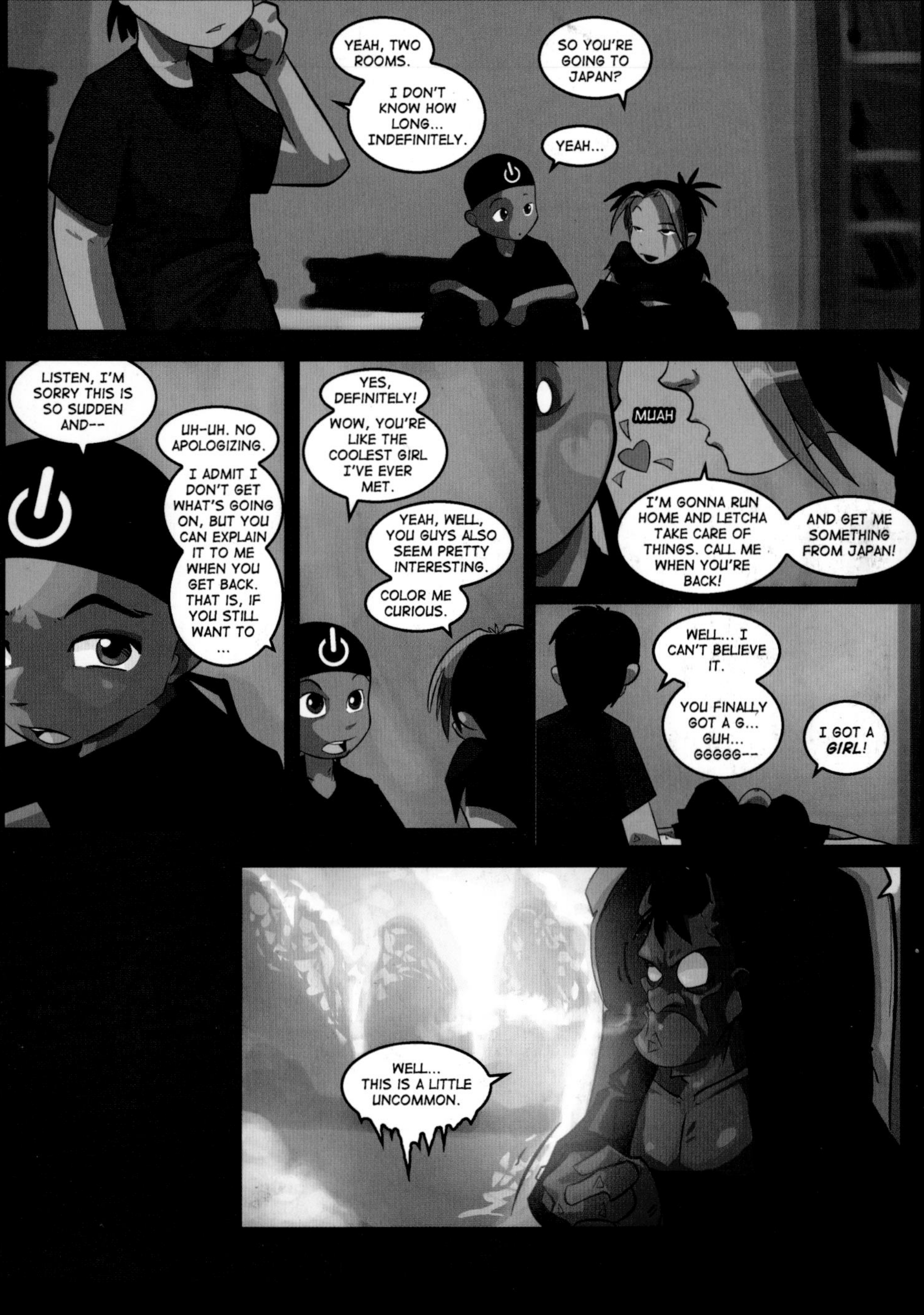
YEAH, TWO ROOMS.
I DON'T KNOW HOW LONG... INDEFINITELY.
SO YOU'RE GOING TO JAPAN?
YEAH...
LISTEN, I'M SORRY THIS IS SO SUDDEN AND--
UH-UH. NO APOLOGIZING.
I ADMIT I DON'T GET WHAT'S GOING ON, BUT YOU CAN EXPLAIN IT TO ME WHEN YOU GET BACK. THAT IS, IF YOU STILL WANT TO ...
YES, DEFINITELY!
WOW, YOU'RE LIKE THE COOLEST GIRL I'VE EVER MET.
YEAH, WELL, YOU GUYS ALSO SEEM PRETTY INTERESTING.
COLOR ME CURIOUS.
MUAH
I'M GONNA RUN HOME AND LETCHA TAKE CARE OF THINGS. CALL ME WHEN YOU'RE BACK!
AND GET ME SOMETHING FROM JAPAN!
WELL... I CAN'T BELIEVE IT.
YOU FINALLY GOT A G... GUH... GGGGG--
I GOT A *GIRL*!
WELL... THIS IS A LITTLE UNCOMMON.

A lot of people were actually pretty surprised that Hawk got the girl! The point, of course, is that you *think* the hard part is asking someone out, but no . . . The hard part is building a relationship. It has a learning curve.

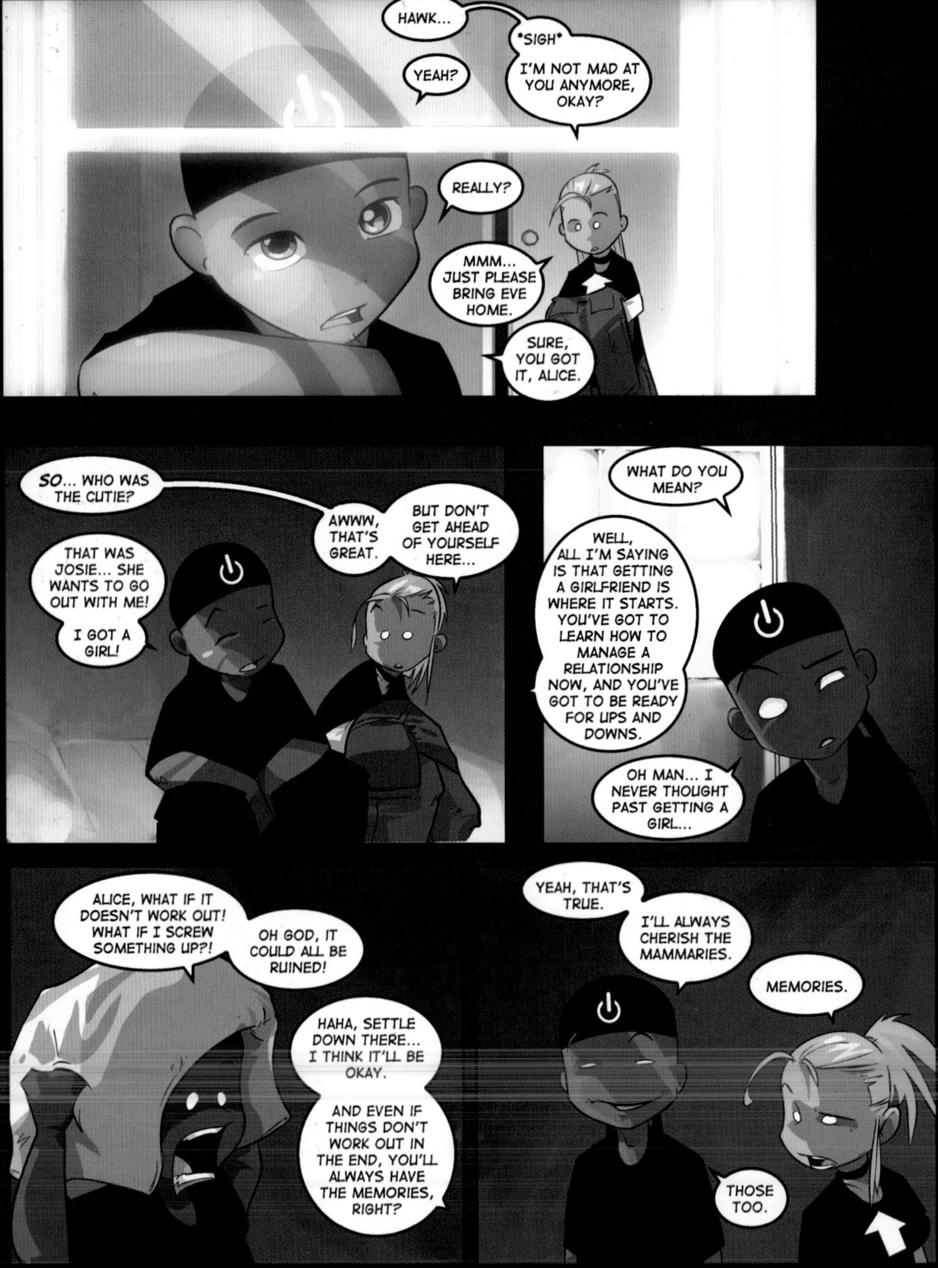
HAWK...
YEAH?
SIGH
I'M NOT MAD AT YOU ANYMORE, OKAY?
REALLY?
MMM... JUST PLEASE BRING EVE HOME.
SURE, YOU GOT IT, ALICE.
SO... WHO WAS THE CUTIE?
THAT WAS JOSIE... SHE WANTS TO GO OUT WITH ME!
I GOT A GIRL!
AWWW, THAT'S GREAT.
BUT DON'T GET AHEAD OF YOURSELF HERE...
WHAT DO YOU MEAN?
WELL, ALL I'M SAYING IS THAT GETTING A GIRLFRIEND IS WHERE IT STARTS. YOU'VE GOT TO LEARN HOW TO MANAGE A RELATIONSHIP NOW, AND YOU'VE GOT TO BE READY FOR UPS AND DOWNS.
OH MAN... I NEVER THOUGHT PAST GETTING A GIRL...
ALICE, WHAT IF IT DOESN'T WORK OUT! WHAT IF I SCREW SOMETHING UP?!
OH GOD, IT COULD ALL BE RUINED!
HAHA, SETTLE DOWN THERE... I THINK IT'LL BE OKAY.
AND EVEN IF THINGS DON'T WORK OUT IN THE END, YOU'LL ALWAYS HAVE THE MEMORIES, RIGHT?
YEAH, THAT'S TRUE.
I'LL ALWAYS CHERISH THE MAMMARIES.
MEMORIES.
THOSE TOO.

Alice brings Hawk back down to earth, and he understandably freaks a bit. Hawk's face in the last panel might be the creepiest face he's made in the comic to date . . . He's just off in his own little world, isn't he?

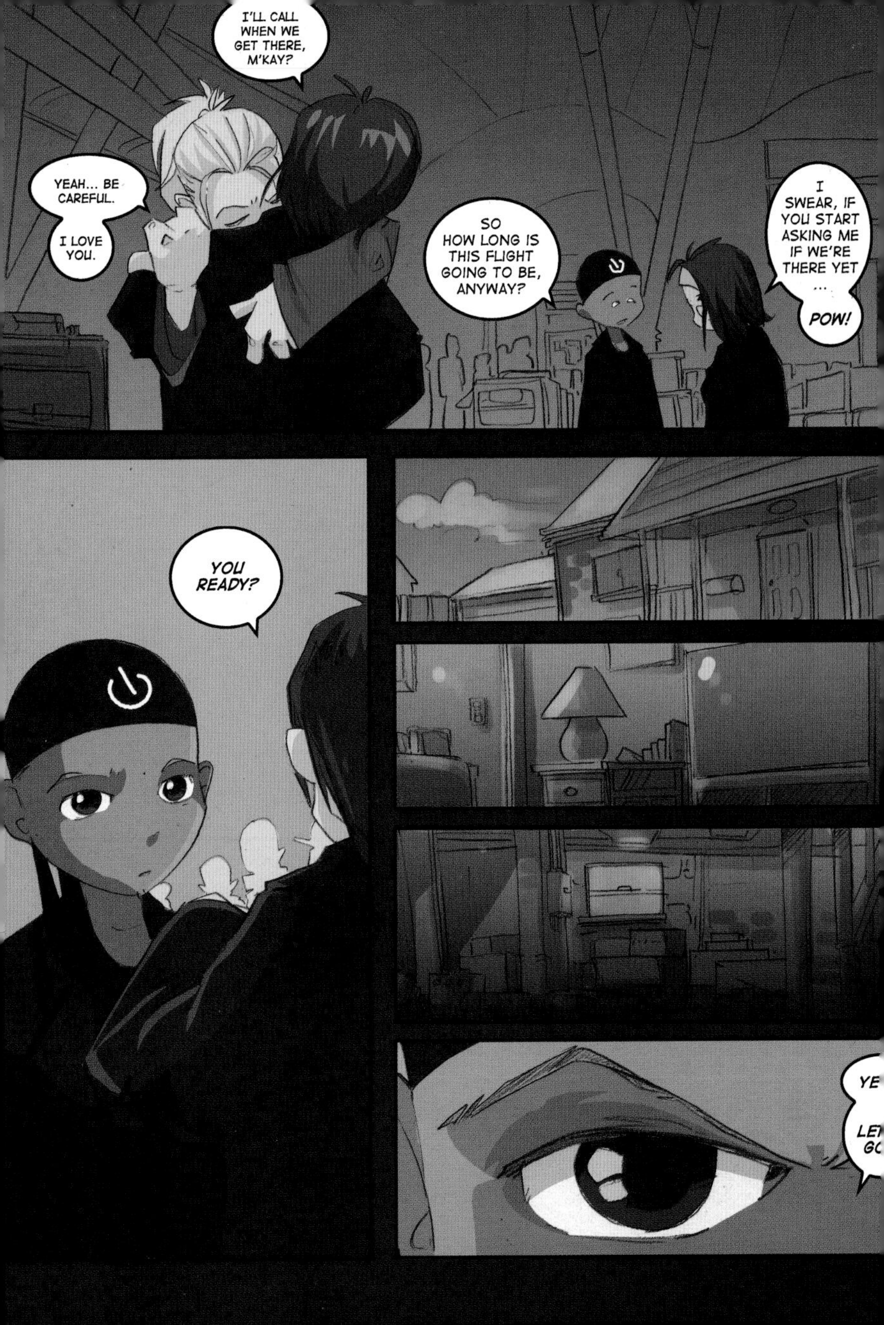
I'LL CALL WHEN WE GET THERE, M'KAY?
YEAH... BE CAREFUL.
I LOVE YOU.
SO HOW LONG IS THIS FLIGHT GOING TO BE, ANYWAY?
I SWEAR, IF YOU START ASKING ME IF WE'RE THERE YET ...
POW!
YOU READY?

e the airport is Reagan (DCA)! That's the airport we fly out of every time we do a show; it's right
and that makes it extra convenient. If you are hungry and have a little time to kill before you pass

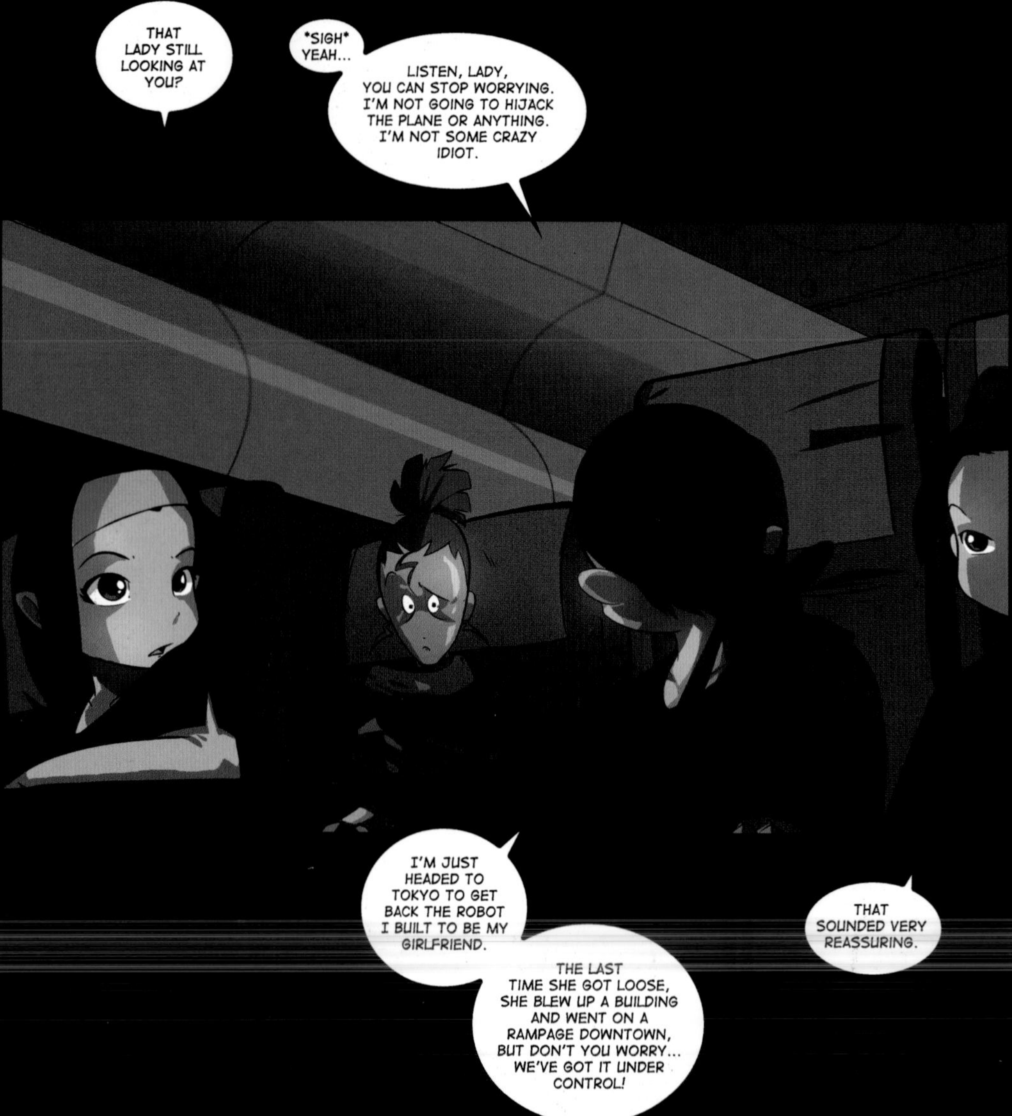
THAT LADY STILL LOOKING AT YOU?
SIGH YEAH...
LISTEN, LADY, YOU CAN STOP WORRYING. I'M NOT GOING TO HIJACK THE PLANE OR ANYTHING. I'M NOT SOME CRAZY IDIOT.
I'M JUST HEADED TO TOKYO TO GET BACK THE ROBOT I BUILT TO BE MY GIRLFRIEND.
THE LAST TIME SHE GOT LOOSE, SHE BLEW UP A BUILDING AND WENT ON A RAMPAGE DOWNTOWN, BUT DON'T YOU WORRY... WE'VE GOT IT UNDER CONTROL!
THAT SOUNDED VERY REASSURING.

Hahaha . . . We can turn it into a joke here, but when we were flying post 9/11, we took extra care in what we said out loud, and specifically what kind of jokes we cracked. Everyone was all ramped up and oversensitive, and it was (and sometimes still is) a huge pain in the ass. There's nothing worse than an overzealous passenger or TSA agent.

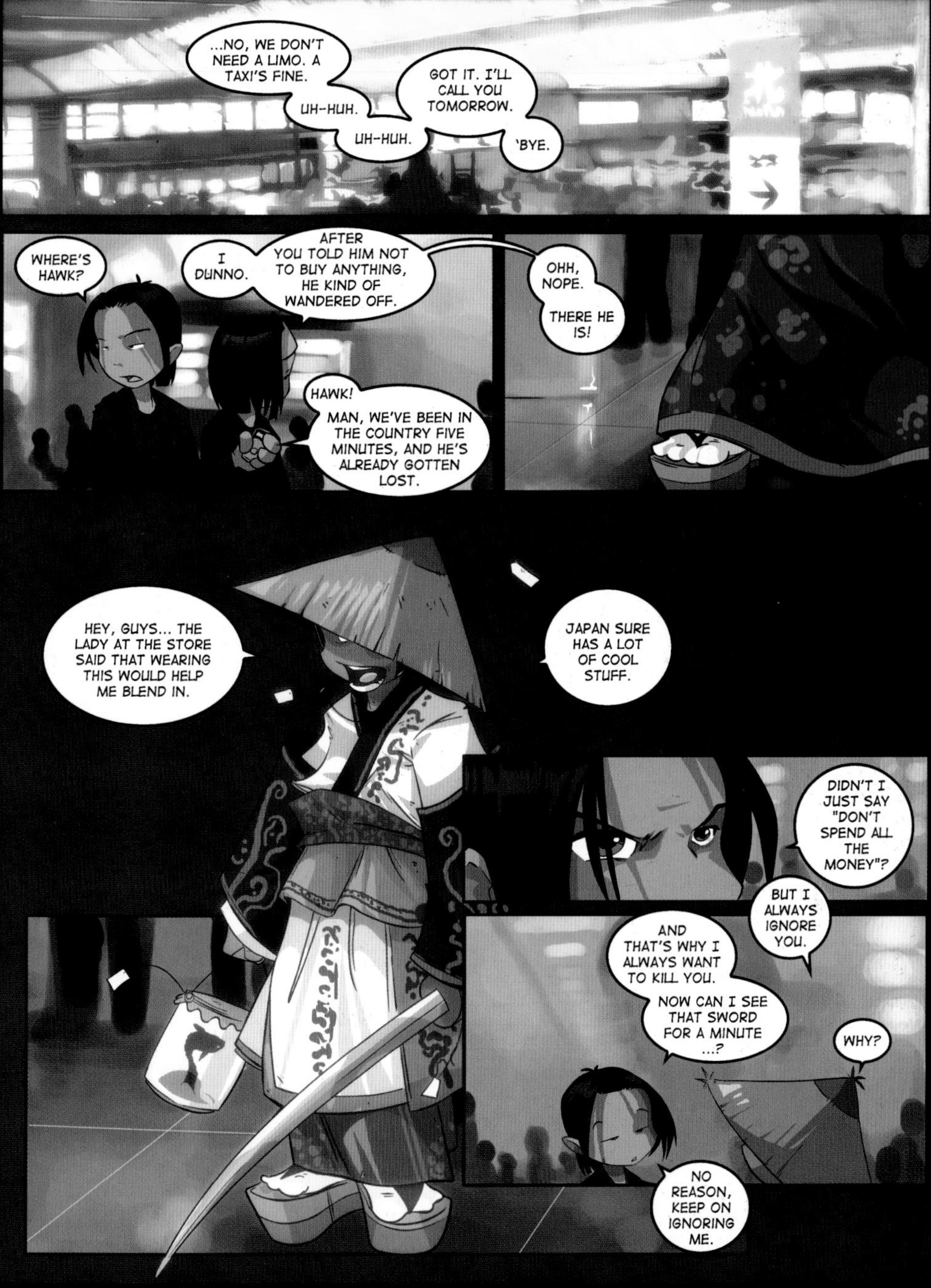
...NO, WE DON'T NEED A LIMO. A TAXI'S FINE.
UH-HUH.
UH-HUH.
GOT IT. I'LL CALL YOU TOMORROW.
'BYE.
WHERE'S HAWK?
I DUNNO.
AFTER YOU TOLD HIM NOT TO BUY ANYTHING, HE KIND OF WANDERED OFF.
HAWK!
MAN, WE'VE BEEN IN THE COUNTRY FIVE MINUTES, AND HE'S ALREADY GOTTEN LOST.
OHH, NOPE.
THERE HE IS!
HEY, GUYS... THE LADY AT THE STORE SAID THAT WEARING THIS WOULD HELP ME BLEND IN.
JAPAN SURE HAS A LOT OF COOL STUFF.
DIDN'T I JUST SAY "DON'T SPEND ALL THE MONEY"?
BUT I ALWAYS IGNORE YOU.
AND THAT'S WHY I ALWAYS WANT TO KILL YOU.
NOW CAN I SEE THAT SWORD FOR A MINUTE ...?
WHY?
NO REASON, KEEP ON IGNORING ME.

Okay, so this comic is grounded in 100 percent fact. We were headed to a show and Hawk turned to me and said, "I'm going to save all of my money this weekend." And he did. He made it past artist's alley and the dealer's room, and resisted all temptation to buy anything at all. On our flight back we had a layover, and I had to make a call, so he wandered off . . . When I found him, he was walking out of a Brookstone with two bags full of electronics. I had to pay for his lunch. Way to go, man.

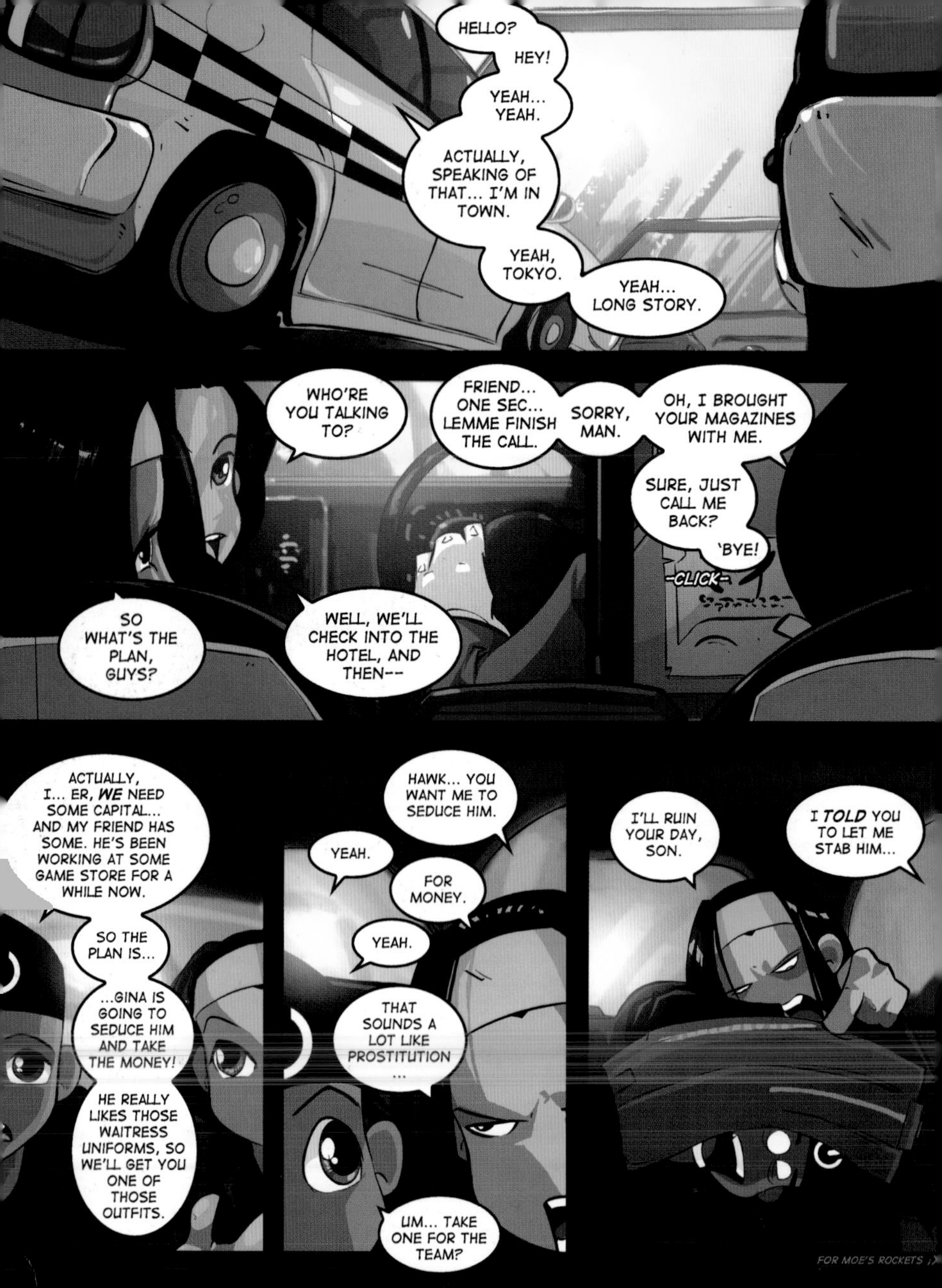
HELLO?
HEY!
YEAH... YEAH.
ACTUALLY, SPEAKING OF THAT... I'M IN TOWN.
YEAH, TOKYO.
YEAH... LONG STORY.
WHO'RE YOU TALKING TO?
FRIEND... ONE SEC... LEMME FINISH THE CALL.
SORRY, MAN.
OH, I BROUGHT YOUR MAGAZINES WITH ME.
SURE, JUST CALL ME BACK?
'BYE!
-CLICK-
SO WHAT'S THE PLAN, GUYS?
WELL, WE'LL CHECK INTO THE HOTEL, AND THEN--
ACTUALLY, I... ER, *WE* NEED SOME CAPITAL... AND MY FRIEND HAS SOME. HE'S BEEN WORKING AT SOME GAME STORE FOR A WHILE NOW.
SO THE PLAN IS...
...GINA IS GOING TO SEDUCE HIM AND TAKE THE MONEY!
HE REALLY LIKES THOSE WAITRESS UNIFORMS, SO WE'LL GET YOU ONE OF THOSE OUTFITS.
HAWK... YOU WANT ME TO SEDUCE HIM.
YEAH.
FOR MONEY.
YEAH.
THAT SOUNDS A LOT LIKE PROSTITUTION ...
UM... TAKE ONE FOR THE TEAM?
I'LL RUIN YOUR DAY, SON.
I *TOLD* YOU TO LET ME STAB HIM...
FOR MOE'S ROCKETS

ase it's not clear, the guy on the other end of that phone call is Piro from *Megatokyo*. The "magazines" refe

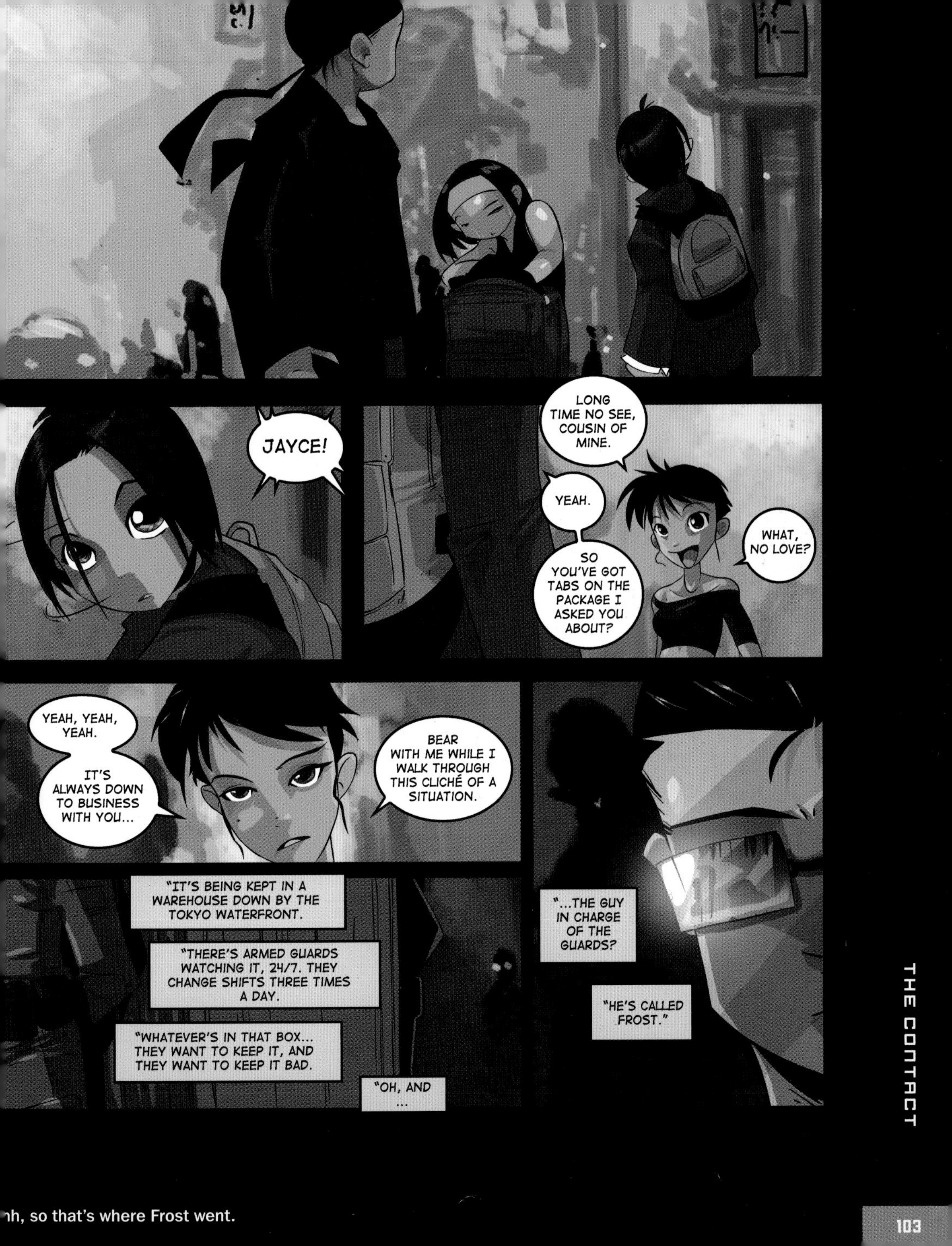
JAYCE!
LONG TIME NO SEE, COUSIN OF MINE.
YEAH.
SO YOU'VE GOT TABS ON THE PACKAGE I ASKED YOU ABOUT?
WHAT, NO LOVE?
YEAH, YEAH, YEAH.
IT'S ALWAYS DOWN TO BUSINESS WITH YOU...
BEAR WITH ME WHILE I WALK THROUGH THIS CLICHÉ OF A SITUATION.
"IT'S BEING KEPT IN A WAREHOUSE DOWN BY THE TOKYO WATERFRONT.
"THERE'S ARMED GUARDS WATCHING IT, 24/7. THEY CHANGE SHIFTS THREE TIMES A DAY.
"WHATEVER'S IN THAT BOX... THEY WANT TO KEEP IT, AND THEY WANT TO KEEP IT BAD.
"OH, AND ...
"...THE GUY IN CHARGE OF THE GUARDS?
"HE'S CALLED FROST."

ıh, so that's where Frost went.

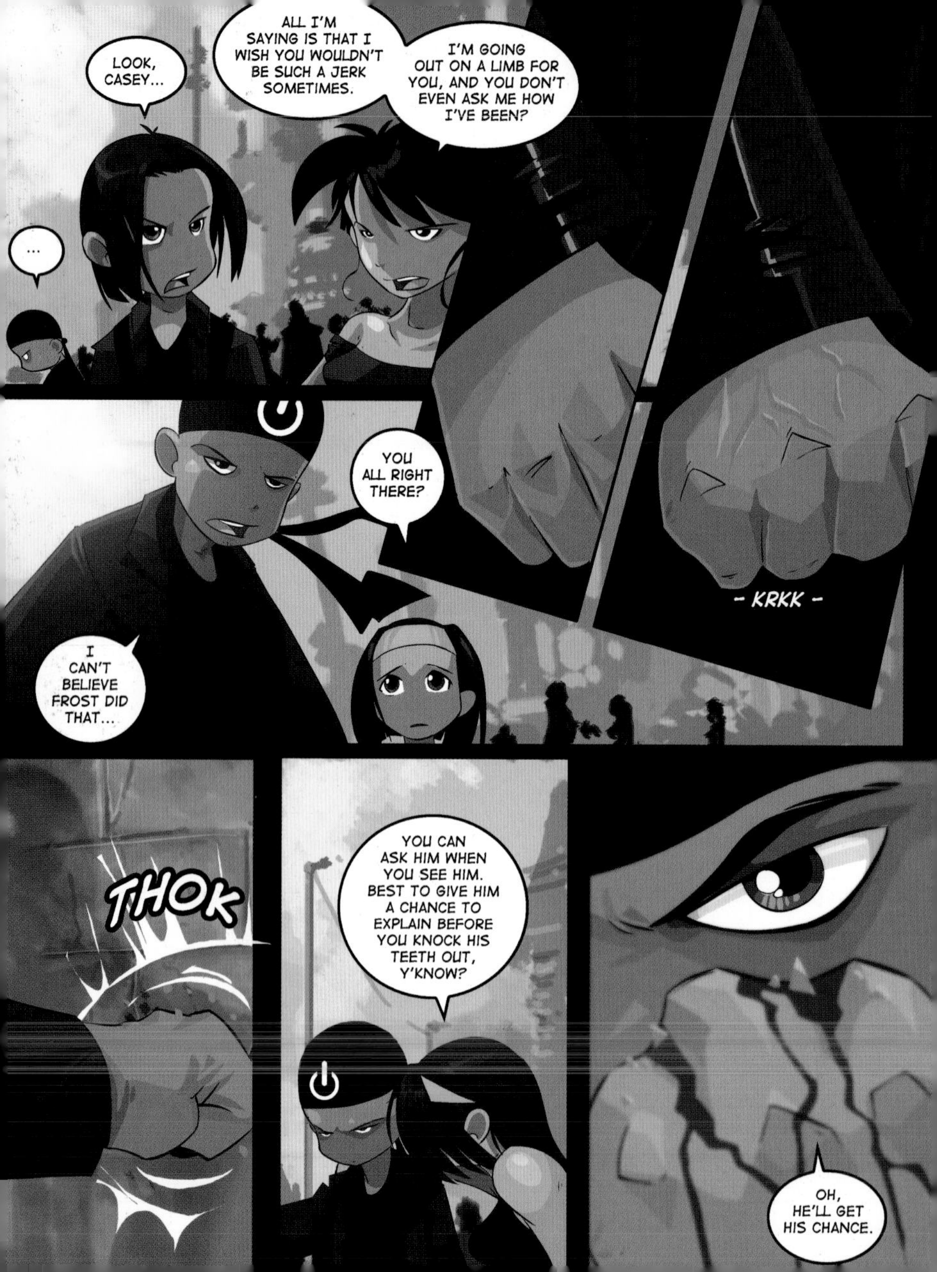
LOOK, CASEY...
ALL I'M SAYING IS THAT I WISH YOU WOULDN'T BE SUCH A JERK SOMETIMES.
I'M GOING OUT ON A LIMB FOR YOU, AND YOU DON'T EVEN ASK ME HOW I'VE BEEN?
...
- KRKK -
YOU ALL RIGHT THERE?
I CAN'T BELIEVE FROST DID THAT...
THOK
YOU CAN ASK HIM WHEN YOU SEE HIM. BEST TO GIVE HIM A CHANCE TO EXPLAIN BEFORE YOU KNOCK HIS TEETH OUT, Y'KNOW?
OH, HE'LL GET HIS CHANCE.

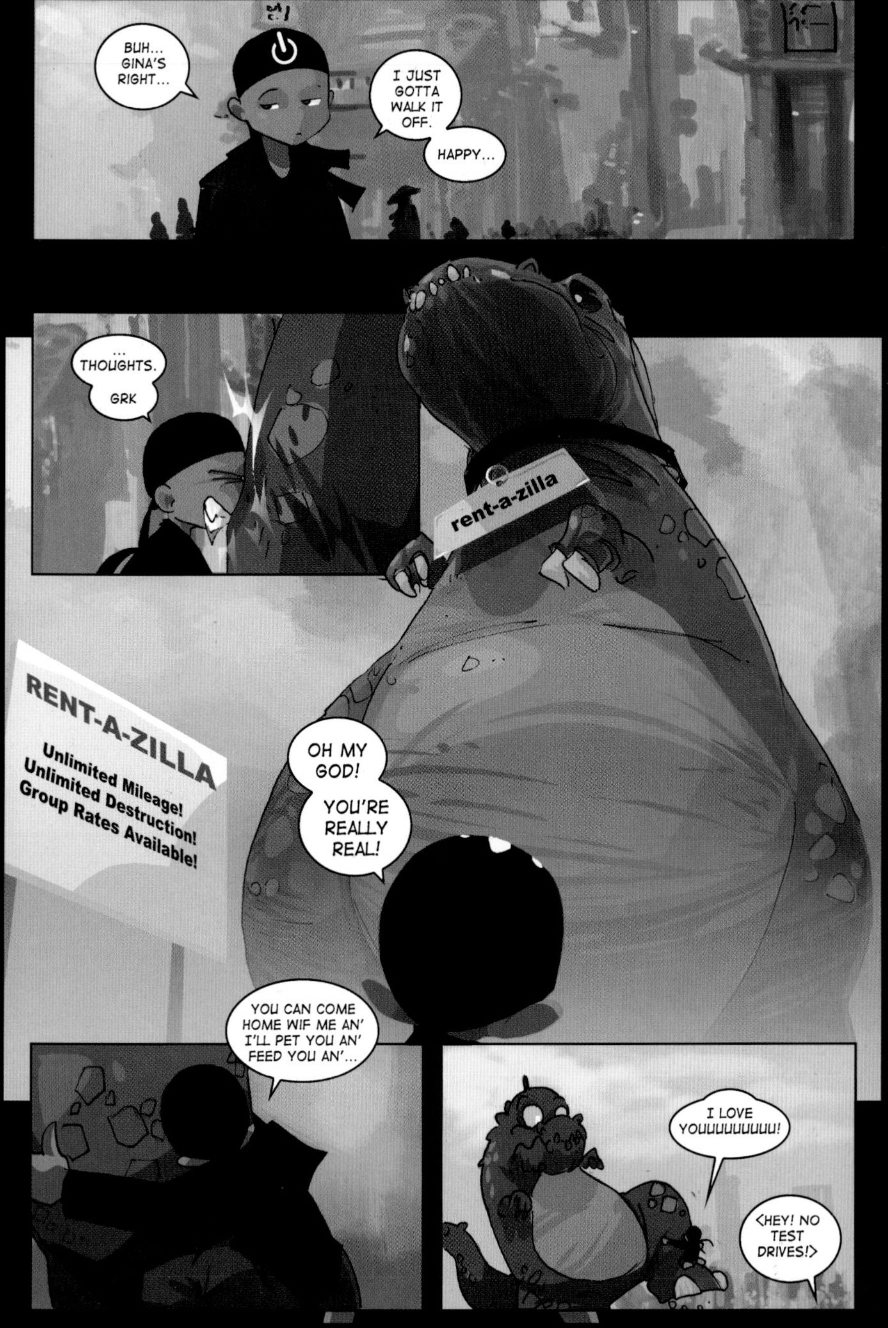
BUH... GINA'S RIGHT...
I JUST GOTTA WALK IT OFF.
HAPPY...
... THOUGHTS.
GRK
rent-a-zilla
RENT-A-ZILLA
Unlimited Mileage!
Unlimited Destruction!
Group Rates Available!
OH MY GOD!
YOU'RE REALLY REAL!
YOU CAN COME HOME WIF ME AN' I'LL PET YOU AN' FEED YOU AN'...
I LOVE YOUUUUUUUUU!
<HEY! NO TEST DRIVES!>

Rent-a-zilla is a character from *Megatokyo* that we *had* to find an excuse to borrow while the *Applegeeks* crew was in Tokyo. Since cartoon Hawk was angry and Fred needed a filler strip, we had Hawk bump into a Rent-a-zilla dealership. I imagine it works a lot like car rentals, only insurance is mandatory and a good deal more than the rental fee.

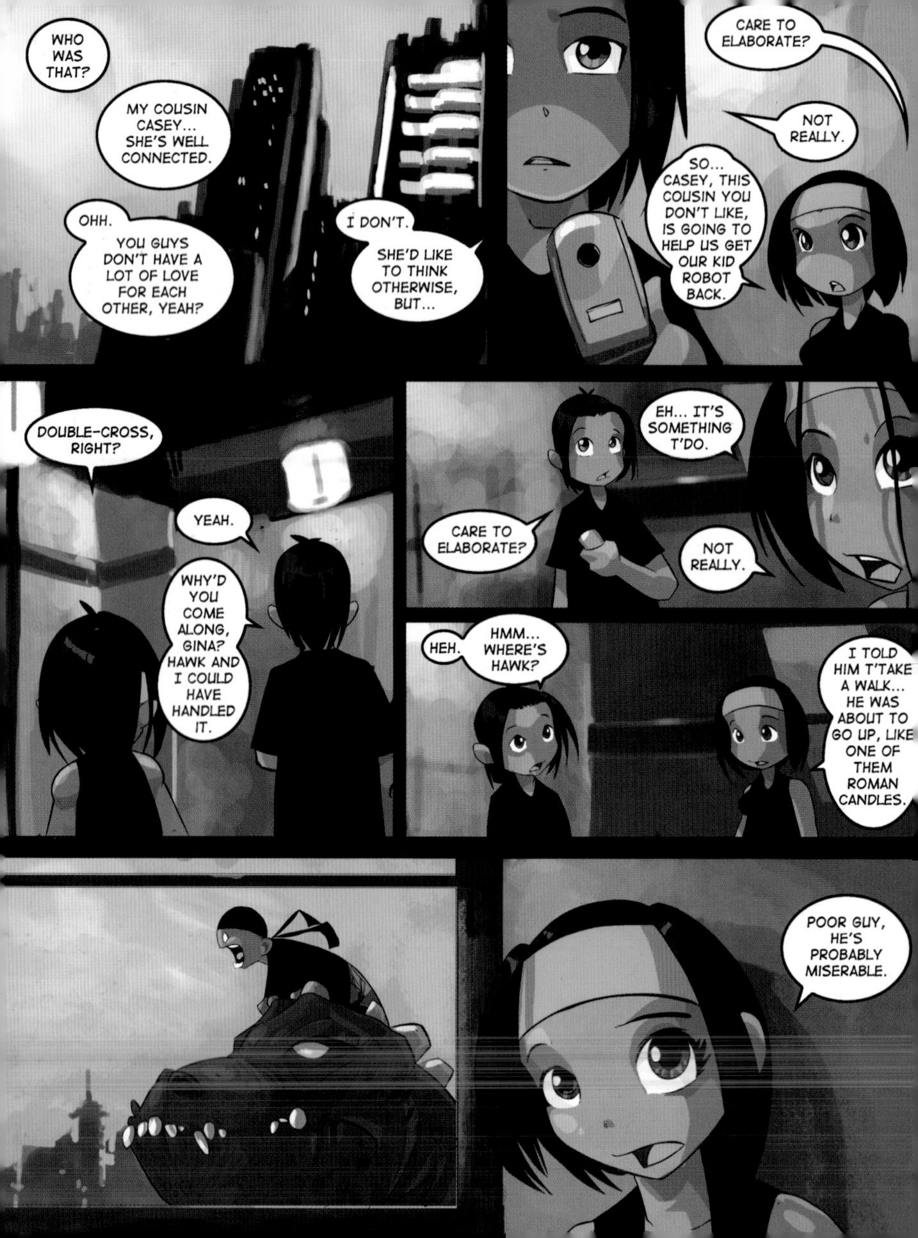
WHO WAS THAT?
MY COUSIN CASEY... SHE'S WELL CONNECTED.
OHH.
YOU GUYS DON'T HAVE A LOT OF LOVE FOR EACH OTHER, YEAH?
I DON'T.
SHE'D LIKE TO THINK OTHERWISE, BUT...
CARE TO ELABORATE?
NOT REALLY.
SO... CASEY, THIS COUSIN YOU DON'T LIKE, IS GOING TO HELP US GET OUR KID ROBOT BACK.
DOUBLE-CROSS, RIGHT?
YEAH.
WHY'D YOU COME ALONG, GINA? HAWK AND I COULD HAVE HANDLED IT.
EH... IT'S SOMETHING T'DO.
CARE TO ELABORATE?
NOT REALLY.
HEH.
HMM... WHERE'S HAWK?
I TOLD HIM T'TAKE A WALK... HE WAS ABOUT TO GO UP, LIKE ONE OF THEM ROMAN CANDLES.
POOR GUY, HE'S PROBABLY MISERABLE.

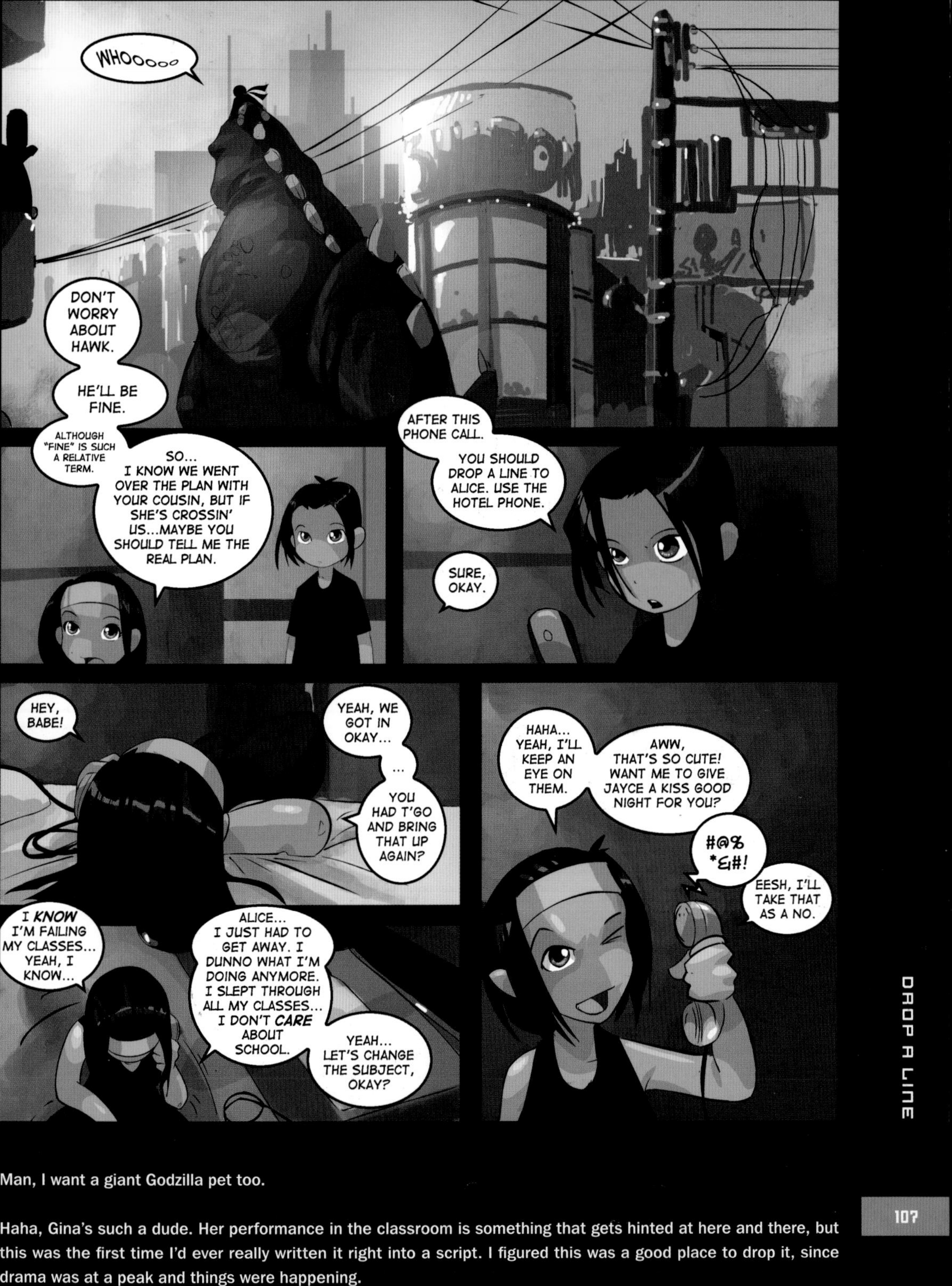
WHOOoooo
DON'T WORRY ABOUT HAWK.
HE'LL BE FINE.
ALTHOUGH "FINE" IS SUCH A RELATIVE TERM.
SO... I KNOW WE WENT OVER THE PLAN WITH YOUR COUSIN, BUT IF SHE'S CROSSIN' US...MAYBE YOU SHOULD TELL ME THE REAL PLAN.
AFTER THIS PHONE CALL.
YOU SHOULD DROP A LINE TO ALICE. USE THE HOTEL PHONE.
SURE, OKAY.
HEY, BABE!
YEAH, WE GOT IN OKAY...
...
YOU HAD T'GO AND BRING THAT UP AGAIN?
I *KNOW* I'M FAILING MY CLASSES... YEAH, I KNOW...
ALICE... I JUST HAD TO GET AWAY. I DUNNO WHAT I'M DOING ANYMORE. I SLEPT THROUGH ALL MY CLASSES... I DON'T *CARE* ABOUT SCHOOL.
YEAH... LET'S CHANGE THE SUBJECT, OKAY?
HAHA... YEAH, I'LL KEEP AN EYE ON THEM.
AWW, THAT'S SO CUTE! WANT ME TO GIVE JAYCE A KISS GOOD NIGHT FOR YOU?
#@% *&#!
EESH, I'LL TAKE THAT AS A NO.

Man, I want a giant Godzilla pet too.

Haha, Gina's such a dude. Her performance in the classroom is something that gets hinted at here and there, but this was the first time I'd ever really written it right into a script. I figured this was a good place to drop it, since drama was at a peak and things were happening.

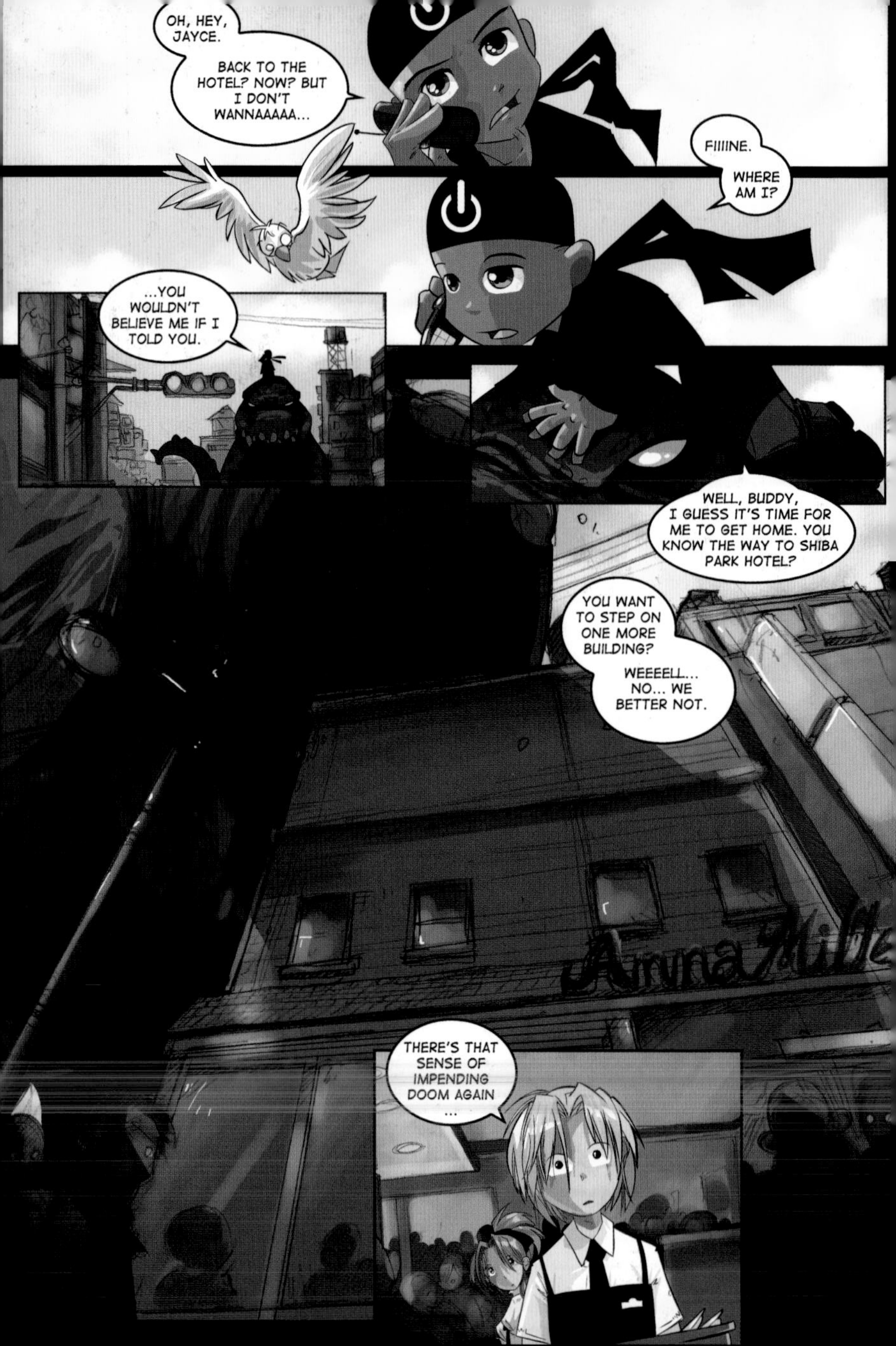
OH, HEY, JAYCE.
BACK TO THE HOTEL? NOW? BUT I DON'T WANNAAAAA...
FIIIINE.
WHERE AM I?
...YOU WOULDN'T BELIEVE ME IF I TOLD YOU.
WELL, BUDDY, I GUESS IT'S TIME FOR ME TO GET HOME. YOU KNOW THE WAY TO SHIBA PARK HOTEL?
YOU WANT TO STEP ON ONE MORE BUILDING?
WEEEELL... NO... WE BETTER NOT.
THERE'S THAT SENSE OF IMPENDING DOOM AGAIN ...

ne is another guest strip that was originally posted on megatokyo.com.

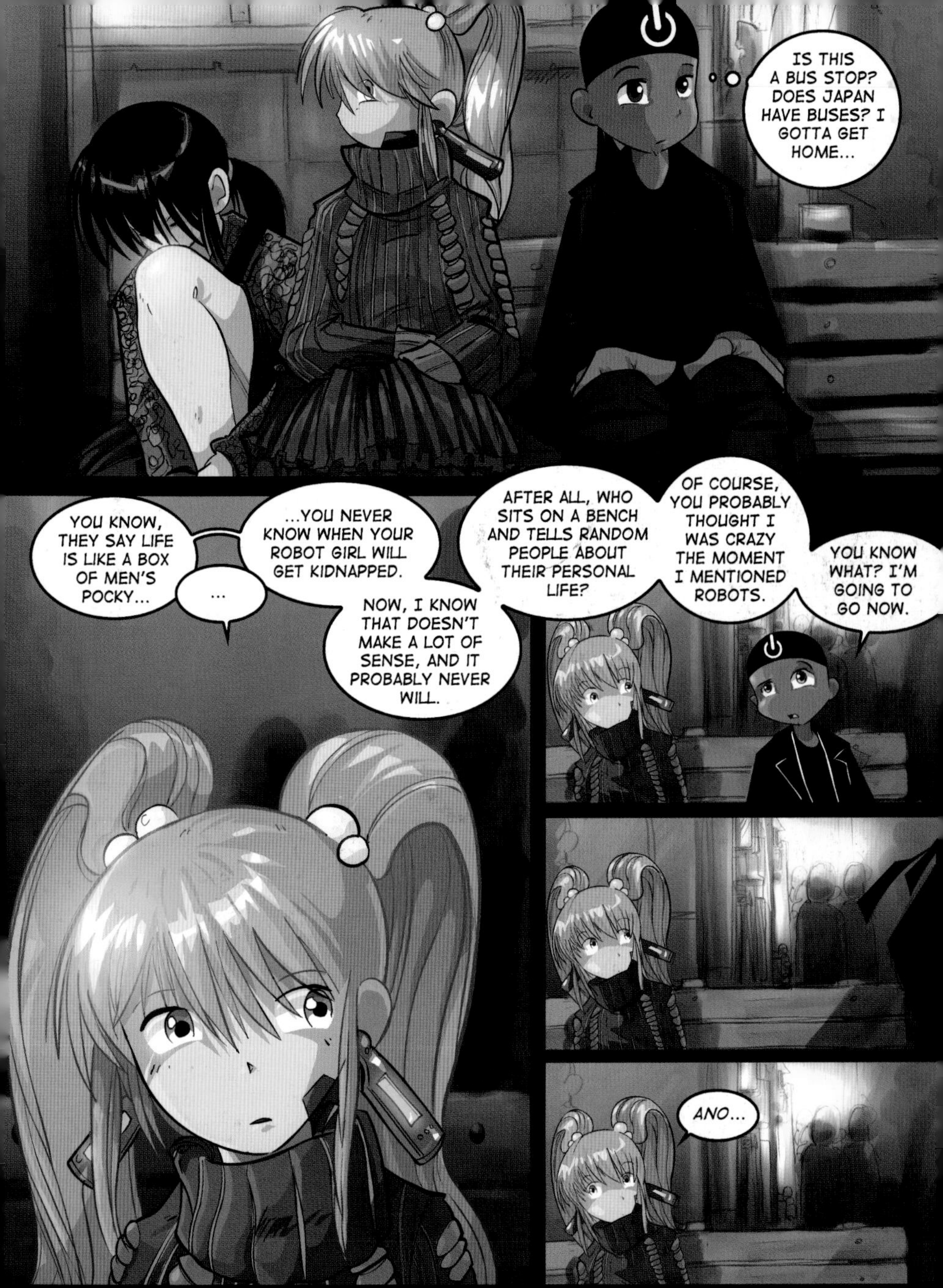
IS THIS A BUS STOP? DOES JAPAN HAVE BUSES? I GOTTA GET HOME...
YOU KNOW, THEY SAY LIFE IS LIKE A BOX OF MEN'S POCKY...
...YOU NEVER KNOW WHEN YOUR ROBOT GIRL WILL GET KIDNAPPED.
...
NOW, I KNOW THAT DOESN'T MAKE A LOT OF SENSE, AND IT PROBABLY NEVER WILL.
AFTER ALL, WHO SITS ON A BENCH AND TELLS RANDOM PEOPLE ABOUT THEIR PERSONAL LIFE?
OF COURSE, YOU PROBABLY THOUGHT I WAS CRAZY THE MOMENT I MENTIONED ROBOTS.
YOU KNOW WHAT? I'M GOING TO GO NOW.
ANO...

ore cameos! Ping is actually the robot PlayStation accessory from *Megatokyo*, so I always thought there were parallel etween her and Eva. I always thought it'd be cool to do a short crossover story with the two of them. Some day!

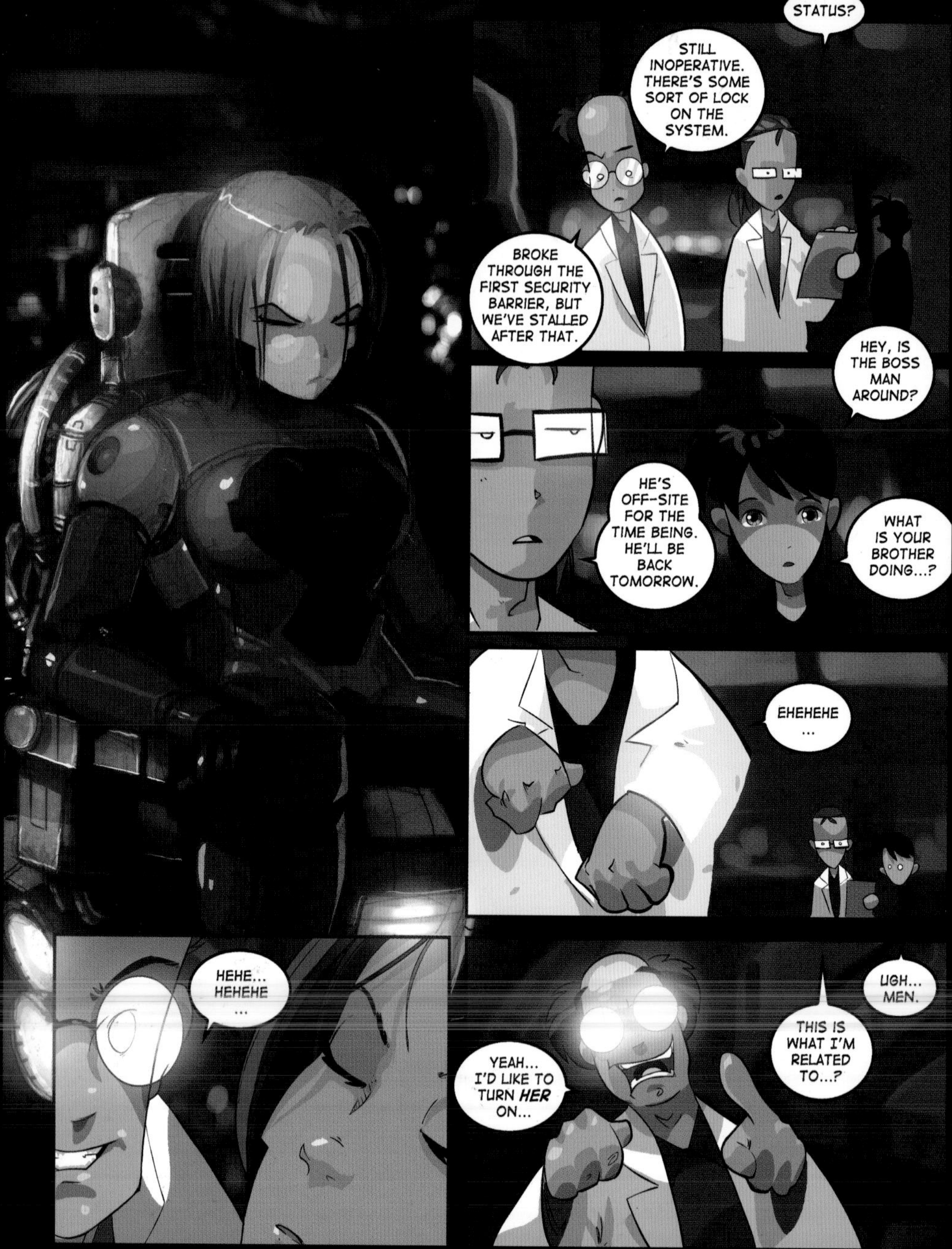
STATUS?
STILL INOPERATIVE. THERE'S SOME SORT OF LOCK ON THE SYSTEM.
BROKE THROUGH THE FIRST SECURITY BARRIER, BUT WE'VE STALLED AFTER THAT.
HEY, IS THE BOSS MAN AROUND?
HE'S OFF-SITE FOR THE TIME BEING. HE'LL BE BACK TOMORROW.
WHAT IS YOUR BROTHER DOING...?
EHEHEHE ...
HEHE... HEHEHE ...
YEAH... I'D LIKE TO TURN *HER* ON...
THIS IS WHAT I'M RELATED TO...?
UGH... MEN.

TURN ON

Casey, you two-timer! Well, Gina and Jayce predicted as much. There's a Frankenstein's monster quality to the way Eve is drawn in the first panel, and she's misunderstood the way Frankenstein's monster was, but I maintain that she is 200 percent more adorable than that big green guy. Frankenstein's monster, if you're out there reading this, no offense, buddy! Don't beat me to a pulp!

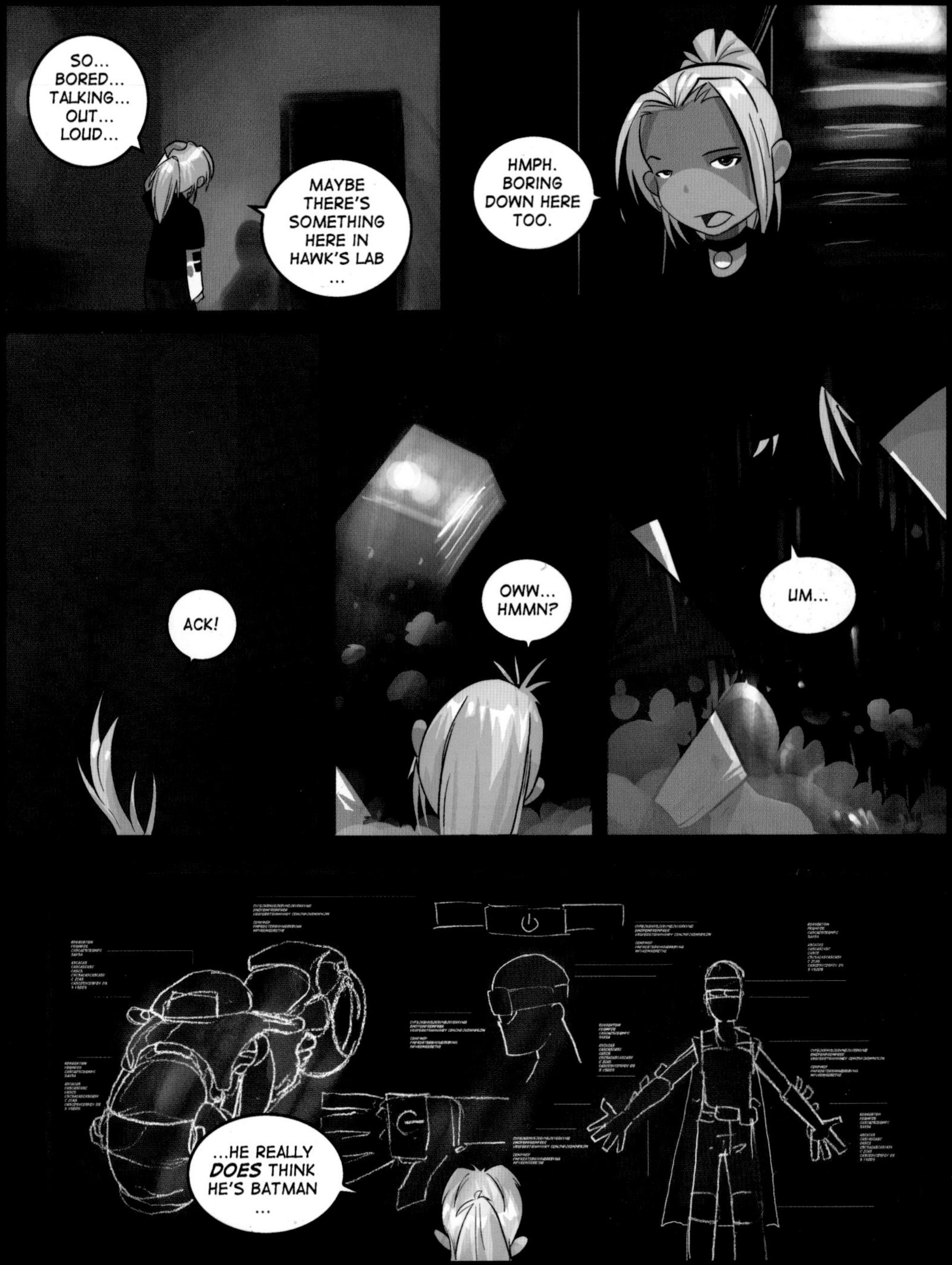
SO... BORED... TALKING... OUT... LOUD...
MAYBE THERE'S SOMETHING HERE IN HAWK'S LAB ...
HMPH. BORING DOWN HERE TOO.
ACK!
OWW... HMMN?
UM...
...HE REALLY ***DOES*** THINK HE'S BATMAN ...

Yes, yes he does.

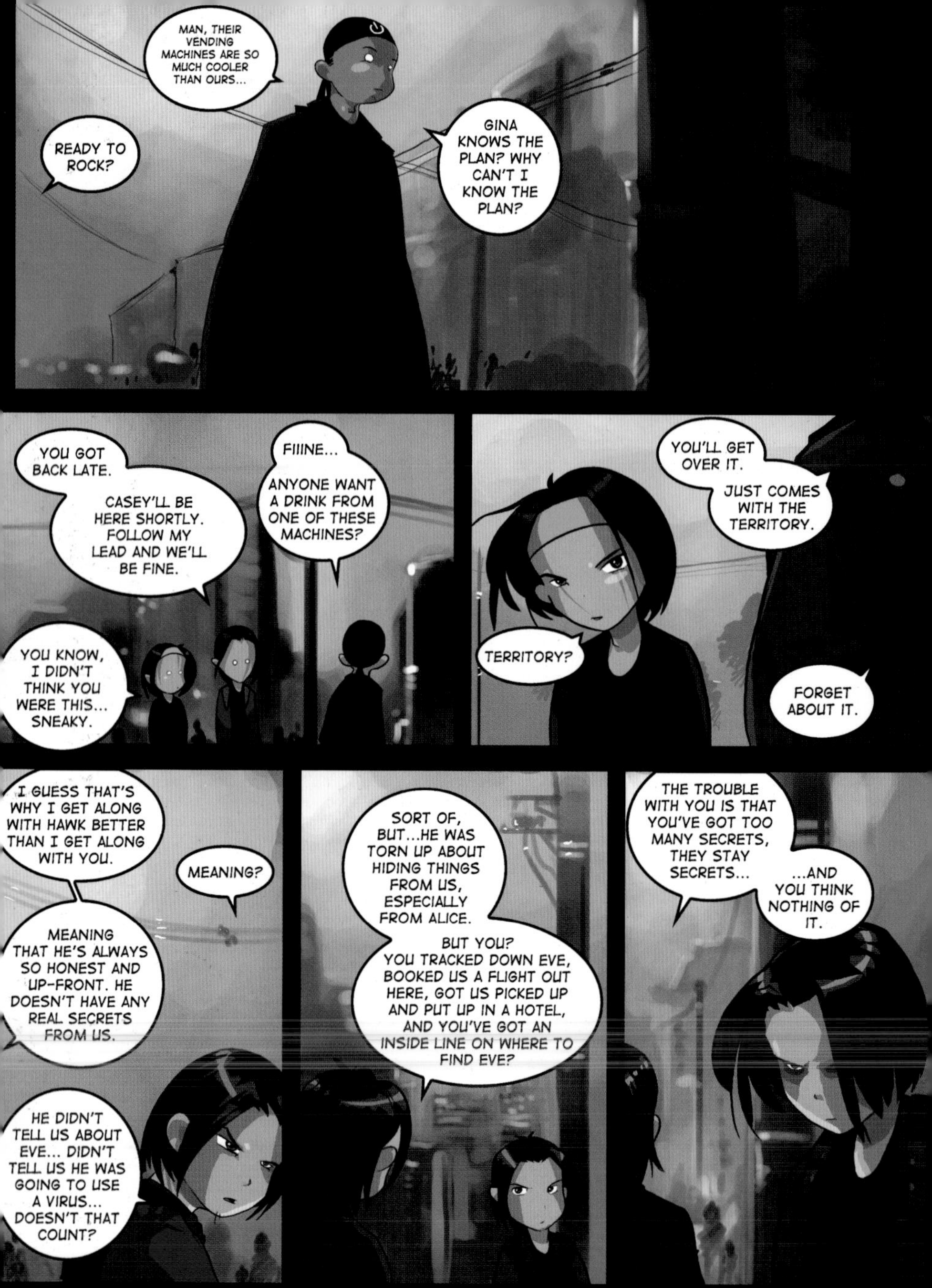
MAN, THEIR VENDING MACHINES ARE SO MUCH COOLER THAN OURS...
READY TO ROCK?
GINA KNOWS THE PLAN? WHY CAN'T I KNOW THE PLAN?
YOU GOT BACK LATE.
CASEY'LL BE HERE SHORTLY. FOLLOW MY LEAD AND WE'LL BE FINE.
FIIINE...
ANYONE WANT A DRINK FROM ONE OF THESE MACHINES?
YOU KNOW, I DIDN'T THINK YOU WERE THIS... SNEAKY.
YOU'LL GET OVER IT.
JUST COMES WITH THE TERRITORY.
TERRITORY?
FORGET ABOUT IT.
I GUESS THAT'S WHY I GET ALONG WITH HAWK BETTER THAN I GET ALONG WITH YOU.
MEANING?
MEANING THAT HE'S ALWAYS SO HONEST AND UP-FRONT. HE DOESN'T HAVE ANY REAL SECRETS FROM US.
HE DIDN'T TELL US ABOUT EVE... DIDN'T TELL US HE WAS GOING TO USE A VIRUS... DOESN'T THAT COUNT?
SORT OF, BUT...HE WAS TORN UP ABOUT HIDING THINGS FROM US, ESPECIALLY FROM ALICE.
BUT YOU? YOU TRACKED DOWN EVE, BOOKED US A FLIGHT OUT HERE, GOT US PICKED UP AND PUT UP IN A HOTEL, AND YOU'VE GOT AN INSIDE LINE ON WHERE TO FIND EVE?
THE TROUBLE WITH YOU IS THAT YOU'VE GOT TOO MANY SECRETS, THEY STAY SECRETS...
...AND YOU THINK NOTHING OF IT.

guys, come on . . . Group hug! Actually, you know who *really* needs a group hug? Batman. He's got Nightwin
mmissioner Gordon, Batgirl, Oracle, Robin, Alfred, and more . . . and yet the guy can't even crack a smile. What

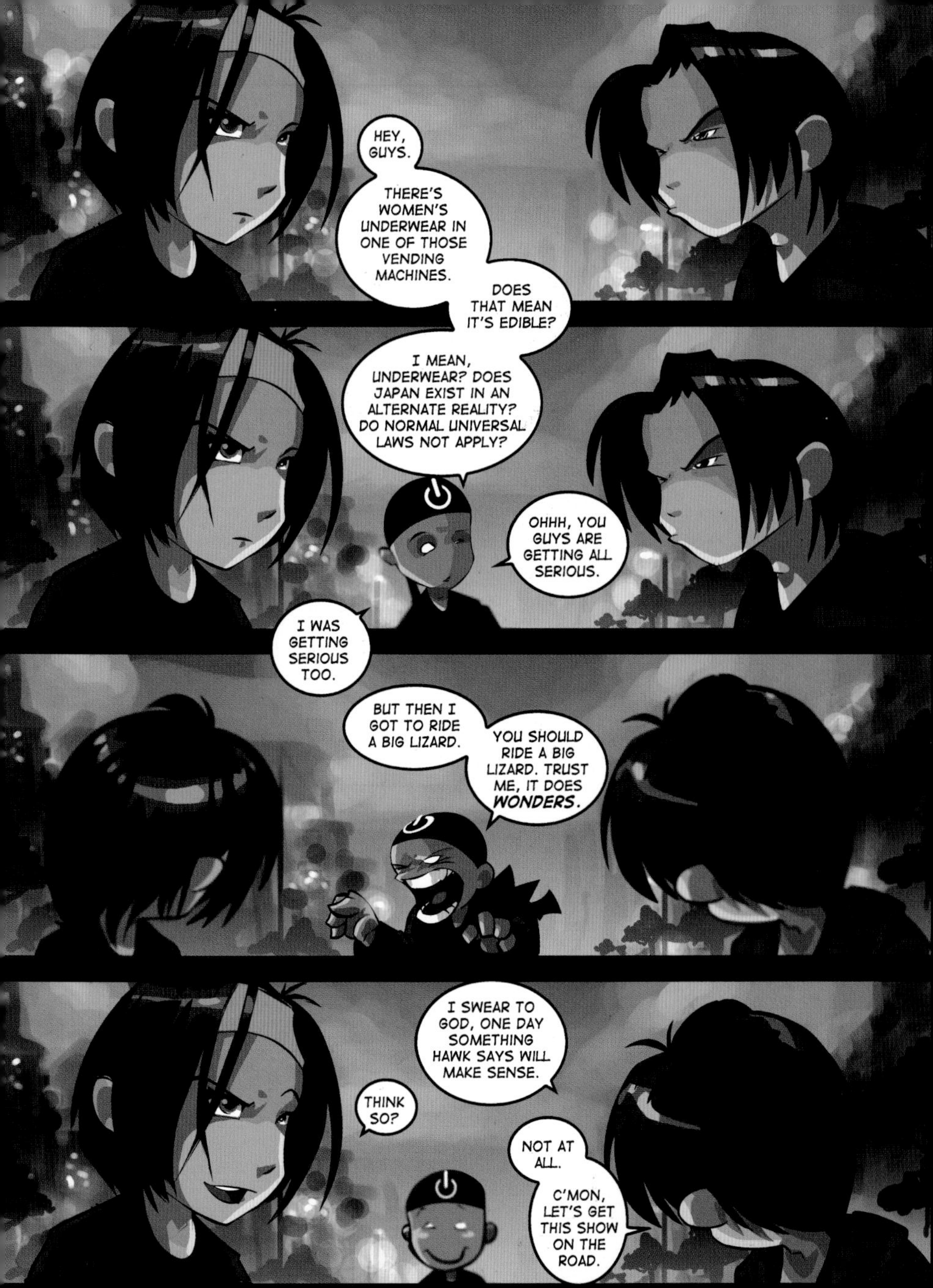
HEY, GUYS.
THERE'S WOMEN'S UNDERWEAR IN ONE OF THOSE VENDING MACHINES.
DOES THAT MEAN IT'S EDIBLE?
I MEAN, UNDERWEAR? DOES JAPAN EXIST IN AN ALTERNATE REALITY? DO NORMAL UNIVERSAL LAWS NOT APPLY?
OHHH, YOU GUYS ARE GETTING ALL SERIOUS.
I WAS GETTING SERIOUS TOO.
BUT THEN I GOT TO RIDE A BIG LIZARD.
YOU SHOULD RIDE A BIG LIZARD. TRUST ME, IT DOES ***WONDERS***.
I SWEAR TO GOD, ONE DAY SOMETHING HAWK SAYS WILL MAKE SENSE.
THINK SO?
NOT AT ALL.
C'MON, LET'S GET THIS SHOW ON THE ROAD.

the six years we've been doing *Applegeeks*, this is hands down one of my favorite pages that Hawk has illustrated.

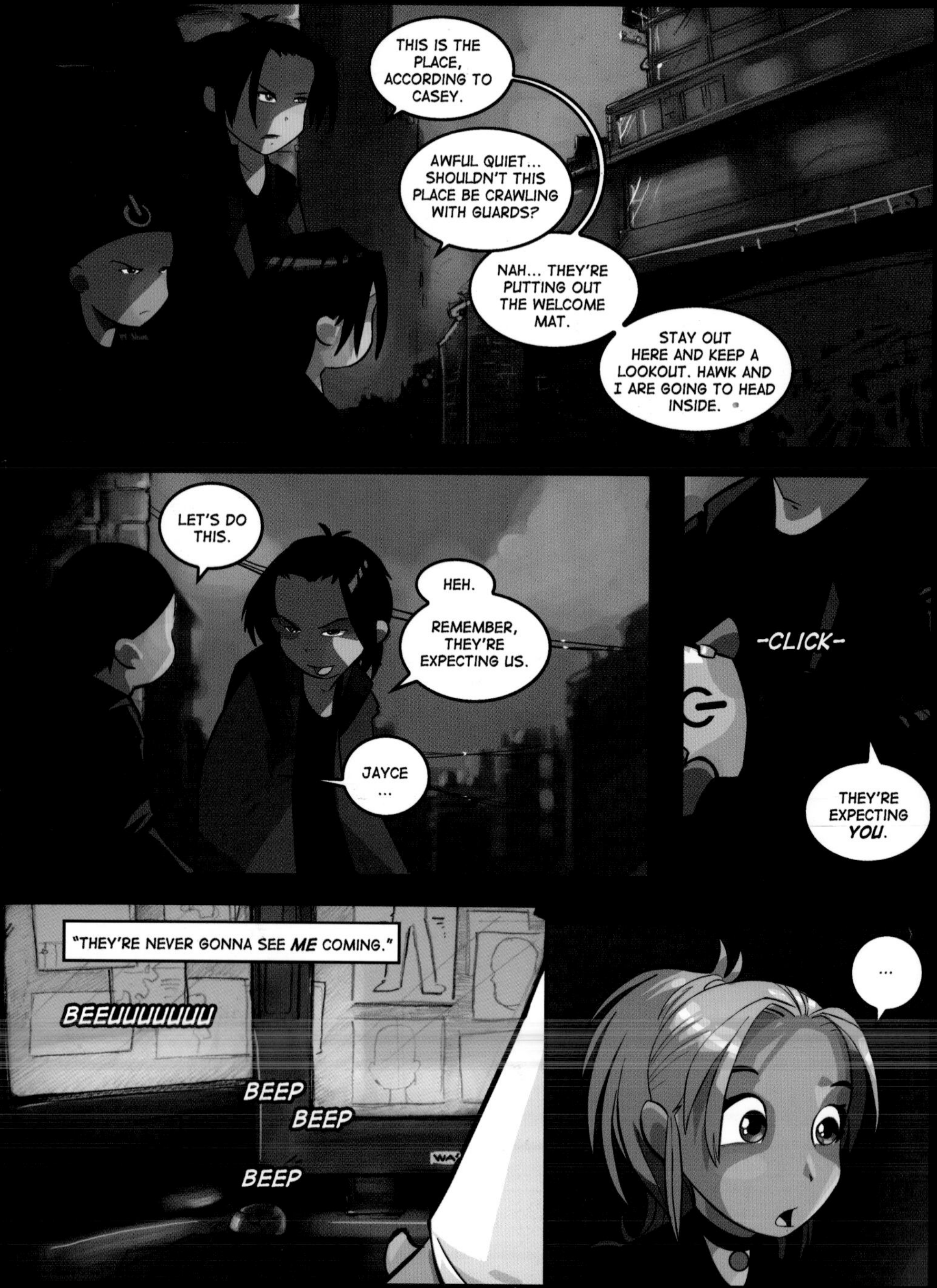
THIS IS THE PLACE, ACCORDING TO CASEY.
AWFUL QUIET... SHOULDN'T THIS PLACE BE CRAWLING WITH GUARDS?
NAH... THEY'RE PUTTING OUT THE WELCOME MAT.
STAY OUT HERE AND KEEP A LOOKOUT. HAWK AND I ARE GOING TO HEAD INSIDE.
LET'S DO THIS.
HEH.
REMEMBER, THEY'RE EXPECTING US.
JAYCE ...
-CLICK-
THEY'RE EXPECTING *YOU*.
"THEY'RE NEVER GONNA SEE *ME* COMING."
BEEUUUUUUU
BEEP
BEEP
BEEP
...

In panel four, the monitor on the right is modeled after the Wacom Cintiq. There are a lot of misconceptions about the Cintiq, the biggest one being that it will make you a better artist. Practice makes you a better artist—a Cintiq will only make you faster. It depends on the task, but with the combination of Photoshop hot keys and the Cintiq, Hawk sometimes manages to cut his work time down to half of what it used to be.

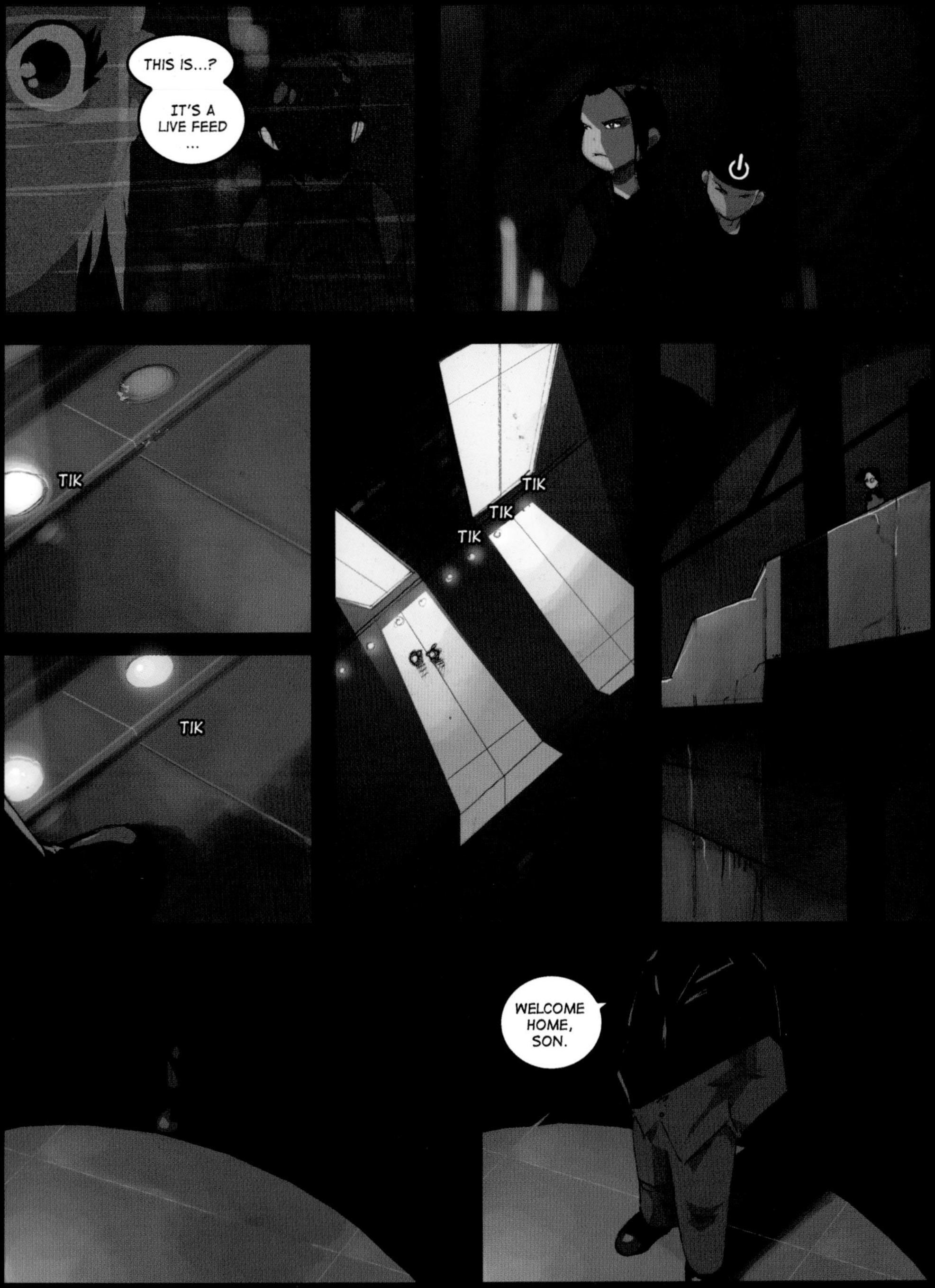
THIS IS...?
IT'S A LIVE FEED ...
TIK
TIK
TIK
TIK
TIK
WELCOME HOME, SON.

People often wonder why *Applegeeks* is a little prone to being heavy on the dialogue. Answer: When you post comics to the web two days a week, those two pages really have to speak until the next time you update. It's rare that we dedicate an entire page to ambience and working up to a moment, but in this case we felt it really behooved us to go that route.

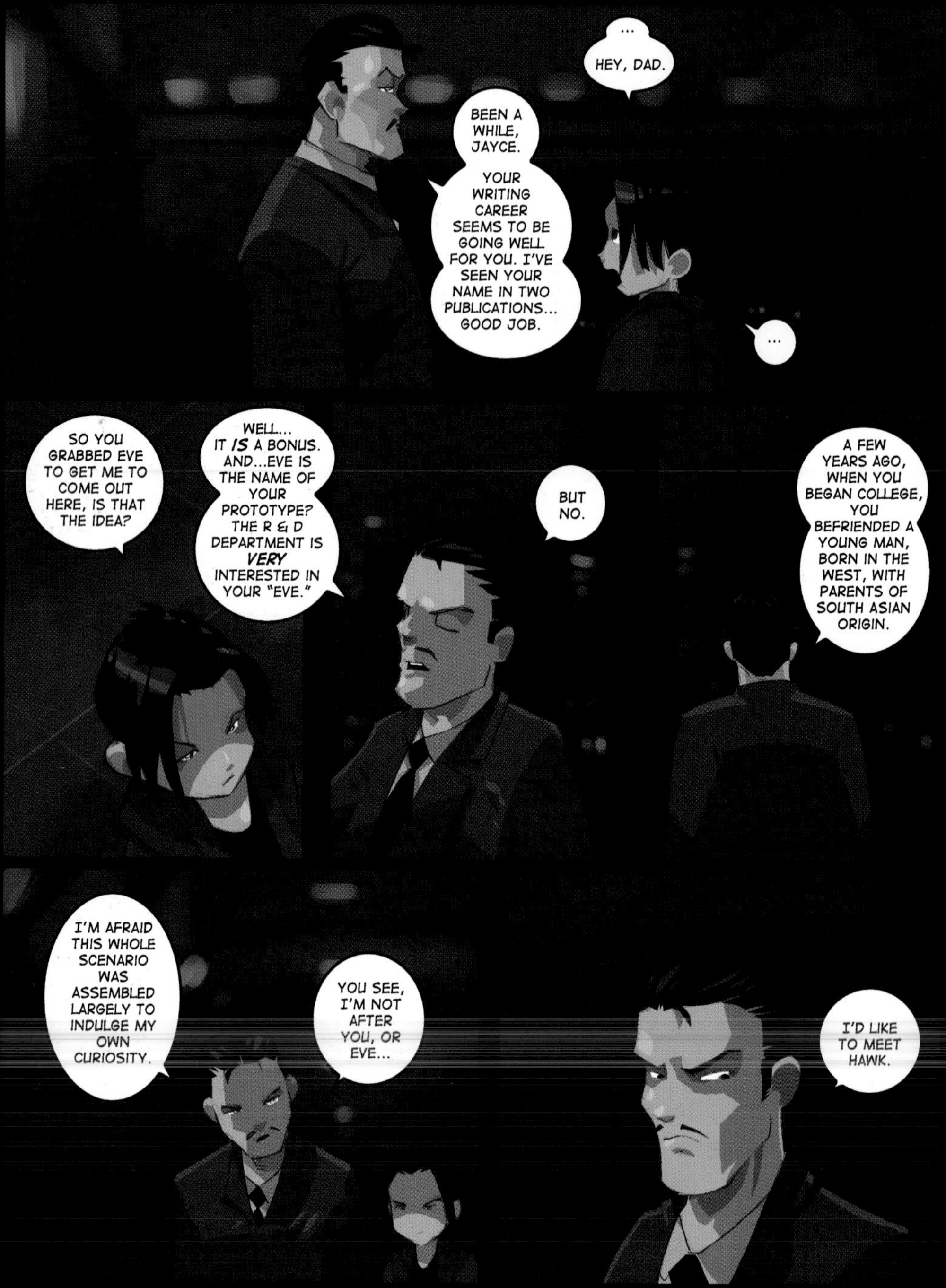
...
HEY, DAD.
BEEN A WHILE, JAYCE.
YOUR WRITING CAREER SEEMS TO BE GOING WELL FOR YOU. I'VE SEEN YOUR NAME IN TWO PUBLICATIONS... GOOD JOB.
...
SO YOU GRABBED EVE TO GET ME TO COME OUT HERE, IS THAT THE IDEA?
WELL... IT *IS* A BONUS. AND...EVE IS THE NAME OF YOUR PROTOTYPE? THE R & D DEPARTMENT IS ***VERY*** INTERESTED IN YOUR "EVE."
BUT NO.
A FEW YEARS AGO, WHEN YOU BEGAN COLLEGE, YOU BEFRIENDED A YOUNG MAN, BORN IN THE WEST, WITH PARENTS OF SOUTH ASIAN ORIGIN.
I'M AFRAID THIS WHOLE SCENARIO WAS ASSEMBLED LARGELY TO INDULGE MY OWN CURIOSITY.
YOU SEE, I'M NOT AFTER YOU, OR EVE...
I'D LIKE TO MEET HAWK.

Dude, all I'm saying is that is the 'stache of an evil man. It's a mustache with strong roots in villainy.

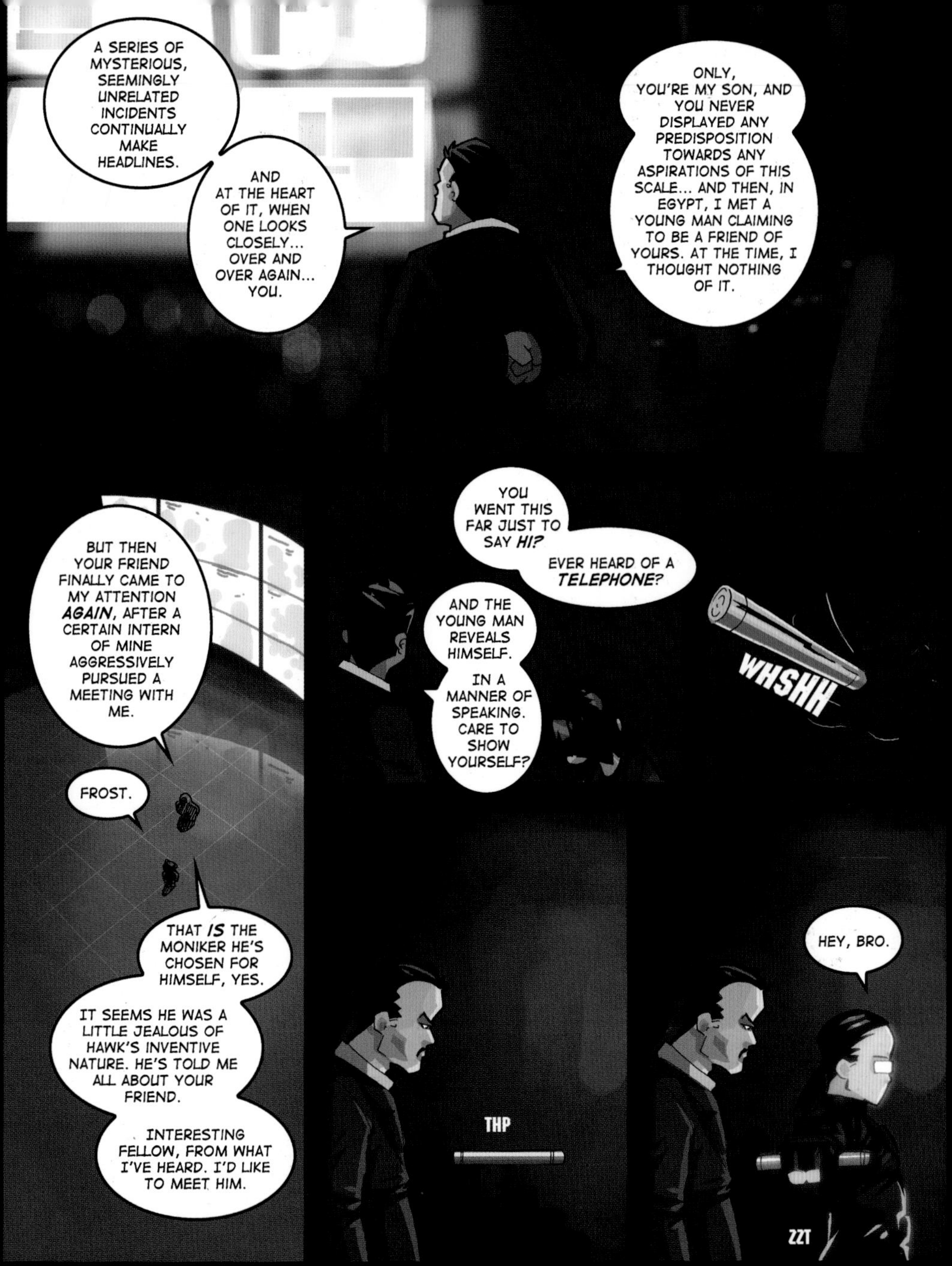
A SERIES OF MYSTERIOUS, SEEMINGLY UNRELATED INCIDENTS CONTINUALLY MAKE HEADLINES.
AND AT THE HEART OF IT, WHEN ONE LOOKS CLOSELY... OVER AND OVER AGAIN... YOU.
ONLY, YOU'RE MY SON, AND YOU NEVER DISPLAYED ANY PREDISPOSITION TOWARDS ANY ASPIRATIONS OF THIS SCALE... AND THEN, IN EGYPT, I MET A YOUNG MAN CLAIMING TO BE A FRIEND OF YOURS. AT THE TIME, I THOUGHT NOTHING OF IT.
BUT THEN YOUR FRIEND FINALLY CAME TO MY ATTENTION *AGAIN*, AFTER A CERTAIN INTERN OF MINE AGGRESSIVELY PURSUED A MEETING WITH ME.
FROST.
THAT *IS* THE MONIKER HE'S CHOSEN FOR HIMSELF, YES.
IT SEEMS HE WAS A LITTLE JEALOUS OF HAWK'S INVENTIVE NATURE. HE'S TOLD ME ALL ABOUT YOUR FRIEND.
INTERESTING FELLOW, FROM WHAT I'VE HEARD. I'D LIKE TO MEET HIM.
YOU WENT THIS FAR JUST TO SAY *HI?*
EVER HEARD OF A *TELEPHONE?*
AND THE YOUNG MAN REVEALS HIMSELF.
IN A MANNER OF SPEAKING. CARE TO SHOW YOURSELF?
WHSHH
THP
HEY, BRO.
ZZT

It's only mentioned in the narration, but Hawk met Jayce's father in Egypt way back when I was filling in on art duties (*Applegeeks* Vol. 1, pages 27–28). I had a lot of this loosely planned out from the beginning of *Applegeeks*, but the details filled themselves in as I went along (for instance, neither Hawk nor I had any idea Eve would join our cast). *Applegeeks* is written page by page due to the nature of updating on the web, and sometimes that makes pacing and continuity tricky.

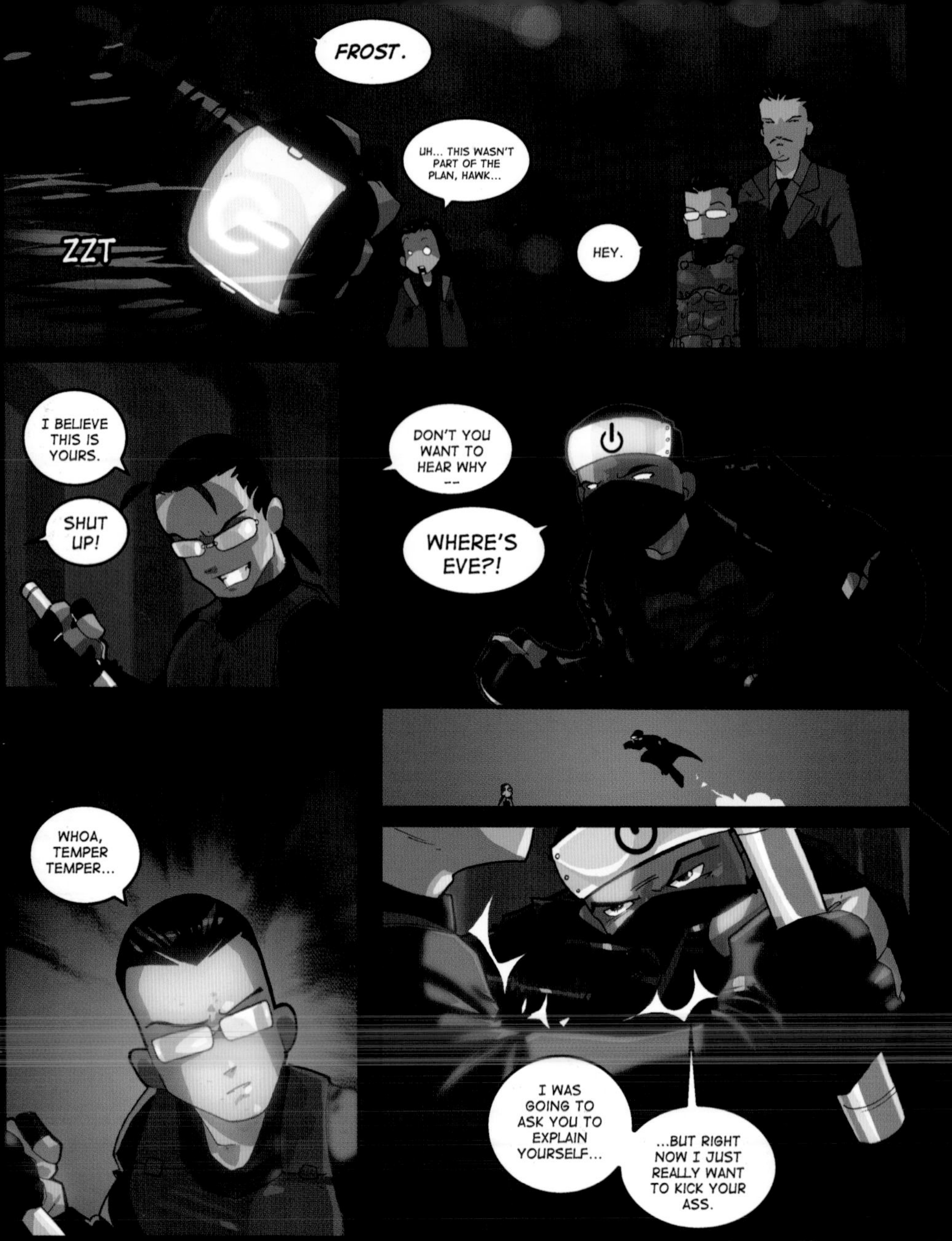
FROST.
UH... THIS WASN'T PART OF THE PLAN, HAWK...
ZZT
HEY.
I BELIEVE THIS IS YOURS.
SHUT UP!
DON'T YOU WANT TO HEAR WHY --
WHERE'S EVE?!
WHOA, TEMPER TEMPER...
I WAS GOING TO ASK YOU TO EXPLAIN YOURSELF...
...BUT RIGHT NOW I JUST REALLY WANT TO KICK YOUR ASS.

You can get the headband that Hawk has on from Jim over at Morlock Enterprises (morlockenterprises.com). We see Jim at almost all of the shows we do, and he is a righteous dude. He is an expert machinist with a heart of gold, and he will build you whatever props or accessories your heart desires.

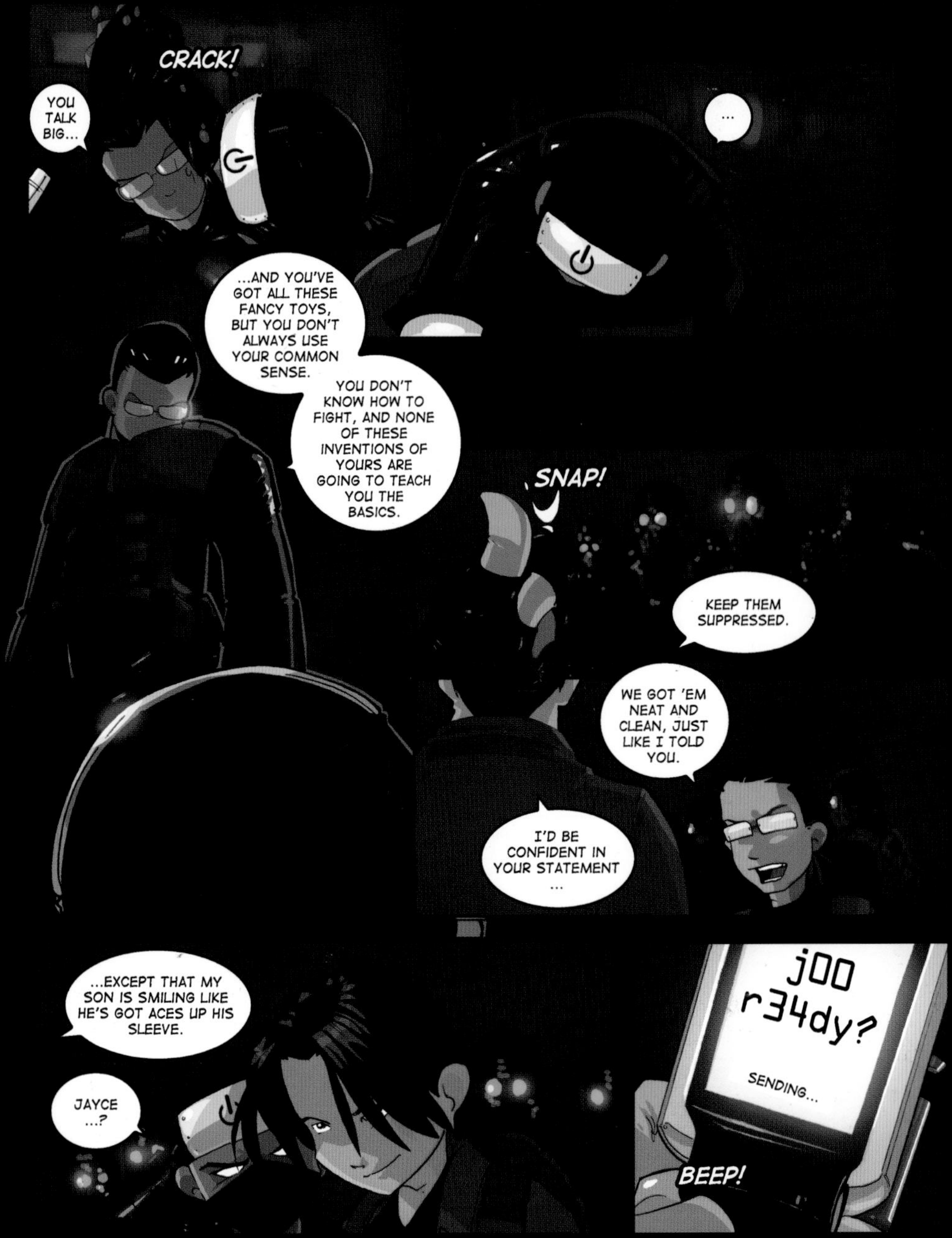
CRACK!
YOU TALK BIG...
...
...AND YOU'VE GOT ALL THESE FANCY TOYS, BUT YOU DON'T ALWAYS USE YOUR COMMON SENSE.
YOU DON'T KNOW HOW TO FIGHT, AND NONE OF THESE INVENTIONS OF YOURS ARE GOING TO TEACH YOU THE BASICS.
SNAP!
KEEP THEM SUPPRESSED.
WE GOT 'EM NEAT AND CLEAN, JUST LIKE I TOLD YOU.
I'D BE CONFIDENT IN YOUR STATEMENT ...
...EXCEPT THAT MY SON IS SMILING LIKE HE'S GOT ACES UP HIS SLEEVE.
JAYCE ...?
j00 r34dy?
SENDING...
BEEP!

A lot of people were expecting Hawk to whup Frost's ass, but for me that crossed the line from fantastic into fantasy. Everyone in the cast fills a role, and Hawk's isn't "ass-kicker." But don't worry . . . That doesn't mean there isn't going to be any ass-kicking. I'm (not so) secretly fifteen, so there will always be ass-kicking.

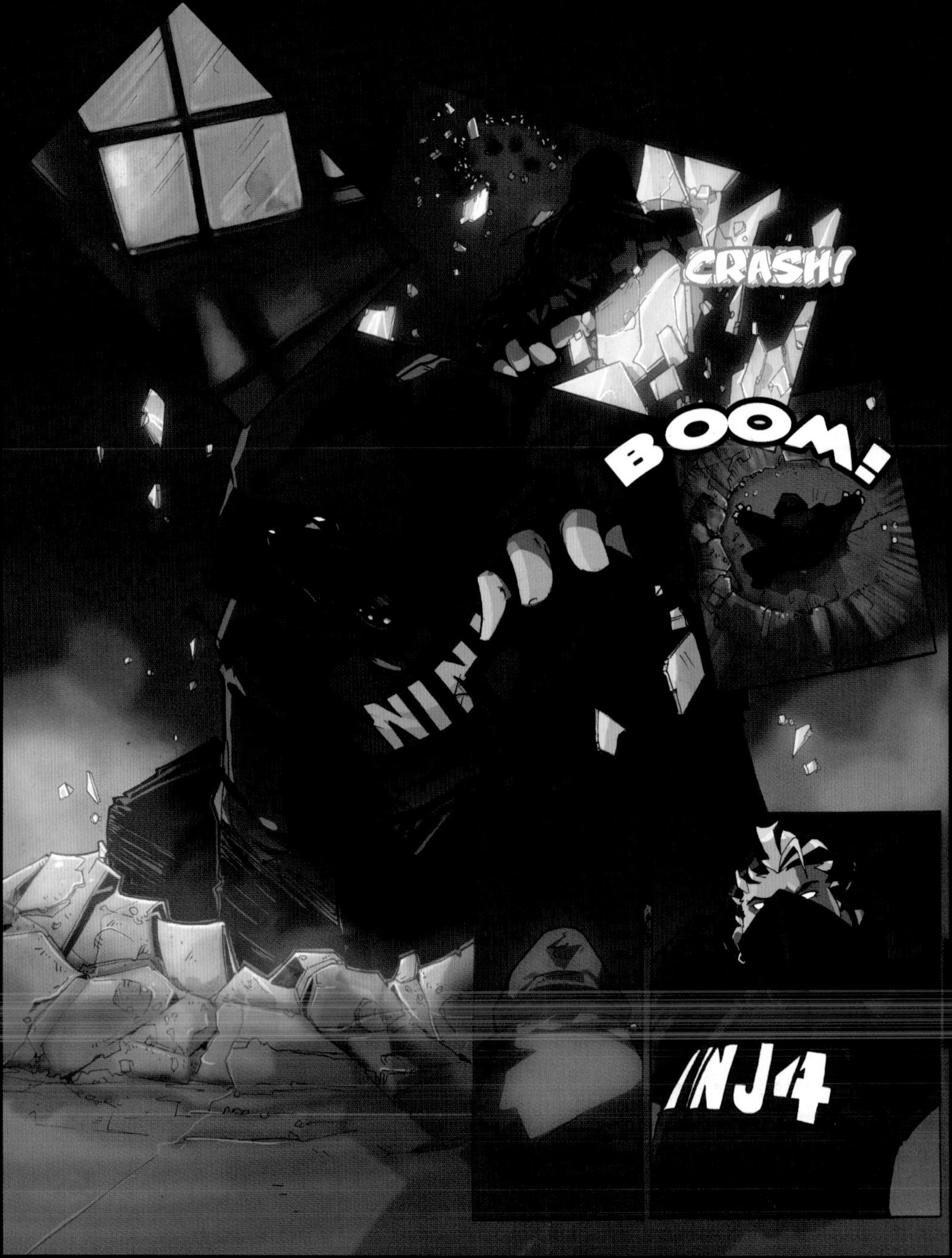
CRASH!
BOOM!

I figured I would leave the ass-kicking to the professionals. Many of you probably recognize Junpei from *Megatokyo* . . . Here he is in full-color glory! Thanks for letting us hire your ninja, Fred! Fan reaction to this page was unbelievable.

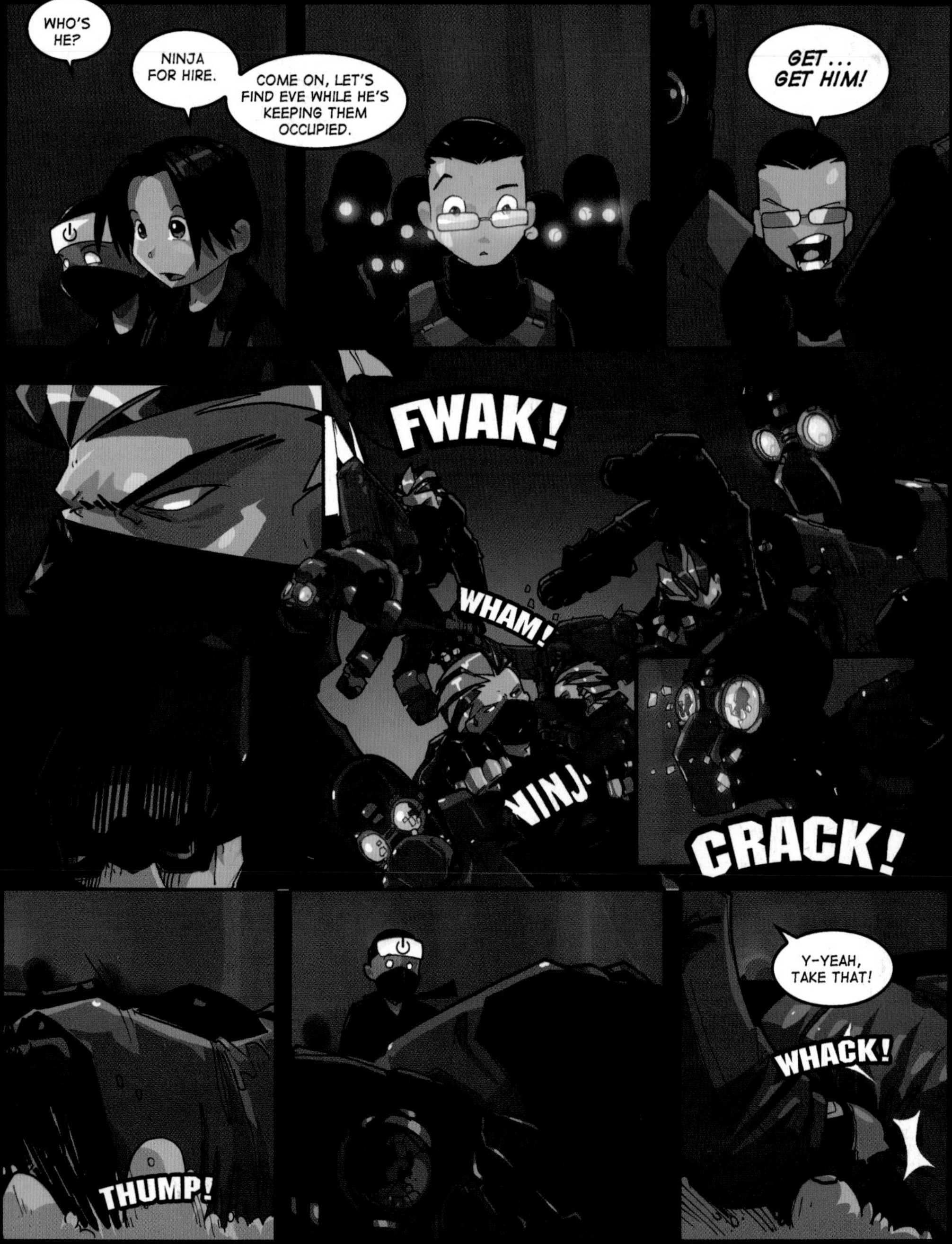
WHO'S HE?
NINJA FOR HIRE.
COME ON, LET'S FIND EVE WHILE HE'S KEEPING THEM OCCUPIED.
GET... GET HIM!
FWAK!
WHAM!
NINJ
CRACK!
THUMP!
Y-YEAH, TAKE THAT!
WHACK!

Good job, Hawk. You really showed that guy who's boss.

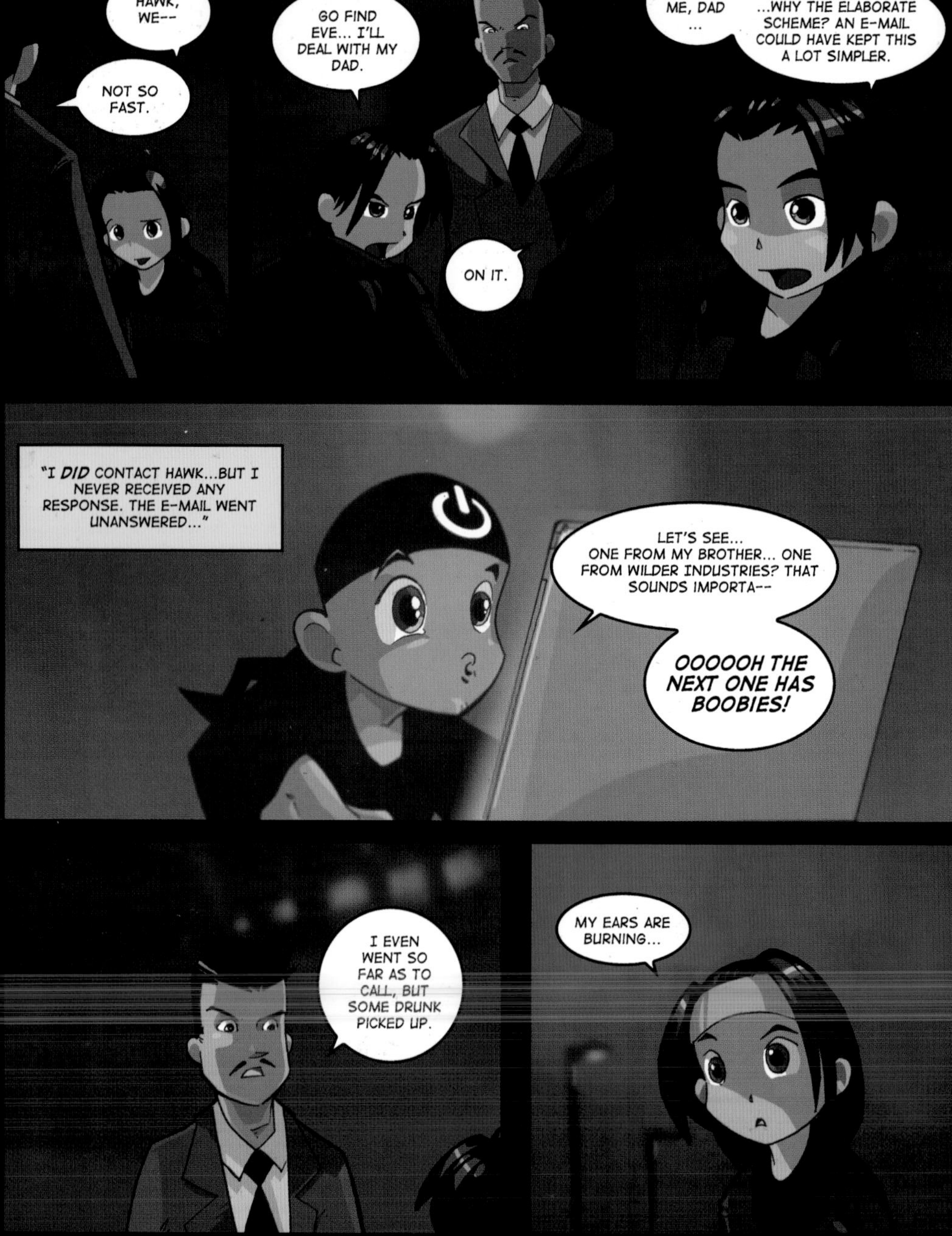
HAWK, WE--
NOT SO FAST.
GO FIND EVE... I'LL DEAL WITH MY DAD.
ON IT.
ME, DAD ...
...WHY THE ELABORATE SCHEME? AN E-MAIL COULD HAVE KEPT THIS A LOT SIMPLER.
"I *DID* CONTACT HAWK...BUT I NEVER RECEIVED ANY RESPONSE. THE E-MAIL WENT UNANSWERED..."
LET'S SEE... ONE FROM MY BROTHER... ONE FROM WILDER INDUSTRIES? THAT SOUNDS IMPORTA--
OOOOOH THE NEXT ONE HAS BOOBIES!
I EVEN WENT SO FAR AS TO CALL, BUT SOME DRUNK PICKED UP.
MY EARS ARE BURNING...

With friends like these, who needs enemies?

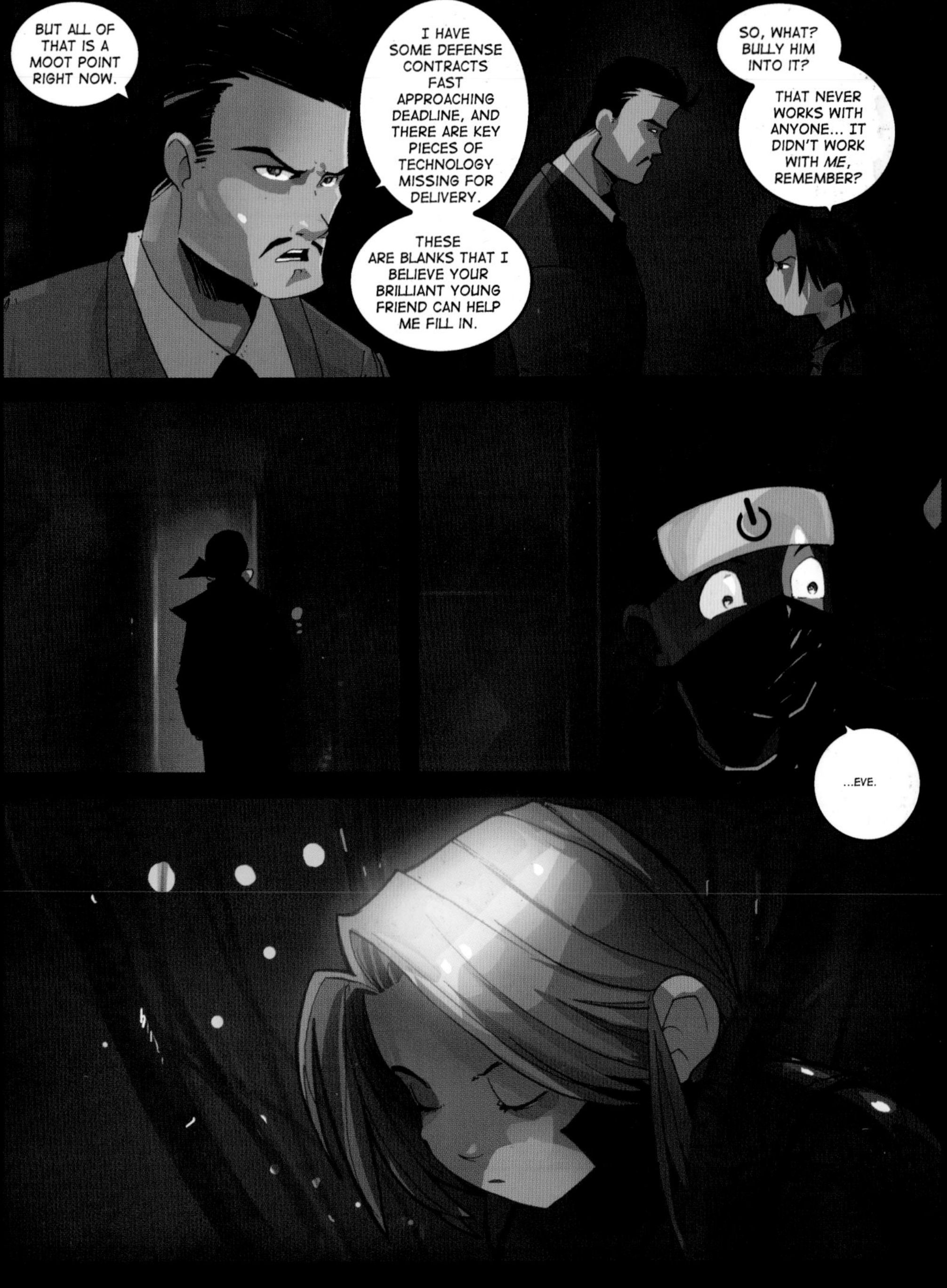
BUT ALL OF THAT IS A MOOT POINT RIGHT NOW.
I HAVE SOME DEFENSE CONTRACTS FAST APPROACHING DEADLINE, AND THERE ARE KEY PIECES OF TECHNOLOGY MISSING FOR DELIVERY.
THESE ARE BLANKS THAT I BELIEVE YOUR BRILLIANT YOUNG FRIEND CAN HELP ME FILL IN.
SO, WHAT? BULLY HIM INTO IT?
THAT NEVER WORKS WITH ANYONE... IT DIDN'T WORK WITH *ME*, REMEMBER?
...EVE.

The last panel is reminiscent of scenes from *Battle Angel Alita* and *Ghost in the Shell*; one cool thing about *Applegeeks* being in color is that when Hawk decides to pay homage to manga, we get to see his interpretation of a manga color palette.

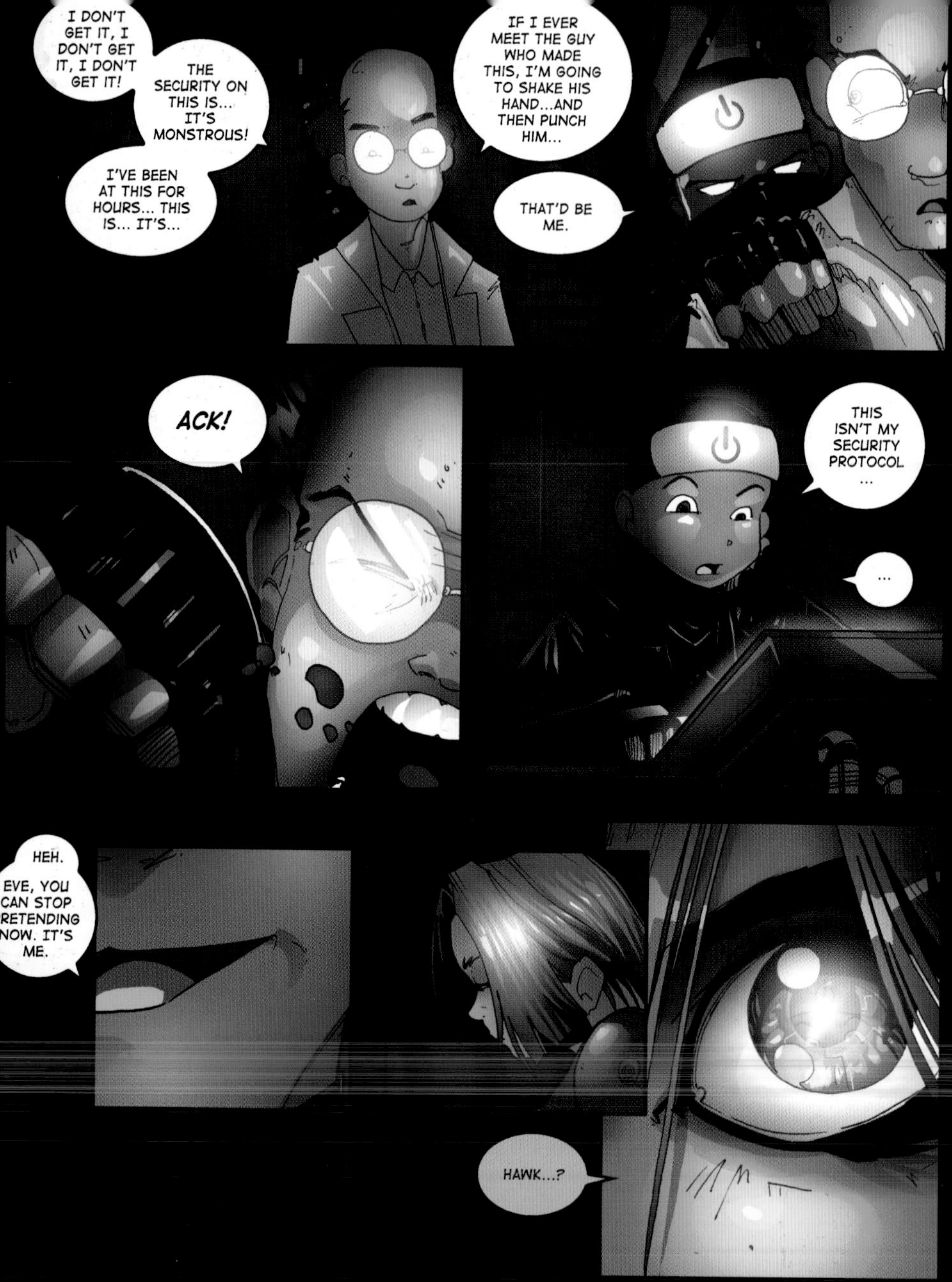
I DON'T GET IT, I DON'T GET IT, I DON'T GET IT!
THE SECURITY ON THIS IS... IT'S MONSTROUS!
I'VE BEEN AT THIS FOR HOURS... THIS IS... IT'S...
IF I EVER MEET THE GUY WHO MADE THIS, I'M GOING TO SHAKE HIS HAND...AND THEN PUNCH HIM...
THAT'D BE ME.
ACK!
THIS ISN'T MY SECURITY PROTOCOL ...
...
HEH.
EVE, YOU CAN STOP PRETENDING NOW. IT'S ME.
HAWK...?

That scientist looks like a very young Dr. Wily from *Mega Man*. All of the strange neuroses are there . . . And the hair! Oh God, the hair. Dr. Wily was apparently loosely based

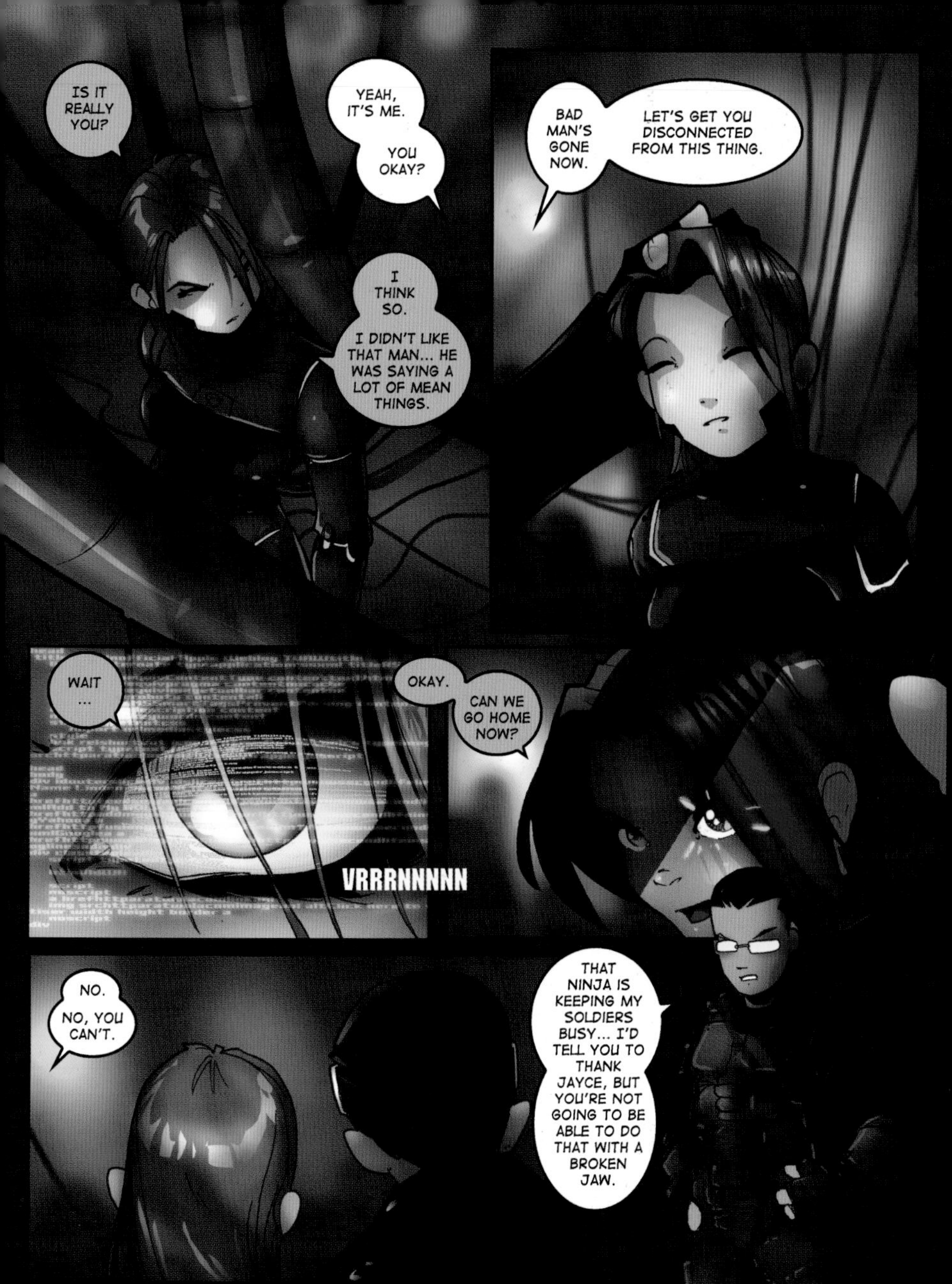

IS IT REALLY YOU?
YEAH, IT'S ME.
YOU OKAY?
I THINK SO.
I DIDN'T LIKE THAT MAN... HE WAS SAYING A LOT OF MEAN THINGS.
BAD MAN'S GONE NOW.
LET'S GET YOU DISCONNECTED FROM THIS THING.
WAIT ...
VRRRNNNNN
OKAY.
CAN WE GO HOME NOW?
NO.
NO, YOU CAN'T.
THAT NINJA IS KEEPING MY SOLDIERS BUSY... I'D TELL YOU TO THANK JAYCE, BUT YOU'RE NOT GOING TO BE ABLE TO DO THAT WITH A BROKEN JAW.

ve been flipping through some old comics, late '80s and early '90s *X-Men* and *Spider-Man* mostly. It seems like a airly common mutant power back then was having extraneous muscles. Lots of them . . . So many . . . Every once in a hile I see a body builder with a physique as defined as a superhero's body, and it always looks so weird. This too must

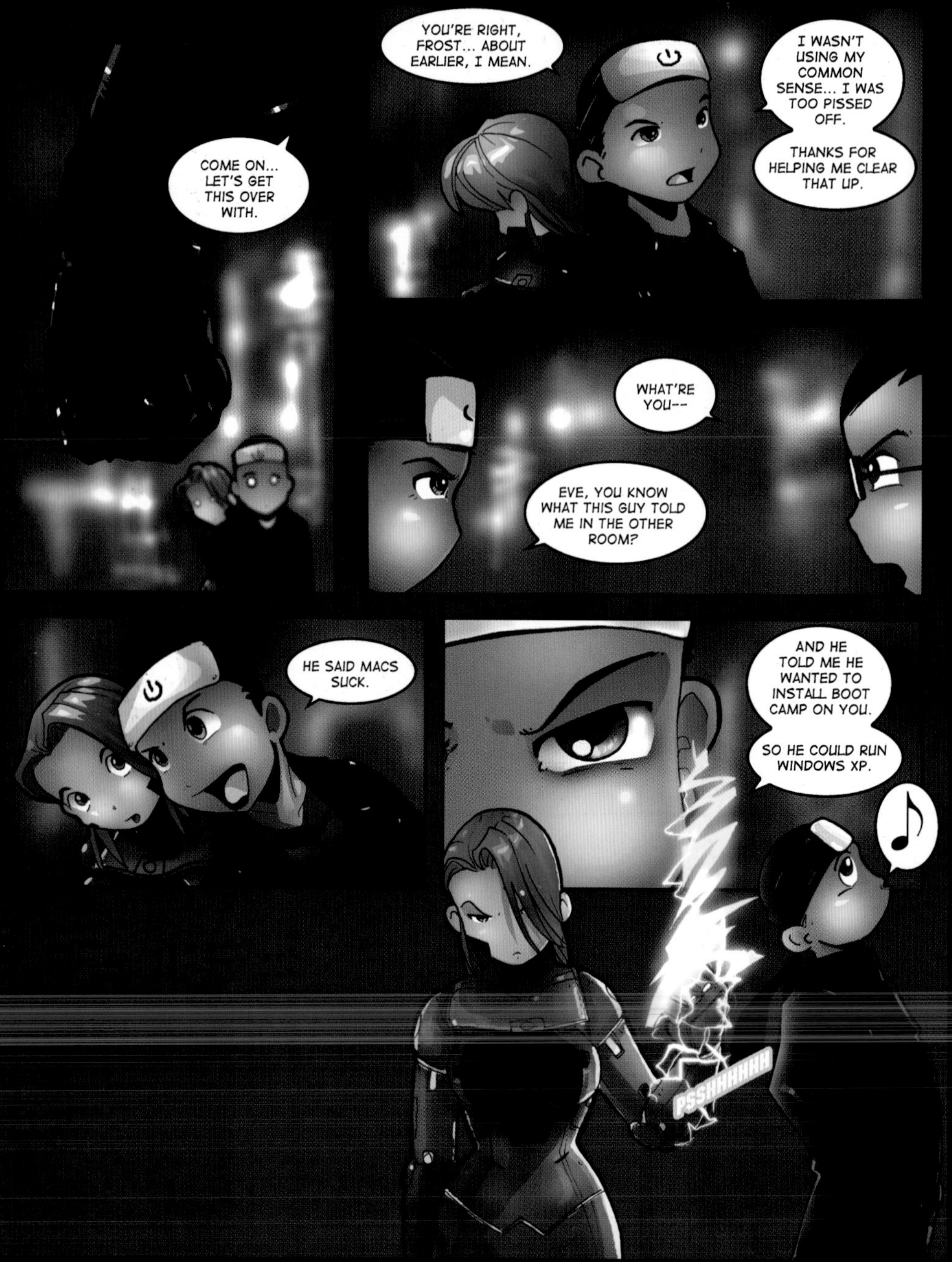
COME ON... LET'S GET THIS OVER WITH.
YOU'RE RIGHT, FROST... ABOUT EARLIER, I MEAN.
I WASN'T USING MY COMMON SENSE... I WAS TOO PISSED OFF.
THANKS FOR HELPING ME CLEAR THAT UP.
WHAT'RE YOU--
EVE, YOU KNOW WHAT THIS GUY TOLD ME IN THE OTHER ROOM?
HE SAID MACS SUCK.
AND HE TOLD ME HE WANTED TO INSTALL BOOT CAMP ON YOU.
SO HE COULD RUN WINDOWS XP.
♪
PSSHHHHHH

That's one way to do it!

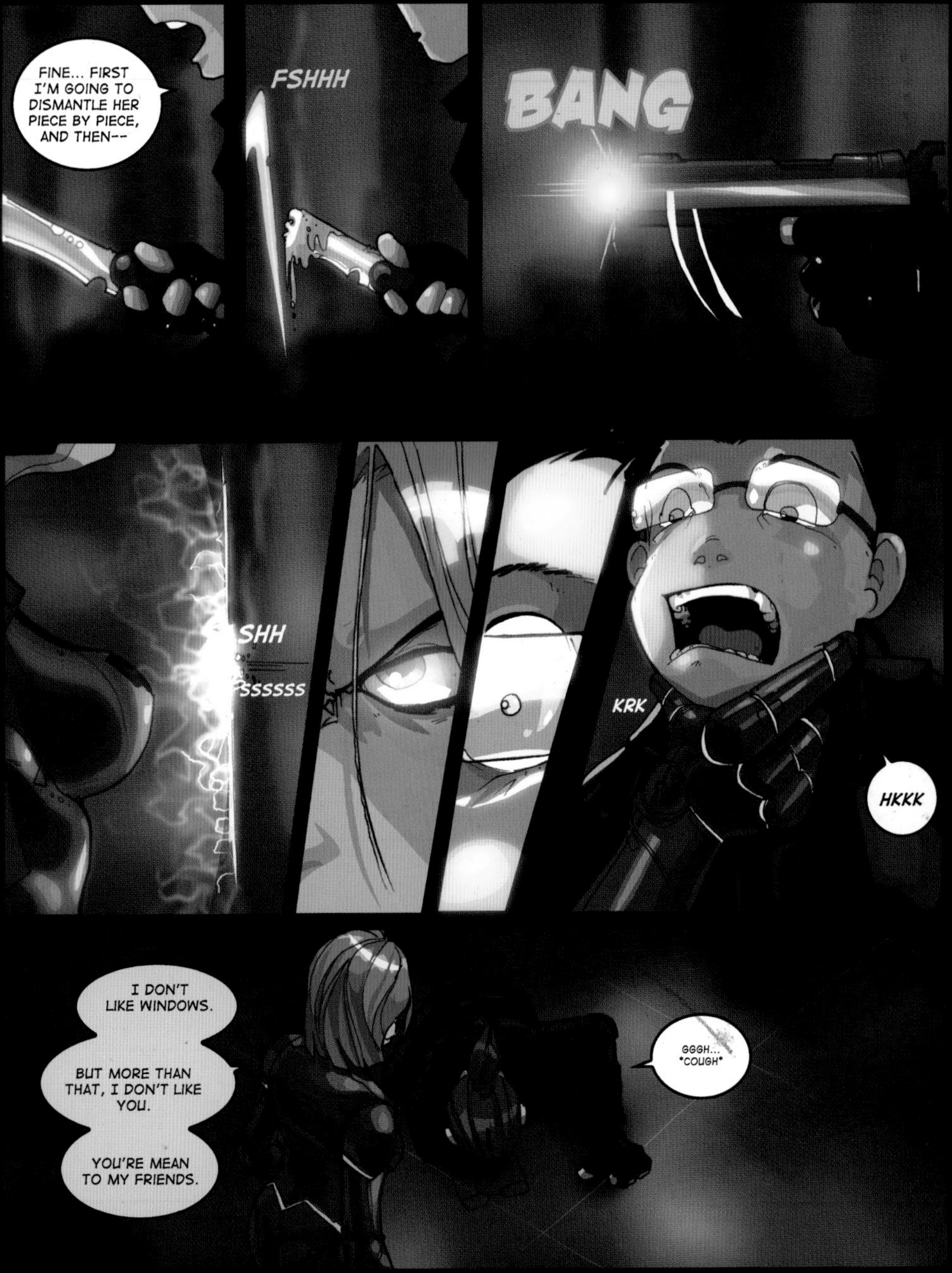
FINE... FIRST I'M GOING TO DISMANTLE HER PIECE BY PIECE, AND THEN--
FSHHH
BANG
SHH
SSSSSS
KRK
HKKK
I DON'T LIKE WINDOWS.
BUT MORE THAN THAT, I DON'T LIKE YOU.
YOU'RE MEAN TO MY FRIENDS.
GGGH... *COUGH*

In the end, Eve became pretty wholesome. I didn't set out with the intent of making her that way, but over time certain themes of friendship, innocence, and honesty just kept making themselves known. It may be strange to say this, but I think that over the course of *Applegeeks*, Eve is the character that has developed the most.

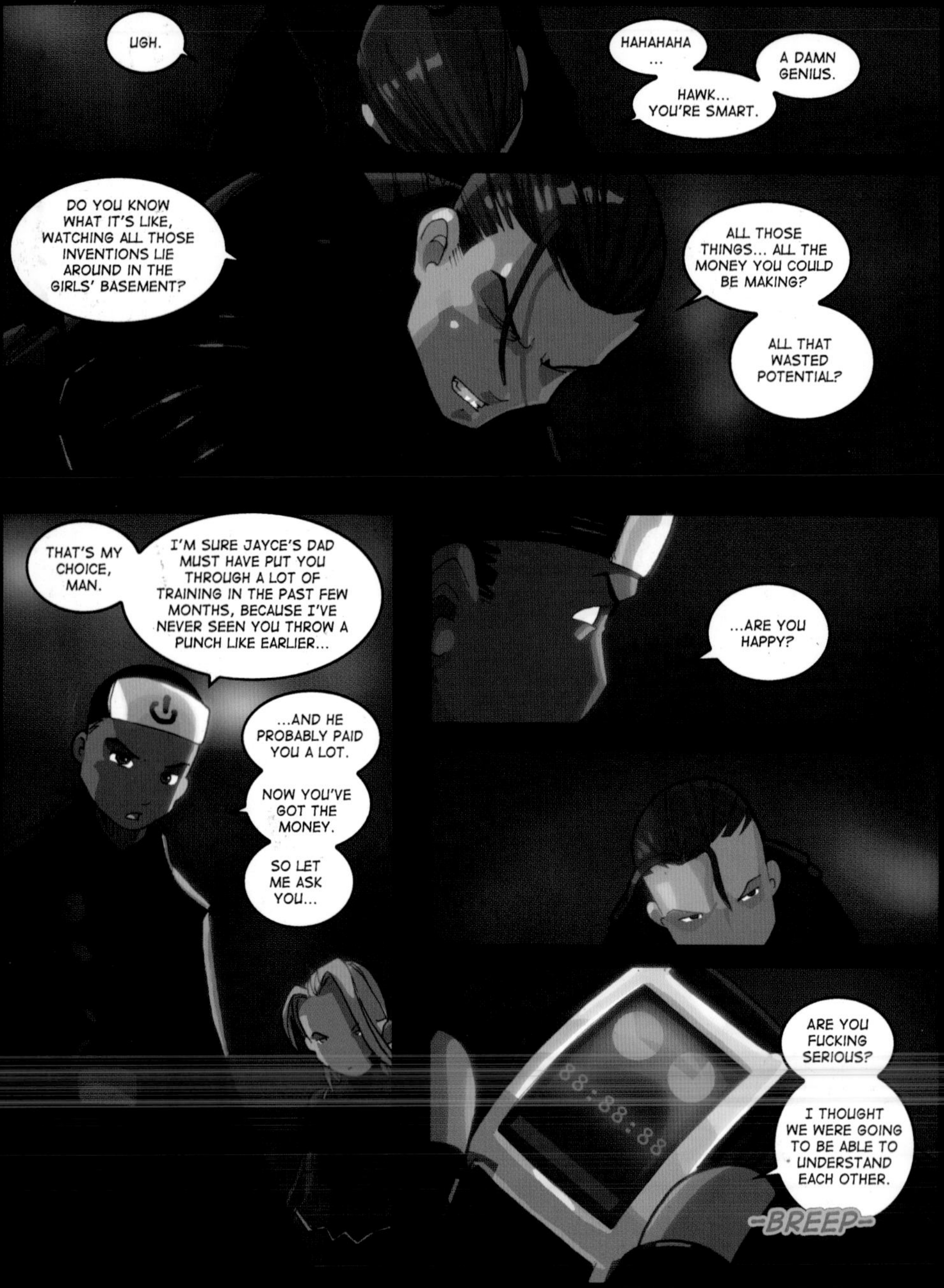
UGH.
HAHAHAHA ...
HAWK... YOU'RE SMART.
A DAMN GENIUS.
DO YOU KNOW WHAT IT'S LIKE, WATCHING ALL THOSE INVENTIONS LIE AROUND IN THE GIRLS' BASEMENT?
ALL THOSE THINGS... ALL THE MONEY YOU COULD BE MAKING?
ALL THAT WASTED POTENTIAL?
THAT'S MY CHOICE, MAN.
I'M SURE JAYCE'S DAD MUST HAVE PUT YOU THROUGH A LOT OF TRAINING IN THE PAST FEW MONTHS, BECAUSE I'VE NEVER SEEN YOU THROW A PUNCH LIKE EARLIER...
...AND HE PROBABLY PAID YOU A LOT.
NOW YOU'VE GOT THE MONEY.
SO LET ME ASK YOU...
...ARE YOU HAPPY?
88:88:88
ARE YOU FUCKING SERIOUS?
I THOUGHT WE WERE GOING TO BE ABLE TO UNDERSTAND EACH OTHER.
-BREEP-

And so the truth finally comes out! I always thought that in some weird, twisted way Frost's heart was in the right place. His methodology sure sucks, though. He should be doing his own work, not stealing from other people. Ambition isn't a bad thing, but it should be tempered with honesty!

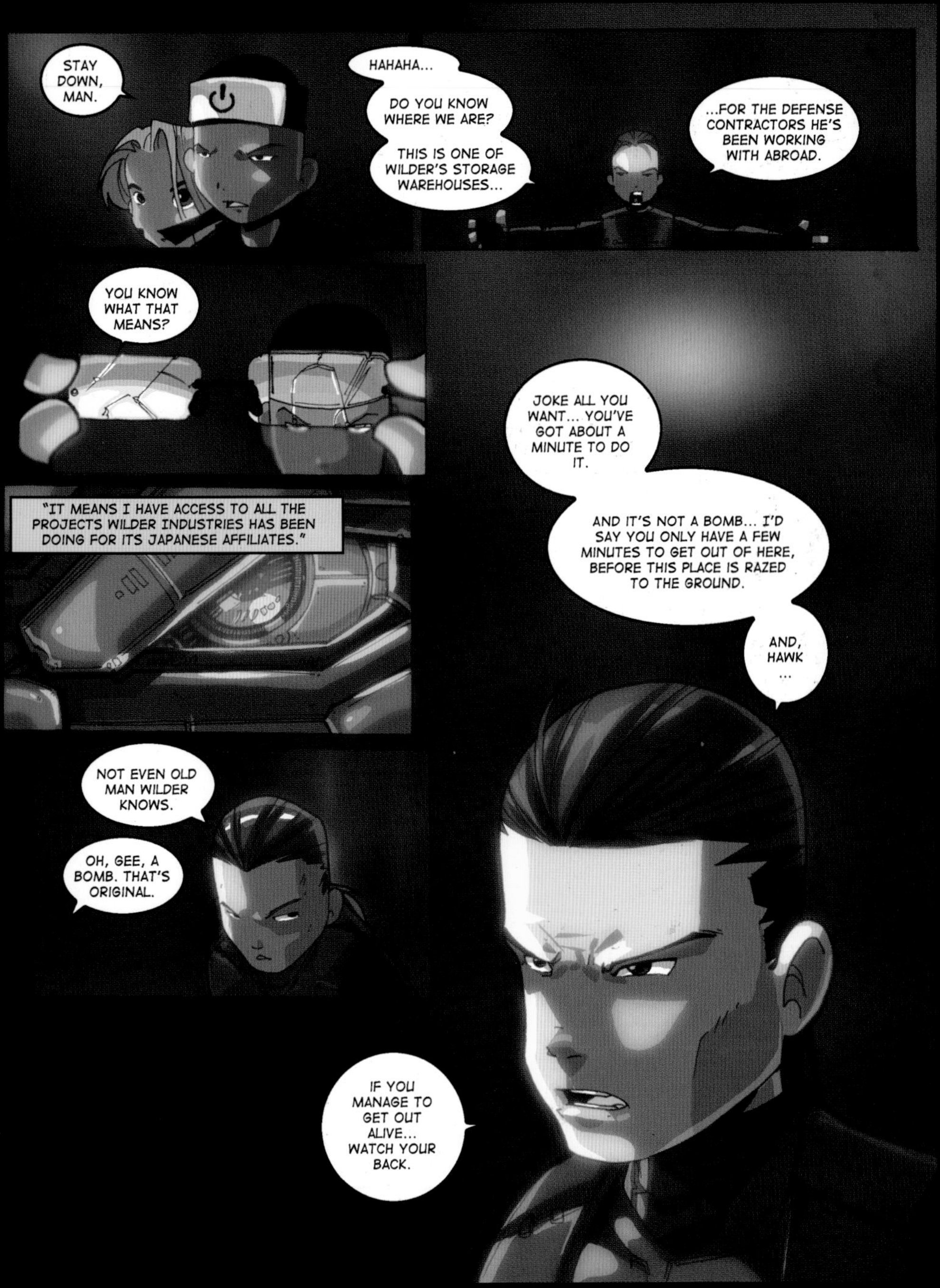
STAY DOWN, MAN.
HAHAHA...
DO YOU KNOW WHERE WE ARE?
THIS IS ONE OF WILDER'S STORAGE WAREHOUSES...
...FOR THE DEFENSE CONTRACTORS HE'S BEEN WORKING WITH ABROAD.
YOU KNOW WHAT THAT MEANS?
"IT MEANS I HAVE ACCESS TO ALL THE PROJECTS WILDER INDUSTRIES HAS BEEN DOING FOR ITS JAPANESE AFFILIATES."
NOT EVEN OLD MAN WILDER KNOWS.
OH, GEE, A BOMB. THAT'S ORIGINAL.
JOKE ALL YOU WANT... YOU'VE GOT ABOUT A MINUTE TO DO IT.
AND IT'S NOT A BOMB... I'D SAY YOU ONLY HAVE A FEW MINUTES TO GET OUT OF HERE, BEFORE THIS PLACE IS RAZED TO THE GROUND.
AND, HAWK ...
IF YOU MANAGE TO GET OUT ALIVE... WATCH YOUR BACK.

In the eyes of the readers, Frost ended up being the real villain of *Applegeeks*. He was there from the start, and his change of heart really got people fired up.

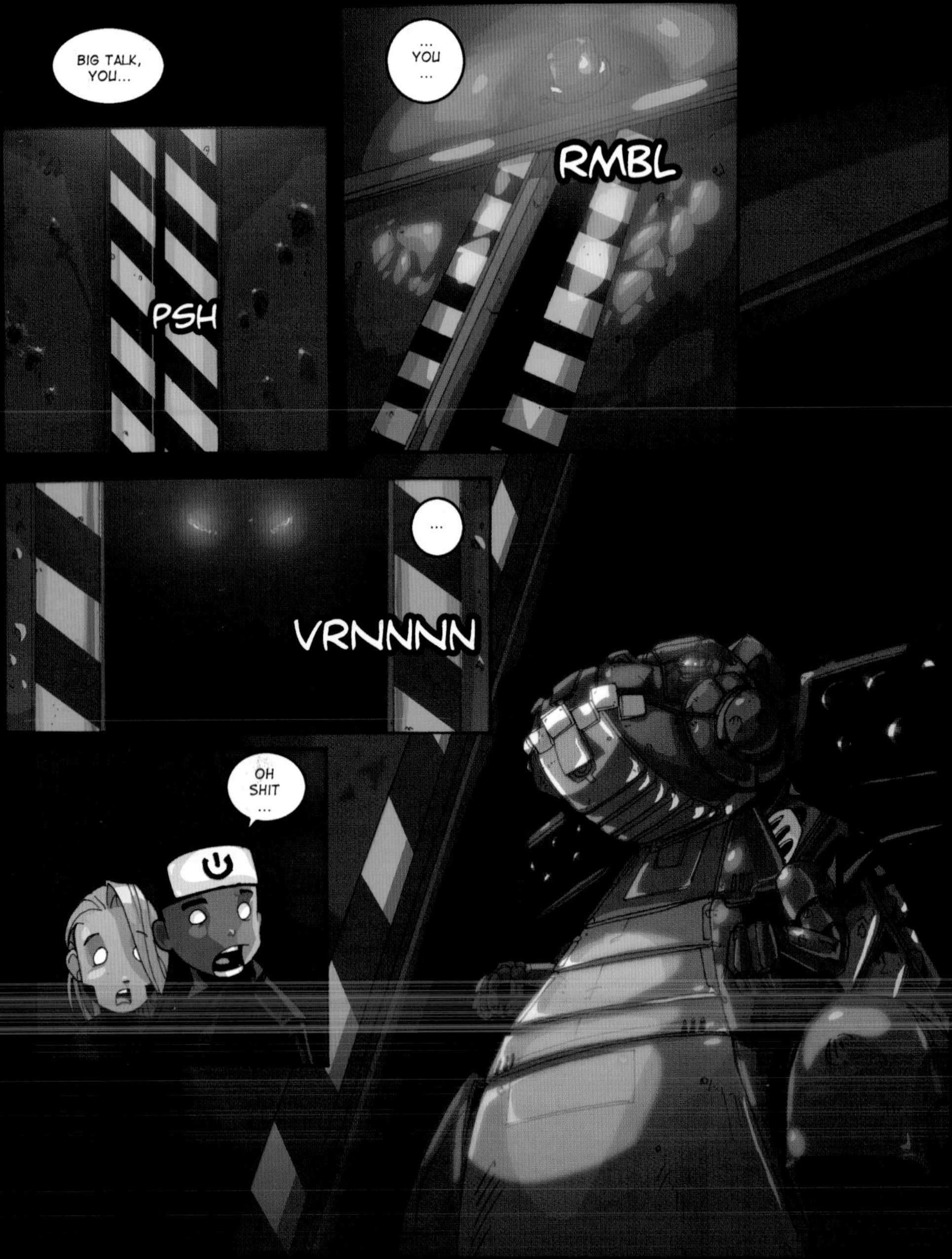
BIG TALK, YOU...
... YOU ...
RMBL
PSH
...
VRNNNN
OH SHIT ...

It's a Mecha-Rent-a-zilla! Since there's a Mecha-Godzilla, it seems only natural that there ought to be a Mecha-Rent-a-zilla. In fact, there definitely seems to be a trope in manga, anime, and Japanese video-game properties to create mecha versions of characters. As a kid, I was all about it. When Mecha-Sonic showed up on the Sega Genesis, we were all like, *WHOAAA*!

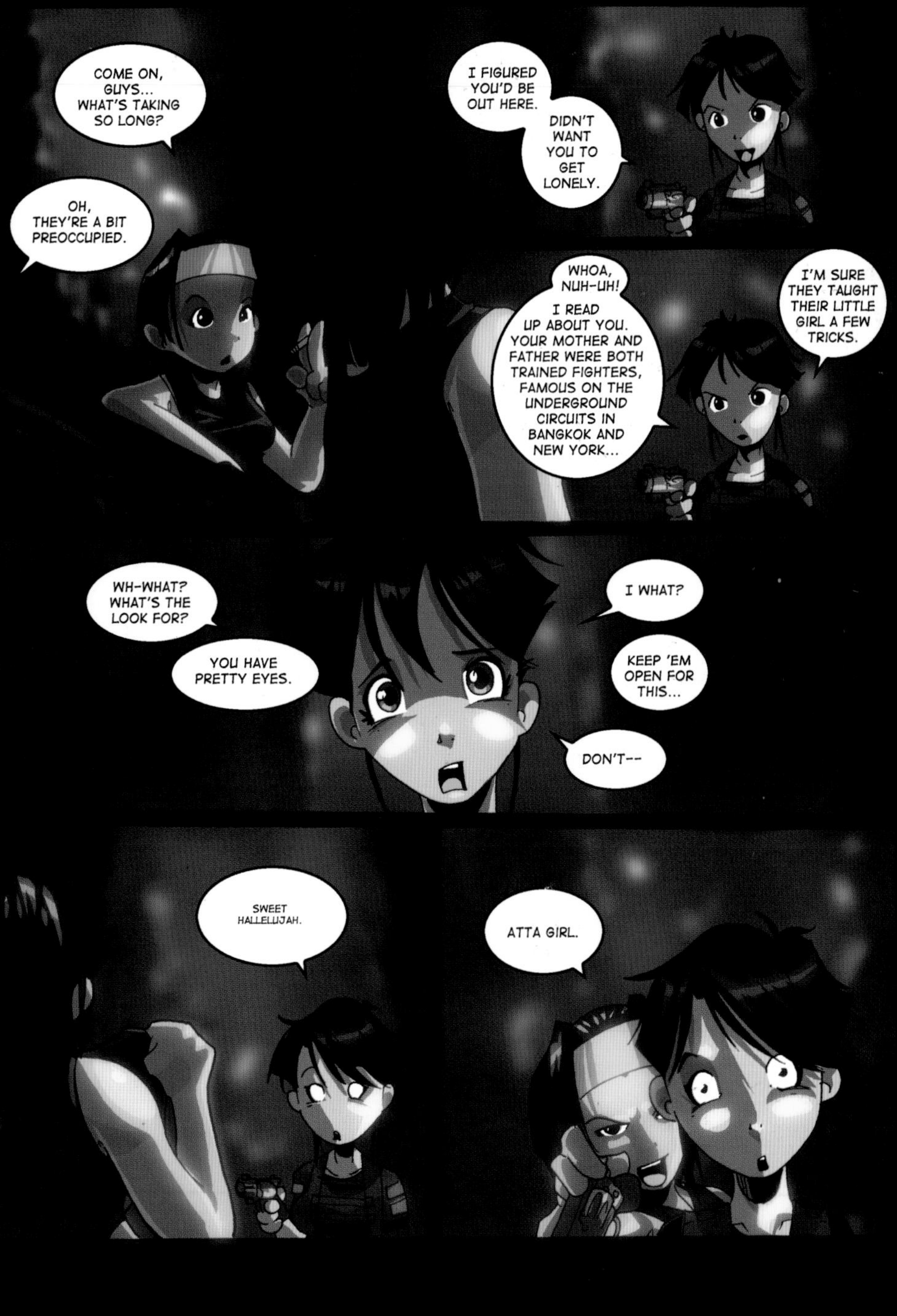
COME ON, GUYS... WHAT'S TAKING SO LONG?
OH, THEY'RE A BIT PREOCCUPIED.
I FIGURED YOU'D BE OUT HERE.
DIDN'T WANT YOU TO GET LONELY.
WHOA, NUH-UH!
I READ UP ABOUT YOU. YOUR MOTHER AND FATHER WERE BOTH TRAINED FIGHTERS, FAMOUS ON THE UNDERGROUND CIRCUITS IN BANGKOK AND NEW YORK...
I'M SURE THEY TAUGHT THEIR LITTLE GIRL A FEW TRICKS.
WH-WHAT? WHAT'S THE LOOK FOR?
YOU HAVE PRETTY EYES.
I WHAT?
KEEP 'EM OPEN FOR THIS...
DON'T--
SWEET HALLELUJAH.
ATTA GIRL.

There were a few people who were puzzled by this comic, so I'll spell it out: Casey likes girls.

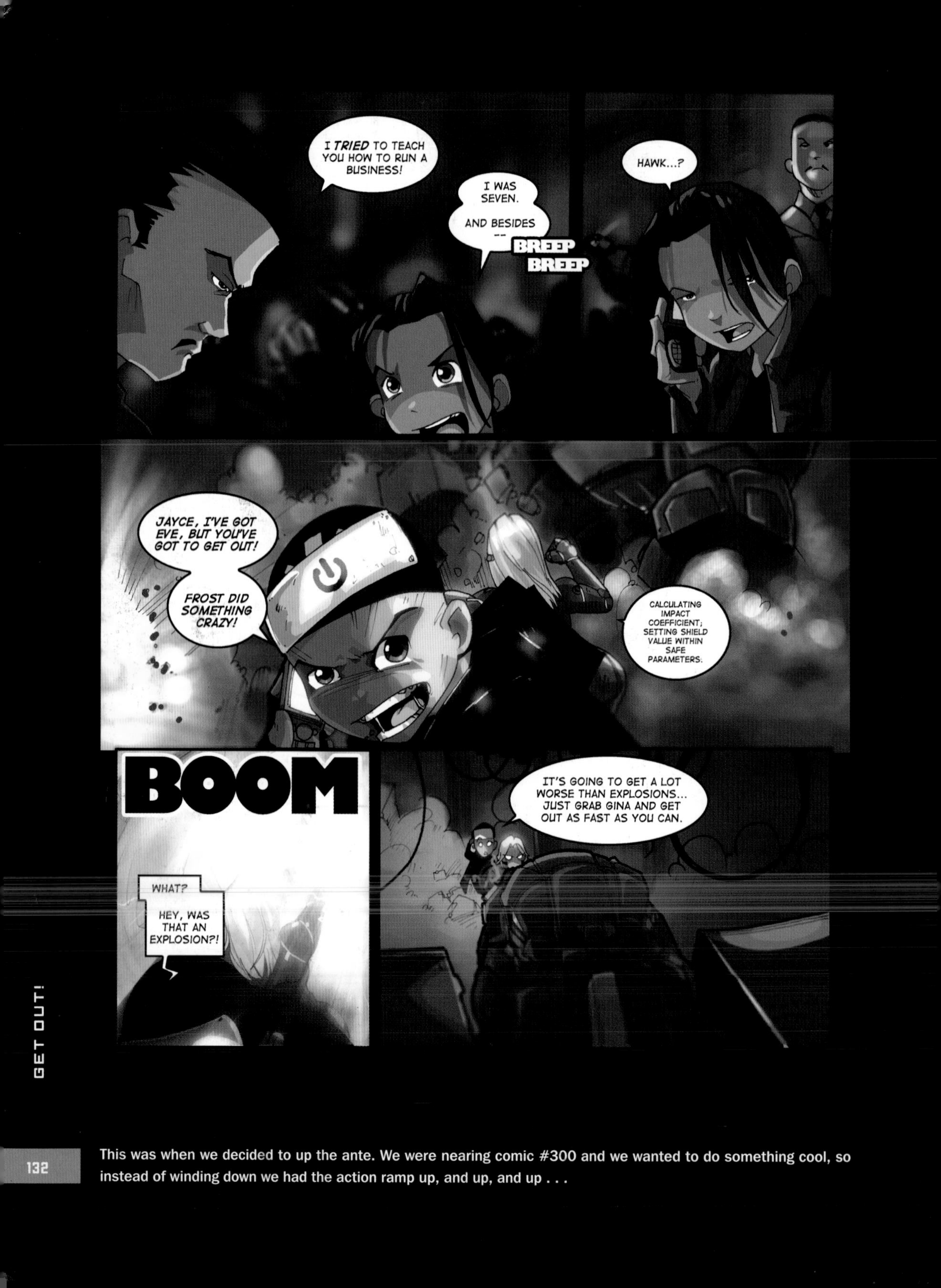
I TRIED TO TEACH YOU HOW TO RUN A BUSINESS!
I WAS SEVEN.
AND BESIDES --
BREEP BREEP
HAWK...?
JAYCE, I'VE GOT EVE, BUT YOU'VE GOT TO GET OUT!
FROST DID SOMETHING CRAZY!
CALCULATING IMPACT COEFFICIENT; SETTING SHIELD VALUE WITHIN SAFE PARAMETERS.
BOOM
WHAT?
HEY, WAS THAT AN EXPLOSION?!
IT'S GOING TO GET A LOT WORSE THAN EXPLOSIONS... JUST GRAB GINA AND GET OUT AS FAST AS YOU CAN.

This was when we decided to up the ante. We were nearing comic #300 and we wanted to do something cool, so instead of winding down we had the action ramp up, and up, and up . . .

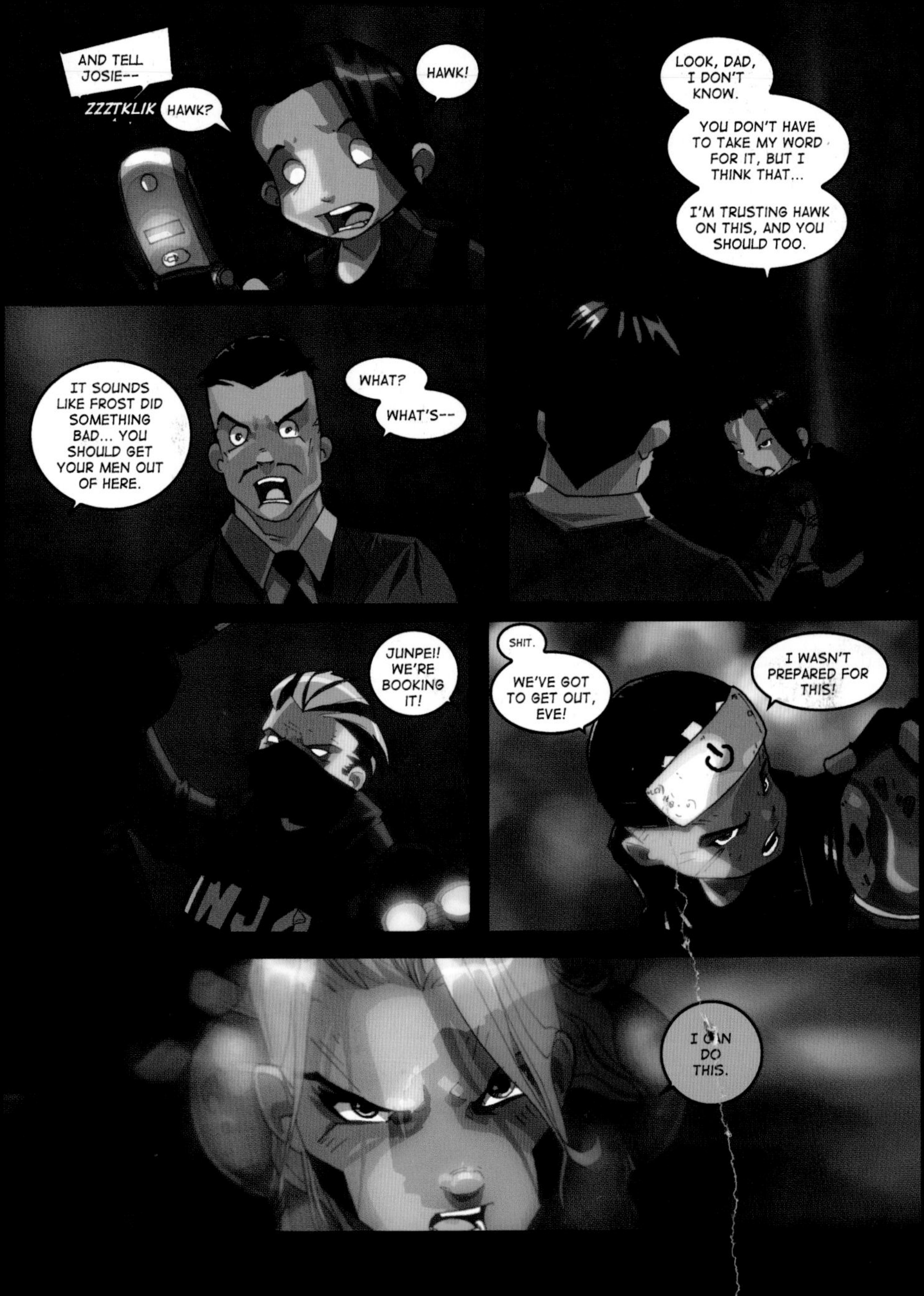
AND TELL JOSIE--
ZZZTKLIK
HAWK?
HAWK!
IT SOUNDS LIKE FROST DID SOMETHING BAD... YOU SHOULD GET YOUR MEN OUT OF HERE.
WHAT?
WHAT'S--
LOOK, DAD, I DON'T KNOW.
YOU DON'T HAVE TO TAKE MY WORD FOR IT, BUT I THINK THAT...
I'M TRUSTING HAWK ON THIS, AND YOU SHOULD TOO.
JUNPEI! WE'RE BOOKING IT!
SHIT.
WE'VE GOT TO GET OUT, EVE!
I WASN'T PREPARED FOR THIS!
I CAN DO THIS.

Amidst all the action and drama, this was an important turning point for Eve. This was the first time she displayed self-confidence—from here on out, she really begins to grow as a character.

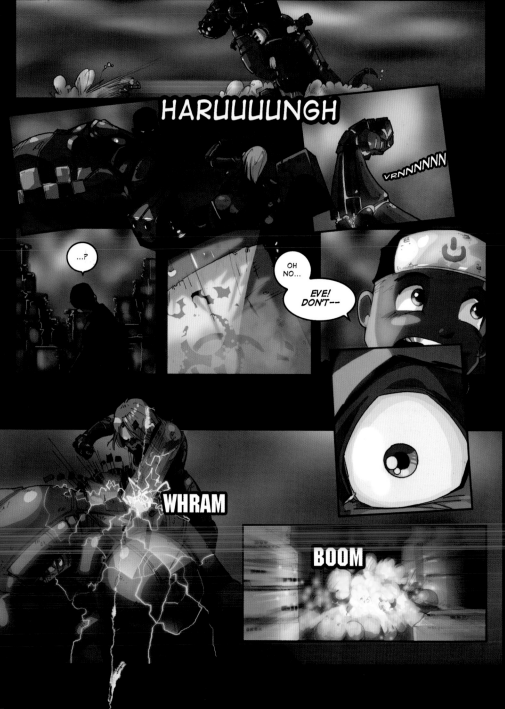

HARUUUUUNGH
VRNNNNNN
...?
OH NO...
EVE! DONT--
WHRAM
BOOM

Everything goes wrong all of the time! After this comic, we took the whole website down for a couple of days. It was replaced with a splash page of a shattered power symbol and the ominous words "Applegeeks: Exodus" hanging on an otherwise-black website.

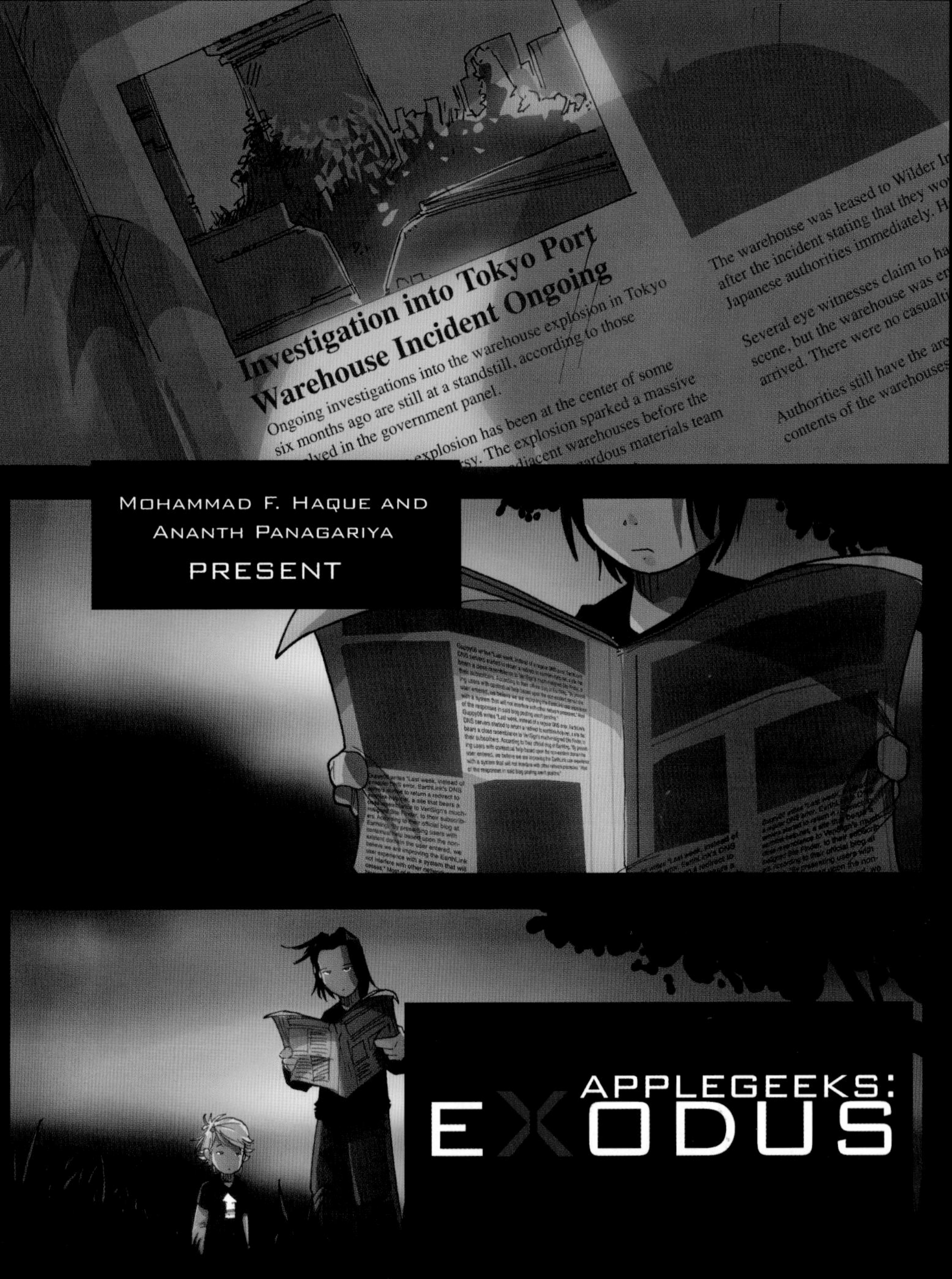
Investigation into Tokyo Port Warehouse Incident Ongoing
Ongoing investigations into the warehouse explosion in Tokyo six months ago are still at a standstill, according to those involved in the government panel.
The warehouse was leased to Wilder In
after the incident stating that they wo
Japanese authorities immediately. H
Several eye witnesses claim to ha
scene, but the warehouse was em
arrived. There were no casualti
Authorities still have the are
contents of the warehouses
Mohammad F. Haque and
Ananth Panagariya
PRESENT
APPLEGEEKS:
EXODUS

he next couple of comics were largely experimental, especially the ones featuring Gina. With Hawk and Eve out of the icture, we were ready to explore the rest of the cast a little bit. Gina ended up getting the most face time, and while any of these comics don't fit the usually goofy tone of *Applegeeks*, Hawk and I had a lot of fun putting them together.

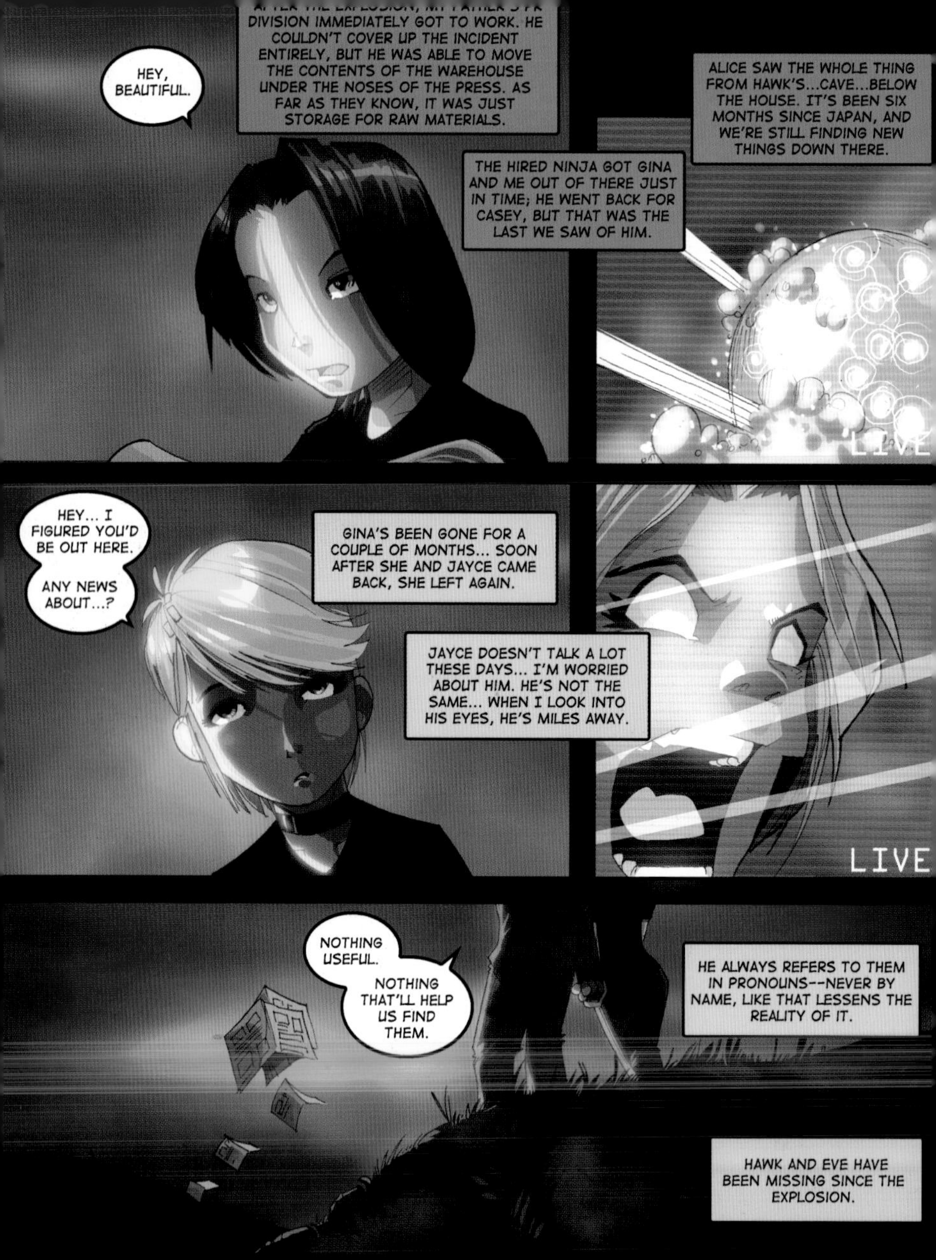
HEY, BEAUTIFUL.
DIVISION IMMEDIATELY GOT TO WORK. HE COULDN'T COVER UP THE INCIDENT ENTIRELY, BUT HE WAS ABLE TO MOVE THE CONTENTS OF THE WAREHOUSE UNDER THE NOSES OF THE PRESS. AS FAR AS THEY KNOW, IT WAS JUST STORAGE FOR RAW MATERIALS.
THE HIRED NINJA GOT GINA AND ME OUT OF THERE JUST IN TIME; HE WENT BACK FOR CASEY, BUT THAT WAS THE LAST WE SAW OF HIM.
ALICE SAW THE WHOLE THING FROM HAWK'S...CAVE...BELOW THE HOUSE. IT'S BEEN SIX MONTHS SINCE JAPAN, AND WE'RE STILL FINDING NEW THINGS DOWN THERE.
LIVE
HEY... I FIGURED YOU'D BE OUT HERE.
ANY NEWS ABOUT...?
GINA'S BEEN GONE FOR A COUPLE OF MONTHS... SOON AFTER SHE AND JAYCE CAME BACK, SHE LEFT AGAIN.
JAYCE DOESN'T TALK A LOT THESE DAYS... I'M WORRIED ABOUT HIM. HE'S NOT THE SAME... WHEN I LOOK INTO HIS EYES, HE'S MILES AWAY.
LIVE
NOTHING USEFUL.
NOTHING THAT'LL HELP US FIND THEM.
HE ALWAYS REFERS TO THEM IN PRONOUNS--NEVER BY NAME, LIKE THAT LESSENS THE REALITY OF IT.
HAWK AND EVE HAVE BEEN MISSING SINCE THE EXPLOSION.

of the things I hate to do is internal narration with text boxes, but you'll notice that most of *Exodus* feat
exact styling. Hawk challenged me to do it, and when a challenge is made it's time to put up your dukes!

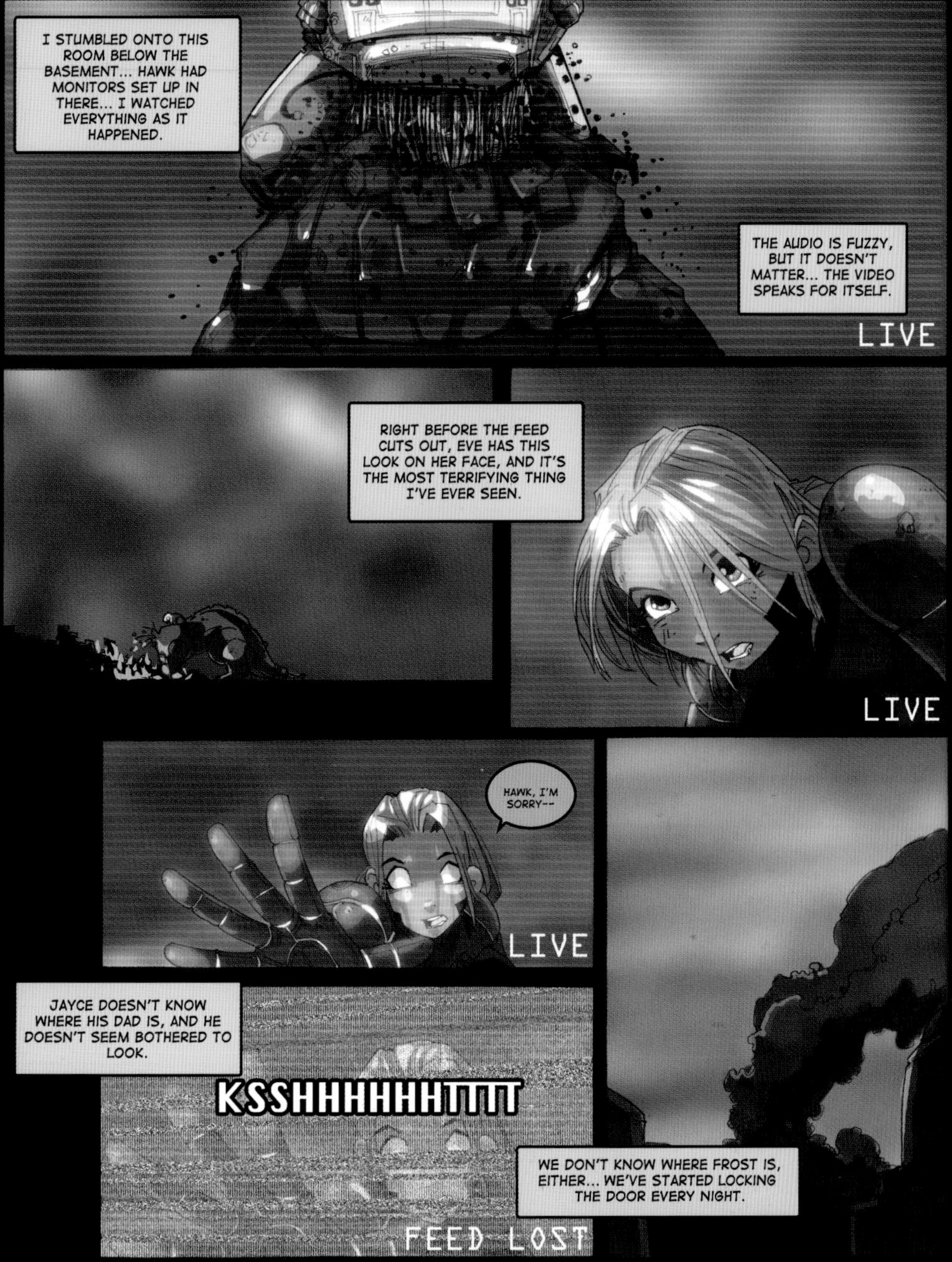
I STUMBLED ONTO THIS ROOM BELOW THE BASEMENT... HAWK HAD MONITORS SET UP IN THERE... I WATCHED EVERYTHING AS IT HAPPENED.
THE AUDIO IS FUZZY, BUT IT DOESN'T MATTER... THE VIDEO SPEAKS FOR ITSELF.
LIVE
RIGHT BEFORE THE FEED CUTS OUT, EVE HAS THIS LOOK ON HER FACE, AND IT'S THE MOST TERRIFYING THING I'VE EVER SEEN.
LIVE
HAWK, I'M SORRY--
LIVE
JAYCE DOESN'T KNOW WHERE HIS DAD IS, AND HE DOESN'T SEEM BOTHERED TO LOOK.
KSSHHHHHHTTTT
WE DON'T KNOW WHERE FROST IS, EITHER... WE'VE STARTED LOCKING THE DOOR EVERY NIGHT.
FEED LOST

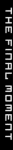

liked the idea of using screen shots from the video feed Alice was watching as panels of the flashback. I didn't

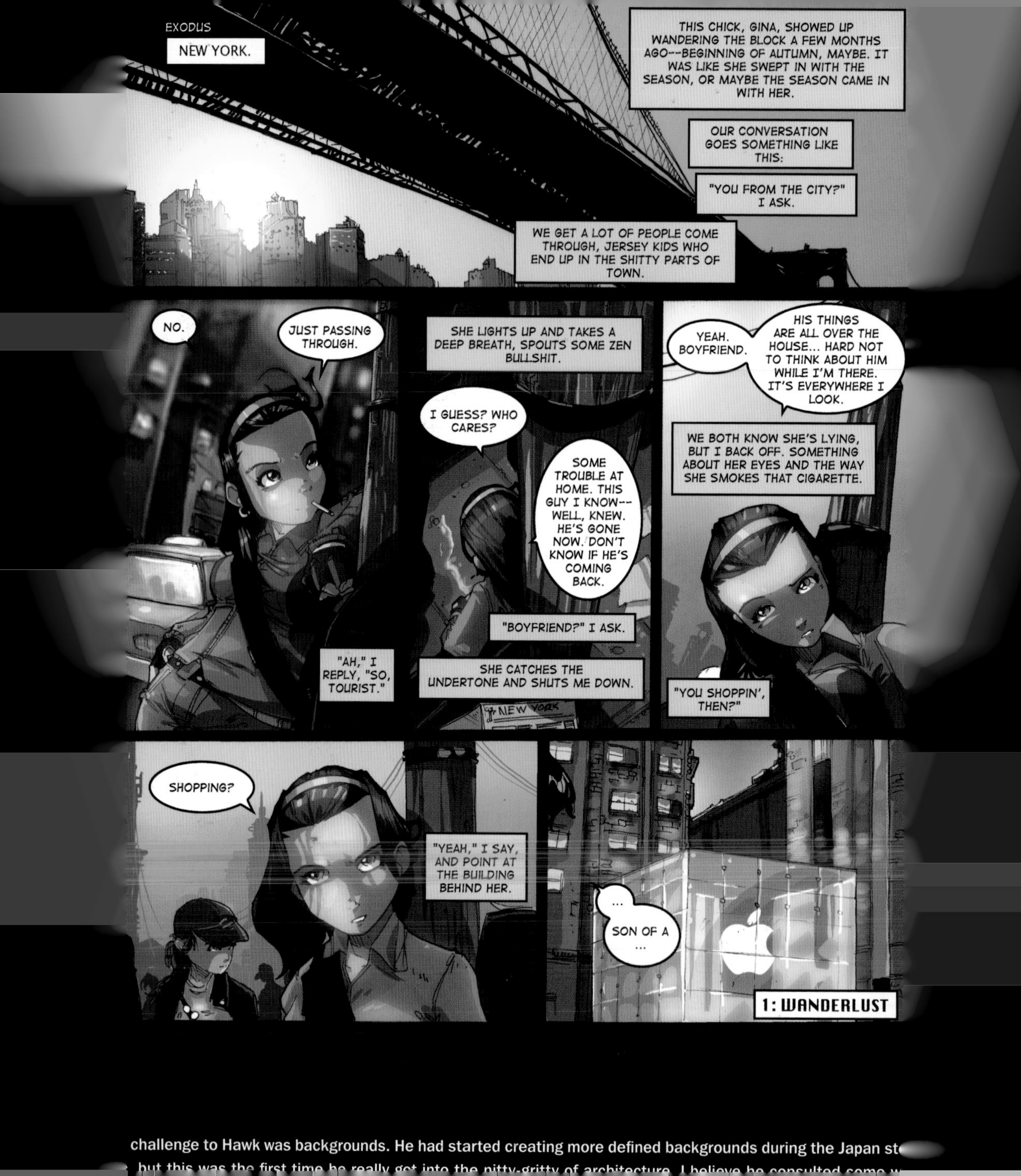
EXODUS
NEW YORK.
THIS CHICK, GINA, SHOWED UP WANDERING THE BLOCK A FEW MONTHS AGO--BEGINNING OF AUTUMN, MAYBE. IT WAS LIKE SHE SWEPT IN WITH THE SEASON, OR MAYBE THE SEASON CAME IN WITH HER.
OUR CONVERSATION GOES SOMETHING LIKE THIS:
"YOU FROM THE CITY?" I ASK.
WE GET A LOT OF PEOPLE COME THROUGH, JERSEY KIDS WHO END UP IN THE SHITTY PARTS OF TOWN.
NO.
JUST PASSING THROUGH.
"AH," I REPLY, "SO, TOURIST."
SHE LIGHTS UP AND TAKES A DEEP BREATH, SPOUTS SOME ZEN BULLSHIT.
I GUESS? WHO CARES?
SOME TROUBLE AT HOME. THIS GUY I KNOW--WELL, KNEW. HE'S GONE NOW. DON'T KNOW IF HE'S COMING BACK.
"BOYFRIEND?" I ASK.
SHE CATCHES THE UNDERTONE AND SHUTS ME DOWN.
NEW YORK
YEAH. BOYFRIEND.
HIS THINGS ARE ALL OVER THE HOUSE... HARD NOT TO THINK ABOUT HIM WHILE I'M THERE. IT'S EVERYWHERE I LOOK.
WE BOTH KNOW SHE'S LYING, BUT I BACK OFF. SOMETHING ABOUT HER EYES AND THE WAY SHE SMOKES THAT CIGARETTE.
"YOU SHOPPIN', THEN?"
SHOPPING?
"YEAH," I SAY, AND POINT AT THE BUILDING BEHIND HER.
...
SON OF A ...
1: WANDERLUST

challenge to Hawk was backgrounds. He had started creating more defined backgrounds during the Japan st
but this was the first time he really got into the nitty-gritty of architecture. I believe he consulted some w

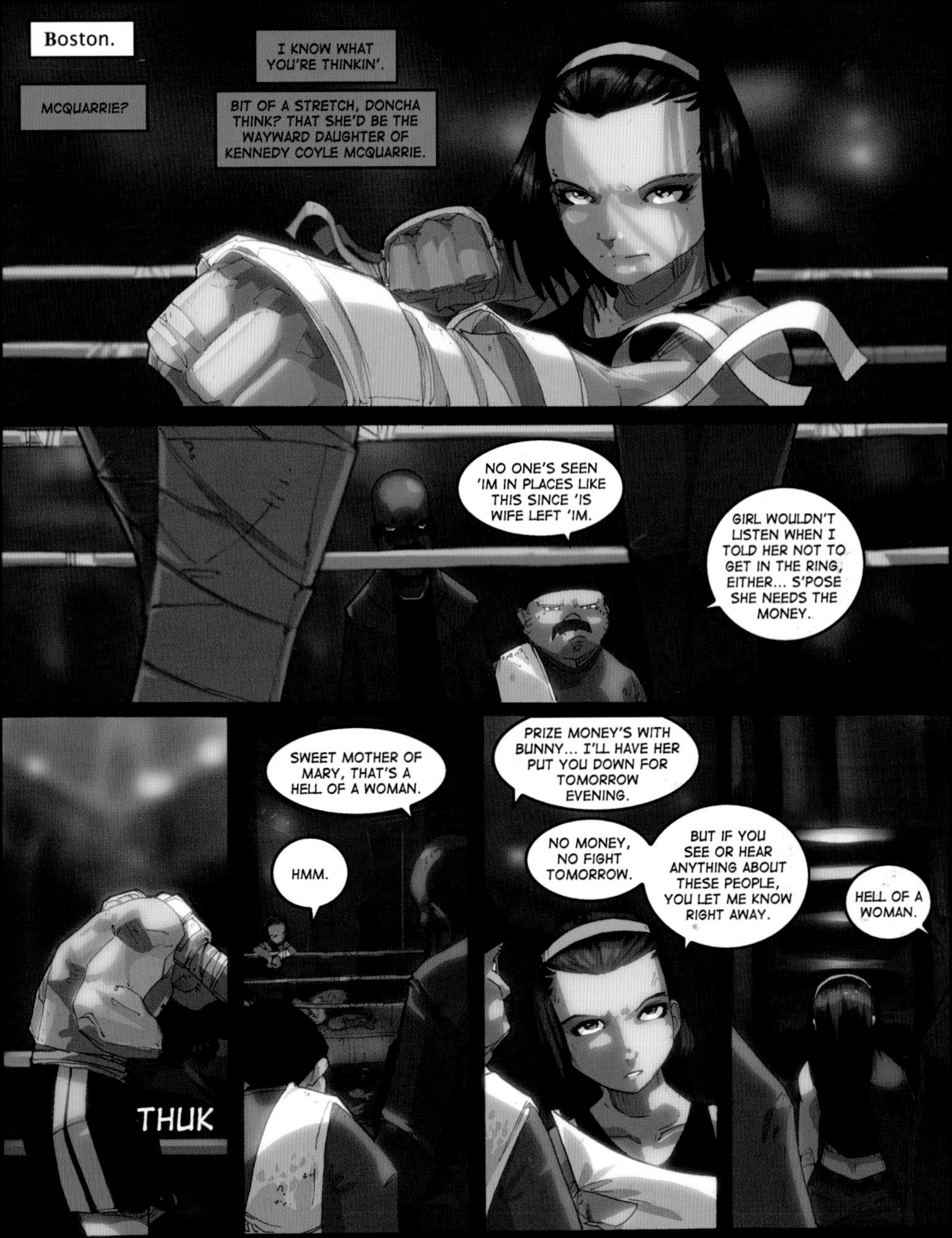
Boston.
MCQUARRIE?
I KNOW WHAT YOU'RE THINKIN'.
BIT OF A STRETCH, DONCHA THINK? THAT SHE'D BE THE WAYWARD DAUGHTER OF KENNEDY COYLE MCQUARRIE.
NO ONE'S SEEN 'IM IN PLACES LIKE THIS SINCE 'IS WIFE LEFT 'IM.
GIRL WOULDN'T LISTEN WHEN I TOLD HER NOT TO GET IN THE RING, EITHER... S'POSE SHE NEEDS THE MONEY.
THUK
SWEET MOTHER OF MARY, THAT'S A HELL OF A WOMAN.
HMM.
PRIZE MONEY'S WITH BUNNY... I'LL HAVE HER PUT YOU DOWN FOR TOMORROW EVENING.
NO MONEY, NO FIGHT TOMORROW.
BUT IF YOU SEE OR HEAR ANYTHING ABOUT THESE PEOPLE, YOU LET ME KNOW RIGHT AWAY.
HELL OF A WOMAN.

I might have been watching too many boxing movies, or maybe too much MMA. If you look closely, you'll notice that Gina is using a *muay thai* move—we were watching a lot of Tony Jaa movies at that point, like *The Bodyguard* and *Ong-Bak*. If you haven't seen them, put down this book and go watch them! *Ong-Bak* will blow your mind!

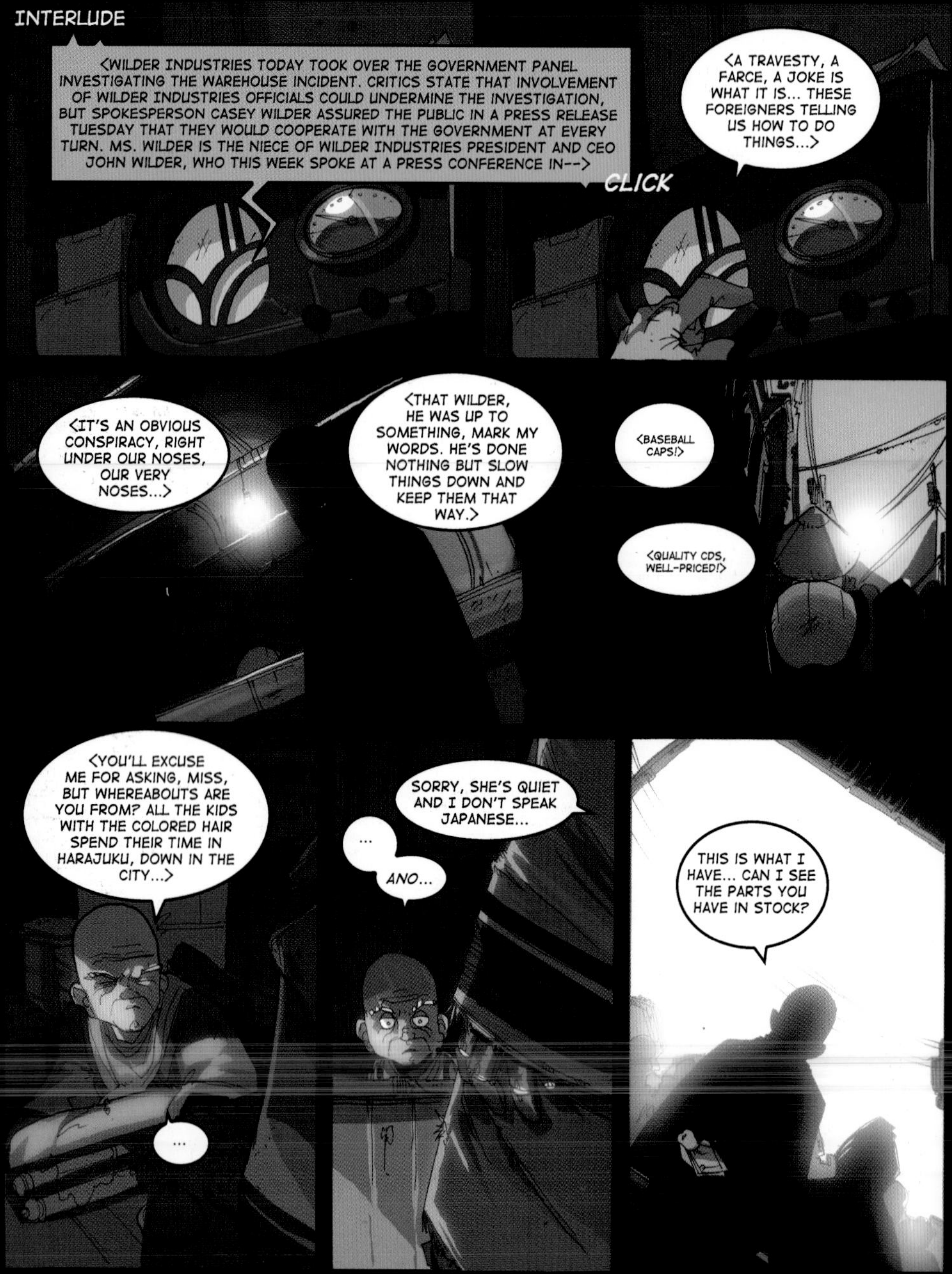
INTERLUDE
<WILDER INDUSTRIES TODAY TOOK OVER THE GOVERNMENT PANEL INVESTIGATING THE WAREHOUSE INCIDENT. CRITICS STATE THAT INVOLVEMENT OF WILDER INDUSTRIES OFFICIALS COULD UNDERMINE THE INVESTIGATION, BUT SPOKESPERSON CASEY WILDER ASSURED THE PUBLIC IN A PRESS RELEASE TUESDAY THAT THEY WOULD COOPERATE WITH THE GOVERNMENT AT EVERY TURN. MS. WILDER IS THE NIECE OF WILDER INDUSTRIES PRESIDENT AND CEO JOHN WILDER, WHO THIS WEEK SPOKE AT A PRESS CONFERENCE IN-->
CLICK
<A TRAVESTY, A FARCE, A JOKE IS WHAT IT IS... THESE FOREIGNERS TELLING US HOW TO DO THINGS...>
<IT'S AN OBVIOUS CONSPIRACY, RIGHT UNDER OUR NOSES, OUR VERY NOSES...>
<THAT WILDER, HE WAS UP TO SOMETHING, MARK MY WORDS. HE'S DONE NOTHING BUT SLOW THINGS DOWN AND KEEP THEM THAT WAY.>
<BASEBALL CAPS!>
<QUALITY CDS, WELL-PRICED!>
<YOU'LL EXCUSE ME FOR ASKING, MISS, BUT WHEREABOUTS ARE YOU FROM? ALL THE KIDS WITH THE COLORED HAIR SPEND THEIR TIME IN HARAJUKU, DOWN IN THE CITY...>
...
SORRY, SHE'S QUIET AND I DON'T SPEAK JAPANESE...
...
ANO...
THIS IS WHAT I HAVE... CAN I SEE THE PARTS YOU HAVE IN STOCK?

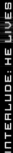

There's an almost wastelander design ethic to the way Hawk draws Japan, very much from the outset. It has a fantasy quality to it, with (surprisingly) lots of browns dominating. I believe he was looking at a lot of stuff by Craig Mullins. If you haven't

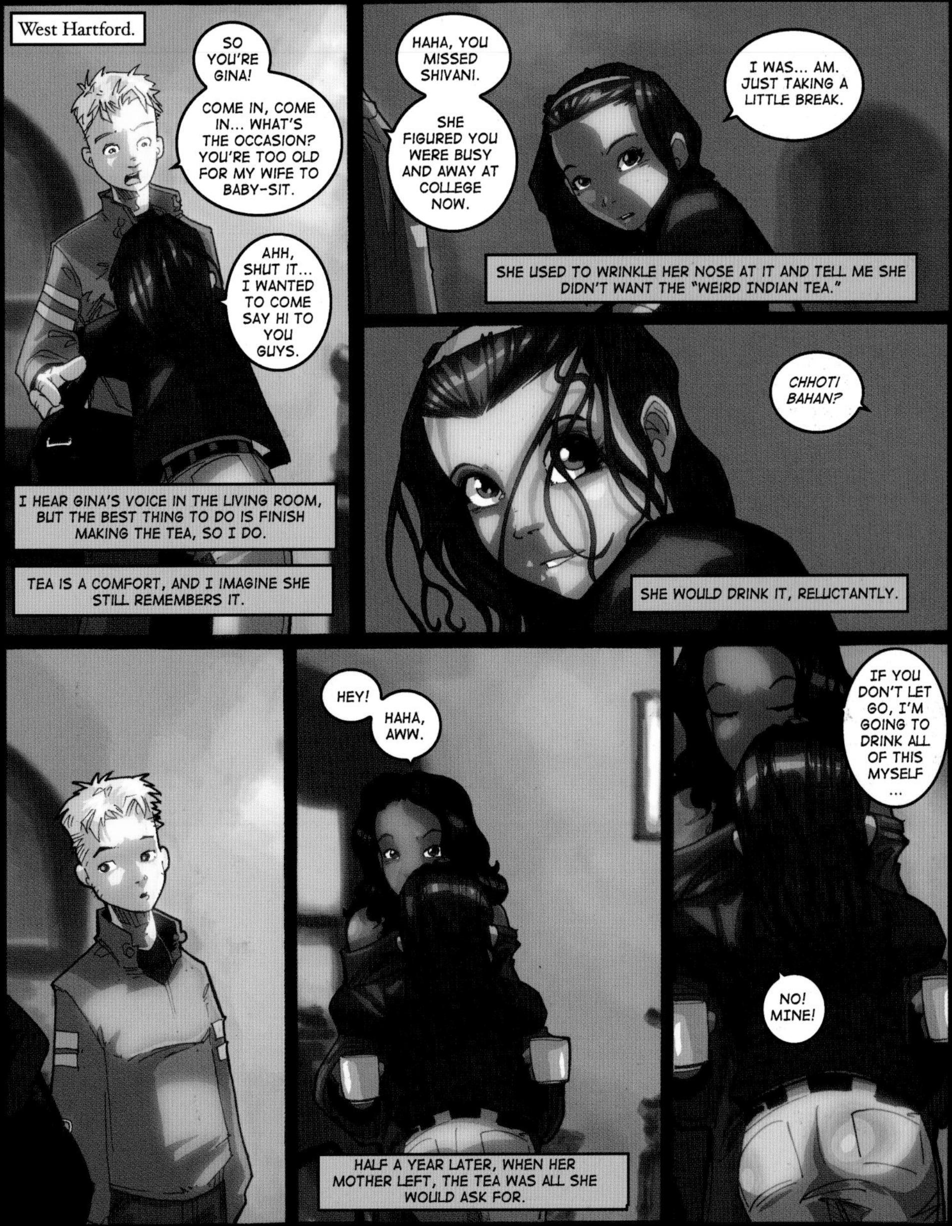
West Hartford.
SO YOU'RE GINA!
COME IN, COME IN... WHAT'S THE OCCASION? YOU'RE TOO OLD FOR MY WIFE TO BABY-SIT.
AHH, SHUT IT... I WANTED TO COME SAY HI TO YOU GUYS.
I HEAR GINA'S VOICE IN THE LIVING ROOM, BUT THE BEST THING TO DO IS FINISH MAKING THE TEA, SO I DO.
TEA IS A COMFORT, AND I IMAGINE SHE STILL REMEMBERS IT.
HAHA, YOU MISSED SHIVANI.
SHE FIGURED YOU WERE BUSY AND AWAY AT COLLEGE NOW.
I WAS... AM. JUST TAKING A LITTLE BREAK.
SHE USED TO WRINKLE HER NOSE AT IT AND TELL ME SHE DIDN'T WANT THE "WEIRD INDIAN TEA."
CHHOTI BAHAN?
SHE WOULD DRINK IT, RELUCTANTLY.
HEY!
HAHA, AWW.
HALF A YEAR LATER, WHEN HER MOTHER LEFT, THE TEA WAS ALL SHE WOULD ASK FOR.
IF YOU DON'T LET GO, I'M GOING TO DRINK ALL OF THIS MYSELF ...
NO! MINE!

Shivani was the first Indian character I added to the cast. She's a secondary character, but I really wanted to leave myself an open avenue to exploring my own cultural background, something that, while having a big influence on me personally, gets glossed over during most of the series.

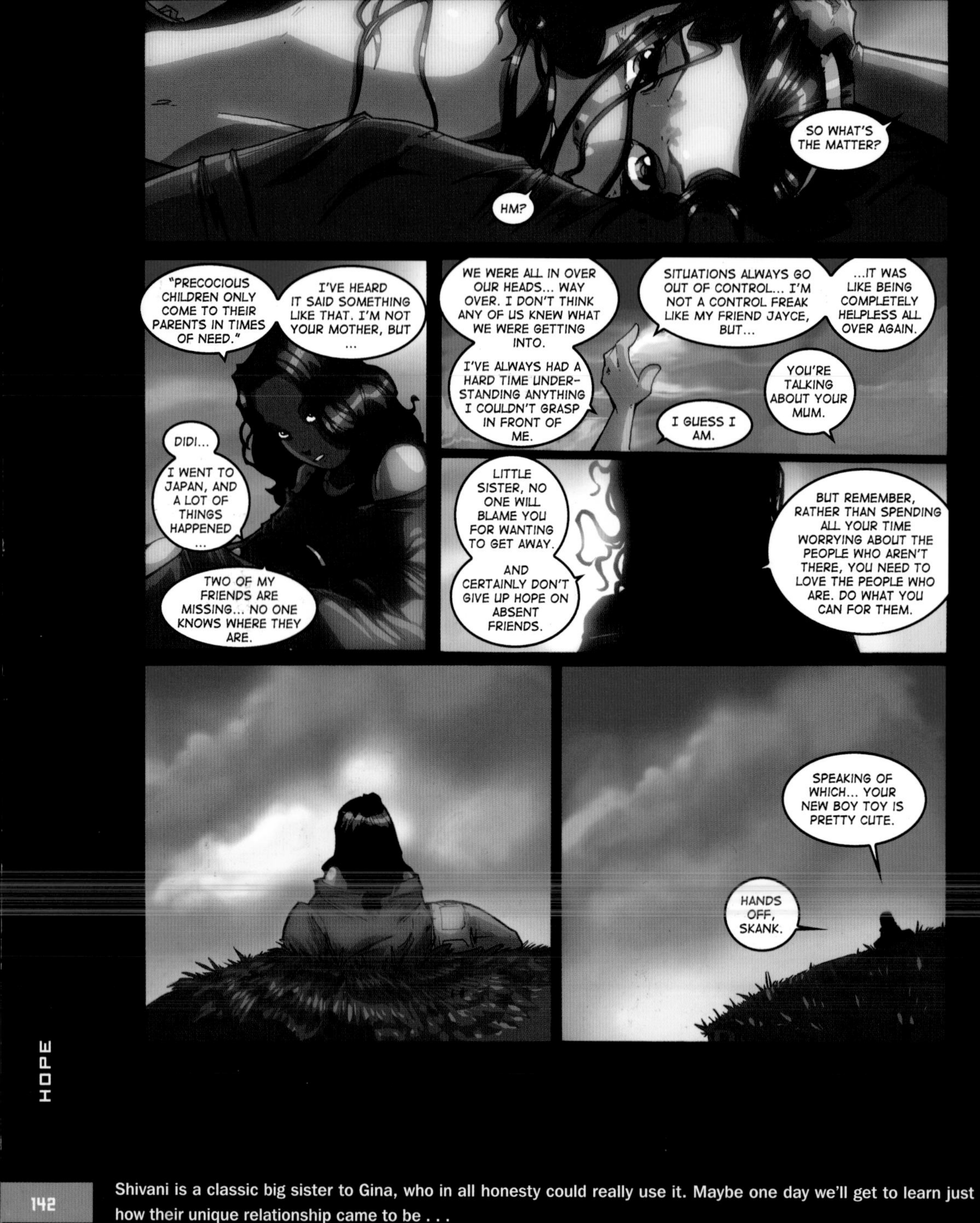
SO WHAT'S THE MATTER?
HM?
"PRECOCIOUS CHILDREN ONLY COME TO THEIR PARENTS IN TIMES OF NEED."
I'VE HEARD IT SAID SOMETHING LIKE THAT. I'M NOT YOUR MOTHER, BUT ...
DIDI...
I WENT TO JAPAN, AND A LOT OF THINGS HAPPENED ...
TWO OF MY FRIENDS ARE MISSING... NO ONE KNOWS WHERE THEY ARE.
WE WERE ALL IN OVER OUR HEADS... WAY OVER. I DON'T THINK ANY OF US KNEW WHAT WE WERE GETTING INTO.
I'VE ALWAYS HAD A HARD TIME UNDER-STANDING ANYTHING I COULDN'T GRASP IN FRONT OF ME.
SITUATIONS ALWAYS GO OUT OF CONTROL... I'M NOT A CONTROL FREAK LIKE MY FRIEND JAYCE, BUT...
...IT WAS LIKE BEING COMPLETELY HELPLESS ALL OVER AGAIN.
YOU'RE TALKING ABOUT YOUR MUM.
I GUESS I AM.
LITTLE SISTER, NO ONE WILL BLAME YOU FOR WANTING TO GET AWAY.
AND CERTAINLY DON'T GIVE UP HOPE ON ABSENT FRIENDS.
BUT REMEMBER, RATHER THAN SPENDING ALL YOUR TIME WORRYING ABOUT THE PEOPLE WHO AREN'T THERE, YOU NEED TO LOVE THE PEOPLE WHO ARE. DO WHAT YOU CAN FOR THEM.
SPEAKING OF WHICH... YOUR NEW BOY TOY IS PRETTY CUTE.
HANDS OFF, SKANK.

Shivani is a classic big sister to Gina, who in all honesty could really use it. Maybe one day we'll get to learn just how their unique relationship came to be . . .

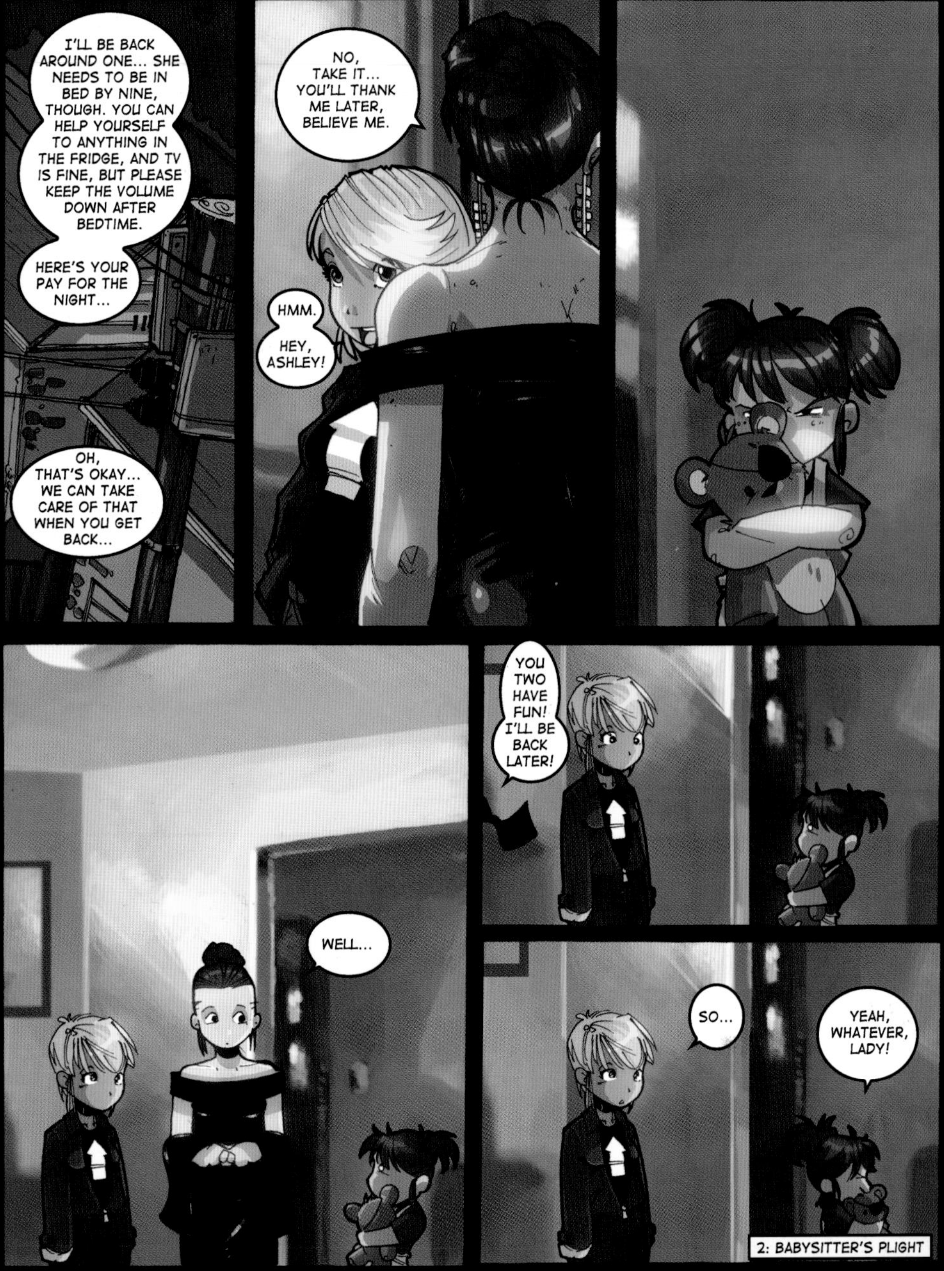
I'LL BE BACK AROUND ONE... SHE NEEDS TO BE IN BED BY NINE, THOUGH. YOU CAN HELP YOURSELF TO ANYTHING IN THE FRIDGE, AND TV IS FINE, BUT PLEASE KEEP THE VOLUME DOWN AFTER BEDTIME.
HERE'S YOUR PAY FOR THE NIGHT...
OH, THAT'S OKAY... WE CAN TAKE CARE OF THAT WHEN YOU GET BACK...
NO, TAKE IT... YOU'LL THANK ME LATER, BELIEVE ME.
HMM.
HEY, ASHLEY!
WELL...
YOU TWO HAVE FUN! I'LL BE BACK LATER!
SO...
YEAH, WHATEVER, LADY!
2: BABYSITTER'S PLIGHT

Thus begins one of my favorite story arcs. After all of the super-serious comics we'd done, we decided it was time for a detox. Enjoy!

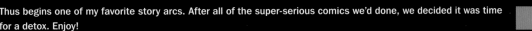

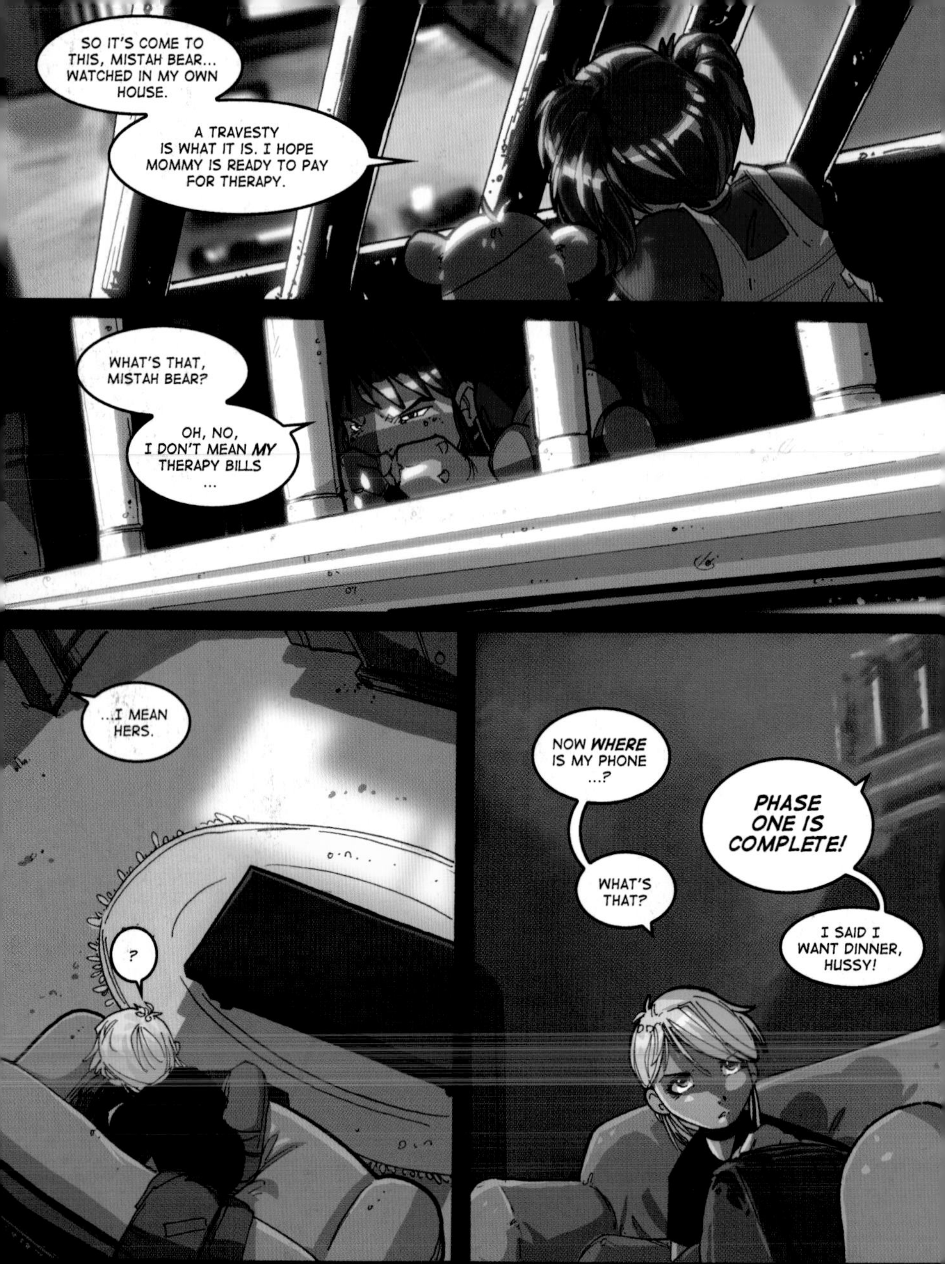
SO IT'S COME TO THIS, MISTAH BEAR... WATCHED IN MY OWN HOUSE.
A TRAVESTY IS WHAT IT IS. I HOPE MOMMY IS READY TO PAY FOR THERAPY.
WHAT'S THAT, MISTAH BEAR?
OH, NO, I DON'T MEAN *MY* THERAPY BILLS ...
...I MEAN HERS.
?
NOW *WHERE* IS MY PHONE ...?
WHAT'S THAT?
PHASE ONE IS COMPLETE!
I SAID I WANT DINNER, HUSSY!

arly Ashley is a bit of a handful. She's capricious, certainly, and she's ready to learn all manner of bad words

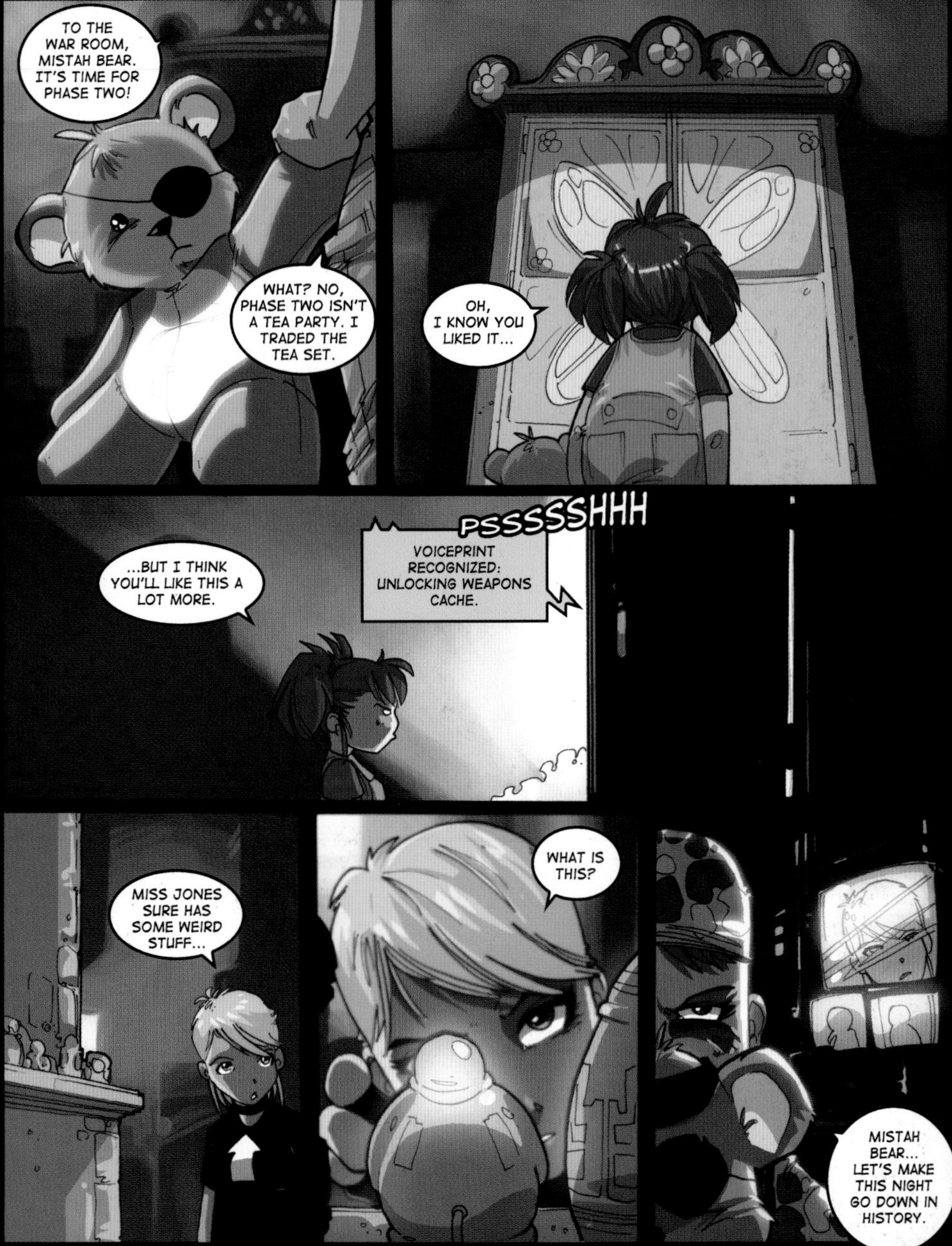
TO THE WAR ROOM, MISTAH BEAR. IT'S TIME FOR PHASE TWO!
WHAT? NO, PHASE TWO ISN'T A TEA PARTY. I TRADED THE TEA SET.
OH, I KNOW YOU LIKED IT...
...BUT I THINK YOU'LL LIKE THIS A LOT MORE.
PSSSSSHHH
VOICEPRINT RECOGNIZED: UNLOCKING WEAPONS CACHE.
MISS JONES SURE HAS SOME WEIRD STUFF...
WHAT IS THIS?
MISTAH BEAR... LET'S MAKE THIS NIGHT GO DOWN IN HISTORY.

If you ignore the fact that she's got a bit of a tyrant complex, she kind of reminds you of someone else we know . . . Who else has a bunch of crazy inventions lying around? I just can't seem to recall.

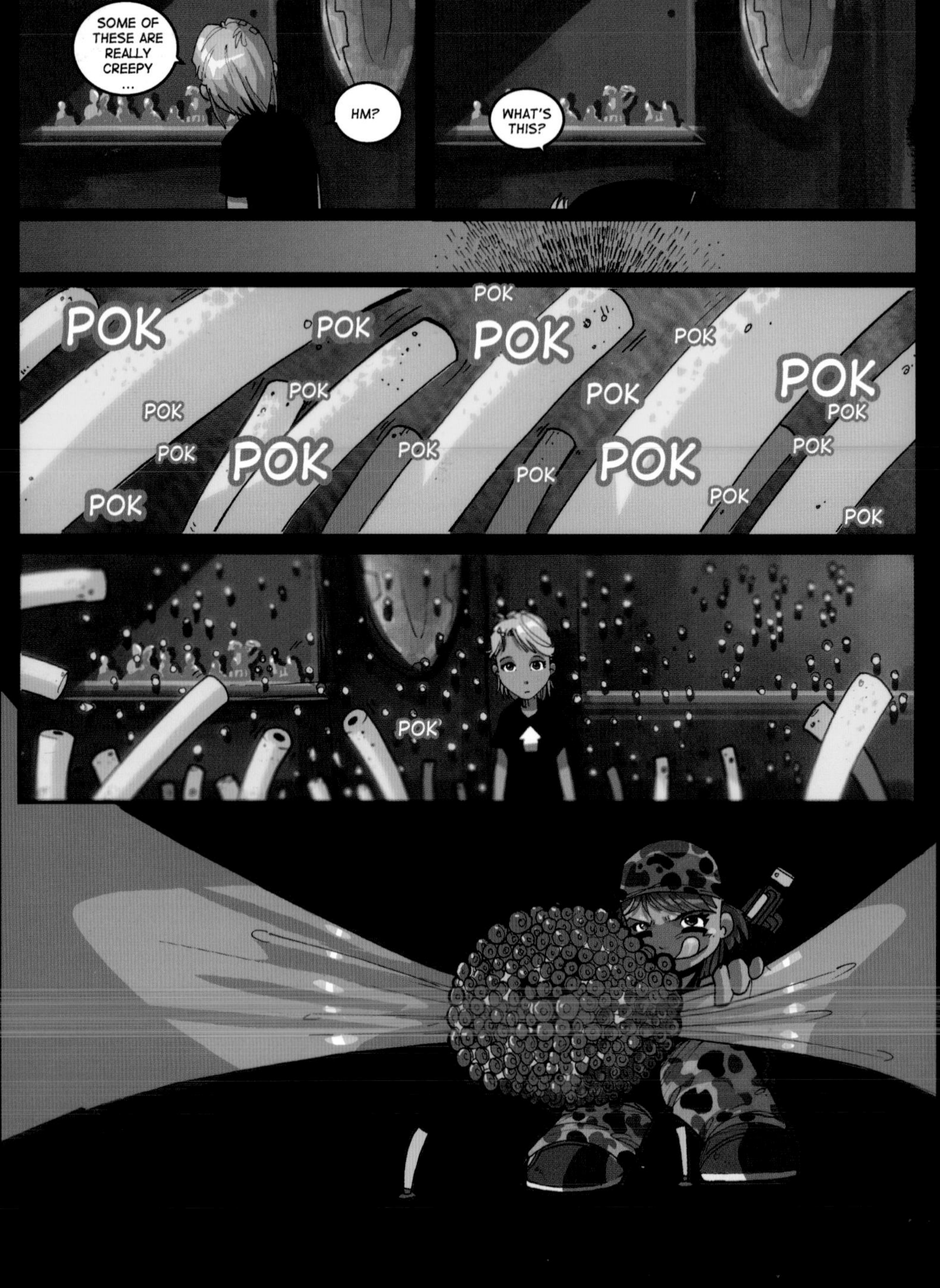
SOME OF THESE ARE REALLY CREEPY ...
HM?
WHAT'S THIS?
POK
POK
POK
POK
POK
POK
POK
POK
POK
POK
POK
POK
POK
POK
POK
POK
POK
POK
POK
POK

We had just watched *Hero*, and Jet Li's famous scene staring down the arrows is what inspired the line of action in this comic. Movies by Yimou Zhang always make beautiful use of colors—they're delicious to watch. IMDb says Sam Raimi is remaking *House of Flying Daggers* . . . So soon?

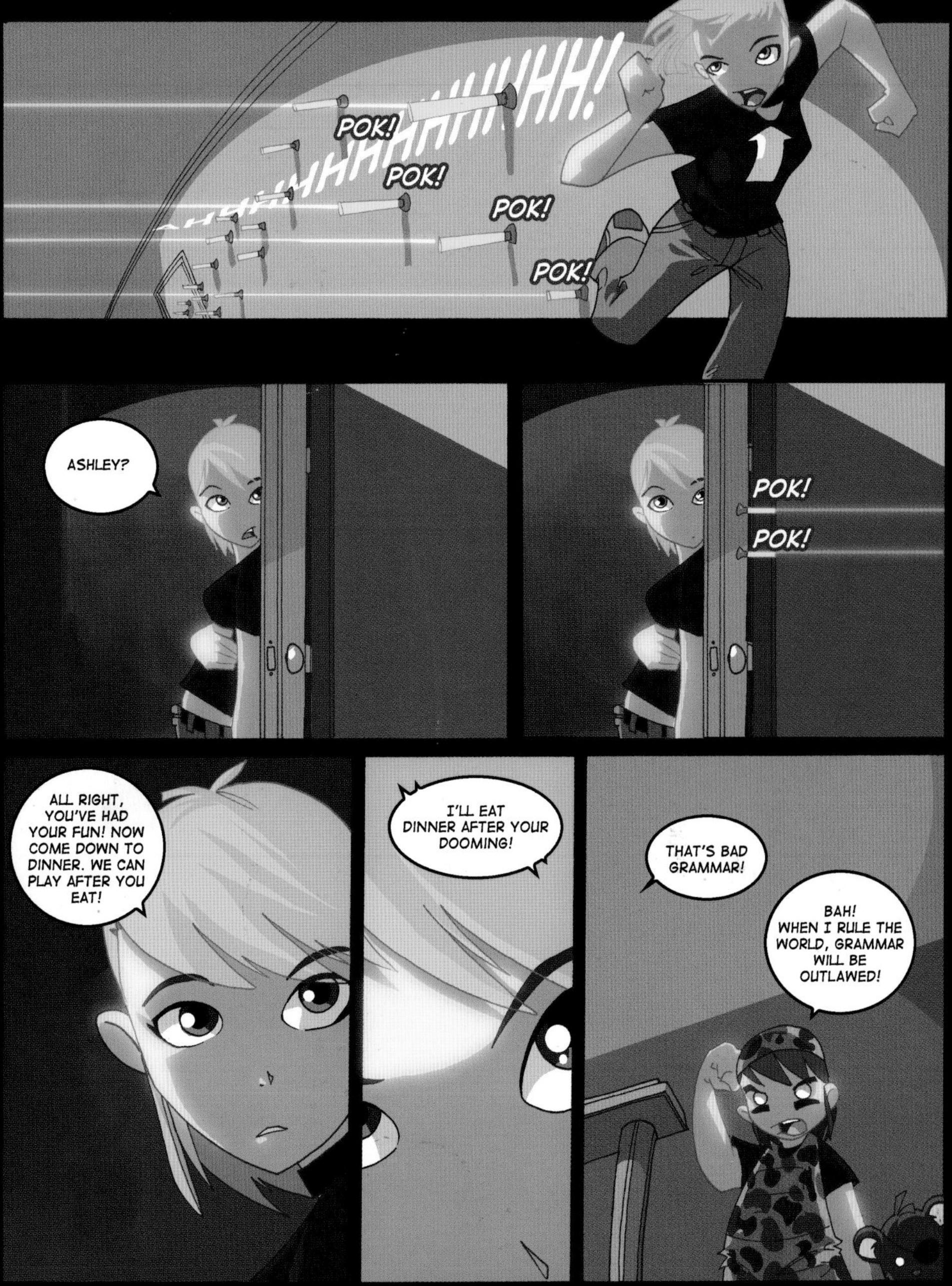
POK!
POK!
POK!
POK!
ASHLEY?
POK!
POK!
ALL RIGHT, YOU'VE HAD YOUR FUN! NOW COME DOWN TO DINNER. WE CAN PLAY AFTER YOU EAT!
I'LL EAT DINNER AFTER YOUR DOOMING!
THAT'S BAD GRAMMAR!
BAH! WHEN I RULE THE WORLD, GRAMMAR WILL BE OUTLAWED!

Ashley's been described as somewhere between *Pinky and the Brain* and *Calvin and Hobbes*. I'll leave it up to you to decide . . . I'm loath to compare anything I do to *Calvin and Hobbes*. That guy is a master. There is a handsome, leather-bound collection of all of the *Calvin and Hobbes* comics in existence, and it's definitely on my wish list.

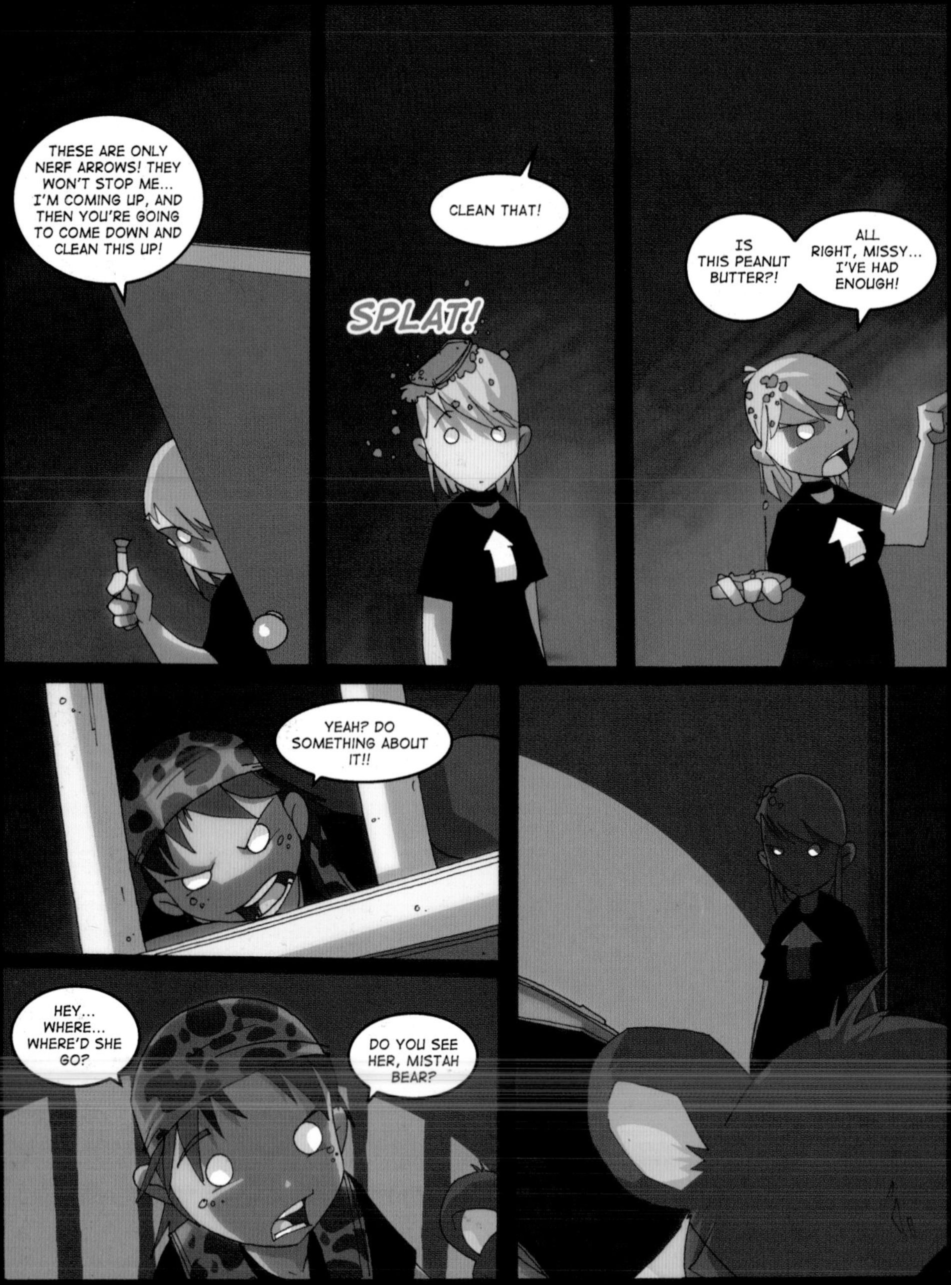
THESE ARE ONLY NERF ARROWS! THEY WON'T STOP ME... I'M COMING UP, AND THEN YOU'RE GOING TO COME DOWN AND CLEAN THIS UP!
CLEAN THAT!
SPLAT!
IS THIS PEANUT BUTTER?!
ALL RIGHT, MISSY... I'VE HAD ENOUGH!
YEAH? DO SOMETHING ABOUT IT!!
HEY... WHERE... WHERE'D SHE GO?
DO YOU SEE HER, MISTAH BEAR?

Uh-oh. Thaaat's a spanking face. I've never baby-sat anyone before, but I've been baby-sat, and one thing that is vivid in my mind is the face my babysitter would make when I was particularly contrary. There's an unfortunate dilemma for the babysitter there, because they can't really smack you, but boy do you deserve it. I did, anyway.

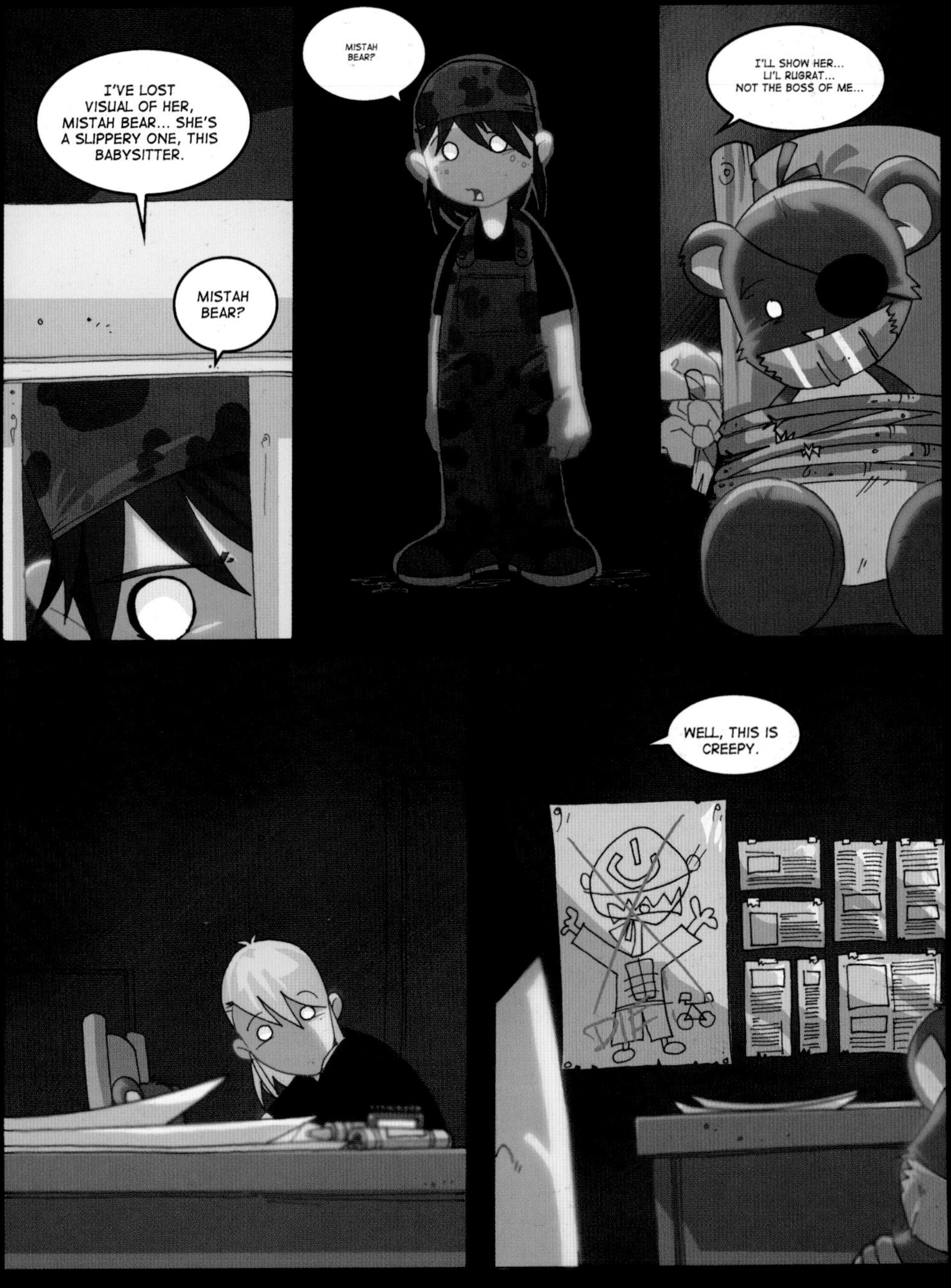
I'VE LOST VISUAL OF HER, MISTAH BEAR... SHE'S A SLIPPERY ONE, THIS BABYSITTER.
MISTAH BEAR?
MISTAH BEAR?
I'LL SHOW HER... LI'L RUGRAT... NOT THE BOSS OF ME...
WELL, THIS IS CREEPY.

Ashley has been obsessing a little bit over her tricycle . . .

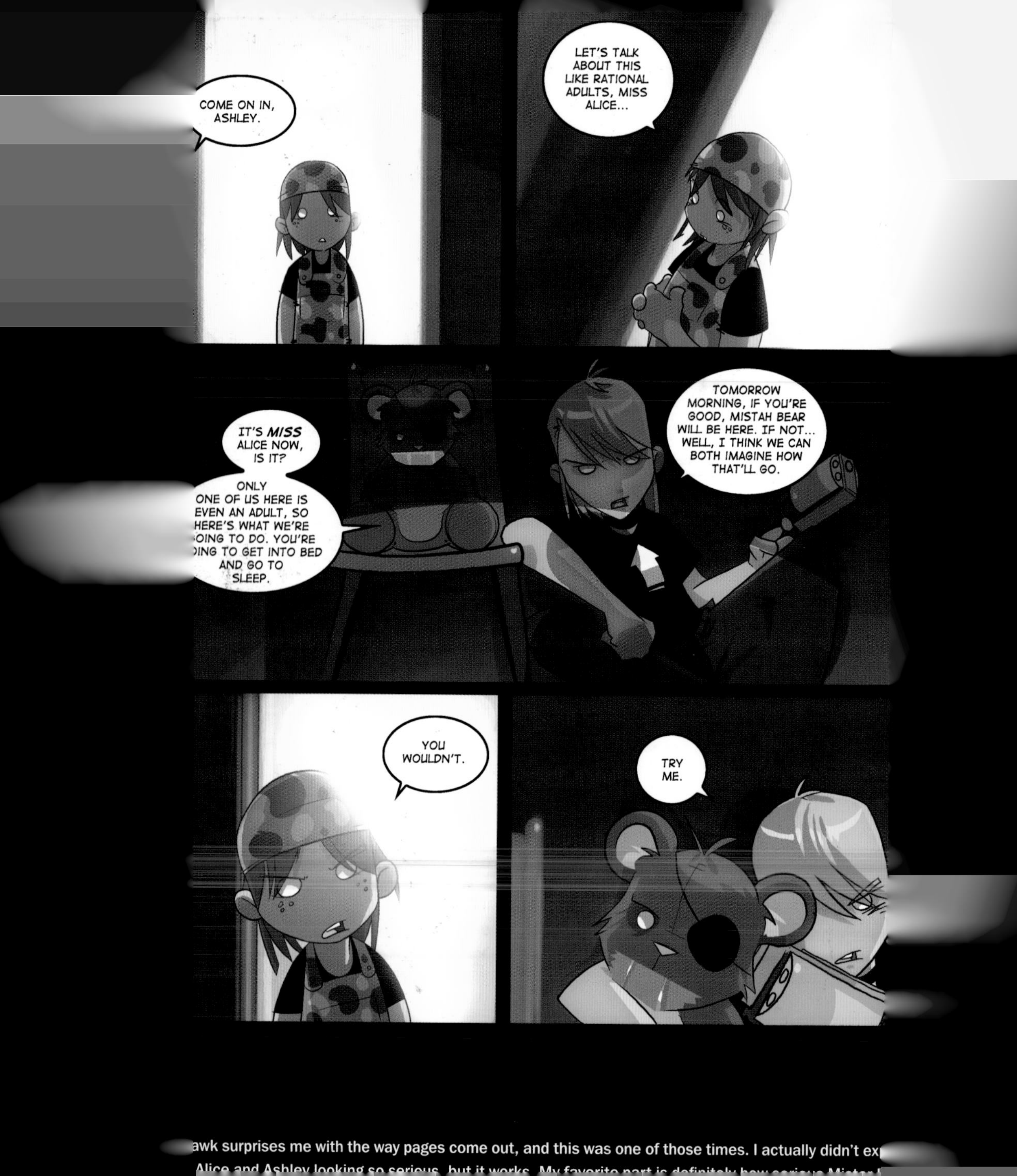
COME ON IN, ASHLEY.
LET'S TALK ABOUT THIS LIKE RATIONAL ADULTS, MISS ALICE...
IT'S *MISS* ALICE NOW, IS IT?
ONLY ONE OF US HERE IS EVEN AN ADULT, SO HERE'S WHAT WE'RE OING TO DO. YOU'RE ING TO GET INTO BED AND GO TO SLEEP.
TOMORROW MORNING, IF YOU'RE GOOD, MISTAH BEAR WILL BE HERE. IF NOT... WELL, I THINK WE CAN BOTH IMAGINE HOW THAT'LL GO.
YOU WOULDN'T.
TRY ME.

awk surprises me with the way pages come out, and this was one of those times. I actually didn't ex
Alice and Ashley looking so serious, but it works. My favorite part is definitely how serious Mister

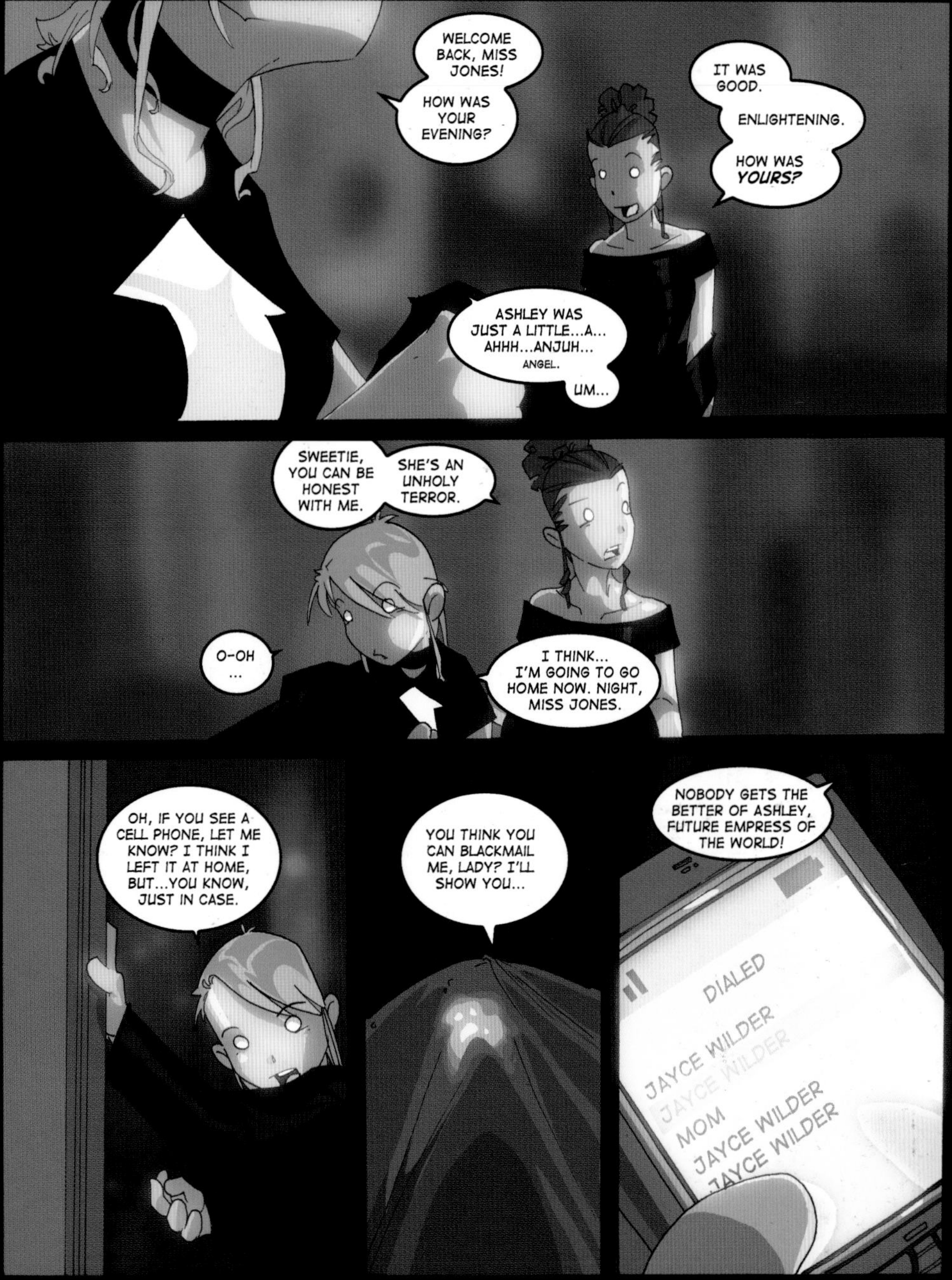
WELCOME BACK, MISS JONES!
HOW WAS YOUR EVENING?
IT WAS GOOD.
ENLIGHTENING.
HOW WAS *YOURS?*
ASHLEY WAS JUST A LITTLE...A... AHHH...ANJUH... ANGEL.
UM...
SWEETIE, YOU CAN BE HONEST WITH ME.
SHE'S AN UNHOLY TERROR.
O-OH ...
I THINK... I'M GOING TO GO HOME NOW. NIGHT, MISS JONES.
OH, IF YOU SEE A CELL PHONE, LET ME KNOW? I THINK I LEFT IT AT HOME, BUT...YOU KNOW, JUST IN CASE.
YOU THINK YOU CAN BLACKMAIL ME, LADY? I'LL SHOW YOU...
NOBODY GETS THE BETTER OF ASHLEY, FUTURE EMPRESS OF THE WORLD!
DIALED
JAYCE WILDER
JAYCE WILDER
MOM
JAYCE WILDER
JAYCE WILDER

I have had a friend's little sister steal my phone and make a couple of phone calls. It was actually pretty funny. In the end, I got her to record a voice-mail message pretending to be me. I accidentally left it that way for a week and got a call back from a job interview . . . Good thing they had a sense of humor.

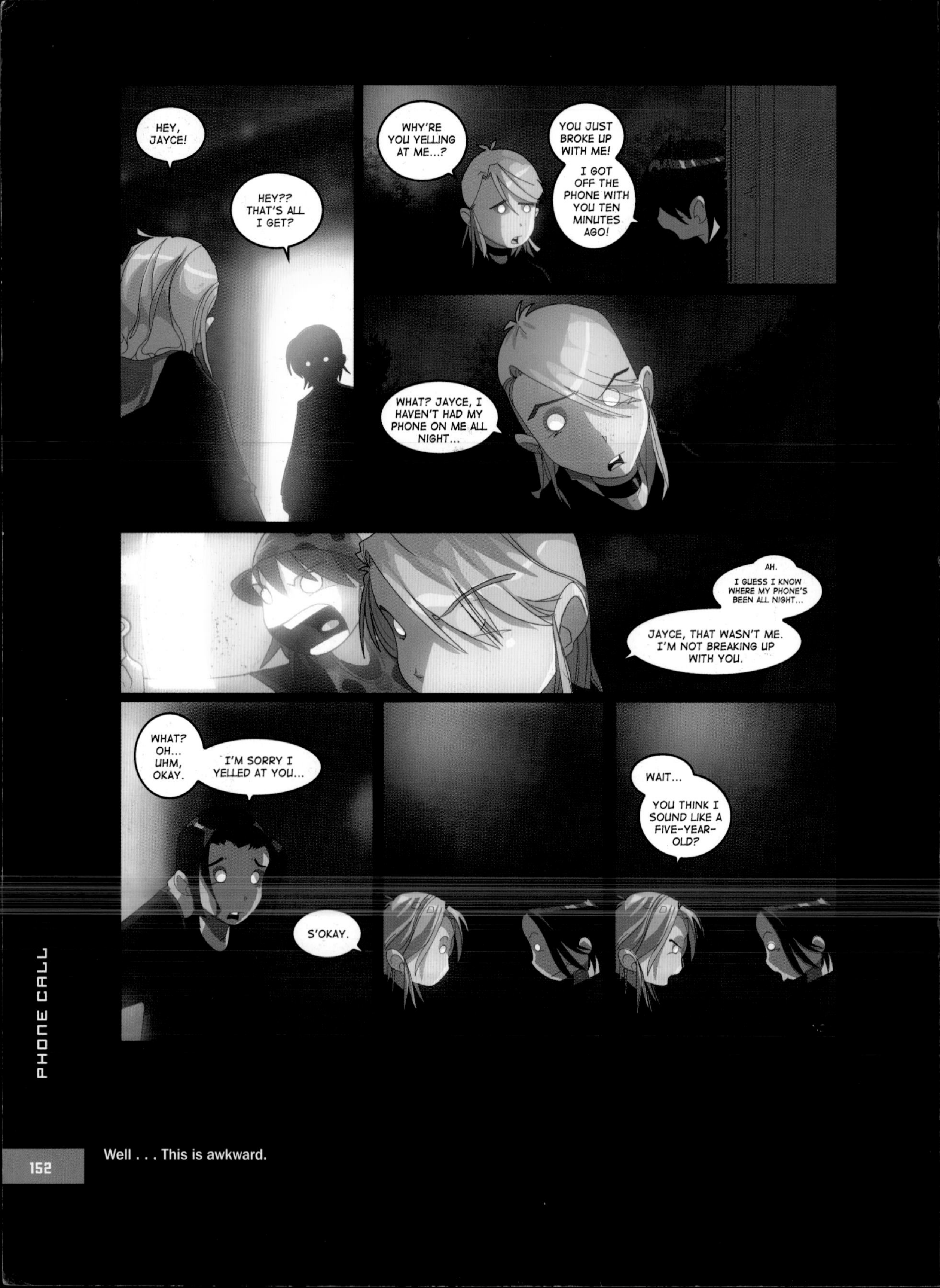
HEY, JAYCE!
HEY?? THAT'S ALL I GET?
WHY'RE YOU YELLING AT ME...?
YOU JUST BROKE UP WITH ME!
I GOT OFF THE PHONE WITH YOU TEN MINUTES AGO!
WHAT? JAYCE, I HAVEN'T HAD MY PHONE ON ME ALL NIGHT...
AH. I GUESS I KNOW WHERE MY PHONE'S BEEN ALL NIGHT...
JAYCE, THAT WASN'T ME. I'M NOT BREAKING UP WITH YOU.
WHAT? OH... UHM, OKAY.
I'M SORRY I YELLED AT YOU...
S'OKAY.
WAIT...
YOU THINK I SOUND LIKE A FIVE-YEAR-OLD?

Well . . . This is awkward.

APPLEGEEKS
1/3/2005-11/13/2006

153 PINUPS.tif

Welcome to the pinup gallery! As was stated in *Applegeeks* Volume 1, some-times work, illness, or some other speed bump prevents me from creating a full-page comic on time. However, I still try my best to put something up for our readers. I know I don't *have* to, since we're putting the comics up for free, but I still feel guilty if I don't. When I look back at these full-page pinups, I can't always recall the exact reason why I had to put each up instead of an actual comic, but I can tell you what I was thinking when I was working on each piece . . .

Choose Wisely—For this piece, I do remember why the comic was late. This was actually our very first poster design! Since it was pretty big, it took a while to finish. By the time the poster was done, it was time for a new comic, so I decided to show our readers a sneak peek of it. If I remember correctly, everyone loved the art, so I was forgiven for not posting a comic.

Katsucon 2005—The reason for this pinup was that Ananth and I were attending an anime convention. When that happens, I don't get the chance to work on a full comic over the week-end. Since this pinup features Ian from *Mac Hall*, he must have been at the convention too.

Unleashed—This time around, I was too busy studying for final exams to work on an actual comic. In the end, this pinup turned out to be a design for an *Applegeeks* T-shirt.

Happy Halloween—I remember coming up with this idea, but I'm not sure why an actual comic wasn't done. Even though I have a Wacom Cintiq, I tend to still draw and ink on paper. For this piece, I remember trying out pen nibs and India ink when it came to inking. It was an interesting process, but took longer than I expected.

Alley—I'll be honest, not one of my favorites. However, it was quick and it went up on time.

Screen tones—I guess I was inspired after reading some manga. I was interested in the look of screen tones, and had never used any on my art before, so I thought I would experiment. Before I applied the screen tones, I used Painter to ink Eve.

Banner Art—For a while, we attended cons without much signage, so the only way a person would see us was if he/she walked up and looked down at the table. So I took about a week to create a large banner that would hang above us. You can view the final banner image on my Flickr page: www.flickr.com/photos/hawkstudios/181033917/.

Ashley World—For this piece, I was inspired by artist Sean Galloway. I thought it would be cool to see what *AG* would look like in his style. Of course I had mixed reviews about it. Oh well.

—Hawk

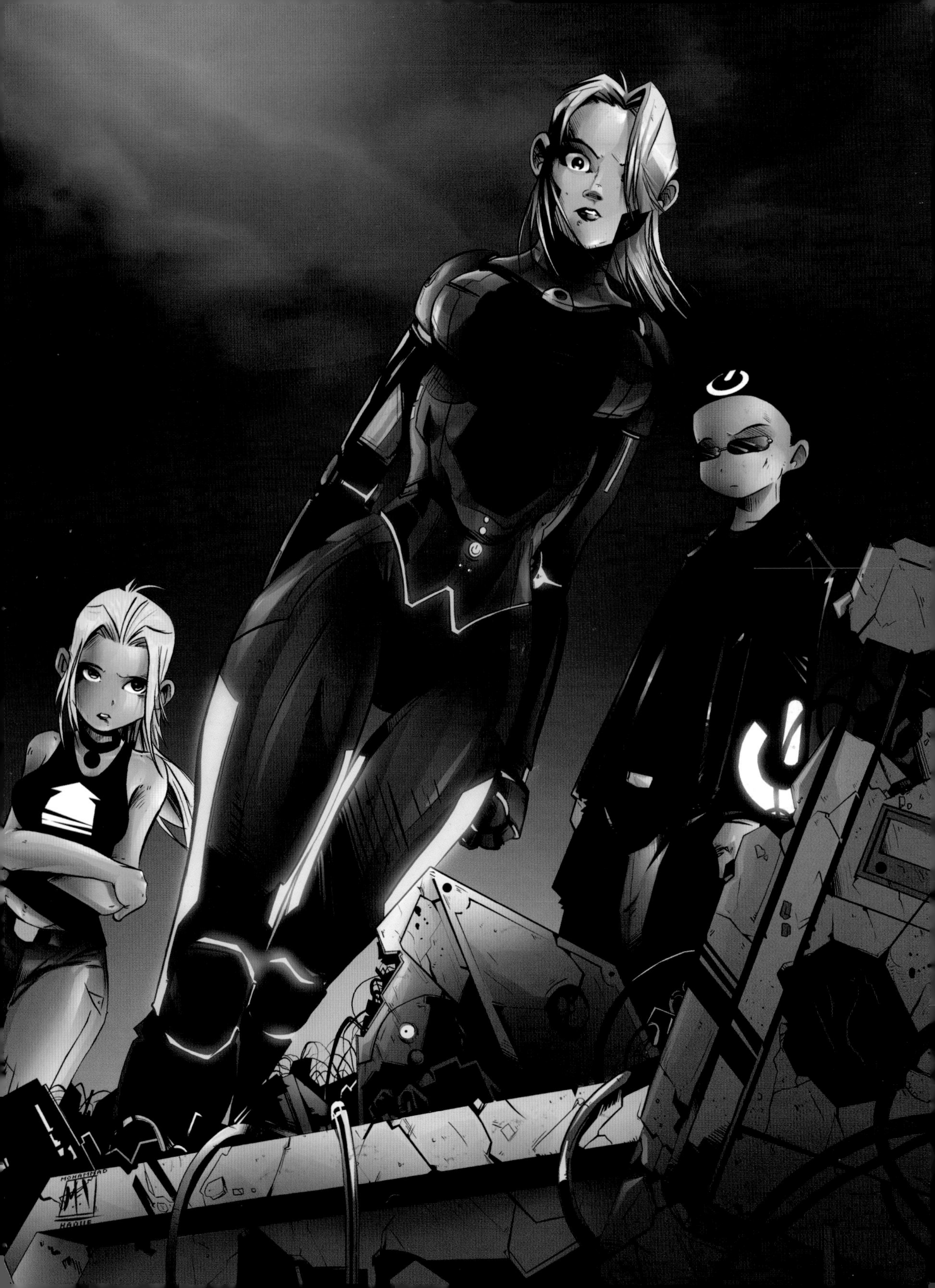

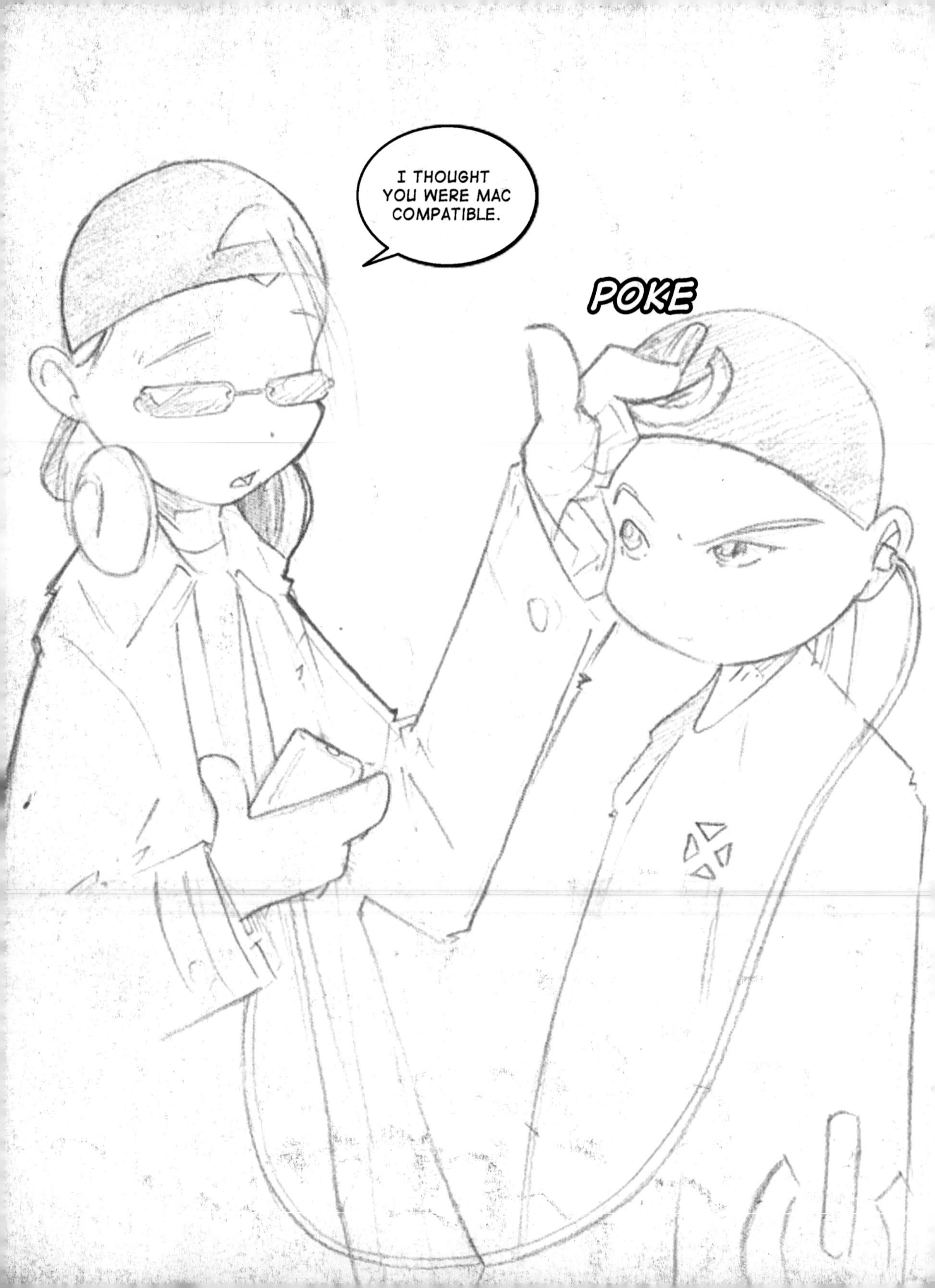
I THOUGHT YOU WERE MAC COMPATIBLE.
POKE

10 rolls of toilet paper for your Mummy costume: $25

Your neighbor's Vampirella costume: $50

Not wearing any pants to her Halloween party: Priceless

HAPPY HALLOWEEN

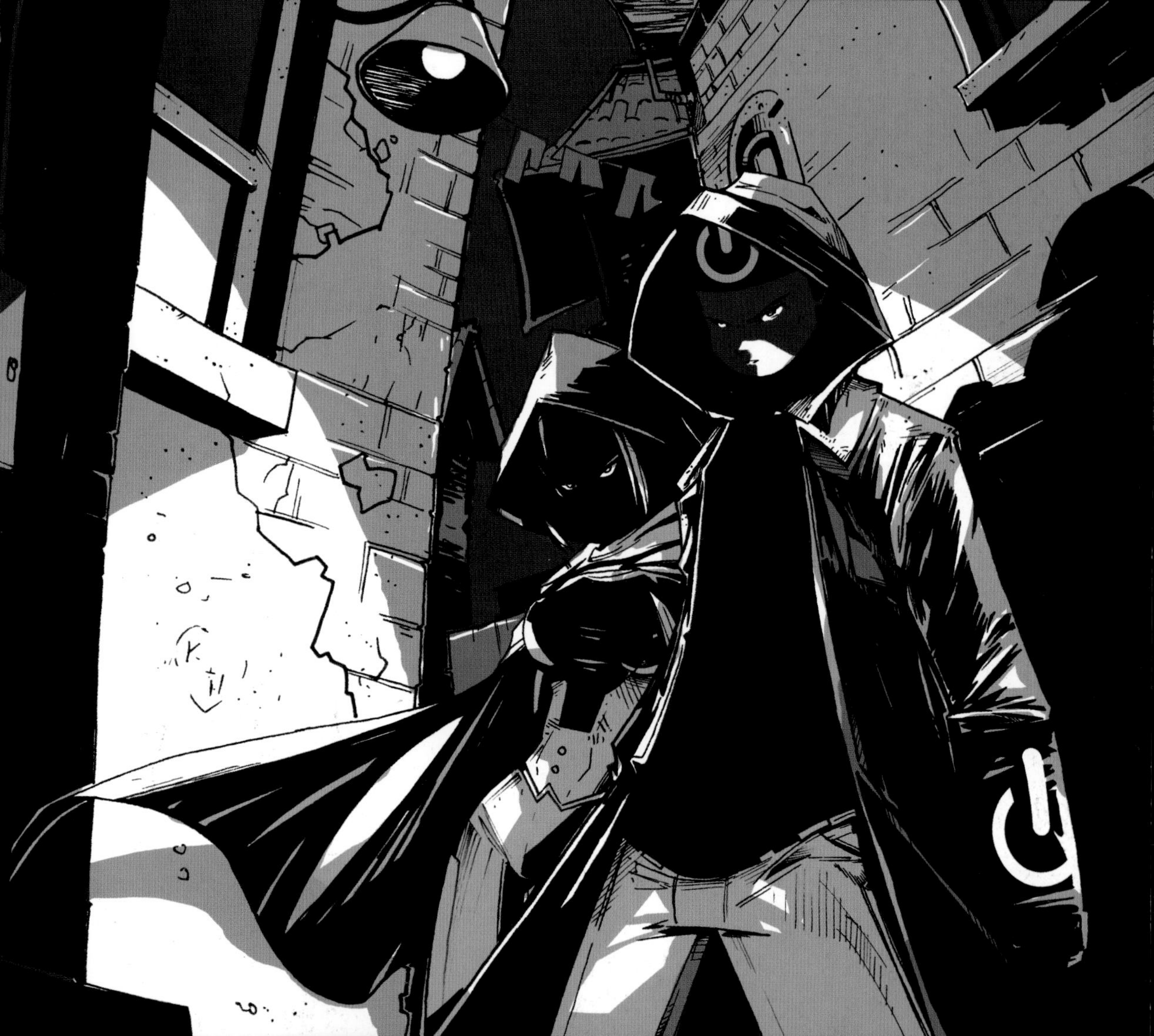

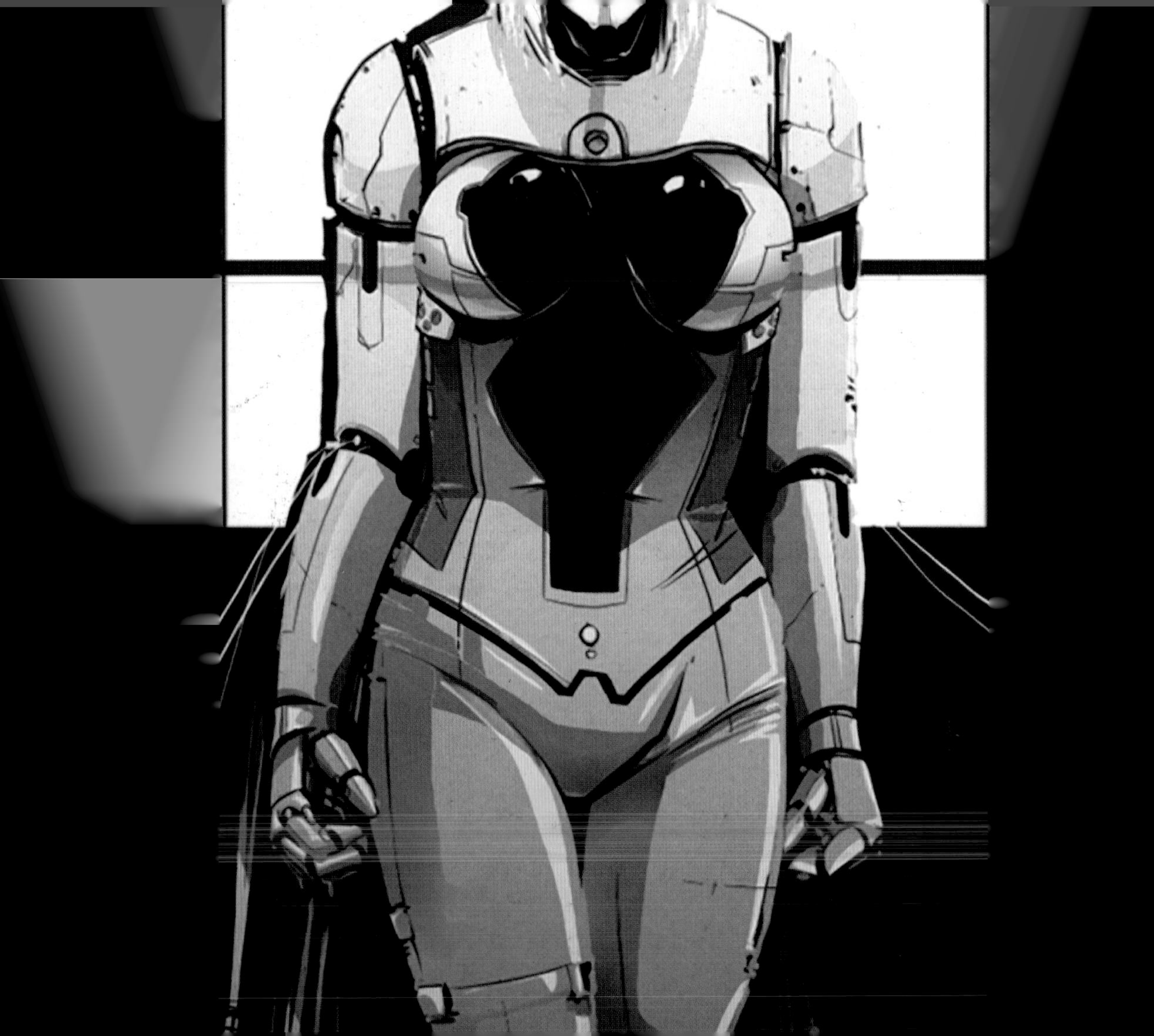

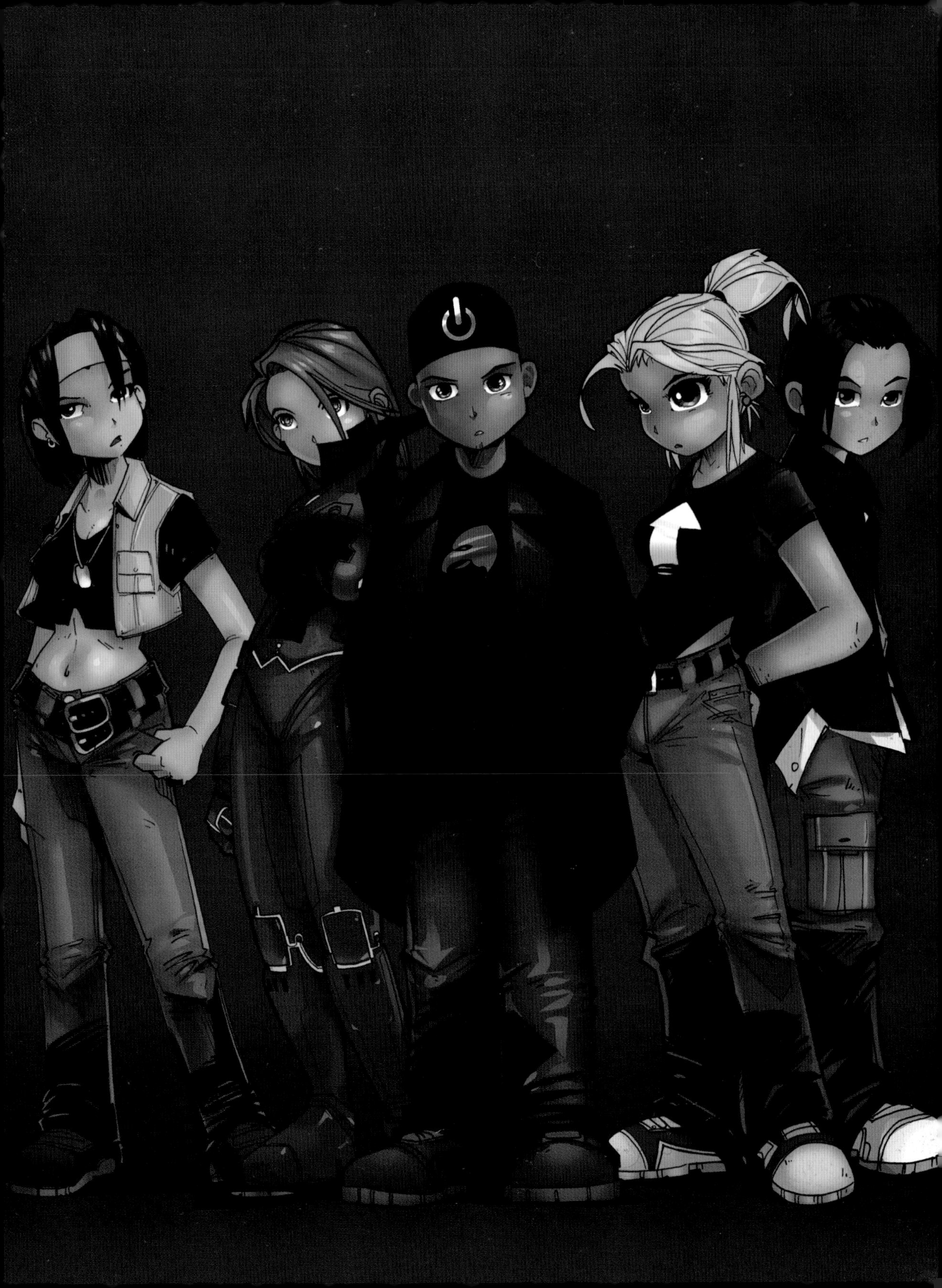

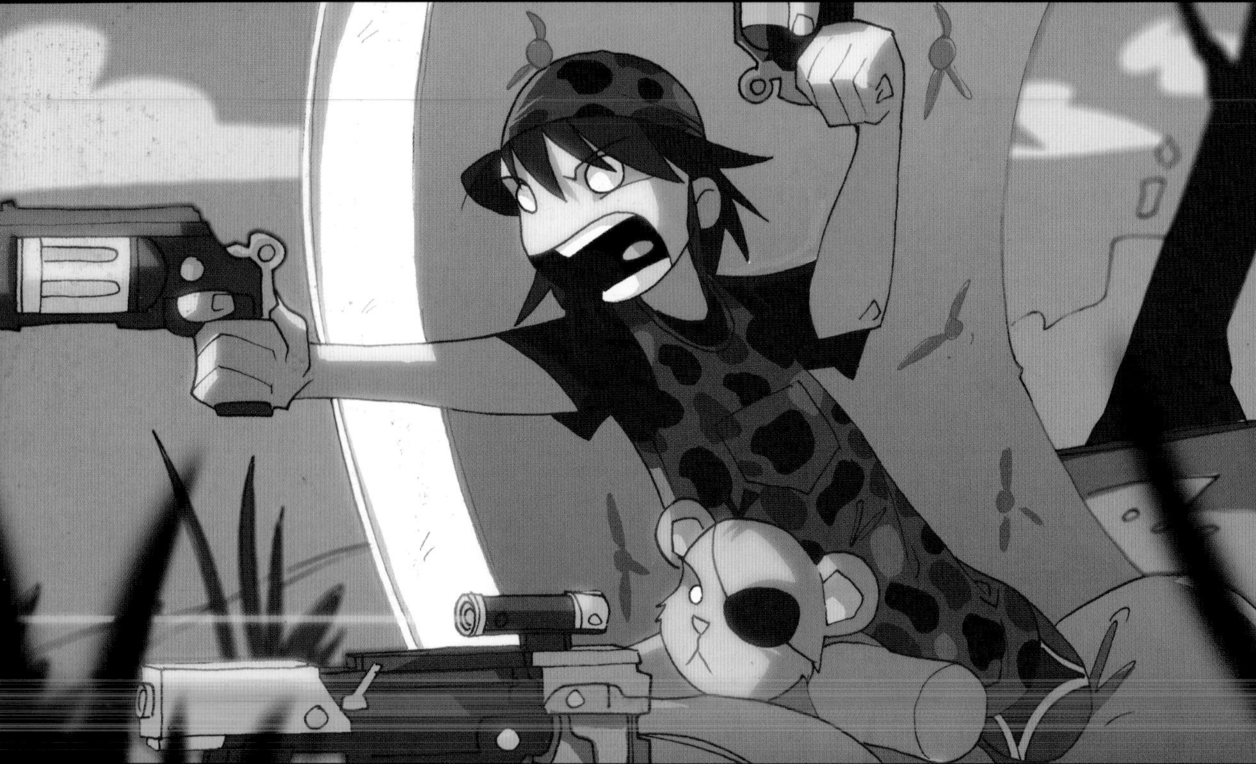

BONUS MATERIAL

163   EVE FIGURINE_DEVELOPMENT JOURNAL.indd

Right around the time work wrapped up on the comics that appear in this volume, a very interesting e-mail exchange kicked off, which would result in the creation of a really sweet limited-edition Eve figurine! Curious about how that all went down? Keep reading!

DECEMBER 18, 2006

We've got a peculiar e-mail in our inbox, from a company called Gensen (gensenfigure.com). They're asking us if we want to produce a figurine of one of our characters. We grew up playing with action figures, but for some reason it's never occurred to us to investigate the possibility of translating our own characters into 3-D. We're positively giddy at the idea—it brings out the kid in each of us!

To get an idea of the kind of product Gensen makes, we've browsed their website, and we're totally blown away. These are the guys who make the figurines you see every-where. The pros. We're sold!

DECEMBER 23, 2006

Hawk just sent in some preliminary sketches. There's a specific format you're sup-posed to use, which you can see illustrated below. Note the floating sketches of the parts hidden in the larger ones.

JANUARY 9, 2007

It's right after the new year, and we're in the thick of a project at work. So thrilled to check out the photos that just arrived of the prototype!

Designed: Applegeeks
Sculptor: www.gensenfigure.com

Designed: Applegeeks

Designed: Applegeeks

Designed: Applegeeks

Designed: Applegeeks

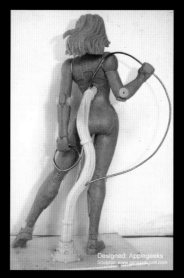

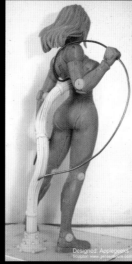

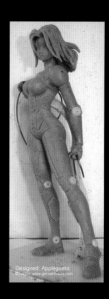

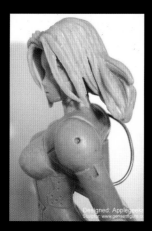

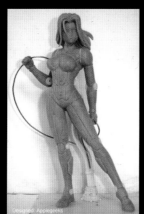

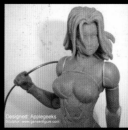

Hawk's sending the photos back with a few notes for changes. Eve's chest is a little too . . . uh . . . detailed.

FEBRUARY 2, 2007

The changes are in, and Gensen's asked Hawk for a color key. He's happy to oblige them and has put together this breakdown of Eve's color scheme . . .

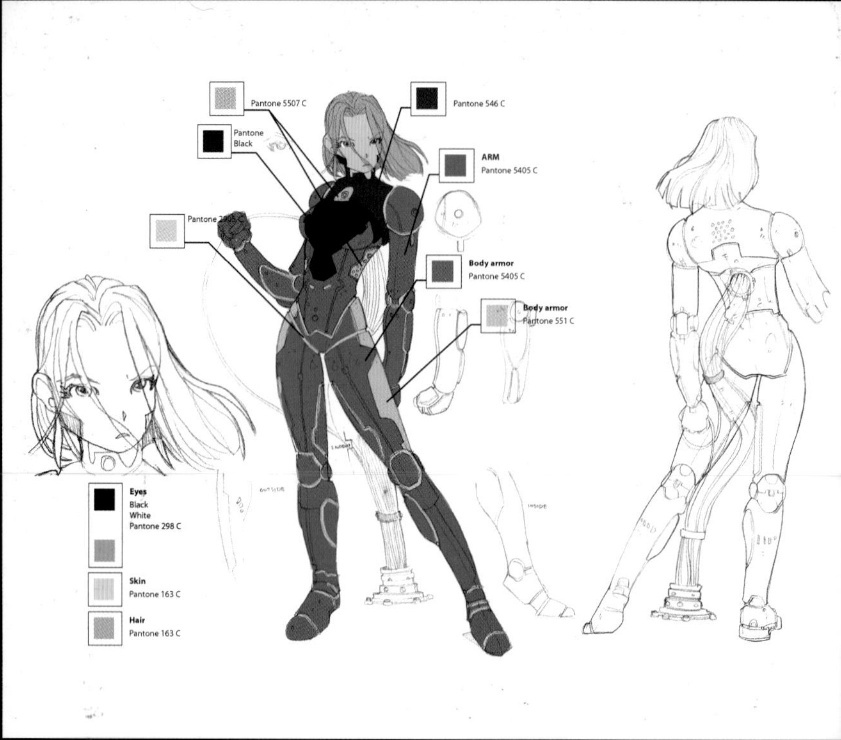
Pantone 5507 C
Pantone 546 C
Pantone Black
ARM
Pantone 5405 C
Pantone 2905 C
Body armor
Pantone 5405 C
Body armor
Pantone 551 C
Eyes
Black
White
Pantone 298 C
Skin
Pantone 163 C
Hair
Pantone 163 C

FEBRUARY 28, 2007

The colored prototype arrived in the mail today! Anyone who has seen one of Gensen's figurines up close can tell you that the attention to detail is exquisite . . . They've really blown our minds with their craftsmanship! What shocks me the most is that they've managed to capture Hawk's specific style, especially in Eve's face.

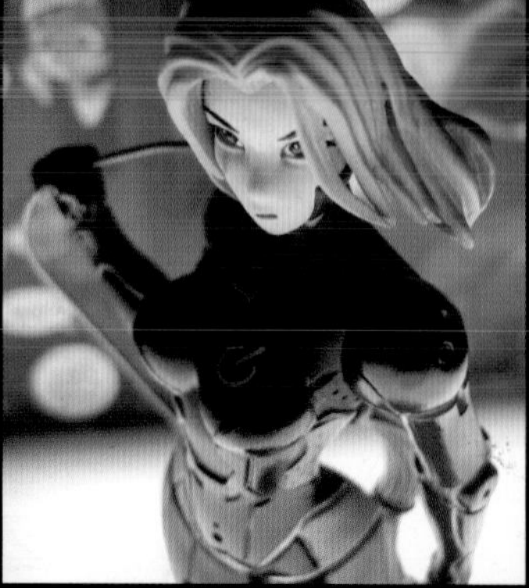

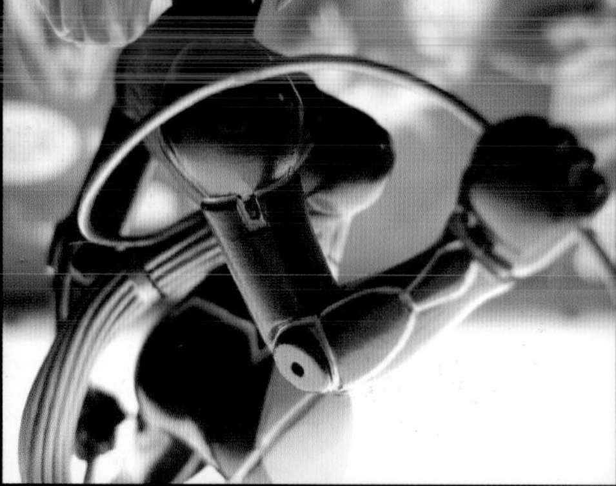

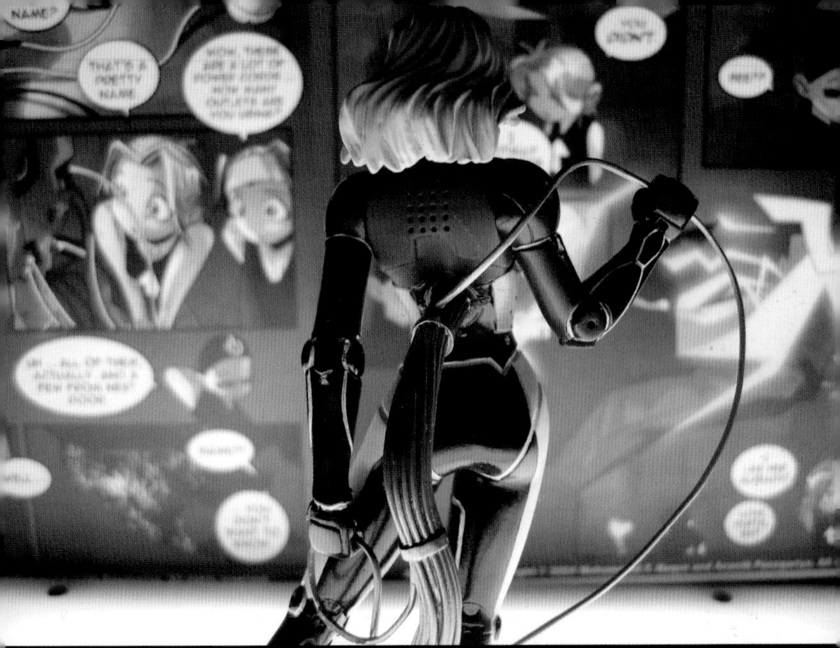

NAME?
THAT'S A PRETTY NAME
YOU DIDN'T

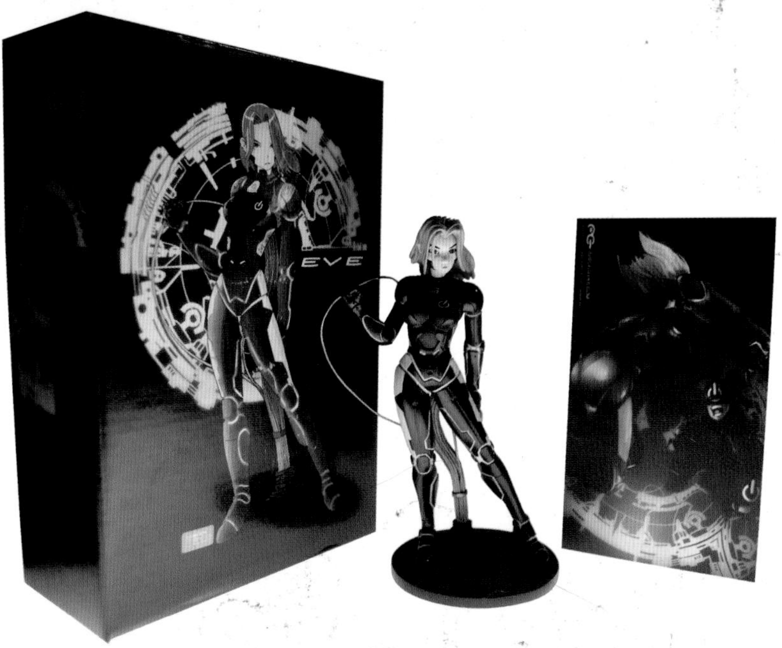

EVE

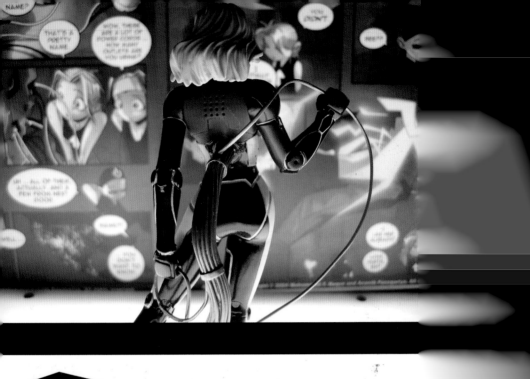

JULY 20, 2007

The Eve figurine debuted today at Otakon 2007 in Baltimore, Maryland. We sold fifty in under ten minutes!

Making the Eve figurine with Gensen was an amazing experience. And, most importantly, our readers really liked how she turned out—that was the icing on the cake for us. To this day we still have people asking us for these, but unfortunately they were restricted to a limited run of five hundred. Maybe we'll just have to make a new one someday!

—Ananth

▼ **BONUS MATERIAL**

169 V2 COVER EVOLUTION.psd

Since Eve really comes into her own in this volume, we wanted to be sure to make her the focus of the cover art this time around.

First, we tossed around a bunch of concept sketches . . .

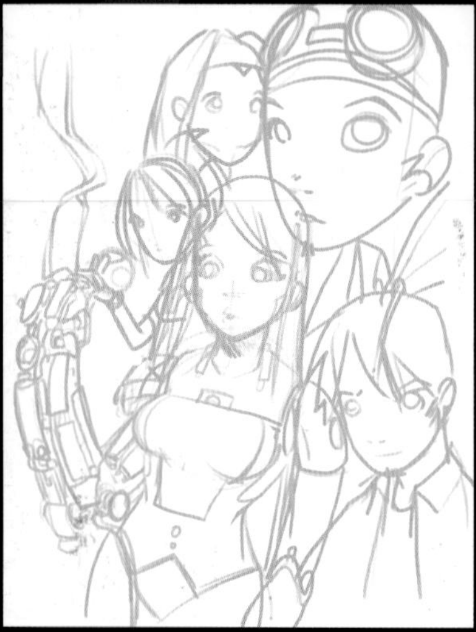

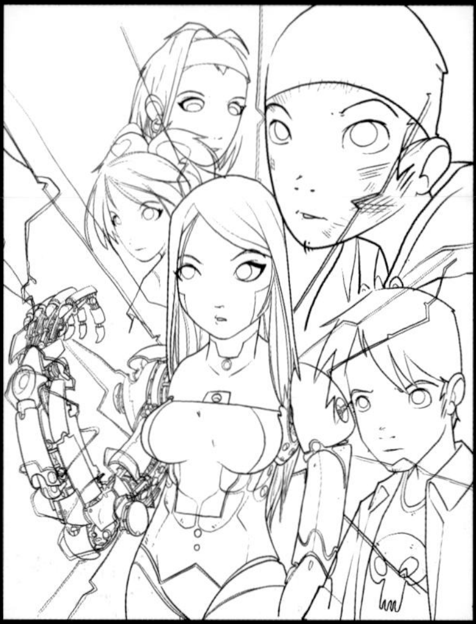

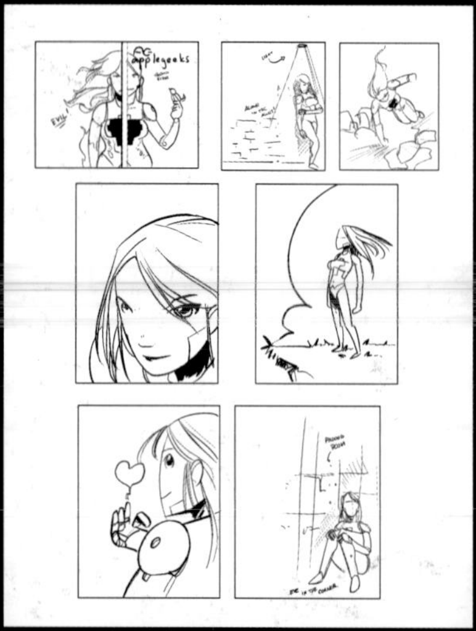
applegeeks
EVIL!

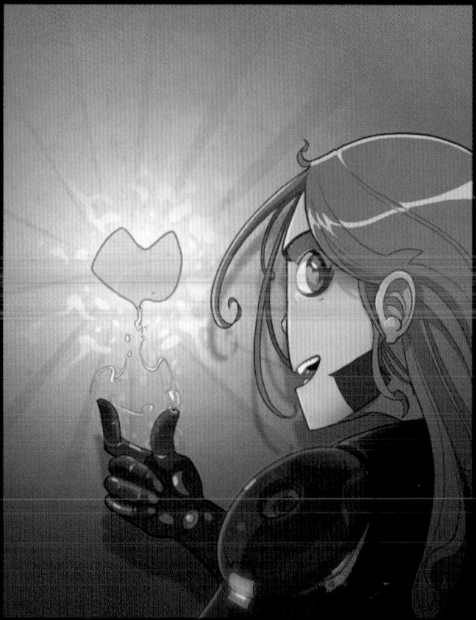

Once we settled on an image, it was time to start playing with details and color schemes. Here's one of the alternate color schemes we came up with. If you look closely, you can spot a bunch of little differences between this version and the illustration as it ended up on the final cover.

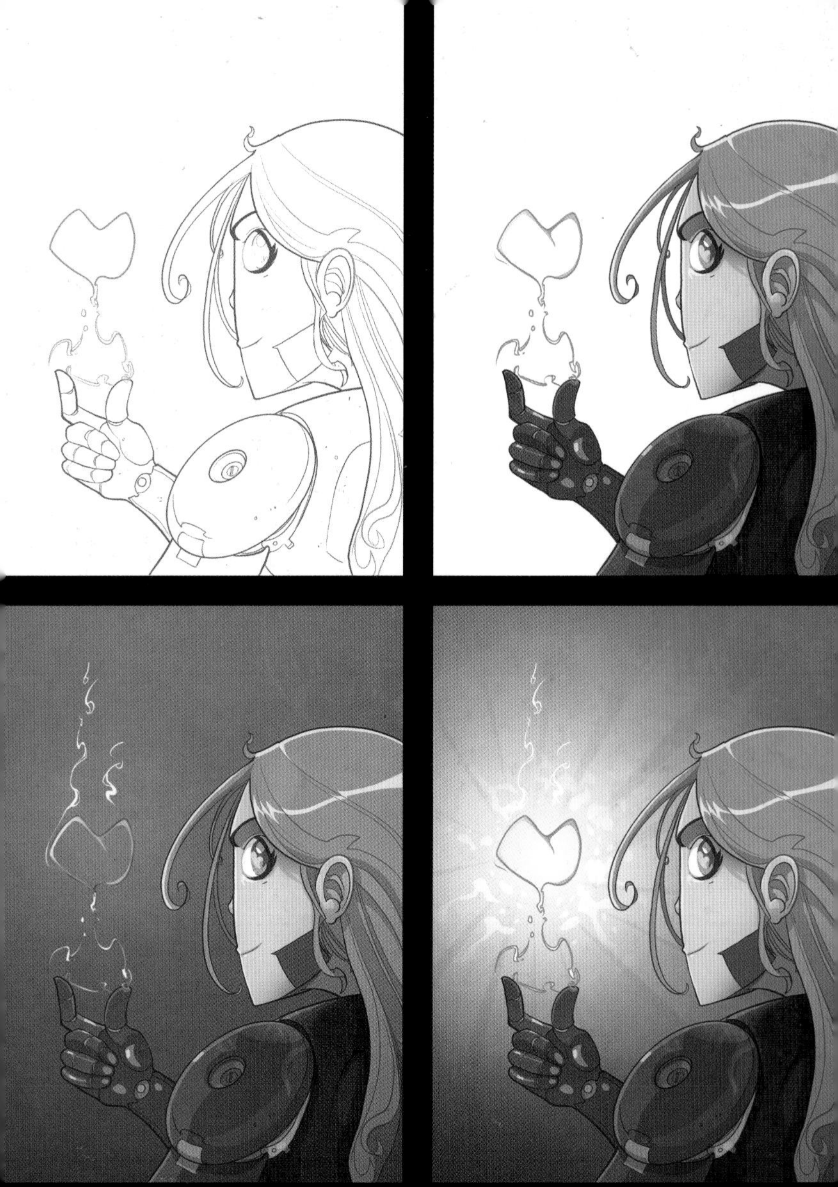

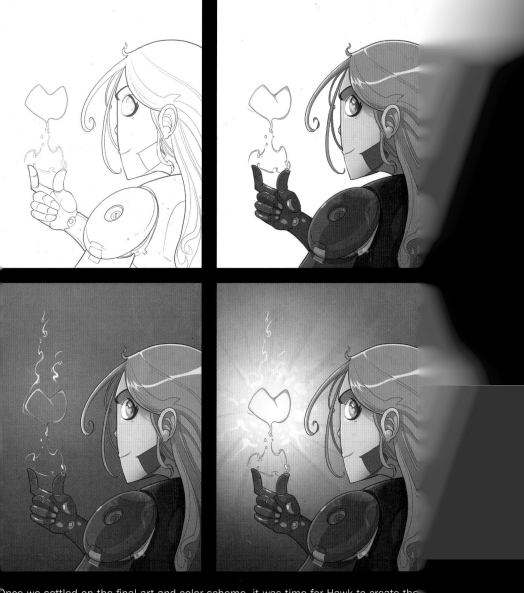

Once we settled on the final art and color scheme, it was time for Hawk to create the

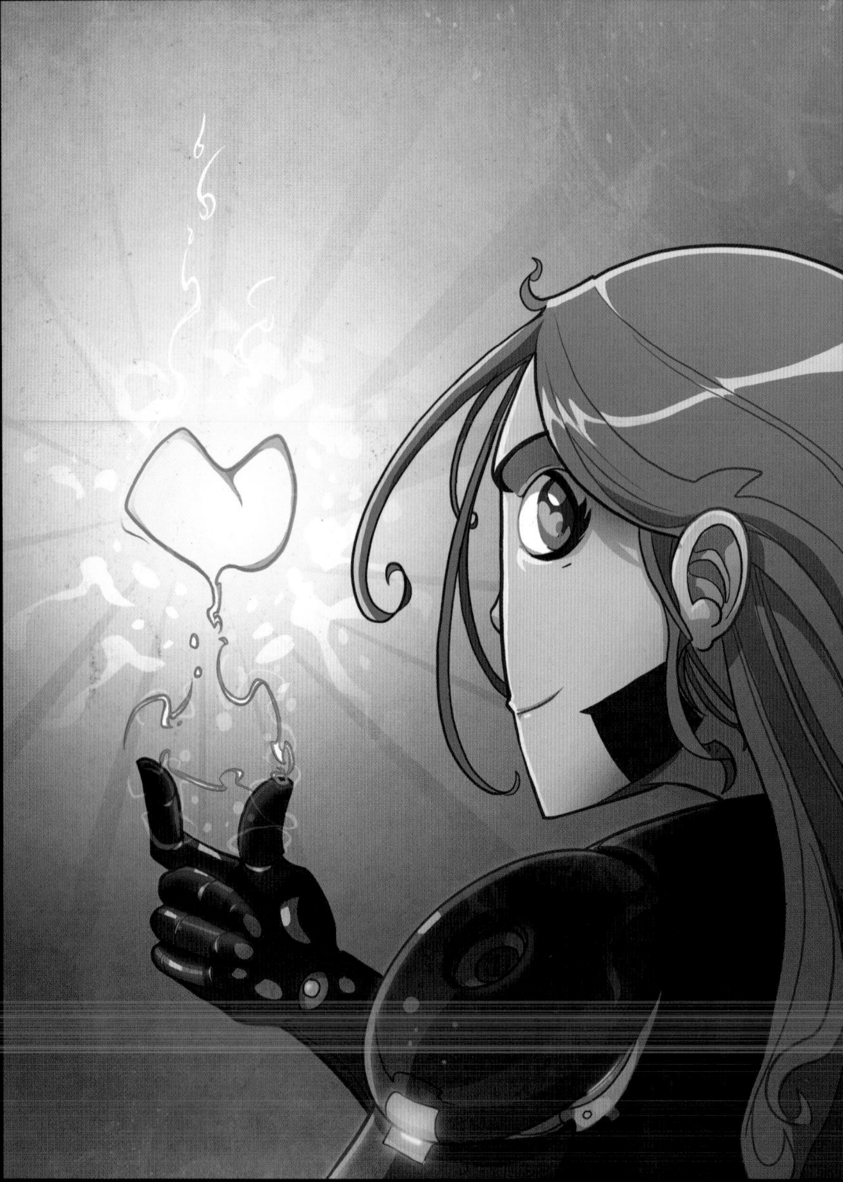

We often chat about how things are going with our work on these volumes over on applegeeks.com. We were really excited about how this cover art turned out, so Hawk posted a sneak peek of it on the site. It got a lot of great response from our readers. Thanks, guys!

—Ananth

▼ BONUS MATERIAL

173 **GUEST PINUPS.tif**

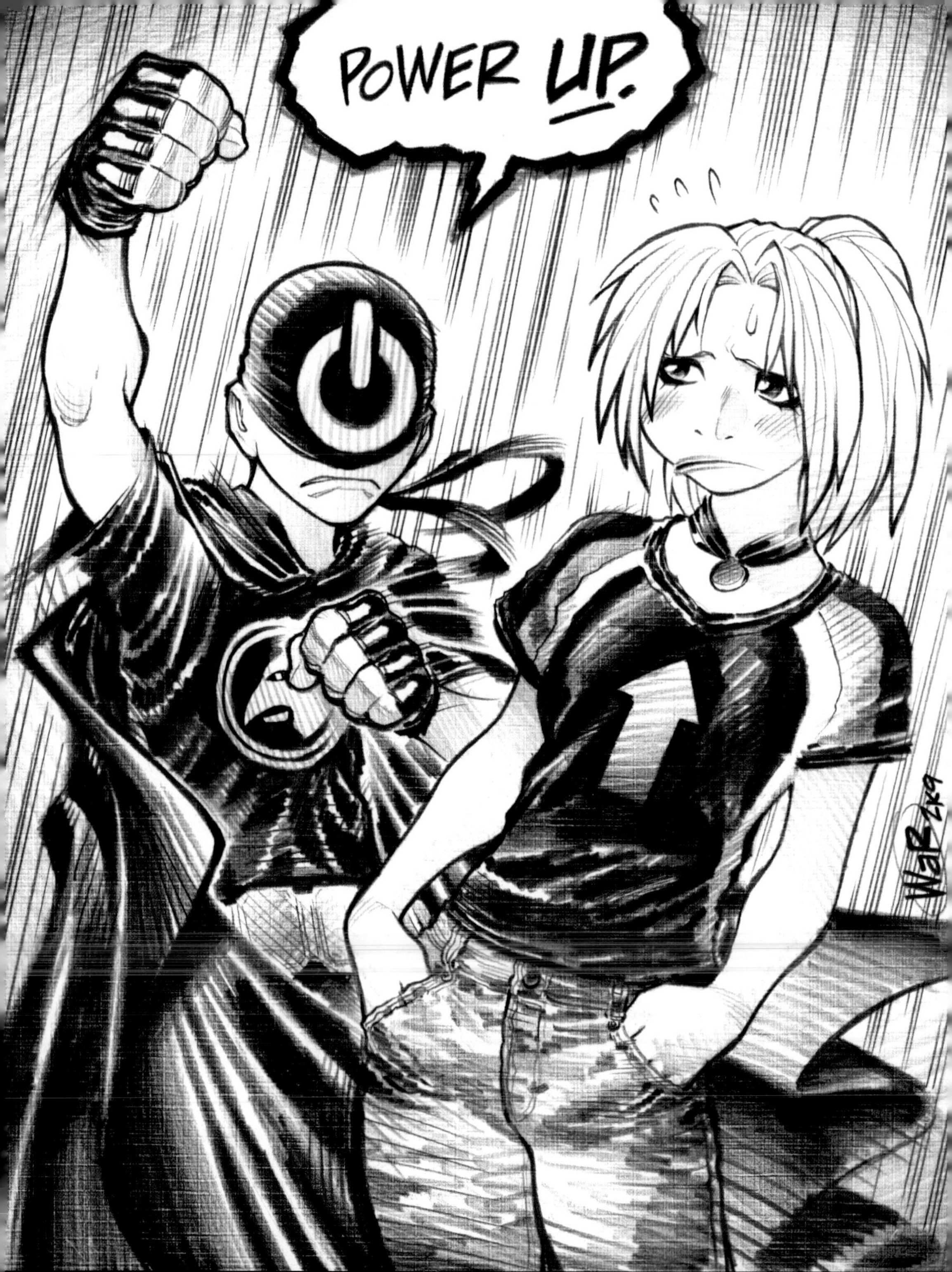
POWER UP.

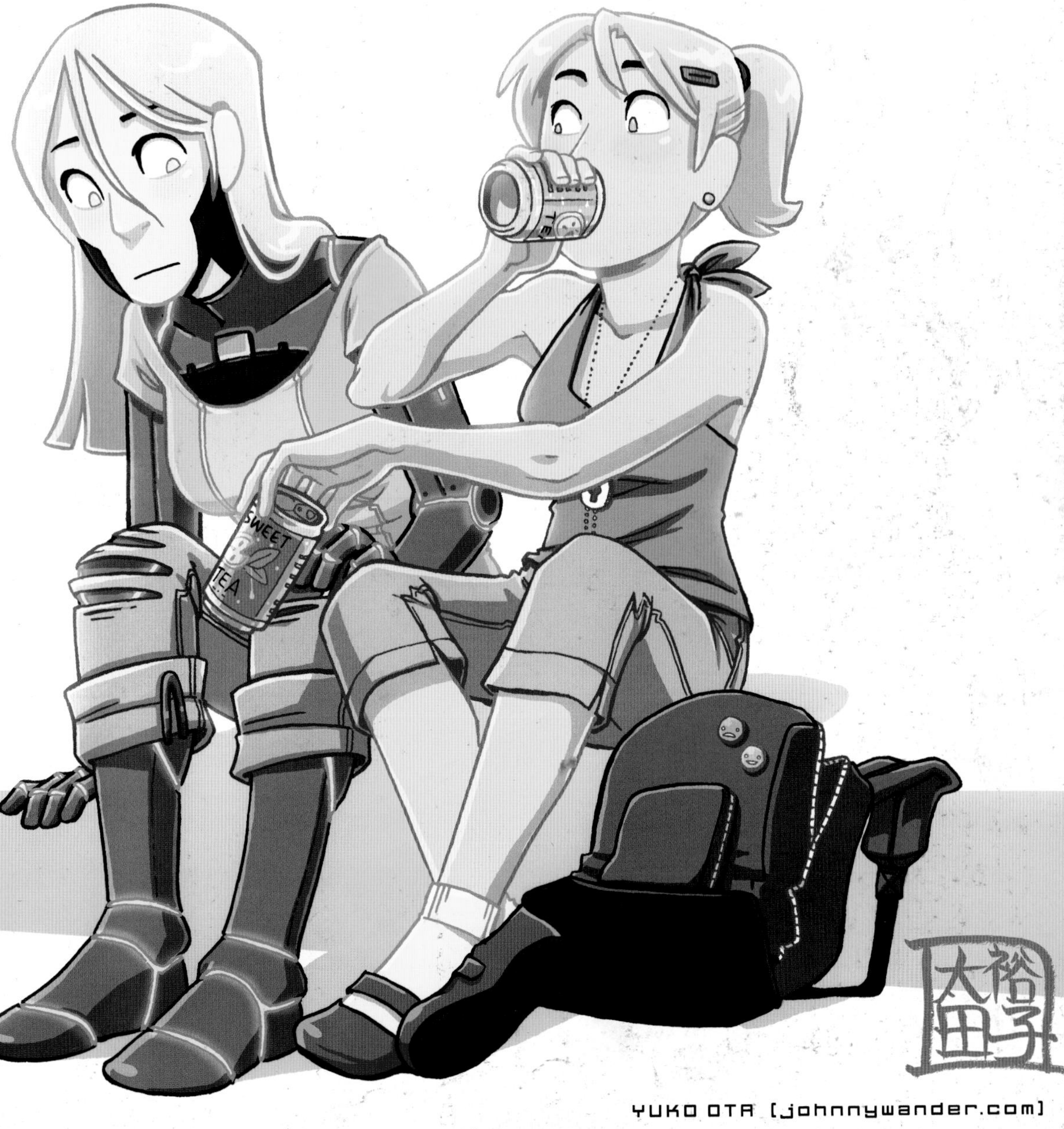
SWEET
TEA

YUKO OTA [johnnywander.com]

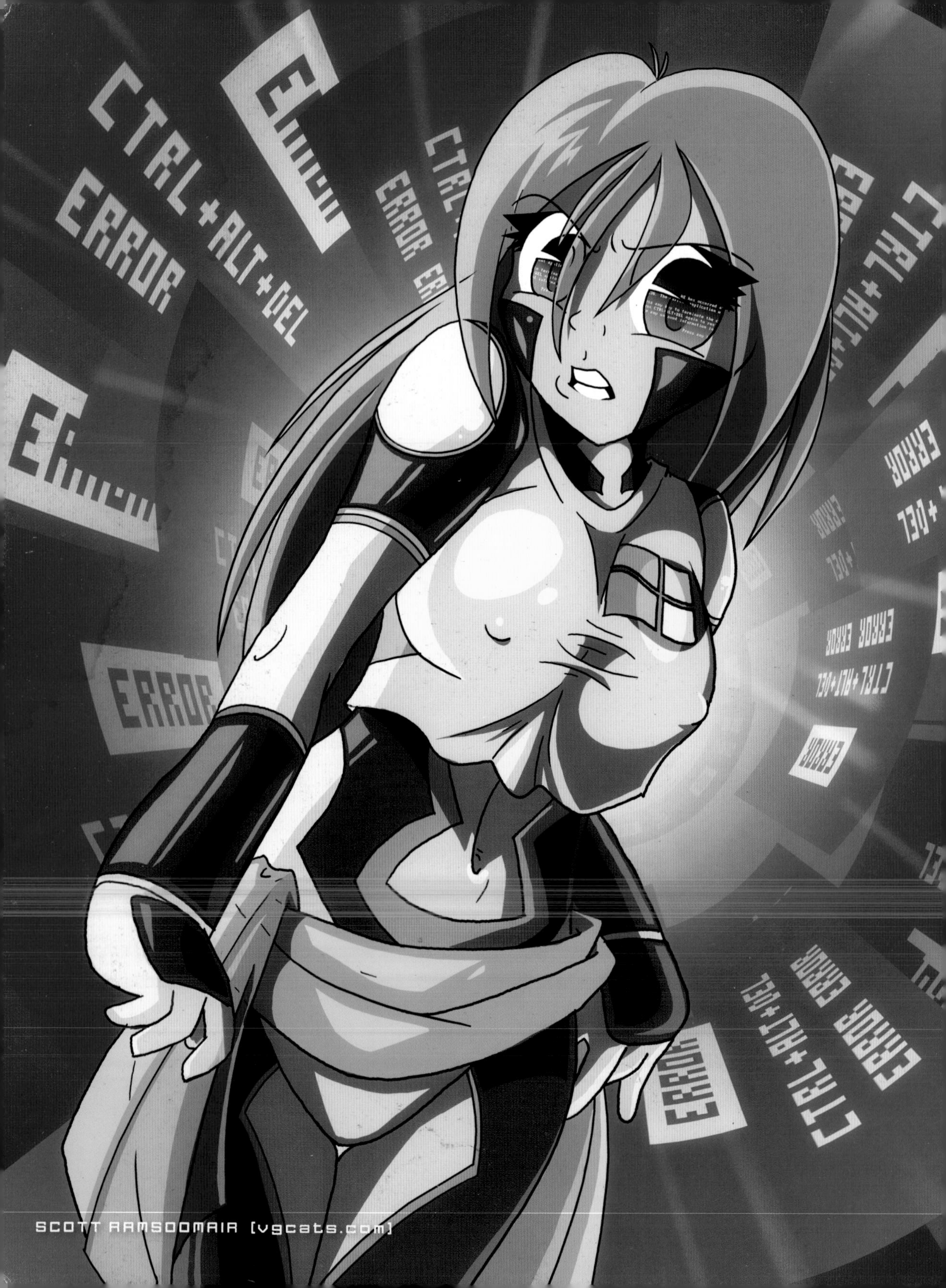
CTRL+ALT+DEL
ERROR
CTRL
ERROR
ERROR
CTRL+ALT+DEL
ERROR
ERROR
+DEL
ERROR ERROR
CTRL+ALT+DEL
ERROR
ERROR ERROR
ERROR ERROR
CTRL+ALT+DEL

SCOTT RAMSOOMAIR [vgcats.com]

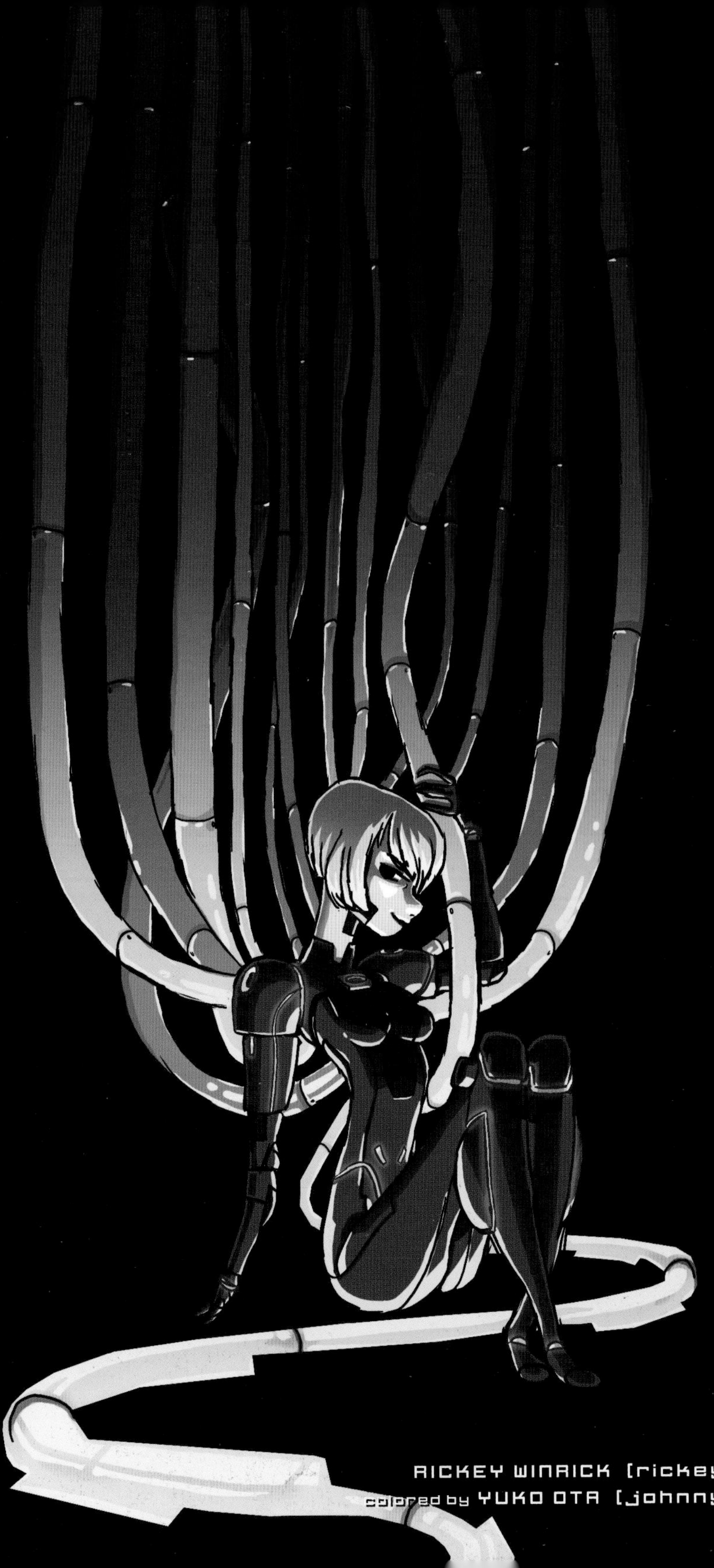

RICKEY WINRICK [rickeywinrick.com]
colored by YUKO OTA [johnnywander.com]

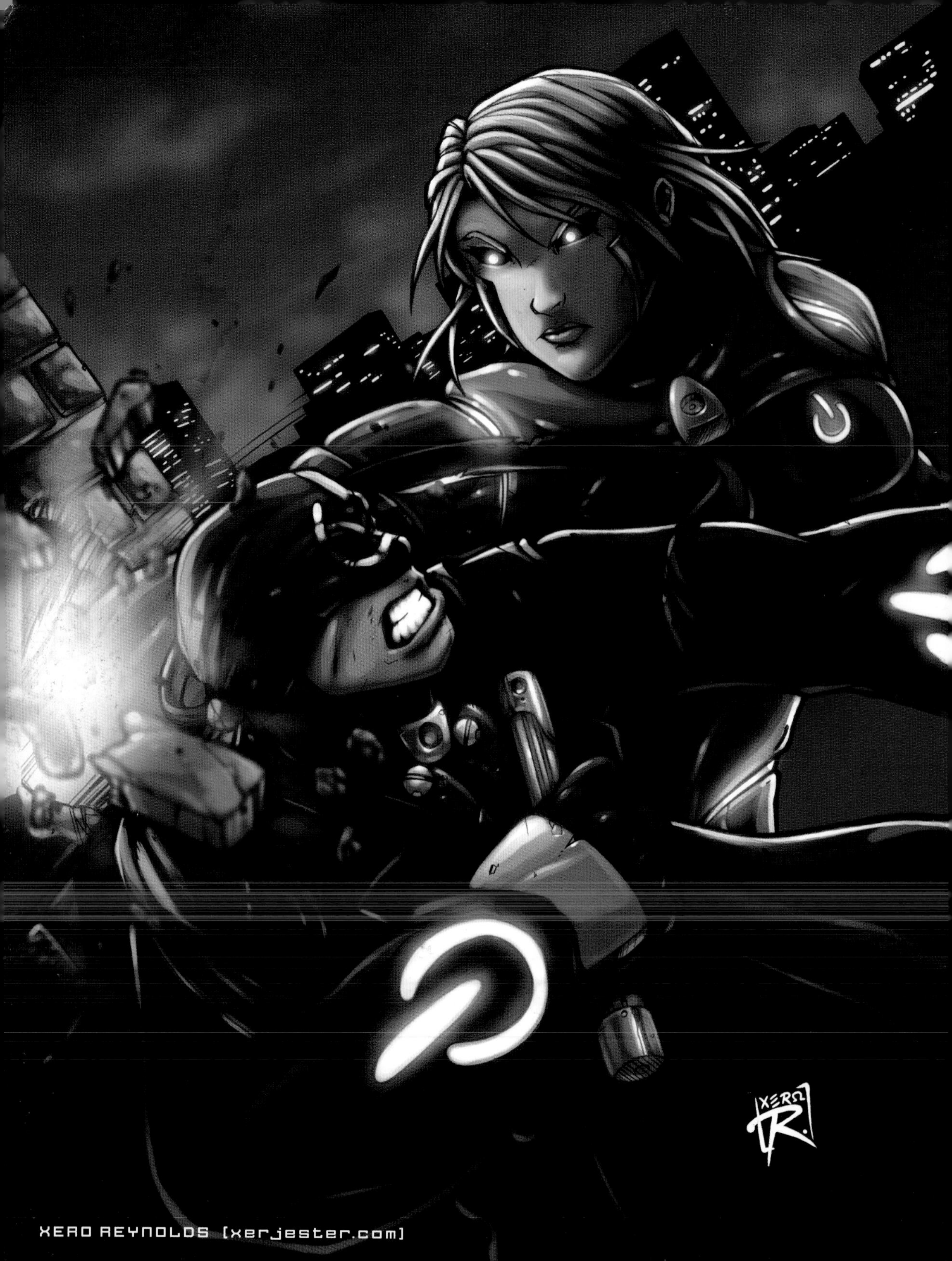

XERO REYNOLDS [xerjester.com]

BONUS MATERIAL

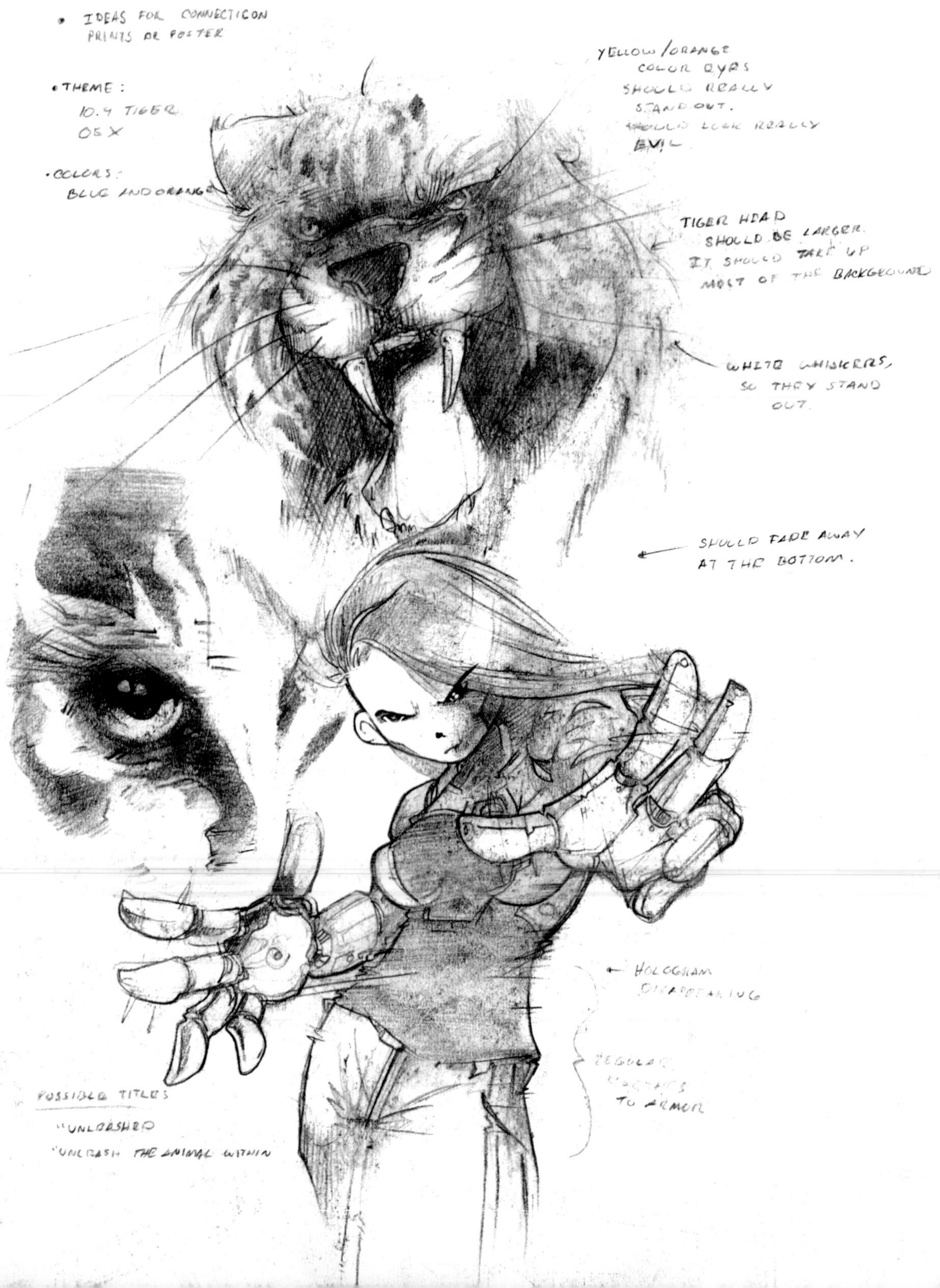
• IDEAS FOR CONNECTICON PRINTS OR POSTER
• THEME: 10.4 TIGER OS X
• COLORS: BLUE AND ORANGE
YELLOW/ORANGE COLOR EYES SHOULD REALLY STAND OUT. SHOULD LOOK REALLY EVIL
TIGER HEAD SHOULD BE LARGER. IT SHOULD TAKE UP MOST OF THE BACKGROUND
WHITE WHISKERS, SO THEY STAND OUT.
SHOULD FADE AWAY AT THE BOTTOM.
HOLOGRAM DISAPPEARING
REGULAR CLOTHES TO ARMOR
POSSIBLE TITLES
"UNLEASHED
"UNLEASH THE ANIMAL WITHIN

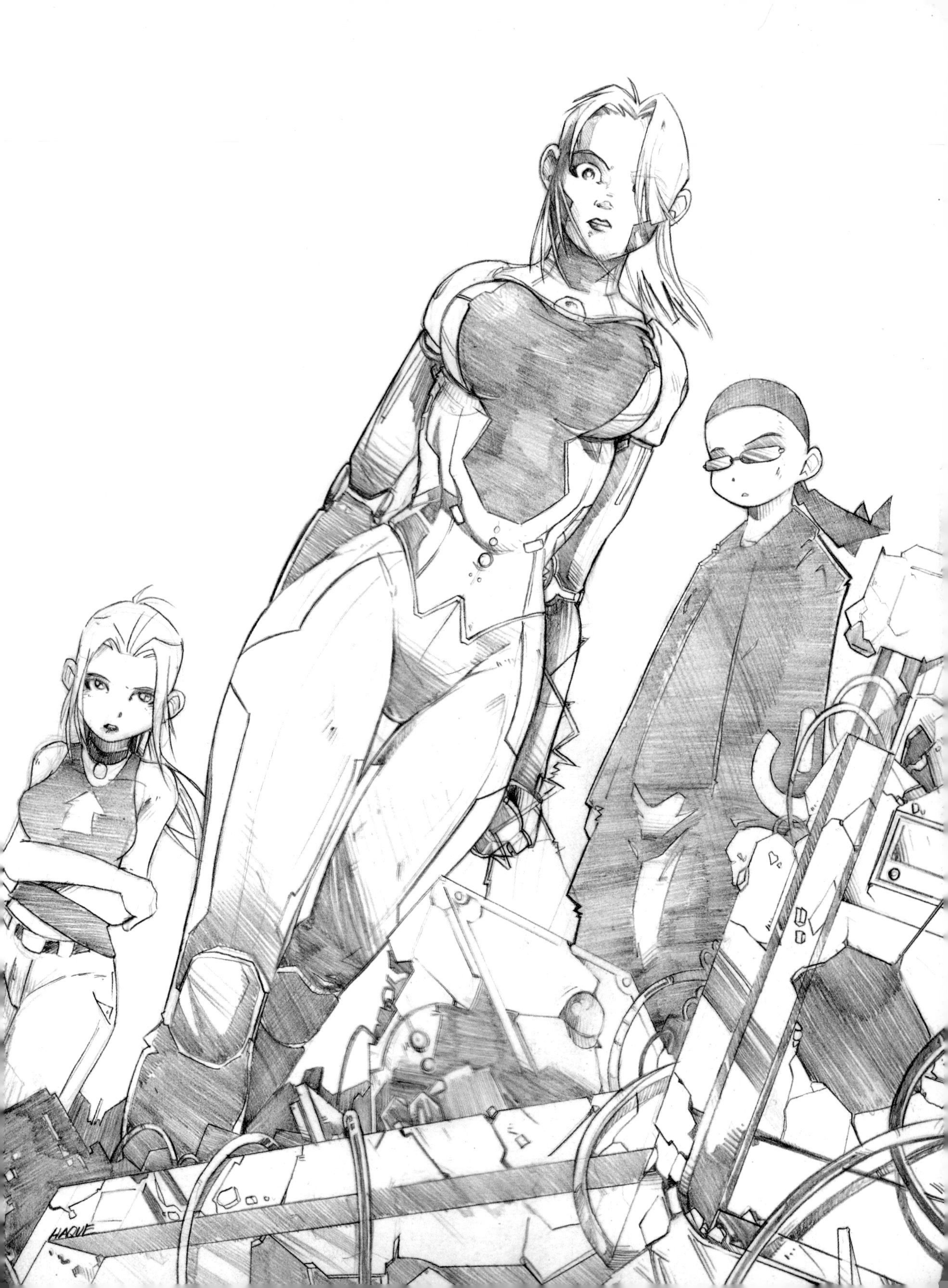
HAQUE

about the creators

Ananth Panagariya is a writer and designer based out of Washington DC. He graduated in 2005 from the University of Maryland, College Park, and since then has worked as an in-house designer for a non-profit, a designer/animator at a firm, and freelanced as a designer, brand identity manager, and developer for, among other things, an iPhone camera application from Snapture Labs. In 2007 he and a team of friends launched Mutagenics, a designer clothing line, which sparked his interest in new business paradigms. In addition to *Applegeeks*, you can also see more of his latest comics work at Johnny Wander (johnnywander.com).

Mohammad F. Haque is a designer, illustrator, and web developer/programmer. His professional career began when he was fifteen, when he started as a programmer but got moved to the design department after his boss caught wind of his sketchbook. From there his work has taken him to nonprofits, firms, and many freelance clients. You can also see his coloring work in the *Penny Arcade* CCG, some of *Megatokyo*'s covers and posters, and the cover of *Ctrl Alt Del* Vol. 1. He's received an award nomination from CGTalk, the popular online digital art forum. Hawk's been drawing since he could hold a pencil, and he'll be drawing until it falls out of his hand. You can see more of his work at his personal site, Hawkstudios (hawkstudios.net).

applegeeks™

written by ananth panagariya • art by mohammad f. haque

Jayce, an introspective writer, and Hawk, an excitable artist and inventor, have unofficially taken up residence in the home of sweet and thoughtful Alice and hard-drinking, hard-hitting Gina. The foursome's busy trying to figure out what to do with the rest of their lives, and how the heck to fit their college classes in around marathon video-game sessions, visits to the comic shop, and offbeat road trips; but when Hawk decides to create the perfect girlfriend in his basement lab, passing classes suddenly becomes the least of the group's worries!

VOLUME ONE
ISBN 978-1-59582-174-4 | $14.95

Dark Horse Comics is proud to bring *Applegeeks* off the Net and into print! *Applegeeks: Freshman Year* includes the first two years of *Applegeeks* comics, as well as extensive creator commentary, a pinup gallery, and lots of other great bonus material!

DARK HORSE BRINGS YOU THE BEST IN WEBCOMICS!

These wildly popular cartoon gems were once only available online, but now can be found through Dark Horse Books with loads of awesome extras!

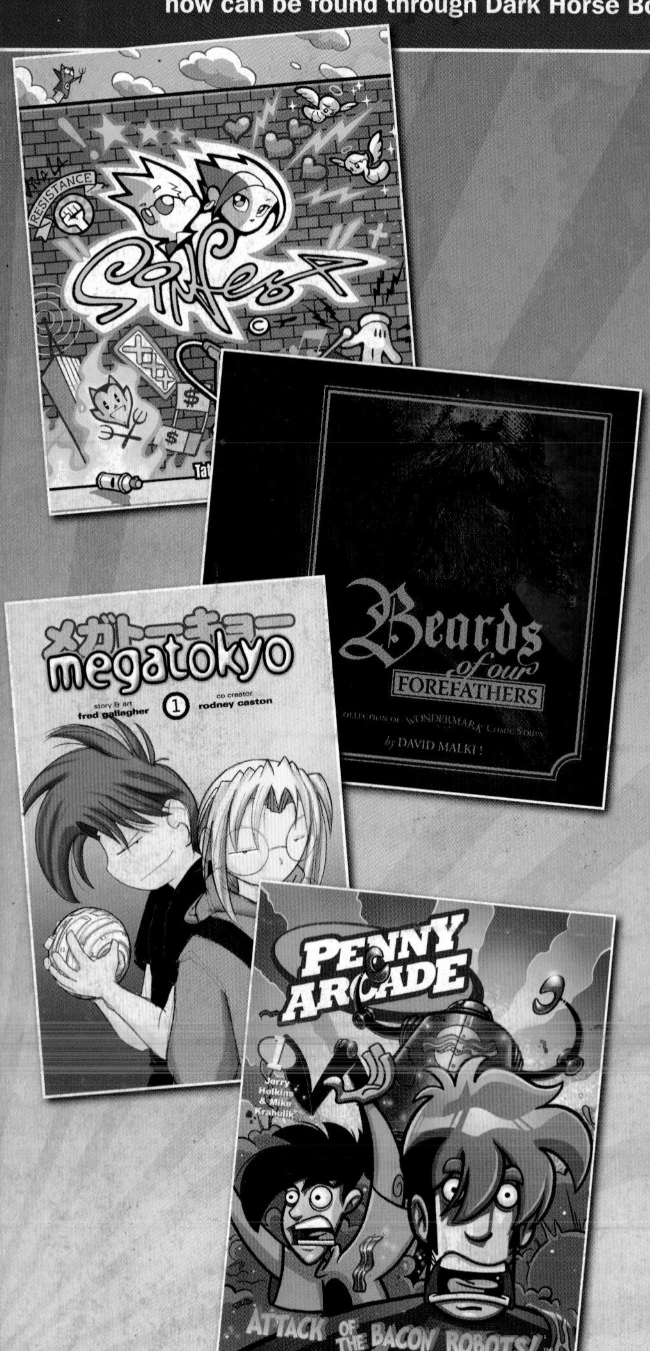
RESISTANCE
Sinfest
メガトーキョー
megatokyo
story & art
fred gallagher
1
co creator
rodney caston
Beards of our FOREFATHERS
A COLLECTION OF WONDERMARK COMIC STRIPS
by DAVID MALKI !
PENNY ARCADE
1
Jerry Holkins & Mike Krahulik
ATTACK OF THE BACON ROBOTS!

SINFEST
Volume One TPB
By Tatsuya Ishida

Sinfest is one of the most-read and longest-running w comics out there, and explores religion, advertising, s and politics in a way fleen.com calls "both brutally fu and devastatingly on-target." The first volume collects first six hundred *Sinfest* strips, introducing the full cas characters and the opening installments of Ninja Thea beat poetry, calligraphy lessons, and the irresistible Po & Percival strips. If your comic-strip craving hasn't be satisfied since the nineties, deliverance is finally at ha

ISBN 978-1-59582-319-9 | $14.95

WONDERMARK
Volume One: Beards of Our Forefathers HC
By David Malki

Dark Horse Comics is proud to present this handsome ha bound collection of David Malki's Ignatz-nominated co strip *Wondermark*. Malki repurposes illustrations a engravings from nineteenth-century books into hilario collage-style comic strips. Beards are just the beginnin

ISBN 978-1-59307-984-0 | $14.95

MEGATOKYO
Volume One TPB
By Fred Gallagher and Rodney Caston

This reissue of the highly successful *Megatokyo* Volu One brings fans a new and revised version of the book w improved print quality and a larger trim size. This book contain all of the comics from Chapter 0 as well as running editorial comments featured in the original lease. Exclusive to the Dark Horse reissue are additio drawings, historical notes, and selected rants from t first developmental year of the *Megatokyo* webcomic.

ISBN 978-1-59307-163-9 | $9.95

PENNY ARCADE
Volume One: Attack of the Bacon Robots! TPB
By Jerry Holkins and Mike Krahulik

Penny Arcade, the comic strip for gamers, by gamers now available in comic shops and bookstores everywhe Experience the joy of being a hardcore gamer as express in hilariously witty vignettes of random vulgarity and mi less violence!

ISBN 978-1-59307-444-9 | $12.95

DARK HORSE BOOKS

darkhorse.com

AVAILABLE AT YOUR LOCAL COMICS SHOP OR BOOKSTORE

To find a comics shop in your area, call 1-888-266-4226

For more information or to order direct: •On the web: darkhorse.com •E-mail: mailorder@darkhorse.com •Phone: 1-800-862-0052 Mon.–Fri. 9AM to 5PM Pacific Time.